CAMBRIDGE GREEK AND

OVID

HEROIDES

SELECT EPISTLES

EDITED BY

PETER E. KNOX

*Associate Professor of Classics in the
University of Colorado at Boulder*

CAMBRIDGE
UNIVERSITY PRESS

PUBLISHED BY THE PRESS SYNDICATE OF THE UNIVERSITY OF CAMBRIDGE
The Pitt Building, Trumpington Street, Cambridge, United Kingdom

CAMBRIDGE UNIVERSITY PRESS
The Edinburgh Building, Cambridge CB2 2RU, UK   http://www.cup.cam.ac.uk
40 West 20th Street, New York, NY 10011–4211, USA   http://www.cup.org
10 Stamford Road, Oakleigh, Melbourne 3166, Australia
Ruiz de Alarcón 13, 28014 Madrid, Spain

First published 1995
Reprinted 2000

A catalogue record for this book is available from the British Library

Library of Congress Cataloguing in Publication data
Ovid, 43 B.C. – 17 or 18 A.D.
[Heroides. Selections]
Heroides : select epistles / Ovid; edited by Peter E. Knox.
p.   cm. – (Cambridge Greek and Latin classics)
Text in Latin; commentary in English.
Includes bibliographical references and indexes.
ISBN 0 521 36279 2. – ISBN 0 521 36834 0 (pbk)
1. Epistolary poetry, Latin.   2. Mythology, Classical – Poetry.
3. Love-letters – Poetry.   4. Love poetry, Latin.   5. Women – Poetry.
I. Knox, Peter E.   II. Title.   III. Series.
PA6519.H5   1995
871'.01–dc20   94-49341
CIP

ISBN 0 521 36279 2 hardback
ISBN 0 521 36834 0 paperback

Transferred to digital printing 2003

For Noriko

prima locum sanctas heroidas inter haberes

CONTENTS

Preface   *page* ix

Introduction   1
  1 *The poet*   1
  2 *The collection*   5
  3 *The* Epistula Sapphus   12
  4 *The epistles*   14
    (a) *The genre*   14
    (b) *The literary background*   18
    (c) *Aspects of language, style, and metre*   25
  5 *The transmission of the text*   34

P. OVIDI NASONIS EPISTVLAE HEROIDVM
  SELECTAE   39
INCERTI AVCTORIS EPISTVLA SAPPHVS AD
  PHAONEM   78

Commentary   86

Bibliography   316
Indexes   325
  1 *Latin words*   325
  2 *General*   326

PREFACE

When this commentary was begun some seven years ago, at the suggestion of Professor E. J. Kenney, it was possible to characterize the *Heroides* as Ovid's most neglected work. In the intervening years interest in these epistles has intensified, and I have benefited greatly from the labours of others who have recognized that this collection is far more subtle and complex than has generally been thought. There is still no full-scale modern commentary on the *Heroides*, but the present edition aims to mitigate this situation by providing the student with a representative selection from the single epistles. I have not avoided the thorny issue of the authenticity of parts of the collection, but since Ovidian authorship of most of the poems in this selection is not disputed, the reader's attention can remain focused on the more important aspects of this poet's art. The *Epistula Sapphus*, which I do not believe to be Ovid's, is an interesting poem in its own right, and I have included it as an illustration of the principle that a judgement against authenticity does not necessarily imply aesthetic condemnation.

It is a pleasure to acknowledge several friends and colleagues whose suggestions have led to a number of improvements in both presentation and substance. Professors Alessandro Barchiesi, D. R. Shackleton Bailey and Richard Thomas read substantial portions of the commentary. I am particularly indebted to Professors Wendell Clausen and James McKeown, who read and commented upon the entire typescript. All contributors to this series benefit from the advice and criticism of the General Editors; I have been especially fortunate because Professor Kenney has shouldered more than a fair share of the burden of trying to rescue me from error. I am grateful for the attention he has lavished on a succession of drafts and for the generous spirit in which he has shared his accumulated store of learning in all things Ovidian. My chief obligation is acknowledged in the dedication.

September 1994   P. E. K.

INTRODUCTION

1. THE POET

In antiquity literary criticism could be written by compiling a string of names. Thus Quintilian on the subject of Latin elegy: *elegia quoque Graecos prouocamus, cuius mihi tersus atque elegans maxime uidetur auctor Tibullus. sunt qui Propertium malint. Ouidius utroque lasciuior, sicut durior Gallus* (10.1.93). Late in Ovid's career, when he defines his own place in Roman literary history by referring to his most important contemporaries, we find that he draws up much the same list:

> Vergilium uidi tantum, nec auara Tibullo
> tempus amicitiae fata dedere meae.
> successor fuit hic tibi, Galle, Propertius illi;
> quartus ab his serie temporis ipse fui. (*Trist.* 4.10.51–4)

The selection is not random. He places himself in the same company at *Trist.* 2.445–66, where he discusses the works of Gallus, Tibullus, and Propertius, concluding (467), *his ego successi.* The literary climate in Rome during the decade following Octavian's victory at Actium was electric. The scene was dominated by the names O. recalls in *Trist.* 4.10: Virgil, who released his *Georgics* in 29 BC, was at work on an epic of Rome's foundation; Horace, the author of two books of satires and a collection of epodes, was nearing completion of the *Odes*;[1] but most importantly for O.'s own career, Tibullus and Propertius were producing books of amatory elegy appealing to the increasingly sophisticated tastes of the literate elite. They followed the example of their predecessor in the genre Cornelius Gallus, whose poetry was much admired by his contemporaries and must certainly have made a great impression on the young O., though it has not

---

[1] O. mentions Horace in the couplet immediately preceding the passage cited here: *et tenuit nostras numerosus Horatius aures, | dum ferit Ausonia carmina culta lyra* (*Trist.* 4.10.49–50). He refers specifically to the *Odes*, and it may be assumed that they were the most potent influence on his own work; cf. A. Zingerle, *Ovidius und sein Verhältnis zu den Vorgängern und gleichzeitigen römischen Dichtern. 3 Heft: Ovidius und Horaz* (Innsbruck 1871).

survived in sufficient quantity to allow us a sure assessment.[2] Suc-
ceeding generations may have looked back at this roster in despair
of emulating their achievements; but in 25 BC, when as a young man
O. gave up his professional ambitions for a life of literature,[3] it may
well have seemed the most obvious choice to make.

O. tells more about himself than we are accustomed to hear from
ancient poets, both in the long autobiographical poem composed to-
wards the end of his life during his exile on the Black Sea (*Trist.* 4.10)
and in numerous revealing remarks scattered throughout his works.
He was born Publius Ovidius Naso on 20 March 43 BC at Sulmo,
one of the chief towns of the Italian people known as the Paeligni,
located in a well-watered valley of central Italy: *Sulmo mihi patria est*
(*Trist.* 4.10.3). The date is significant, for as O. reminds us (*Trist.*
4.10.6) it was in this year that the two consuls Hirtius and Pansa both
fell in the campaign against Mark Antony at the head of the last
army of the Roman Republic to take the field. O.'s life and career
belong entirely to the early empire; his first public literary per-
formances probably occurred at least five years after the battle of
Actium and the fall of Alexandria (31–30 BC). And his death came
only a few years after that of the emperor who exiled him: no poet
so fully merits the epithet 'Augustan' as O., all of whose works were
conceived in, and inspired by, the era that bears that name.

O.'s family background marked him out for special preferment.

_____

[2] Only two fragments of his poetry survive: one pentameter quoted by Vi-
bius Sequester and substantial parts of nine lines preserved on papyrus, first
edited by R. D. Anderson, P. J. Parsons, and R. G. M. Nisbet, 'Elegiacs by
Gallus from Qaṣr Ibrîm', *J.R.S.* 69 (1979) 125–55. Gallus is often mentioned
by Propertius (e.g. 2.34.91–2) and O. (e.g. *Am.* 1.15.29–30), and Virgil pays
tribute to his poetry by incorporating Gallus as a character in his *Eclogues*
(6.64–73, 10.9–74). The discovery of the papyrus from Qaṣr Ibrîm has done
nothing to diminish the importance of Ross (1975), a highly suggestive study
of the role of Gallus in Augustan poetry. For a convenient summary of his
life and works, see E. Courtney, *The fragmentary Latin poets* (Oxford 1993) 259–
70, who somewhat optimistically includes *Ecl.* 10.42–63 as a third 'fragment'.

[3] The date can only be approximate. It derives from *Trist.* 4.10.57–8,
where O. describes his first performances as a poet: *carmina cum primum populo
iuuenalia legi,* | *barba resecta mihi bisue semelue fuit.* The reference is to the *depositio
barbae*, which provides no precise date: we may suppose O. to have been
about 18 years old. On this question and others in the life of the poet, cf.
Wheeler (1925) 11–17.

He was the second son of an old and wealthy equestrian family of some standing locally. Only a few generations before the birth of the poet, Sulmo had stood with the rest of the Paeligni against Rome in the general revolt of the Italian allied cities (91–89 BC). It was precisely communities such as Sulmo from which Augustus was eager to draw support for his new regime; and it was to ambitious local families such as O.'s that he would look to recruit new magistrates and senators. O. embarked on a career that might well have led to high public office. He studied rhetoric at Rome and Athens, and served in two administrative posts in the vigintivirate.[4] On his own testimony his earliest efforts in poetry must have taken place during this false start at an official career, which he threw over for the life of letters. It was not a choice calculated to please a father: O.'s had hoped for a more lucrative career for his son (*Trist.* 4.10.21–2), and Augustus, if he had noticed, would not have approved.

Over the next two decades, from *c.* 20 BC to AD 2, O. produced a remarkable series of elegiac works: during this time he composed the *Amores, Heroides, Ars amatoria,* and *Remedia amoris,* along with assorted minor works in elegy and one in another genre, the important tragedy *Medea,* now lost. There is no consensus about the relative chronology of this phase of O.'s career.[5] His poetry treats of life in the everyday world or in the realm of myth; there are very few datable references in the poems and they tell us little. The question is further complicated by the fact that his earliest collection, the *Amores,* comes down to us in an abridged edition of three books reduced from the original five: as O. wryly puts it in a prologue to the revised work, *leuior demptis poena duobus erit.* That the process of revision consisted exclusively of removal of certain poems and rearrangement of the survivors seems likely from the testimony of the poet and the texture of the work.[6] O.'s fluent manner of composition, often attested by

---

[4] On his early education and training, see Wheeler (1925) 4–11. O. probably served as one of the *tresuiri capitales,* but the evidence (*Trist.* 4.10.33–4) is not explicit; cf. Kenney (1969) 244. Later, he tells us (*Fast.* 4.383–4), he held a seat among the *decemuiri stlitibus iudicandis.*

[5] Earlier views are summarized in the standard surveys by Martini (1933) and Kraus (1968). More recent discussions can be found, e.g., in Jacobson (1974) 300–18, Syme (1978) 1–20, and McKeown (1987) 74–89.

[6] Cf. A. Cameron, 'The first edition of Ovid's *Amores*', *C.Q.* 18 (1968) 320–

the poet himself, led more easily to abandoning false starts than to careful re-working:

> multa quidem scripsi, sed, quae uitiosa putaui,
> emendaturis ignibus ipse dedi. (*Trist.* 4.10.61–2)

We can never know anything about the content of this first five-book collection. That it was a more diverse assortment than the final version is a reasonable surmise. The almost exclusive concentration on the themes of love and courtship in the *Amores* contrasts sharply with the diversity of the collections of elegies by Propertius and Tibullus, and is doubtless the result of conscientious editing. O. chose to explore a variety of themes in independent books of elegy before turning to a different genre altogether in the *Metamorphoses*.

In the years immediately preceding his exile O. seems to have been occupied primarily with the composition of narrative on a large scale in the *Fasti* and the *Metamorphoses*. His career, and life, changed abruptly with Augustus' edict in AD 8 relegating him to the town of Tomi located on the shores of the Black Sea. The reasons given by O. are the composition of the *Ars amatoria* and an unspecified affront to the emperor, *carmen et error* (*Trist.* 2.207). About the first charge O. is eloquent in his own defence: he devotes a book-length elegy (*Trist.* 2) to vindication of his work, and never wavers in his insistence on the integrity of his poetic enterprise. On the second count of the indictment O. maintains a steadfast silence, but the suspicion imposes itself that his disgrace was somehow related to the fall of Augustus' granddaughter Julia, exiled on a charge of adultery in the same year.[7] Life at Tomi did not suit O., but it did not break his commitment to the art that had called him as a young man. A

---

33. This position remains controversial and arguments for a more complex re-working of the *Amores* with the addition of new material can be found in A. S. Hollis, *Ovid: Ars amatoria book I* (Oxford 1977) 150–1 and McKeown (1987) 86–9.

[7] The subject of O.'s exile has attracted, and will continue to attract speculation because of his own silence. J. C. Thibault, *The mystery of Ovid's exile* (Berkeley 1964) catalogues hypotheses advanced up to his time. More recently, Syme (1978) 215–29 makes the case for O.'s involvement in a political conspiracy against Augustus, while G. P. Goold, 'The cause of Ovid's exile', *I.C.S.* 8 (1983) 94–107 argues the position adopted here, that O. was involved in a scandal of a more personal nature.

steady stream of innovative new works poured from his pen: *Tristia* in five books and *Epistulae ex Ponto* in four, chronicling his personal experiences in exile as no poet in antiquity had done before; the *Ibis*, a bizarre display of erudition in a unique poem of invective; and the revision of the *Fasti*, undertaken but never completed. O. died in exile during the winter of AD 17–18.

2. THE COLLECTION

The twenty-one poems that today constitute the collection known generally as the *Epistulae Heroidum* or *Heroides* are a diverse group.[8] They comprise fourteen fictional epistles from heroines of Greek and Roman mythology to the men they loved, one further such epistle by the early Greek lyric poet Sappho, and three pairs of letters by famous couples of myth and literature: Paris and Helen, Leander and Hero, Acontius and Cydippe. The circumstances surrounding the composition of the collection and its transmission from antiquity through the Middle Ages raise troubling questions on three issues important for literary history: (1) the dates of individual epistles or groups of epistles and their relative position in the chronology of O.'s career; (2) the publication of the collection and O.'s role in arranging the poems; and (3) the authenticity of individual epistles. O.'s own testimony offers an appropriate starting-point for inquiry.

In an elegy from the second book of the *Amores* O. addresses a friend, the poet Macer, who is writing epic verse and in this context describes some of his own poetic efforts (*Am.* 2.18.19–26):

> quod licet, aut artes teneri profitemur Amoris
> (ei mihi, praeceptis urgeor ipse meis),
> aut quod Penelopes uerbis reddatur Vlixi
> scribimus et lacrimas, Phylli relicta, tuas,

---

[8] They were probably called *Heroides* or *Heroidum liber* by O., a title that had been used (Ἡρωῖναι) by the Greek poets Philochorus (*Suda* s.v.) and Theocritus (*Suda* s.v.) for works of unknown content now lost. O.'s poems are cited under this title by Priscian (*Inst.* 10.54 = *GLK* II 544.4) and the scholia to the *Ibis* (357, 589). O. himself refers to a single poem from the *Heroides* as an *epistula* (*Ars* 3.345); cf. Martini (1933) 18, Kraus (1968) 89, N. Horsfall, 'Some problems of titulature in Roman literary history', *B.I.C.S.* 28 (1981) 107.

> quod Paris et Macareus et quod male gratus Iason
>   Hippolytique parens Hippolytusque legant,
> quodque tenens strictum Dido miserabilis ensem
>   dicat et †Aoniae Lesbis amata lyrae.†

This passage appears to refer to a 'published work',[9] and thus provides the only external evidence for the date of composition of the *Heroides* listed here. The only collection of *Heroides* attested by O. therefore antedates at least the second edition of the *Amores* (*c.* 2 BC), and probably the first (*c.* 16 BC), if we accept the view that his revision of the *Amores* involved only the elimination of some poems with rearrangement of the remainder.[10] What poems were included in this early edition of *Heroides*?

The so-called double epistles (*Her.* 16–21) are nowhere mentioned by O., and this omission is curious. In addition, as a group they contain a number of lexical and metrical traits otherwise characteristic of O.'s later elegiac poetry written in exile (AD 8–17). If they come from his hand, they are likely to belong to this later period and cannot have belonged to the collection described in *Am.* 2.18.[11] This enlargement of the corpus, whether it was performed by O. or a later editor, consisted simply in adding one rather long (*c.* 1,564 lines) papyrus roll to the existing collection of *Heroides*. It is only a guess, but a plausible one, that this was the work not of O., but of an editor. For one thing, O. cannot have called this collection, which included epistles by male characters, *Heroides*. As a practical consequence, problems involving the authorship, language, and literary purpose of the double epistles must be separated from consideration of 1–15.

Am. 2.18 refers to an epistle by Sappho as part of what we may

---

[9] Modern terminology of this type must be used with caution in discussing the circumstances of ancient book production and circulation: once a book was released to the public its author had no further control over its fate; cf. E. J. Kenney, 'Books and readers in the Roman world', E. J. Kenney and W. V. Clausen (edd.) *The Cambridge history of classical literature.* II *Latin literature* (Cambridge 1982) 15–22. This point is especially relevant when considering the ways in which the corpus of the *Heroides* might have taken shape.

[10] See p. 3.

[11] Cf. M. Pohlenz, 'Die Abfassungszeit von Ovids Metamorphosen', *Hermes* 48 (1913) 3–4, Kraus (1968) 56.

call the first collection, and it is reasonable to associate the extant *Epistula Sapphus* with this reference. This association, however, is fraught with complications. Ovidian authorship of this poem is suspect on a number of grounds both internal, regarding its language and content, and external, due to the circumstances of its transmission. Convincing arguments against identifying O. as its author have been advanced over a long period, and this position is adopted in the present edition (see p. 13) . This creates as many complications as it resolves, but for the present it is necessary only to consider the consequences for our understanding of *Am.* 2.18; for if the *ES* is not by O., there must either once have been another poem written by O., now lost, or the references to Sappho's epistle in lines 26 and 34 of this elegy are also spurious. However improbable, this may well be the truth, for the *ES* is undoubtedly an early imitation of the *Heroides*, if imitation it is, and the interpolated notices of its existence in *Am.* 2.18 might be the product of editorial marginalia adding a notice of an epistle supposed to be by O. but absent from the catalogue of titles.[12]

How much of the rest of the corpus may be ascribed to O. is an open question. The scepticism advocated by Karl Lachmann may seem extreme,[13] but proceeds from the safest assumption warranted by the evidence, that only the poems mentioned by O. in the uncorrupted portion of *Am.* 2.18 are unquestionably authentic: *Her.* 1–2, 4–7, and 10–11. Despite occasional protests,[14] however, Ovidian

[12] Cf. Tarrant (1981) 148–52. Ascription of spurious works to O. began very early. The *Halieutica* was thought to be Ovidian by Pliny the Elder (*c.* AD 77), but is certainly not from O.'s hand: cf. J. Richmond, 'The authorship of the Halieuticon ascribed to Ovid', *Philol.* 120 (1976) 92–106. For medieval poems incorrectly attributed to O., see P. Lehman, *Pseudo-antike Literatur des Mittelalters* (Leipzig and Berlin 1927). The *ES* may have been thought to be O.'s by Ausonius (4th cent. AD), who seems to refer to the *Heroides* (*Epigr.* 23.12–13): *quod sibi suaserunt, Phaedra et Elissa dabunt, | quod Canace Phyllisque et fastidita Phaoni.* But this is a selective list of famous suicides that might be a conflation of several sources. Ausonius did know the *ES*, but nothing proves that he knew it as part of the *Heroides*.

[13] Lachmann (1848).

[14] E.g. Courtney (1965), D. W. T. C. Vessey, 'Notes on Ovid, *Heroides* 9', *C.Q.* 19 (1969) 349–61, and P. E. Knox, 'Ovid's *Medea* and the authenticity of *Heroides* 12', *H.S.C.P.* 90 (1986) 207–23. For a different view of these issues,

authorship of *Her.* 1–14 is assumed by most modern scholars. The
last word has not been said, but future discussions of this vexed issue
will need to consider closely the problems posed by the concentra-
tion of lexical oddities in the poems not listed in *Am.* 2.18. An ap-
parent exception is the third epistle, Briseis to Achilles, which few
have doubted is O.'s.

An illustration of the difficulties involved in resolving such doubts
may be provided from the eighth epistle, Hermione to Orestes,
composed while she is being held captive by Pyrrhus. For Arthur
Palmer this poem is 'the feeblest and least poetical of all the *Heroides*,
and has certain solecisms in diction and metre, which are either
spurious or show that the epistle is an unfinished and careless per-
formance'.[15] Subjective judgements of quality are not a valid basis
for disputing the attributions of the manuscript tradition. But if the
number of questionable words, phrases, or lines exceeds the toler-
ance level, doubts may legitimately harden to conviction.

In lines 75–81 of this epistle Palmer and other editors have argued
for substantial interpolation, but the lines which precede also pose
problems. Hermione digresses on the apparently inescapable fate of
the female descendants of Tantalus constantly to be the victims of
abduction or rape. Her list of victims includes Leda, Hippodamia,
and Helen's two abductions by Theseus and Paris. This is how the
passage (*Her.* 8.65–74) is transmitted in the MSS:

> num generis fato, quod nostros errat in annos,   65
>   Tantalides matres apta rapina sumus?
> non ego fluminei referam mendacia cycni
>   nec querar in plumis delituisse Iouem.
> qua duo porrectus longe freta distinet Isthmos,
>   uecta peregrinis Hippodamia rotis;   70
> Castori Amyclaeo et Amyclaeo Polluci
>   reddita Mopsopia Taenaris urbe soror;
> Taenaris Idaeo trans aequor ab hospite rapta
>   Argolicas pro se uertit in arma manus.

see S. Hinds, 'Medea in Ovid: scenes from the life of an intertextual heroine',
M.D. 30 (1993) 9–47 and T. Heinze, 'The authenticity of Ovid *Heroides* 12 re-
considered', *B.I.C.S.* 38 (1991–3) 94–8.
    [15] In his edition, p. 351.

Most modern editors athetize the couplet 71–2, which refers to the
return of Helen to her brothers after her abduction to Athens by
Theseus. The hexameter contains three metrical irregularities: the
hiatus at the third-foot caesura, the fourth-foot spondee, and the
elision in the first foot. The hiatus before *et* is without parallel in
O.'s elegiac verse, and there is no other example in O.'s elegies of a
hexameter ending with three spondees.[16] Further, the elision of *Cas-
tori* cannot be ascribed to O. Elision of a final long vowel in a word
of this shape (cretic) is very rare in Latin poetry, and never occurs in
O.[17] In addition the repetition of *Taenaris* of line 72 in the following
hexameter is impossibly awkward. This couplet (71–2) is bracketed as
an interpolation by most editors after Palmer – with some justice,
since it cannot be by O., although if the author of this poem is not
O. perhaps it should not be excised. For the problems in this passage
are more extensive.

In the previous two verses (69–70) Hippodamia is introduced into
the list of victims of abduction. The pentameter, *uecta peregrinis Hip-
podamia rotis*, appears in exactly this form early in the second book of
the *Ars amatoria*. There O. compares the glee of the successful lover
who has applied the precepts of book 1 to Paris and to Pelops after
they won their brides (*Ars* 2.5–8):

> talis ab armiferis Priameius hospes Amyclis
> candida cum rapta coniuge uela dedit;
> talis erat qui te curru uictore ferebat,
> uecta peregrinis Hippodamia rotis.

[16] There are parallels for the hiatus in the *Metamorphoses* (5.312, 8.310), as
Courtney (1965) 65 remarks. It is perhaps significant that the only other in-
stance of hiatus in the third foot also occurs in an epistle not registered in *Am.*
2.18, i.e. 9.131 *forsitan et pulsa Aetolide Deianira*. Courtney also notes that the
fourth-foot spondee in 8.71 may be defended by *Met.* 1.117; but while each
peculiarity can be separately accounted for, the accumulation of anomalies in
a single verse cannot.

[17] The problem cannot be explained away by trying to turn *Castori* into a
dactyl, as was attempted by L. Mueller, *De re metrica* (Leipzig 1894) 342 and
Platnauer (1951) 73n. 3. The vowel would be short in Greek, but that form of
the declension is used only by Catullus and Statius (N–W 1 457) and, as
Housman notes on Manil. 4.597 *add.*, neither poet elides the vowel.

This represents a characteristically Ovidian recasting of a Propertian pentameter (1.2.19–20):

> nec Phrygium falso traxit candore maritum
>   auecta externis Hippodamia rotis.

The elision in the second foot of line 20 is of a type relatively common in Propertius, where it is found in 7.5% of his pentameters, but it is avoided by Tibullus, who has it only half as often (3.7%), and especially by O., who has such elision in only 1.3% of his elegiac pentameters.[18] O. eliminates the unwanted elision by using the uncompounded form of the participle and filling out the line with a synonymous adjective *peregrinis*. The pentameter, which constitutes the subject of the phrase in Propertius, is adapted to its new context in the *Ars amatoria* by its forming a vocative in an apostrophe to Hippodamia with *uecta* functioning as a participle like its counterpart in Propertius. In *Her.* 8.70 *uecta* must do duty for a finite verb, a slight awkwardness not characteristic of O.'s adaptations of other poets. Further, the entire couplet is out of place in this context. Hermione purports to be giving examples from among the female descendants of Tantalus, to whom she somewhat oddly refers as *Tantalides matres* in line 66. Hippodamia, however, was not a descendant of Tantalus; rather she was later married to one. And although Hermione makes a great point of verifying her descent from Pelops by reference to this list, none of the women she names is actually a descendant of Tantalus or Pelops. O. could not have blundered so: genealogical relationships were the sort of material he took great care with. Furthermore, it is not clear how the victory of Pelops could be considered in the same category as the two abductions of Helen or the rape of Leda. Hippodamia was, of course, only figuratively carried off by Pelops, who won her in a chariot race, while the author of these lines apparently means the phrase to be taken literally.

This passage appears to be an imitation of the *Ars amatoria*, and the imitator cannot be O.: the metrical correction of Propertius' elision could not have been performed by the same poet who elided *Castori*.[19] Palmer advocated bracketing only lines 71–2, and later 75–

---

[18] Cf. Platnauer (1951) 90.

[19] This assertion, though it borders on the subjective, draws upon methods of stylistic analysis applied by scholars since Alexandrian times in detecting

81 as interpolations, but the difficulties in this passage are more ex-
tensive than he suspected and excision, if that is the answer, should
be extended at least back to line 65. This remedy, however, is not
necessary. The metrical and lexical anomalies of these nine couplets
are consistent with the remainder of the poem, and in such a situa-
tion they should not necessarily be removed by emendation or ex-
cision. For example, this epistle offers us *Orestis* as the genitive form
of the name of Pyrrhus' competitor for Hermione not once, but
twice at lines 9 and 115, the only examples of such a genitive for this
type of Greek name in Latin poetry. As Housman puts it, 'its author,
if he was capable of the elision *Castori Amyclaeo* ... may also be
thought capable of nonconformity in the declension of nouns'.[20]
Perhaps his conjugation of verbs may be added to this dossier; for at
line 21 we find the form *stertisset* for *stertuisset* in some MSS. Most
editors bracket the couplet 21–2, while those who do not, print the
variant *plorasset* or the emendation *sedisset*. But if this poem is the
work of a later imitator of O., the lines and the form may stand: it is
paralleled by the equally nonconformist *occulerat* found in Valerius
Flaccus or *occulerunt* of Arnobius.[21] Another indication of composi-
tion at a date later in the first century AD is the use of the plural in
the phrase *numeros Danai militis* in line 24. As Heinsius noticed, this is
an instance of the use of *numeri* for *cohortes*, which is found regularly
in later Latinity, beginning with Tacitus and the younger Pliny; its
occurrence in a work by O. would be extraordinary.

The proliferation of such anomalies in the epistles not specifically
attested as O.'s work in *Am.* 2.18 obliges us to treat seriously the pos-
sibility that the collection of *Heroides* as we know it is vastly different
from the collection composed by O. Of the original form of the
collection envisaged by O. the surviving poems give no indication:
there is no evidence of division into books nor are there any signs of
a designed sequence. The fourteen poems assumed to be O.'s could
not have been accommodated in a single papyrus roll: they contain

forgeries or pseudepigrapha. For an accessible survey of the subject, see A.
Grafton, *Forgers and critics: creativity and duplicity in western scholarship* (Princeton
1990) esp. 69–98.

[20] Housman (1910) 251–2 (= *Class. pap.* 828). Heinsius emends to *-ae*
(adopted by Goold). See also Housman (1910) 252 (= *Class. pap.* 828–9) for
the dative *Oresti* at line 59.

[21] Val. Flacc. 2.280; Arnob. 5.53; cf. N–W III 397.

approximately 2,192 verses, far more than the 1,457 lines of Lucre-
tius' fifth book, the longest in Latin poetry. So large a collection of
poems on diverse subjects was vulnerable to alteration in the condi-
tions of book manufacture and circulation prevailing in antiquity.[22]
Whether the copying was done onto papyrus rolls or from rolls to
codex, an otherwise well-intentioned reader might make unfortunate
editorial decisions as he assembled the amatory epistles known to
him as O.'s. A final decision, if one is ever reached, will come only
after a complete stylistic and lexical investigation of the corpus, and
the importance of the inquiry resides in what more might be learned
about O.'s technique as a poet.

And so we are left with the evidence of the *Heroides*. The first
poem is Penelope's epistle to Ulysses, and it is the first mentioned in
the list in *Am.* 2.18. That is probably not mere chance: it is likely that
O. intended this poem to introduce the collection. He hints at this in
a poem addressed to his wife (*Trist.* 1.6), where he says that if she
had found her Homer (instead of O.) she would be as famous as
Penelope (21–2), and, he goes on,[23]

> prima locum sanctas heroidas inter haberes,
>   prima bonis animi conspicerere tui.

In other words she, not Penelope, would stand at the head of the
Heroides. The suggestion is neither ironic nor romantic; it is an asser-
tion of O.'s own worth as an artist, deserving to be mentioned in the
same breath as Homer.

3. THE *EPISTVLA SAPPHVS*

The epistle of Sappho to Phaon was not part of the medieval collec-
tion of *Heroides* (see below, p. 36) and after it came to light in the

---

[22] The eight epistles mentioned in 2.18 (1–2, 4–7, 10–11) with the addition
of Briseis (*Her.* 3) could easily have been accommodated in a single roll of
approximately 1,392 lines. The intrusion of spurious works might have begun
very early, as happened in the case of Theocritus, after which the collection
of single *Heroides* could have been carried on two rolls of approximately 1,100
lines each. The present edition includes only seven of the epistles whose
Ovidian authorship has never been disputed and the curious *Epistula Sapphus*.

[23] Lines 33–4 are transposed to follow 22 in the Venetian edition of 1486
and the arrangement has been adopted by most modern editors (e.g. Luck,

fifteenth century it attracted the considerable attention that attended
the discovery of a new text. Opinions varied both as to whether
the work was correctly ascribed to O. and whether it represented a
translation from Sappho. Important commentaries were produced
by Giorgio Merula (Venice 1471) and Domizio Calderini (Brescia
1476), and Angelo Poliziano lectured on the poem in 1481.[24] The work
of critical and textual exegesis that began with them developed into
a consensus in favour of Ovidian authorship which was not seriously
challenged until the nineteenth century. One scholar published the
suggestion that the epistle was a Renaissance forgery, and touched
off an interesting debate, which was dampened somewhat by news
of the existence of a thirteenth-century MS (F).[25] The more cogent
points raised by Karl Lachmann had greater effect,[26] but once again
the consensus of scholarly opinion swung back in the latter part of
the nineteenth century towards accepting the work as O.'s, a view
that prevailed through most of the twentieth century.[27]

A different view is adopted in this edition. Attention has long
focused on verbal similarities between the *ES* and the certainly
genuine *Heroides* as well as O.'s other works, but these parallels have
usually been adduced as evidence of Ovidian authorship.[28] Most re-
cently the case against Ovidian authorship has been argued by R. J.
Tarrant, who subjects the verbal evidence to a close analysis in an
effort to determine the relative chronology of the related passages.[29]

Goold). See E. J. Kenney, 'The poetry of Ovid's exile', *P.C.P.S.* 11 (1965) 39–
41 on the significance of this poem in the first book of the *Tristia*.

[24] His notes survive in Munich, Staatsbibliothek cod. lat. 754 and have re-
cently been published in E. Lazzeri, *Angelo Poliziano: commento inedito all'epistola
ovidiana* (Florence 1971).

[25] F. W. Schneidewin, 'Ovids fünfzehnter Brief', *Rh.M.* 2 (1843) 138–44.
See his further remarks in *Rh.M.* 3 (1845) 144–6, and the response by J.
Mähly, *Rh.M.* 9 (1854) 623–5.

[26] See above, p. 7.

[27] Especially influential were D. Comparetti, *Sull'autenticità della epistola
ovidiana di Saffo a Faone* (Florence 1876) and de Vries (1885), in addition to the
remarks of L. C. Purser in Palmer's edition, pp. 419–24.

[28] Especially de Vries (1885), W. Zingerle, *Untersuchungen zur Echtheitsfrage
der Heroiden Ovids* (Innsbruck 1878), and B. Eschenburg, *Wie hat Ovid einzelne
Wörter und Wortklassen im Verse verwandt? Ein Beitrag zur Echtheitsfrage der Heroides*
(Lübeck 1886).

[29] Tarrant (1981), supported by C. E. Murgia, 'Imitation and authenticity
in Ovid's *Metamorphoses* 1.477 and *Heroides* 15', *A.J.P.* 106 (1985) 456–74; but

The conclusions he reaches tend to confirm the indications of other metrical and lexical anomalies that the poem is later than O.'s exile poetry, and consequently cannot be by him.

If the poem is not by O., then by whom? The question has troubled many scholars who have dealt with this question, since it has seemed unlikely that its author could have remained anonymous. That the author was in many respects a talented poet is clear; but the finished product is a very different kind of poem from the *Heroides*. In all of the other epistles, including those whose authenticity has been disputed, the poem represents a character taken from an earlier narrative and depicted at a crucial juncture of her story. Although it is clear that the author of the *ES* knew Sappho's poetry, the narrative setting of this poem is not drawn from any work of literature, but from the biography of Sappho and the later traditions surrounding her life. It was an ingenious idea, but it was not O.'s.

4. THE EPISTLES

(a) The genre

The collection of *Heroides* is unique among the works of elegy surviving from Greek and Roman antiquity. In the *Ars amatoria* O. asserts the novelty of these epistles when he recommends his own poetry as reading material for women (3.345–6)

> uel tibi composita cantetur Epistula uoce:
>   ignotum hoc aliis ille nouauit opus.

The implications of this straightforward statement have sometimes been denied, but there is no reason to believe that any Greek or Roman poet wrote epistles like the *Heroides* before O.[30] As in the case of Latin love elegy, the originality of the *Heroides* consists primarily

---

the opposite conclusion is reached by E. Courtney, 'Ovid and an epigram of Philodemus', *L.C.M.* 15 (1990) 117–18.

[30] As Kenney (1982) 455 observes, such innovation characterizes O.'s entire poetic career: 'Every one of his surviving works represents a new literary departure, an unpredictable and individual variation on inherited themes and techniques.' Cf. Jacobson (1974) 319–22, with reference to earlier literature, and F. Spoth, *Ovids Heroides als Elegien* (Munich 1992) 22–8.

in the combination of features from other literary forms, and in this respect they may represent the most interesting example in Roman poetry of innovation in genre.[31] Detailed study of the collection reveals elements traceable to different branches of the rhetorical and literary traditions, although none can adequately account in and of itself for O.'s achievement in the *Heroides*.

There are few readers of the *Heroides* who would now accept at face value the old view of these poems as versified rhetorical set pieces.[32] But it would be a mistake to ignore completely the influence of O.'s early training in declamation. In his poetic autobiography O. relates how, thanks to the considerate attention of his parents, both he and his brother were able to study with the finest professors of rhetoric in Rome (*Trist.* 4.10.15–16). That O. preferred a literary career to a forensic one did not mean that he rejected his intellectual roots. On the contrary, the elder Seneca informs us (*Contr.* 2.2.8) of O.'s relationship as young man with the rhetor M. Porcius Latro: 'He was an admirer of Latro, though his style of speech was different. He had a neat, seemly and attractive talent. Even in those days his speech could be regarded as simply poetry put into prose. Moreover, he was so keen a student of Latro that he transferred many epigrams (*sententias*) into his own verse.' It would be an easy task to add to the examples adduced by Seneca of rhetorically inspired *sententiae* to be found in O.'s poetry.[33] Much has been made of Seneca's other recollection about O.'s performances in the rhetorical schools, that he 'rarely declaimed *controuersiae*, and only ones involving portrayal of character (*non nisi ethicas*). He preferred *suasoriae*, finding all argumentation tiresome.' It has often been argued that the *Heroides*

---

[31] The phenomenon which received its classic formulation in W. Kroll, *Studien zum Verständnis der römischen Literatur* (Stuttgart 1924) 202–24, in a chapter titled 'Die Kreuzung der Gattungen'. The terms in which Kroll opened this line of interpretation are perhaps too mechanical, but the questions he posed about the nature of genre in Roman poetry remain at the heart of critical inquiry into the *Heroides*; cf. G. B. Conte, *Generi e lettori* (Milan 1991) 163.

[32] To be found, e.g., in L. C. Purser's introduction to Palmer's commentary; cf. Martini (1933) 17, Wilkinson (1955) 5–10. Again, for earlier literature Jacobson (1974) 322–30 provides a judicious summary. Maurer (1990) 49–76 revisits the issue of rhetorical influences in the *Heroides*.

[33] Cf. S. F. Bonner, *Roman declamation* (Liverpool 1949) 152–6.

derive their content and structure from the style of the *suasoriae*.[34] To the extent that persuasion is an objective in some of the *Heroides* comparison with this type of rhetorical exercise is relevant, but the more important point that Seneca makes is about O.'s interest in character.

There was another type of exercise practised in the schools of rhetoric known as *ethopoeia*, or 'speech in character'. Quintilian (*Inst.* 3.8.52) considered the *ethopoeia* to be closely related to the *suasoria*. This exercise required the student to imagine himself in the situation of a famous figure from history or mythology, and frame a speech appropriate to the moment: for example, Sulla on abdicating the dictatorship, Priam to Achilles, or Niobe after the death of her children.[35] The impact of this form of schooling on the representation of character in Roman literature has been amply documented.[36] The nature of the *ethopoeia* as an imaginary speech suited to a character's circumstances clearly has special relevance for the fictional epistles of the *Heroides*, adapted to the crises in which the heroines find themselves.[37] But it is possible to find close analogies in many other types of poetry, especially in those that take the form of a monologue.

Because a number of the epistles of the *Heroides* are drawn from the characters of epic or tragedy, attention has naturally focused upon the monologues of drama for comparison with O.[38] Such models were important for O., but it is appropriate to call attention to other poems in which the identity of the poet is concealed behind

---

[34] E.g. H. Dörrie, 'Die dichterische Absicht in den Epistulae Heroidum', *A.&A.* 13 (1967) 45–6, A.-F. Sabot, 'Les Héroides d'Ovide', *A.N.R.W.* II 31.4 (1981) 2553–5.

[35] See S. F. Bonner, *Education in ancient Rome* (Berkeley 1977) 267–70.

[36] Jacobson (1974) 325–30 surveys the topic, while emphasizing the differences between the rhetorical exercise and the *Heroides*; cf. Kraus (1968) 90–1, Maurer (1990) 66–70.

[37] Nicolaus (*Rhet. Gr.* III 489) offers what became the standard definition of the form: ἠθοποιία ἐστὶ λόγος ἁρμόζων τοῖς ὑποκειμένοις. Comparisons have been made between the *Heroides* and *ethopoeiae* since Richard Bentley, *Dissertations upon the Epistles of Phalaris*, ed. A. Dyce (reprint, Hildesheim 1971) 83.

[38] E.g. Wilkinson (1955) 86.

the voice of a character.[39] Examples of such poetry are common in Hellenistic Greece. Theocritus' second *Idyll*, for example, represents the lament of a woman who has been betrayed by her lover. And other poems in the Theocritean corpus (3, 11, 12, and 23) contain monologues on similar amatory themes. The so-called 'Fragmentum Grenfellianum' (*CA*, pp. 177–8) is a lyric poem of the late Hellenistic period containing the lament of an anonymous female lover. And a curious piece of *c.* 100 BC may represent a lament by Helen of Troy (*CA*, p. 185).[40] There is evidence that Greek poets adapted this form to elegy as well. Fragments of elegiac verse from the early empire that seem to consist of monologue suggest a background for the development of Roman elegy somewhat broader than on the traditional view.[41] So too does the incorporation of such monologues into Greek Romances.[42] These works contain many of the features that distinguish Roman love elegy – the references to mythological examples, the identification of the poet and the speaker – but none combines all of these elements in the manner familiar from Latin elegy, and none makes use of the epistolary form.

This last innovation was probably first introduced by Propertius, who in his last book casts one poem (4.3) in the form of a letter from a woman he calls Arethusa to her lover Lycotas, a soldier who is away on campaign. Its opening verses (1–6) strike a note that becomes familiar in the *Heroides*:[43]

> haec Arethusa suo mittit mandata Lycotae,
>   cum totiens absis, si potes esse meus.
> si qua tamen tibi lecturo pars oblita derit,
>   haec erit e lacrimis facta litura meis:
> aut si qua incerto fallet te littera tractu,
>   signa meae dextrae iam morientis erunt.

---

[39] Jacobson (1974) 343–4 rightly emphasizes the importance of this tradition, which certainly influenced the development of Latin subjective elegy.

[40] Jacobson (1974) adduces both these fragments.

[41] For example, *SH* 962, 964, and *P.Oxy.* 54 (1987) no. 3723; cf. P. J. Parsons, 'Eine neugefundene griechische Liebeselegie', *M.H.* 45 (1988) 65–74.

[42] E.g. Chariton 1.14.6–10, 3.10.4–8, 5.1.4–7, 5.10.6–9, 6.6.2–5.

[43] Cf. 11.1n.

It seems clear that O. was influenced in his conception of the *Heroides* by this poem.[44] For the idea of drafting a love letter in verse, Propertius may have drawn on traditions of narrative in Hellenistic verse.[45] The inspiration to adapt this experiment in representing the character of heroines from literature seems to have come from O. alone. For the distinguishing feature of O.'s *Heroides* is their inspiration from works of literature: O.'s Dido is not a mythological figure, she is the heroine of Virgil's *Aeneid* 4. And, as far as we can tell, each of the single *Heroides* has a similar point of reference.

(b) *The literary background*

Each of the heroines' epistles refers self-consciously to a specific source in earlier literature; they represent episodes set in the interstices of the literary tradition. The reader finds himself in book 19 of the *Odyssey*: Penelope cannot sleep after her interview with the stranger who speaks with such assurance of her absent husband. How did she fill the hours till morning? O. knows: she wrote the letter that is *Heroides* 1.[46] In the anxious moments as dawn breaks over Libya, Dido knows that Aeneas and the Trojan fleet are putting to sea. She considers using force to stop him, but rejects it; instead, she writes our seventh epistle. This use of literary models represents a very different approach to the process of allusion or imitation ob-

---

[44] Since Heinsius first made the suggestion in his introductory note to *Her.* 1, it has sometimes been argued that Propertius imitated O.: e.g. R. Bürger, *De Ovidi carminum amatoriorum inventione et arte* (Wolfenbüttel 1901) 27–9; M. Pohlenz, *De Ovidi carminibus amatoriis* (Göttingen 1913) 14–17; H. Mersmann, *Quaestiones Propertianae* (diss. Münster 1931). While the possibility that Propertius imitated O. cannot be dismissed out of hand, it represents a less plausible scenario than the younger poet employing Propertius' unique example of an elegiac epistle as a springboard for a new poetic venture. Most of the specific arguments for Ovidian priority have been effectively refuted by E. Reitzenstein, *Wirklichkeitsbild und Gefühlsentwicklung bei Properz*, Philol. Suppl. 29.2 (Leipzig 1936) 17–34. Cf. also C. Becker, 'Die späten Elegien des Properz', *Hermes* 99 (1971) 469–70.

[45] Cf. Maurer (1990) 38–45.

[46] Cf. Kennedy (1984) on the setting of the first epistle in the context of *Od.* 19. As A. Barchiesi remarks in 'Narratività e convenzione nelle Heroides', *M.D.* 19 (1987) 66, 'la poetica delle *Eroidi* suggerisce, più semplicemente, che è possibile aprire nuove finestre su storie già compiute'.

servable elsewhere in the mythological narratives of Roman poetry.
In the *Heroides* O. does not re-create his heroines from the broad
range of traditional material available to him; he begins with his
characters as they have already been constituted in the works of his
predecessors.

In the third epistle, Briseis pleads with Achilles to take her back,
by force if necessary, for if he does not, he might as well ask her to
die. She then intensifies her rhetoric and suggests that he do the job
himself (145–8):

> cur autem iubeas? stricto pete corpora ferro;
>   est mihi qui fosso pectore sanguis eat.
> me petat ille tuus qui, si dea passa fuisset,
>   ensis in Atridae pectus iturus erat.

These lines refer to the scene in the opening of the *Iliad* when
Achilles in his rage is about to draw his sword to kill Agamemnon,
but is restrained by Athena (1.188–222). Since, as Homer describes
the moment, the goddess appeared only to Achilles and her presence
was not revealed to anyone else but the poet, we may well ask how
O.'s Briseis knows about this. Because she has read, so to speak, the
Iliad.

This allusive play on the text of the *Iliad* is paralleled elsewhere in
the epistle, where O.'s Briseis tries to persuade Achilles to relent in
his anger, both toward the Greeks and, as she imagines it, toward
her (91–3):

> nec tibi turpe puta precibus succumbere nostris;
>   coniugis Oenides uersus in arma prece est.
> res audita mihi, nota est tibi.

Briseis refers to the story of Meleager, who would not aid his people
after his mother had cursed him and was finally prevailed upon by
his wife. It was recounted to Achilles as a cautionary tale in *Il.*
9.529–99 by his old tutor Phoenix, and thus became known (*nota*) to
him; it can only have been heard by Briseis (*audita*) in a reading of
Homer.

This method provides O. with a framework for developing serious
issues raised by his models from an entirely new perspective. What
has not been generally recognized by critics is the extent to which in

the *Heroides* O. compels his readers to confront his literary models as critics, so to speak. He does this by seizing upon moments in the narrative in which his abandoned women may reassemble the components of the original narratives in new and sometimes arresting combinations. In these moments O. causes the reader to separate his reactions from the original model and to question the values represented there. He effects this separation by endowing his heroines with a new voice fashioned out of his experience as an elegist.

In lines 133–8 of the seventh epistle, Dido reminds Aeneas and the reader that she may be pregnant and that by driving her to suicide Aeneas will also be responsible for the death of his unborn child:

> forsitan et grauidam Dido, scelerate, relinquas
> parsque tui lateat corpore clausa meo.
> accedet fatis matris miserabilis infans,
> et nondum nato funeris auctor eris,
> cumque parente sua frater morietur Iuli,
> poenaque conexos auferet una duos.

O. is working from a passage in the *Aeneid* where Dido's anger with Aeneas has given way momentarily to pleading (4.327–30):

> saltem si qua mihi de te suscepta fuisset
> ante fugam suboles, si quis mihi paruulus aula
> luderet Aeneas, qui te tamen ore referret,
> non equidem omnino capta ac deserta uiderer.

Critical reaction has not always been favourable to O.'s more blunt reformulation of these lines where Dido expresses only the wish that she had had a child by him.[47] But in O.'s elegiac world sex has consequences, as we see elsewhere in the *Heroides*. In the emotional intensity of the language employed here (cf. 7.135, 136, 138nn.) O. underlines the seriousness of Dido's claim. The impact of her final words with the pathetic juxtaposition of numerals (*una duos*) is a startling and effective reworking of an elegiac cliché that two lovers are as one. O. interprets the *Aeneid* in terms of the values espoused in

---

[47] 'Vulgar' is the assessment of R. G. Austin, *Aeneidos liber quartus* (Oxford 1955) 105. Williams (1968) 383–4 is more sympathetic to O.'s intentions here, noting that his 'purpose is almost the opposite of Virgil's'.

love elegy, and the portrait that his Dido draws of Aeneas is correspondingly harsher than Virgil's.

O. can adapt his Virgilian model to this purpose in a variety of ways, altering the rhetorical emphases to score a point. In the *Aeneid* Dido threatens that her spirit will haunt Aeneas after his death (4.384-7):

> sequar atris ignibus absens
> et, cum frigida mors anima seduxerit artus,
> omnibus umbra locis adero. dabis, improbe, poenas.
> audiam et haec Manis ueniet mihi fama sub imos.

O.'s Dido employs a softer tone: she is convinced that she has been lied to and in the moments before the violent death that she hopes will not befall him, Aeneas will remember this and suffer. As she puts it (67-70):

> protinus occurrent falsae periuria linguae
> et Phrygia Dido fraude coacta mori.
> coniugis ante oculos deceptae stabit imago
> tristis et effusis sanguinolenta comis.

There is no hint of vengeance in O.'s treatment, the emphasis falls on the remorse that Aeneas will feel. The ambiguity of the phrasing in O.'s poem encourages hesitation about the actions of Aeneas. We are reminded that in the *Aeneid* he has already been visited by the shade of a lost wife at the end of book 2: *infelix simulacrum atque ipsius umbra Creusae | uisa mihi ante oculos et nota maior imago* (772-3). Commentators ancient and modern have been worried by the possible implications of Aeneas' last words to his wife as he flees Troy with his family, reported indirectly by Virgil, *longe seruet uestigia coniunx* (2.711).[48] How Aeneas lost Creusa and how the reader is to judge him

---

[48] Servius comments that Aeneas' strategy of splitting the party is sound since a large group might more easily be captured, while Serv. auct. notes: *uel* longe *ideo ut sit pro oeconomia, quod errare potuerit.* Austin remarks (*ad loc.*) that *longe* can only mean 'at a distance'. Heinze (1915) 59-62 takes pains to interpret the appearance of Creusa's ghost as a device to absolve Aeneas of any possible blame for her disappearance. O.'s adaptation of this part of the *Aeneid* anticipates the 'negative' reading of R. O. A. M. Lyne, *Further voices in the Aeneid* (Oxford 1987) 151, who, while conceding that Aeneas' treatment of

are questions enjoined by the ambiguities in Virgil's portrayal of this scene in the *Aeneid*. O.'s answer, through the voice of Dido, is unambiguous (81–4):

> omnia mentiris; neque enim tua fallere lingua
> > incipit a nobis, primaque plector ego.
> si quaeras, ubi sit formosi mater Iuli,
> > occidit a duro sola relicta uiro.

It is O.'s achievement to have engaged the text of the *Aeneid* on this point, and to treat directly the questions implicitly posed by Virgil.

A further illustration of the dynamic relationship between O.'s epistle and the *Aeneid* can be found in the way his Dido represents the moment when she and Aeneas are left alone in a cave after they have been caught out in a storm. The scene is portrayed by Virgil in a characteristically suggestive manner, as lightning flashes and thunder roars (4.165–8):

> speluncam Dido dux et Troianus eandem
> deueniunt. prima et Tellus et pronuba Iuno
> dant signum; fulsere ignes et conscius aether
> conubiis summoque ulularunt uertice Nymphae.

For Virgil's blurred images O. substitutes graphic language (7.91–2):

> his tamen officiis utinam contenta fuissem,
> > nec mea concubitu fama sepulta foret!

Knowing what she knows now, O.'s Dido wishes that she had avoided sex. On the signs that accompanied this union Virgil is also suggestive, but only suggestive: Juno and Tellus are in attendance, and the nymphs howl from the mountain-top.[49] *ulularunt*, the verb he uses here, has troubled commentators since Servius, for it connotes lamentation or ill-omen, while the context in Virgil seems, at least initially, to call for celebration. Any such suggestion is immediately dispelled by Virgil's own comment (169–70): *ille dies primus leti pri-*

---

his wife in this scene may in some respects accord with Roman priorities, argues that it none the less 'facilitates, if not causes, Creusa's death'.

[49] As Clausen (1987) 24 shows, Virgil refers to Apollonius' depiction of the wedding of Jason and Medea on Corcyra. The allusion to another cave-wedding that went wrong helps to determine the reader's response.

musque malorum | causa fuit. This account is transposed by O. to Dido as she recalls the experience (7.93–6):

> illa dies nocuit, qua nos decliue sub antrum
> caeruleus subitis compulit imber aquis.
> audieram uocem: nymphas ululasse putaui;
> Eumenides fati signa dedere mei.

O.'s Dido, to borrow G. B. Conte's terms,[50] has lived this experience in Virgil's poem, and she remembers the sound she heard: she thought it was the nymphs who delivered the ill-omened sign, but now she realizes that it was worse than that, it was the Eumenides. If a parallel is needed to confirm that this is indeed O.'s understanding of *ululare*, compare *Her.* 2.117, where Phyllis maintains that her marriage to Demophoon was also ill-omened: *pronuba Tisiphone thalamis ululauit in illis.* The so-called 'negative' reading of the *Aeneid* associated with modern criticism began almost simultaneously with the release of the poem. If O.'s reading of Dido has met with small critical success, it is at least partly because this aspect of the poem has not been recognized, and critics with overly fixed notions of Virgil's intentions in *Aeneid* 4 have imported their prejudices to the interpretation of the *Heroides*. What they have missed is the degree to which O. has seen and made explicit ideas that are only implied in Virgil's text.

This approach to *Heroides* 7 as an elegiac commentary on Virgil's *Aeneid* is paralleled by O.'s treatment of his other sources in the collection.[51] With Dido and several other heroines, O.'s method of translation into elegy can be examined with some confidence. His models are well-known to us and survive intact. When O. separates his heroines from their literary bases and endows them with an elegiac voice, the discontinuities are obvious. However, in the case of

---

[50] Conte discusses a similar reference to an earlier text (Cat. 64) by an Ovidian Ariadne at *Fast.* 3.469–75 in his *Memoria dei poeti e sistema letterario* (Turin 1974) 38–9 (= *The rhetoric of imitation* (Ithaca 1986) 60–1). This type of allusion is common in O.: see J. F. Miller, 'Ovidian allusion and the vocabulary of memory', *M.D.* 30 (1993) 153–64.

[51] The idea of such a relationship between works of literature was not unknown to ancient literary critics, who could characterize the *Odyssey*, for example, as Homer's device to fill in the blanks left by the *Iliad*: cf. W. Bühler, *Beiträge zur Erklärung der Schrift vom Erhabenen* (Göttingen 1964) 46–7.

several of the poems, for example the epistles of Phyllis, Oenone, and Canace, we are on less sure ground, for we do not have the texts that O. was working from. This is an important issue, one that critics of these poems have misjudged in assessing their originality. For example, the disparaging remark of one critic that *Her.* 7 is 'a bad poem and would be judged so even if the *Aeneid* had not survived', misses the point.[52] The focus of *Her.* 7 is clear precisely because we have the *Aeneid*. The novelty of the *Heroides* consists in their concentration on works of literature: O. is not interested in re-creating a Dido of his own, he is interested in Virgil's Dido.[53] For several of the poems in the collection we are not so fortunate in the matter of access to O.'s sources, but we may find traces of the same processes at work even in cases where we have no source for direct comparison.

O. never abandoned his legacy as a love elegist. It was his particular achievement to have recognized elegy's representation of emotional conflict as the distinctive contribution of the Roman practioners of the genre. That said, it was also O. who took the matter to the next stage and successfully negotiated the transfer of the elegiac voice to regions beyond the subjective portrayal of a poet-lover. The *Heroides* should be viewed as an important first step in this development which culminates in the *Metamorphoses*.[54] Some sense of their role in his development lies behind O.'s claim to originality in these poems. O.'s heroines are defined by this distinctly elegiac perspective as constituting a unique critical commentary on the Greek and Roman traditions of narrative verse. O.'s innovative reformulation of the heroines' voices in the *Heroides* provides a taste of what is possible in narrative verse when the elegiac perspective is em-

---

[52] Jacobson (1974) 76.

[53] The remarks on this point by L. Kaufman, *Discourses of desire: gender, genre, and epistolary fiction* (Ithaca and London 1986) 20 are apt: 'in his portrait of Dido, Ovid is not striving to represent the central core of woman's self, or "woman's essence"... Instead, Ovid's portrait is a critique of a previous representation of Dido: Virgil's.'

[54] The letter written by Byblis to her brother Caunus in *Met.* 9.530–63 is a concrete illustration of the technique employed in the *Heroides*. Coming at a crucial juncture in the narrative, that epistle provides a vehicle for Byblis' commentary on her own situation. In this case the wit resides in the fact that O. provides not only the epistle, but also the surrounding narrative.

ployed in the service of a critical commentary on the traditions of
the past.

(c) Aspects of language, style, and metre

In the first book of his *Ars amatoria* O. encourages his young readers
to study rhetoric, not for the usual reasons such as success in the law
courts, but in order to win over members of the opposite sex. He
then describes the appropriate style for a love letter (463–8):

> sed lateant uires, nec sis in fronte disertus;
>   effugiant uoces uerba molesta tuae.
> quis, nisi mentis inops, tenerae declamat amicae?
>   saepe ualens odii littera causa fuit.
> sit tibi credibilis sermo consuetaque uerba,
>   blanda tamen, praesens ut uideare loqui.

As O. puts it, the trick is to conceal the artfulness of the composition
by avoiding affected diction (*uerba molesta*).[55] The desired end is
plausibility (*credibilis sermo*), which is created by the use of familiar
language (*consueta uerba*). O.'s guidelines apply familiar rhetorical
precepts,[56] with a slight twist: to be convincing a lover must also be
enticing (*blanda*).[57] To a considerable extent the epistles that O.
writes for his heroines in the *Heroides* adhere to these precepts.

O. is very restrained in his use of archaisms in general and in his
elegiac poetry in particular.[58] But while avoiding the archaic, he is
perhaps less reluctant than his contemporaries to employ language
without poetic colour, often introducing expressions rarely found in
other Roman poets, if at all.[59] Often this involves both word choice

[55] For *molestus* in this context, cf. *TLL* s.v. 1354.46.

[56] As Hollis notes on this passage, with reference to Demetr. *Eloc.* 223–35
on the theory of epistolography; cf. also Maurer (1990) 14–30. On the avoid-
ance of unusual words as a point of rhetorical theory, the remark by Caesar
(Gellius 1.10.4) was famous: *tamquam scopulum, sic fugias inauditum atque insolens
uerbum.*

[57] On *blanditiae* as a characteristic of love elegy, see Smith on Tibullus
1.1.72.

[58] See Kenney (1973) 120–2 on his usage in the *Metamorphoses*.

[59] I avoid the term 'prosaic' here to characterize O.'s deviations from
standard poetic diction, although it will be used for the sake of convenience

and syntax intended to suggest everyday speech. So in Briseis' epistle to Achilles, she concedes that he may have been compelled to give her up to Agamemnon, but complains that he has allowed so much time to pass without trying to reclaim her (21–2):

> sed data sim, quia danda fui: tot noctibus absum,
>   nec repetor. cessas, iraque lenta tua est.

The concessive perfect subjunctive, 'grant that I was given up', is a common idiom in prose first found in poetry in Horace's *Satires* (1.1.45) and O.;[60] while the ablative *tot noctibus* in place of the more regular accusative for extent of time apparently reflects a development in conversational Latin that is first attested in poetry in Propertius and O.[61] Briseis' complaint that Achilles has not reclaimed her is made in language that sounds a bit like everyday Latin. Into this mix he introduces a note from the law courts: *repeto* is the technical term for reclaiming in a court of law property wrongfully acquired.[62] The legal metaphor is sustained in *cessas*, which suggests default in a legal action.[63]

O. has a unique talent for combining the poetic with the familiar. His Briseis adapts a famous passage from the *Iliad*, where Andromache reminds Hector that she has no family left because they have all been slain by Achilles (6.429–30):[64]

> Ἕκτορ, ἀτὰρ σύ μοί ἐσσι πατὴρ καὶ πότνια μήτηρ
> ἠδὲ κασίγνητος, σὺ δέ μοι θαλερὸς παρακοίτης.
>
> Hektor, thus you are father to me, and my honoured mother, | you are my brother, and you it is who are my young husband. (Lattimore)

in the commentary. Axelson (1945) has achieved justifiable celebrity as the fundamental work on the subject. Like most scholarly works that break new ground it is not impervious to criticism: see, e.g., Williams (1968) 743–50 and P. Watson, 'Axelson revisited: the selection of vocabulary in Latin poetry', *C.Q.* 35 (1985) 430–48. Although the discussion of these issues by Lyne (1989) 1–19 refers primarily to the *Aeneid*, his observations are also relevant to O.

[60] H–S 332, K–S I 190.
[61] E.g. Prop. 1.1.7, 1.6.7, 2.24.27, Ov. *Trist.* 5.10.3, *Pont.* 4.10.3.
[62] *OLD* s.v. 9, 10.
[63] *OLD* s.v. 3b.
[64] On O.'s adaptation here, see Barchiesi (1992) 29–32.

Briseis, too, enumerates the deaths of her brothers and husband, killed by Achilles when he captured her (51–2):

> tot tamen amissos te compensauimus uno:[65]
> tu dominus, tu uir, tu mihi frater eras.

In introducing this Homeric imitation, O. explains it by using an expression with an everyday legalistic ring: *compensare* is a common technical term in law and accounting for offsetting a deficit.[66] It is found only here in O., and is rare in Roman poetry,[67] an example of how O. enlivens the representation of his heroines by writing for them in familiar idiom.[68]

The *Heroides* are composed for characters taken primarily from the higher genres of epic, tragedy, and other types of narrative verse, whose expressions are accommodated to the elegiac style. Phaedra's epistle, for example, strikes a note familiar from earlier Roman elegy, and is not simply a reconstituted dramatic monologue. As part of her argument to win Hippolytus, she describes her new interest in hunting (37–40):

> iam quoque (uix credes) ignotas mittor in artes:
> est mihi per saeuas impetus ire feras.
> iam mihi prima dea est arcu praesignis adunco
> Delia; iudicium subsequor ipsa tuum.

Readers will recognize the imitation of Euripides' *Hippolytus* 215–22, where Phaedra imagines herself following Hippolytus into the woods. As Kenney notes,[69] this is part of Euripides' depiction of her delirium; O. represents the motif as part of a topos familiar in Roman love poetry, the lover's willingness to be subservient to please his or her partner (*obsequium*).[70] In this connection the hunting motif

---

[65] The text incorporates Heinsius' emendation for *amissis ... unum* of the MSS.

[66] *OLD* s.v. 1, *TLL* s.v. 2047.50ff.

[67] Elsewhere it is attested only at Hor. *Serm.* 1.3.70, and in a different sense at Sen. *Phaedr.* 84, Luc. 8.249.

[68] See further on O.'s exceptionally frequent use of legal terminology, Kenney (1969) and e.g. 1.96, 2.34, 5.36nn.

[69] Kenney (1982) 423.

[70] See 6.17–18n.

is widely attested in Roman poetry,[71] but its most prominent occurrence is in the opening poem of Propertius' *Monobiblos* in characterizing the steadfastness of Milanion in winning the love of Atalanta (9–10):

> nam modo Partheniis amens errabat in antris,
> ibat et hirsutas ille uidere feras.

The echo of Prop. 1.1.10 in line 38 of Phaedra's epistle clearly sets the motif within the sphere of Roman love elegy. This tone is underscored by the language in which it is couched.

The conversational tone is signalled by the parenthetical comment, *uix credes*, in 37. The expression *est impetus* with an infinitive was apparently coined by O. to describe wild emotion.[72] The adjective *praesignis* with the intensifying prefix *prae-* is first attested here, and adjectives thus compounded are not frequently found in Roman poetry, though they were not uncommon in ordinary prose.[73] Taken with the phrase *adunco arcu* it renders in distinctive fashion a common Greek epithet for Artemis, τοξοφόρος 'bow-bearing'. Such verbal innovation within familiar types of formation is a constant feature of O.'s style. Other uncommon words which are first attested in this selection of single *Heroides* include adjectives *semisepultus* (1.55), *intumulatus* (2.136), *capistratus* (2.80), *sepulcralis* (2.120), *medicabilis* (5.149), *peruigil* (6.13), *conubialis* (6.41), *spectabilis* (6.49), *Cytheriacus* (7.60), *semirefectus* (7.176), *semisupinus* (10.10), *puellaris* (10.20), *Ogygius* (10.48), and *pudibundus* (11.81); nouns *electus* (2.144), *munitor* (5.139), and *subnuba* (6.153); and verbs *spumesco* (2.87), *retempto* (10.12), *combibo* (11.54), and *reuelo* (11.73). It is likely that many, if not most, of these words occurred in lost texts, but the number of words first found in O. is indicative of his flexibility in the matter of word choice.[74]

---

[71] E.g. *Ars* 2.185–6, *Met.* 10.535–41, Prop. 2.19.17–24,Tib. 1.4.49–50, [Tib.] 4.3.11–18.

[72] Cf. 5.64n. After O. it is not attested until Seneca's *Phaedra* 518, a play much influenced by this poem.

[73] Cf. H–S 164. In the *Her.* we find only *praegrauis* (9.98) and *praeualidus* (9.80), and elsewhere in O., *praeacutus*, *praediues*, *praedurus*, *praefrigidus*, *praelustris*, and *praenubilus*. See 6.115–16n.

[74] Linse (1891) and A. Draeger, *Ovid als Sprachbildner* (1888) provide lists but little discussion: see Kenney (1973) 120–8.

Like his other heroines, 'O.'s Phaedra is envisaged very much as an elegiac figure.'[75] This is clearly reflected in the language the poet ascribes to her. Hippolytus is characterized by *ferreus* (14), *durus* (85), *rusticus* (102), and other stock terminology from the elegiac vocabulary of love, while she speaks of her own *nequitia* (17).[76] All of the characters in O.'s epistles have been similarly transformed to resemble the women of Roman elegy. Thus, when O. writes Briseis' epistle to Achilles, he imitates his earlier *Amores* to evoke the world of elegiac love. She reproaches him for not rejoining the battle and taking her back, suggesting that he is simply idling by his tent (117–20):

> tutius est iacuisse toro, tenuisse puellam,
>   Threiciam digitis increpuisse lyram,
> quam manibus clipeos et acutae cuspidis hastam,
>   et galeam pressa sustinuisse coma

The first couplet is repeated with a slight change from *Am.* 2.11.31–2, where O. laments his mistress' departure on a sea voyage:

> tutius est fouisse torum, legisse libellos,
>   Threiciam digitis increpuisse lyram.

The addition of martial images in 3.119–20 serves forcefully to juxtapose the epic background of O.'s Homeric model with this elegiac world. In the *Heroides* O. often evokes the higher stylistic register of his models by a judicious admixture of epic language: in Penelope's epistle, for example, *coniunx* (30), the periphrasis *Sigeia tellus* (33), the archaic genitive *uirum* (55), and the grand epithet *longaeuus* (103).

The essence of O.'s style in the *Heroides*, as in his other works, is wit, not as it is understood today, but in the sense common in seventeenth- and eighteenth-century criticism: 'a propriety of Thoughts and Words; or in other terms, Thought and Words elegantly adapted to the Subject' (Dryden). In O.'s style the play of words reflects an intellectual process that compels thought on the part of the reader by unexpected verbal effects. One of the most characteristic is the

[75] Kenney (1982) 423.
[76] Cf. Pichon (1902) 202.

figure of speech known as syllepsis. By this figure two words are joined with a third that must be construed in a slightly different, but appropriate sense, with each.[77] An example is found in Phyllis' complaint to Demophoon (2.25):

> Demophoon, uentis et uerba et uela dedisti.

The verb *dedisti* must be understood in a different sense with each object, *uerba* (abstract) and *uela* (concrete). *uentis uerba dare* is a proverbial expression for making empty promises,[78] while *uentis uela dare* simply means 'to set sail' (*OLD* s.v. *do* 18f). O. uses the same figure less wittily to describe Ariadne abandoned by Theseus (*Am.* 1.7.15–16):

> talis periuri promissaque uelaque Thesei
> fleuit praecipites Cressa tulisse Notos.

The play on the different senses of the verb compels thought about the actions described. The response elicited by this device is intellectual rather than emotional.

This is not to suggest that syllepsis is an entirely unaffective device. O. can use it in quite arresting combinations, as he does at the end of Phyllis' epistle, in the epitaph she provides for herself (147–8):

> PHYLLIDA DEMOPHOON LETO DEDIT HOSPES AMANTEM
> ILLE NECIS CAVSAM PRAEBVIT IPSA MANVM

Here O. employs a number of verbal devices to elicit an emotional response (see comm.), combined with the effect of the verb in the pentameter (*praebuit*) being taken (ἀπὸ κοινοῦ) with the abstract noun (*causam*) and the concrete (*manum*). The result is a kind of

---

[77] Syllepsis is to be distinguished from zeugma, a less common figure in O., by which a different *and* inappropriate sense must be supplied for the third term. An example of zeugma is Virg. *Geo.* 1.92–3 *ne tenues pluuiae rapidiue potentia solis | acrior aut Boreae penetrabile frigus adurat*, where some sense like *diluant* must be supplied for *pluuiae* from *adurat*; see Kenney on Lucr. 3.614, Bell (1923) 304–14, and H–S 831–4. I note no examples of zeugma in the *Her.*, and indeed it is not common in O.: many of the instances adduced by Bömer on, e.g., *Met.* 2.601 may be better classified as syllepsis.

[78] See Otto (1890) s.v. *verbum*.

syllepsis, requiring a slightly different sense with each object, but
focusing on Demophoon's culpability in causing her suicide. O.'s
manner inspired many imitators among later Latin poets, but rarely
were any able to approximate his wit in harmonizing thought and
expression.[79]

In creating verbal effects O. is more prone than earlier Latin poets
to departing from the natural word-order. Such distortions were
called 'hyperbaton' by the grammarians.[80] O. is often characterized
as especially fond of this device, a generalization which contains an
important grain of truth. Examples of syntactically disruptive word-
order are relatively rare. In *Her.* 3 Briseis tells how she feared that
she would be caught by the Trojans if she tried to slip out of Aga-
memnon's camp at night (19):

> si progressa forem caperer ne nocte timebam.

Editors generally provide commas around *nocte* to signal that it
should be construed with *progressa forem*, but 'ancient readers did not
need it nor should a modern reader who is conscious that Latin is
not English ... and who has trained himself to go on until *the poet*
tells him, by providing the awaited syntactical/rhetorical dénoue-
ment, that he may stop'.[81] And here the dislocation of *nocte* together
with its juxtaposition with *timebam* lends emphasis to her fears of get-
ting lost in the dark. Examples of such hyperbata are relatively in-
frequent in the *Heroides*.[82] More commonly his arrangement of words
in the line serves to arrest the progress of thought and focuses the
reader on an image. That is a procedure closely related to the metre
in which the *Heroides* were composed.

---

[79] See F. Leo, *De Senecae tragoediis observationes criticae* (Berlin 1878) 197–200
for examples of syllepsis in Seneca and Flavian epic.

[80] On hyperbaton in general, see H–S 689–94 and, for a collection of ex-
amples from Latin poetry, A. E. Housman, 'Horatiana', *J.Ph.* 18 (1890) 6–7
(= *Class. pap.* 140–1). For O.'s practice, especially in the *Met.*, see Kenney
(1973) 128–30.

[81] Kenney (1973) 130.

[82] 3. 56 *et mecum fugias quae tibi dantur opes*, where the dislocation of *mecum*
adds to Briseis' tone of indignation. See notes on 7.143–4, 10.110, *ES* 103–4.
For hyperbaton in the elegists, see Platnauer (1951) 104–8.

A complete analysis of O.'s management of the elegiac couplet is not possible here.[83] It is important to realize that the quantities of statistics assembled by scholars on various aspects of his practice reflect choices made by the poet that cannot be easily distinguished from other features of his verse style. O.'s light touch is often remarked upon: in this he continues trends already discernible in his predecessors. The diminished use of elision is a feature in this development, which is illustrated by the following figures taken from 300 lines of representative elegiac texts:[84]

	Cat.	Prop. I	Tib. I	*Her.*	*Am.* I
short vowel	41	36	15	9	19
-*m*	43	11	4	4	5
prodelision	21	7	6	9	9
long vowel	29	1	4	7	2
diphthong	2	20	0	0	0

The lightness and smoothness of O.'s elegiac couplet is assisted by his tendency to treat each couplet as a distinct unit of composition. Sense pauses most commonly fall at line-end, especially in the pentameter. As a consequence, enjambment of couplets is severely limited, and rarely involves more than addition to the sentence, for example, of a relative clause or coordinate phrase. It is especially in the pentameter, then, which rounds off the unit of composition, where O. focuses the attention of the reader. For example, when Phaedra tries to tempt Hippolytus into a love affair, she illustrates her offer by emphasizing the attractions of forbidden fruit (4.29–30):

> est aliquid plenis pomaria carpere ramis,
>   et tenui primam delegere ungue rosam.

[83] See Platnauer (1951) with the reviews by E. J. Kenney, *J.R.S.* 43 (1953) 230–1 and R. J. Getty, *C.P.* 48 (1953) 189–92. For the *Amores* the discussion by McKeown (1987) 108–23 is an excellent introduction.

[84] To the figures collected by McKeown (1987) 114, I have added a sample of 300 lines from *Her.* 1, 2, and 5. See too Platnauer (1951) 72–90.

The pentameter is carefully constructed with two adjectives and two nouns grouped around a verb in the pattern abAB.[85] The image suggested in the hexameter of picking from an orchard is carefully shifted to a more detailed image in the pentameter. A similar effect is achieved as Phaedra contemplates Hippolytus' appearance (77–8):

> te tuus iste rigor positique sine arte capilli
> et leuis egregio puluis in ore decet.

The couplet is arranged in three units of increasing length, a tricolon that rises to a climax in the final clause which fills out the pentameter. Here the two adjectives and two nouns are arranged in a pattern abAB which precedes the verb. Although sometimes viewed as purely ornamental, such 'patterned lines' in O. often contribute strikingly to the tone. Here, the characterization of Phaedra is surely further elaborated by showing her lingering over the detail of the dust clinging to Hippolytus' face after exercise.[86]

Style, metre, and language are not easily separable elements in the analysis of O.'s technique as a poet. In the *Heroides* he manages to endow his characters with the distinctive elegiac voice familiar from the *Amores* and the *Ars amatoria* in particular, and yet through the careful deployment of language manages to evoke the literary models from which he draws. These poems attracted imitators almost as soon as they appeared, if we can trust O., who describes his friend Sabinus composing 'replies' for some of the epistles (*Am.* 2.18.27–32):

> quam cito de toto rediit meus orbe Sabinus
> scriptaque diuersis rettulit ipse locis!
> candida Penelope signum cognouit Vlixis,
> legit ab Hippolyto scripta nouerca suo;

---

[85] Commonly known as a 'golden line' from a famous characterization by Dryden. Other veins of ore are mined by the poets, who arrange the epithets and nouns in chiastic order abBA, sometimes called a 'silver line', as by L. P. Wilkinson, *Golden Latin artistry* (Cambridge 1963) 216. This type of patterning admits of much variation, but the distinctions are less important than the overall effect of such 'patterned lines' as they will be termed here. Important discussions of this feature of poetic style, especially in hexameter poetry, can be found in Norden (1927) 393–8 and Ross (1969) 132–7. We lack a thorough examination of the elegists.

[86] For other examples of such effects, see, e.g., 1.36, 2.94, 7.94, 10.28nn.

iam pius Aeneas miserae rescripsit Elissae,
    quodque legat Phyllis, si modo uiuit, adest.

The genre remained popular through the Middle Ages, when the
Heroides were read and commented upon for their rhetorical value.[87]
Imitations, adaptations, and continuations of the *Heroides* appeared
in great numbers after the Renaissance until the eighteenth cen-
tury.[88] If they have not shared in the general appreciation accorded
O.'s other poetry in more recent times, it is worth listening to the
verdict of Dryden, recorded in his preface to a translation of the
Heroides by several hands (1683), that they are 'generally granted to
be the most perfect piece of O.'

5. THE TRANSMISSION OF THE TEXT

The text of the *Heroides* has suffered more during the passage from
antiquity than any of O.'s other surviving works.[89] The collection is
not transmitted in any medieval manuscript in the form in which it
is printed in modern editions. For *Her.* 1–14 our knowledge of the
text depends in the first instance upon a ninth-century manuscript,
known as the *Puteaneus* (*P*). It has suffered considerable damage, in-
cluding the loss of several leaves, but it is the only MS of the *Heroides*
of Carolingian date, and where extant (2.14–4.47, 4.104–5.96, 6.50–
20.175) it provides a text less affected by interpolation than later wit-
nesses.[90] Of the approximately 100 remaining medieval MSS editors

[87] See R. J. Hexter, *Ovid and medieval schooling: studies in medieval school com-
mentaries on Ovid's Ars Amatoria, Epistulae ex Ponto, and Epistulae Heroidum* (Munich
1986) 137–204.
[88] Much information can be mined from H. Dörrie, *Der heroische Brief.
Bestandsaufnahme, Geschichte, Kritik einer humanistisch-barocken Literaturgattung*
(Berlin 1968). See also R. Trickett, 'The *Heroides* and the English Augustans',
in C. Martindale (ed.), *Ovid renewed* (Cambridge 1988) 191–204.
[89] For a summary account of the transmission, see Tarrant (1983). The
most extensive study of the MSS is by Dörrie (1960a) and (1960b), to be sup-
plemented by the review of E. J. Kenney, *Gnomon* 33 (1961) 478–87. See too
Dörrie (1972).
[90] See D. S. McKie, 'Ovid's *Amores*: the prime sources for the text', *C.Q.* 36
(1986) 224–6 for a description of the condition of *P*. He also provides con-
vincing arguments against the hypothesis, advanced by S. Tafel, *Die Über-
lieferungsgeschichte von Ovids carmina amatoria verfolgt bis zum 11. Jahrhundert* (diss.

have depended primarily upon two products of the late eleventh and twelfth centuries, Eton College 150 (*E*), which is also incomplete (it ends at 7.159) and Wolfenbüttel, Extrav. 260 (*G*).[91] These MSS have undergone varying degrees of correction and interpolation, like the remaining crowd of *recentiores*. In this tradition it is impossible to construct a stemma that would allow the elimination of later manuscripts in reconstructing O.'s text: 'all inherently plausible readings, whatever their source, must be taken seriously, and sense and usage are the only sure criteria for deciding among them'.[92]

The transmission of the so-called double epistles is of less concern here, except in so far as the vicissitudes suffered by these poems indicate the hazards to which the entire collection has been exposed. The text of these epistles rests in the main on the same body of manuscript evidence as *Her.* 1–14. For two long passages in the epistles of Paris (16.39–144) and Cydippe (21.145–248) the only witness is the printed edition produced at Parma in 1477.[93] In addition, most MSS of the *Heroides* break off at 21.12; only three fifteenth-century MSS and the early editions printed at Rome (1471) and Venice (1474) preserve lines 21.13–144.[94] The authenticity of the passages transmitted only in the Parma edition has often been disputed,[95] a question that is unrelated to the authorship of the double epistles themselves. If, as seems likely, they come from the same hand as the remainder of *Her.* 16–21, they must derive from a lost exemplar that survived unnoticed until it or one of its offspring was used for the edition of 1477.[96] The fact that such a MS went unnoticed for so long

Tübingen 1910) 26–32 and supported by Kenney and Dörrie, that the *Heroides* were transmitted to the Carolingian era joined with O.'s other amatory elegies in a single tradition. If that theory is no longer tenable it is easier to comprehend the considerable disfiguration of the text.

[91] The *Heroides* were also translated by the Byzantine scholar Maximus Planudes (13th cent.), and it is occasionally worthwhile to try to recover the readings of the MS he used.

[92] Tarrant (1983) 270.

[93] Dörrie (1960b) 377–9.

[94] Dörrie (1960b) 379–84.

[95] See most recently Reeve (1973) 334–7; there is a fuller discussion in Fischer (1969) 132–51, 196–222.

[96] The ascription of these passages to the author of the double *Heroides* has been vigorously defended by Kenney (1979), who also provides considerable grounds for believing that author to be O. It is likely that the MS that pre-

serves as a caution against summarily rejecting doubtfully attested
lines elsewhere in the collection. External evidence alone cannot
prove interpolation.

A number of couplets in the *Heroides* were clearly not extant in the
mainstream of the tradition, although they are attested in one or
more medieval MSS. In the single *Heroides* they are found after 2.17,
4.132, 7.23, 7.96, 8.18, 9.114, 12.158, and 13.73. These are either gen-
uine verses, carried by some source independent of the main line of
transmission, or interpolations: each case must be judged on its own
merits.[97] These observations are also valid for the introductory cou-
plets found preceding *Her.* 5–12 among the single epistles. Some of
these couplets are obviously spurious, and those present in *E*, one of
the oldest MSS, have no special authority:[98] all can best be ex-
plained as interpolations supplied in those epistles whose openings
were deemed at some point in the transmission to be insufficiently
'epistolary'.[99]

The epistle of Sappho to Phaon is not found in any medieval MS
in its present position as the fifteenth poem in the collection. It owes
its location in modern editions to Daniel Heinsius, who placed it
before the double epistles in his edition of 1629. In this he was ap-
parently anticipated by the compiler of the the twelfth-century an-
thology known as the *Florilegium Gallicum*, which includes excerpts of
Sappho's epistle between those from *Her.* 14 and 16.[100] The only sur-

served these lines was complete, but given its selective use in producing the
Parma edition, this cannot be proved.

[97] See Housman (1897) 200–2 (= *Class. pap.* 388–92), M. Sicherl, 'Ver-
meintliche Versinterpolationen in Ovids Heroiden', *Hermes* 91 (1963) 190–212,
and the notes in the commentary to 2.17, 7.23, and 7.96.

[98] I.e. the couplets preceding *Her.* 5–7. *E* breaks off after 7.159.

[99] Different conclusions are reached by J. Vahlen, 'Über die Anfänge der
Heroiden des Ovid', *Abhandlungen der kgl. Akad. der Wiss. zu Berlin* (1881) 1–40,
W. Schmitz-Cronenbroeck, *Die Anfänge der Heroiden des Ovid*, diss. Cologne
(Düsseldorf 1937) and E. A. Kirfel, *Untersuchungen zur Briefform der Heroiden
Ovids*, Noctes Romanae 11 (Berne and Stuttgart 1969). The more sceptical ap-
proach taken by E. J. Kenney, *Gnom.* 33 (1961) 485, Jacobson (1974) 404–9,
and Tarrant (1983) 271 seems warranted by the circumstances, although the
argument that each letter would have contained a superscription (e.g. *Penelope
Vlixi*) is not compelling: cf. G. P. Goold, *Gnom.* 46 (1974) 483–4.

[100] See R. Burton, *Classical poets in the Florilegium Gallicum* (Berne and Frank-
furt 1983) 16–17.

viving medieval manuscript to transmit the poem, Frankfurt, Univ. Barth. 110 (*F*), places it before the *Heroides*, and there are indications that it was copied from a different source than the other epistles.[101] From the evidence available it is impossible to believe that the *Epistula Sapphus* was transmitted to the Middle Ages as part of the Ovidian corpus. In addition to *F*, the poem is found in about 150 MSS of the fifteenth century descended from an independent source. Their evidence therefore cannot be ignored.

The text of the present edition is based on earlier editions and an unpublished apparatus prepared by E. J. Kenney. The apparatus is intended to signal only those places where there is significant variation in the tradition, or where several editors have disagreed about what to print.

[101] Tarrant (1983) 272.

EPISTVLAE HEROIDVM SELECTAE

SIGLA

P = Parisinus Latinus 8242 (Puteaneus), saec. ix
E = Coll. Etonensis 150 (Bl. 6.5), saec. xi
G = Guelferbytanus extrav. 260, saec. xii
F = Francofurtanus Barth. 110, saec. xii/xiii
Plan. = Metaphrasis Planudis

ω = codices recentiores omnes uel plures
ς = codices recentiores aliquot uel pauci uel unus
codd. = codicum omnium consensus

*** lacuna
[ ] delenda

P. OVIDI NASONIS
EPISTVLAE HEROIDVM SELECTAE

I
PENELOPE VLIXI

Haec tua Penelope lento tibi mittit, Vlixe;
    nil mihi rescribas attinet: ipse ueni.
Troia iacet certe, Danais inuisa puellis;
    uix Priamus tanti totaque Troia fuit.
o utinam tum, cum Lacedaemona classe petebat,   5
    obrutus insanis esset adulter aquis!
non ego deserto iacuissem frigida lecto,
    nec quererer tardos ire relicta dies,
nec mihi quaerenti spatiosam fallere noctem
    lassaret uiduas pendula tela manus.   10
quando ego non timui grauiora pericula ueris?
    res est solliciti plena timoris amor.
in te fingebam uiolentos Troas ituros,
    nomine in Hectoreo pallida semper eram.
siue quis Antilochum narrabat ab hoste reuictum,   15
    Antilochus nostri causa timoris erat;
siue Menoetiaden falsis cecidisse sub armis,
    flebam successu posse carere dolos.
sanguine Tlepolemus Lyciam tepefecerat hastam;
    Tlepolemi leto cura nouata mea est.   20
denique, quisquis erat castris iugulatus Achiuis,
    frigidius glacie pectus amantis erat.
sed bene consuluit casto deus aequus amori:
    uersa est in cinerem sospite Troia uiro.

---

1 1 haec *Palmer*: hanc *codd.*   2 attinet *Apthonius* (*GLK* VI 109.33, 111.24):
attamen *Gω*: sed tamen *Eς*   15 ab hoste reuictum *Housman*: ab Hectore
uictum *codd.*   24 cinerem *Eς*: cineres *Gω*

Argolici rediere duces, altaria fumant,   25
    ponitur ad patrios barbara praeda deos.
grata ferunt nuptae pro saluis dona maritis;
    illi uicta suis Troica fata canunt.
mirantur iustique senes trepidaeque puellae,
    narrantis coniunx pendet ab ore uiri.   30
iamque aliquis posita monstrat fera proelia mensa,
    pingit et exiguo Pergama tota mero:
'hac ibat Simois, haec est Sigeia tellus,
    hic steterat Priami regia celsa senis.
illic Aeacides, illic tendebat Vlixes;   35
    hic lacer admissos terruit Hector equos.'
omnia namque tuo senior te quaerere misso
    rettulerat nato Nestor, at ille mihi.
[rettulit et ferro Rhesum Dolonaque caesos,
    utque sit hic somno proditus, ille dolo.]   40
ausus es, o nimium nimiumque oblite tuorum,
    Thracia nocturno tangere castra dolo
totque simul mactare uiros, adiutus ab uno!
    at bene cautus eras et memor ante mei.
usque metu micuere sinus, dum uictor amicum   45
    dictus es Ismariis isse per agmen equis.
sed mihi quid prodest uestris disiecta lacertis
    Ilios et, murus quod fuit, esse solum,
si maneo, qualis Troia durante manebam,
    uirque mihi dempto fine carendus abest?   50
diruta sunt aliis, uni mihi Pergama restant,
    incola captiuo quae boue uictor arat.
iam seges est ubi Troia fuit, resecandaque falce
    luxuriat Phrygio sanguine pinguis humus.
semisepulta uirum curuis feriuntur aratris   55
    ossa, ruinosas occulit herba domos.

---

27 nuptae *Heinsius*: nymphae *codd.*   31 iamque *G*ς: atque *E*ς   36 lacer
admissos ς: alacer missos *EG*ω   37–40 *del. Bentley*, 39–40 *delendos censeo*
48 esse *G*ς *Plan.*: ante *E*ω

uictor abes, nec scire mihi, quae causa morandi
    aut in quo lateas ferreus orbe, licet.
quisquis ad haec uertit peregrinam litora puppim,
    ille mihi de te multa rogatus abit,   60
quamque tibi reddat, si te modo uiderit usquam,
    traditur huic digitis charta notata meis.
nos Pylon, antiqui Neleia Nestoris arua,
    misimus; incerta est fama remissa Pylo.
misimus et Sparten; Sparte quoque nescia ueri.   65
    quas habitas terras aut ubi lentus abes?
utilius starent etiamnunc moenia Phoebi.
    irascor uotis, heu, leuis ipsa meis!
scirem ubi pugnares, et tantum bella timerem,
    et mea cum multis iuncta querela foret.   70
quid timeam, ignoro; timeo tamen omnia demens,
    et patet in curas area lata meas.
quaecumque aequor habet, quaecumque pericula tellus,
    tam longae causas suspicor esse morae.
haec ego dum stulte metuo, quae uestra libido est,   75
    esse peregrino captus amore potes.
forsitan et narres, quam sit tibi rustica coniunx,
    quae tantum lanas non sinat esse rudes.
fallar, et hoc crimen tenues uanescat in auras,
    neue, reuertendi liber, abesse uelis.   80
me pater Icarius uiduo discedere lecto
    cogit et immensas increpat usque moras.
increpet usque licet: tua sum, tua dicar oportet;
    Penelope coniunx semper Vlixis ero.
ille tamen pietate mea precibusque pudicis   85
    frangitur et uires temperat ipse suas.
Dulichii Samiique et quos tulit alta Zacynthos,
    turba ruunt in me luxuriosa, proci,
inque tua regnant nullis prohibentibus aula;
    uiscera nostra, tuae dilacerantur opes.   90

75 metuo *G*ς: meditor *E*ω   83–4 *del. Bentley*   85–6 *del. Sedlmayer*

quid tibi Pisandrum Polybumque Medontaque dirum
    Eurymachique auidas Antinoique manus
atque alios referam, quos omnes turpiter absens
    ipse tuo partis sanguine rebus alis?
Irus egens pecorisque Melanthius actor edendi   95
    ultimus accedunt in tua damna pudor.
tres sumus imbelles numero, sine uiribus uxor
    Laertesque senex Telemachusque puer.
ille per insidias paene est mihi nuper ademptus,
    dum parat inuitis omnibus ire Pylon.   100
di, precor, hoc iubeant, ut euntibus ordine fatis
    ille meos oculos comprimat, ille tuos!
hac faciunt custosque boum longaeuaque nutrix,
    tertius immundae cura fidelis harae;
sed neque Laertes, ut qui sit inutilis armis,   105
    hostibus in mediis regna tenere ualet.
Telemacho ueniet (uiuat modo) fortior aetas;
    nunc erat auxiliis illa tuenda patris.
nec mihi sunt uires inimicos pellere tectis.
    tu citius uenias, portus et ara tuis.   110
est tibi, sitque precor, natus, qui mollibus annis
    in patrias artes erudiendus erat.
respice Laerten: ut tu sua lumina condas,
    extremum fati sustinet ille diem.
certe ego, quae fueram te discedente puella,   115
    protinus ut redeas, facta uidebor anus.

---

95 actor *G*ς: auctor *E*ω   103 hac *Tyrrell*: haec *EG*ς: hoc ς   105 armis
ς: annis *EG*ω   106 ualet *E*ς *Plan.*: potest *G*ω   110 ara ς: aura *EG*ω
113 tu *Bentley*: iam *codd.*   116 redeas *E*ω: uenias *G*ς

II
PHYLLIS DEMOPHOONTI

Hospita, Demophoon, tua te Rhodopeia Phyllis
    ultra promissum tempus abesse queror.
cornua cum lunae pleno semel orbe coissent,
    litoribus nostris ancora pacta tua est.
luna quater latuit, toto quater orbe recreuit, 5
    nec uehit Actaeas Sithonis unda rates.
tempora si numeres, bene quae numeramus amantes,
    non uenit ante suam nostra querela diem.
spes quoque lenta fuit. tarde, quae credita laedunt,
    credimus: inuita nunc es amante nocens. 10
saepe fui mendax pro te mihi, saepe putaui
    alba procellosos uela referre Notos.
Thesea deuoui, quia te dimittere nollet,
    nec tenuit cursus forsitan ille tuos.
interdum timui, ne, dum uada tendis ad Hebri, 15
    mersa foret cana naufraga puppis aqua.
saepe deos supplex, ut tu, scelerate, ualeres,
    cum prece turicremis sum uenerata focis;
saepe uidens uentos caelo pelagoque fauentes,
    ipsa mihi dixi, 'si ualet ille, uenit.' 20
denique fidus amor, quidquid properantibus obstat,
    finxit, et ad causas ingeniosa fui.
at tu lentus abes; nec te iurata reducunt
    numina, nec nostro motus amore redis.
Demophoon, uentis et uerba et uela dedisti; 25
    uela queror reditu, uerba carere fide.
dic mihi, quid feci, nisi non sapienter amaui?
    crimine te potui demeruisse meo.

II 10 inuita *Eω*: inuito *G*   es amante *F²*: et amante *Eω*: et amore *G*   nocens
EF²: nocent ω: noces *Gς*   14 *incipit P*   17 deos *PGω*: deo ς: diis *E*   18–
19 *habent* ς: *om. PEGω*   18 cum … sum uenerata ς: sum … deuenerata ς
19 fauentes ς: secundos ς   25 uerba et uela *PEω*: uela et uerba *Gς*

unum in me scelus est, quod te, scelerate, recepi;
    sed scelus hoc meriti pondus et instar habet.   30
pacta fides ubi nunc commissaque dextera dextrae
    quique erat in falso plurimus ore deus?
promissus socios ubi nunc Hymenaeus in annos,
    qui mihi coniugii sponsor et obses erat?
per mare, quod totiens uentis agitatur et undis,   35
    per quod nempe ieras, per quod iturus eras,
perque tuum mihi iurasti (nisi fictus et ille est),
    concita qui uentis aequora mulcet, auum,
per Venerem nimiumque mihi facientia tela,
    altera tela arcus, altera tela faces,   40
Iunonemque, toris quae praesidet alma maritis,
    et per taediferae mystica sacra deae.
si de tot laesis sua numina quisque deorum
    uindicet, in poenas non satis unus eris.
at laceras etiam puppes furiosa refeci,   45
    ut, qua desererer, firma carina foret.
remigiumque dedi, quo me fugiturus abires.
    heu, patior telis uulnera facta meis!
credidimus blandis, quorum tibi copia, uerbis;
    credidimus generi nominibusque tuis;   50
credidimus lacrimis. an et hae simulare docentur?
    hae quoque habent artes, quaque iubentur, eunt?
his nos credidimus. quo iam tot pignora nobis?
    parte satis potui qualibet inde capi.
nec moueor quod te iuui portuque locoque: 55
    debuit haec meriti summa fuisse mei.

31 pacta fides *Bentley*: iura fides *codd.*: iura fidesque *Heinsius*   35 totiens
Knaack: totum *codd.*   36 nempe *Bentley*: saepe *codd.*   45 at *P(ut uid.)Eς*:
ha *Gω*: a *D. Heinsius*   47 quo ... abires *Eω*: quod ... haberes *PGς*   50
nominibusque *Plan.*: numinibusque *PEGω*: muneribusque *ς*   52 quaque
codd.: cumque *Slichtenhorst*   53 his nos *Kenney*: dis quoque *codd.* quo *Hein-sius*: quod *P*: quid *P²EGω* nobis *PEGω*: prosunt *ς*

turpiter hospitium lecto cumulasse iugali
   paenitet et lateri conseruisse latus.
quae fuit ante illam, mallem suprema fuisset
   nox mihi, dum potui Phyllis honesta mori.   60
speraui melius, quia me meruisse putaui.
   quaecumque ex merito spes uenit, aequa uenit.
fallere credentem non est operosa puellam
   gloria; simplicitas digna fauore fuit.
sum decepta tuis et amans et femina uerbis.   65
   di faciant, laudis summa sit ista tuae!
inter et Aegidas media statuaris in urbe,
   magnificus titulis stet pater ante suis.
cum fuerit Sciron lectus toruusque Procrustes
   et Sinis et tauri mixtaque forma uiri   70
et domitae bello Thebae fusique bimembres
   et pulsata nigri regia caeca dei,
hoc tua post illos titulo signetur imago:
   HIC EST CVIVS AMANS HOSPITA CAPTA DOLO EST.
de tanta rerum turba factisque parentis   75
   sedit in ingenio Cressa relicta tuo.
quod solum excusat, solum miraris in illo;
   heredem patriae, perfide, fraudis agis.
illa (nec inuideo) fruitur meliore marito
   inque capistratis tigribus alta sedet.   80
at mea despecti fugiunt conubia Thraces,
   quod ferar externum praeposuisse meis,
atque aliquis 'iam nunc doctas eat', inquit, 'Athenas;
   armiferam Thracen qui regat, alter erit.
exitus acta probat.' careat successibus, opto,   85
   quisquis ab euentu facta notanda putat.
at si nostra tuo spumescant aequora remo,
   iam mihi, iam dicar consuluisse meis.

57 hospitium *PG*ω: officium *E*ς   82 ferar *PG*ς: feror *EG²*ω

sed neque consului, nec te mea regia tanget
    fessaque Bistonia membra lauabis aqua. 90
illa meis oculis species abeuntis inhaeret,
    cum premeret portus classis itura meos.
ausus es amplecti colloque infusus amantis
    oscula per longas iungere pressa moras
cumque tuis lacrimis lacrimas confundere nostras, 95
    quodque foret uelis aura secunda, queri
et mihi discedens suprema dicere uoce:
    'Phylli, fac exspectes Demophoonta tuum.'
exspectem, qui me numquam uisurus abisti?
    exspectem pelago uela negata meo? 100
et tamen exspecto; redeas modo serus amanti,
    ut tua sit solo tempore lapsa fides.
quid precor infelix? iam te tenet altera coniunx
    forsitan et, nobis qui male fauit, Amor;
iamque tibi excidimus, nullam, puto, Phyllida nosti. 105
    ei mihi, si quae sim Phyllis et unde rogas!
quae tibi, Demophoon, longis erroribus acto
    Threicios portus hospitiumque dedi,
cuius opes auxere meae, cui diues egenti
    munera multa dedi, multa datura fui; 110
quae tibi subieci latissima regna Lycurgi,
    nomine femineo uix satis apta regi,
qua patet umbrosum Rhodope glacialis ad Haemum,
    et sacer admissas exigit Hebrus aquas;

*   *   *

cui mea uirginitas auibus libata sinistris 115
    castaque fallaci zona recincta manu!
pronuba Tisiphone thalamis ululauit in illis,
    et cecinit maestum deuia carmen auis.

89 tanget *P(ut uid.)G*: tangit *Eω*   103 iam te *E²(te om. E¹)Gω*: te iam *Pς*
105 iamque *Housman*: utque *codd.*   108 hospitiumque *PGω*: officiumque *E*
110 multa datura *PEω*: plura datura *Eς*   114 *lacunam post hunc uersum statui*

adfuit Allecto breuibus torquata colubris,
  suntque sepulcrali lumina mota face.   120
maesta tamen scopulos fruticosaque litora calco;
  quaque patent oculis aequora lata meis,
siue die laxatur humus, seu frigida lucent
  sidera, prospicio, quis freta uentus agat,
et quaecumque procul uenientia lintea uidi,   125
  protinus illa meos auguror esse deos.
in freta procurro, uix me retinentibus undis,
  mobile qua primas porrigit aequor aquas.
quo magis accedunt, minus et minus utilis asto:
  linquor et ancillis excipienda cado.   130
est sinus, adductos modice falcatus in arcus;
  ultima praerupta cornua mole rigent.
hinc mihi suppositas immittere corpus in undas
  mens fuit, et, quoniam fallere pergis, erit.
ad tua me fluctus proiectam litora portent,   135
  occurramque oculis intumulata tuis:
duritia ferrum ut superes adamantaque teque
  'non tibi sic', dices, 'Phylli, sequendus eram.'
saepe uenenorum sitis est mihi, saepe cruenta
  traiectam gladio morte perire iuuat.   140
colla quoque, infidis quia se nectenda lacertis
  praebuerunt, laqueis implicuisse iuuat.
stat nece matura tenerum pensare pudorem.
  in necis electu parua futura mora est.
inscribende meo causa inuidiosa sepulcro,   145
  aut hoc aut simili carmine notus eris:
PHYLLIDA DEMOPHOON LETO DEDIT HOSPES AMANTEM
ILLE NECIS CAVSAM PRAEBVIT IPSA MANVM.

---

122 quaque *Eω*: qu(a)eque *PGς*   aequora ς: litora *PEGω*   lata *PEω*: nota *Gς*
141 quia *PGω*: que ς   142 praebuerunt *P*: -erant *P²Gω*: -erint ς iuuat
PGς: libet ς   145 inscribende *Heinsius*: inscribere *codd.*   148 ipsa *Pς*: illa
P²(in marg.)EGω

V
OENONE PARIDI

Perlegis? an coniunx prohibet noua? perlege: non est
    ista Mycenaea littera facta manu.
Pegasis Oenone, Phrygiis celeberrima siluis,
    laesa queror de te, si sinis ipse, meo.
quis deus opposuit nostris sua numina uotis?   5
    ne tua permaneam, quod mihi crimen obest?
leniter, ex merito quidquid patiare, ferendum est;
    quae uenit indigno poena, dolenda uenit.
nondum tantus eras, cum te contenta marito,
    edita de magno flumine nympha, fui.   10
qui nunc Priamides (absit reuerentia uero),
    seruus eras; seruo nubere nympha tuli.
saepe greges inter requieuimus arbore tecti,
    mixtaque cum foliis praebuit herba torum;
saepe super stramen faenoque iacentibus alto   15
    defensa est humili cana pruina casa.
quis tibi monstrabat saltus uenatibus aptos
    et tegeret catulos qua fera rupe suos?
retia saepe comes maculis distincta tetendi,
    saepe citos egi per iuga longa canes.   20
incisae seruant a te mea nomina fagi
    et legor Oenone falce notata tua,
[populus est, memini, fluuiali consita riuo,
    est in qua nostri littera scripta memor.]
et quantum trunci, tantum mea nomina crescunt.   25
    crescite et in titulos surgite recta meos!

---

ante v 1 nympha suo paridi quamuis suus esse recuset | mittit ab ideis uerba legenda iugis *E*ς: *om. PG*ω   3 Pegasis *P²EG*ω: Pegagis *P*: Pedasis *Micyllus* 4 ipse *EG*ω: ipsa *P*ς: esse ς   8 indigno *P*ς: indigna ς: indigne *EG*ω   11 absit *PEG*ω: adsit ς   uero *PEG*ω: ueri ς   16 defensa *Parrhasius*: depressa *PE*ς: deprensa *G*ς   23–4 *del. Jahn*: *om. PG*: *hic habent E*ω: *post* 26 ς

popule, uiue, precor, quae consita margine ripae
  hoc in rugoso cortice carmen habes:
CVM PARIS OENONE POTERIT SPIRARE RELICTA
  AD FONTEM XANTHI VERSA RECVRRET AQVA.   30
Xanthe, retro propera, uersaeque recurrite lymphae:
  sustinet Oenonen deseruisse Paris.
illa dies fatum miserae mihi dixit, ab illa
  pessima mutati coepit amoris hiems,
qua Venus et Iuno sumptisque decentior armis   35
  uenit in arbitrium nuda Minerua tuum.
attoniti micuere sinus, gelidusque cucurrit,
  ut mihi narrasti, dura per ossa tremor.
consului (neque enim modice terrebar) anusque
  longaeuosque senes: constitit esse nefas.   40
caesa abies, sectaeque trabes, et classe parata
  caerula ceratas accipit unda rates.
flesti discedens: hoc saltem parce negare;
  praeterito magis est iste pudendus amor.
et flesti et nostros uidisti flentis ocellos;   45
  miscuimus lacrimas maestus uterque suas.
non sic appositis uincitur uitibus ulmus,
  ut tua sunt collo bracchia nexa meo.
a quotiens, cum te uento quererere teneri,
  riserunt comites! ille secundus erat.   50
oscula dimissae quotiens repetita dedisti!
  quam uix sustinuit dicere lingua 'uale'!
aura leuis rigido pendentia lintea malo
  suscitat, et remis eruta canet aqua.
prosequor infelix oculis abeuntia uela   55
  qua licet, et lacrimis umet harena meis.
utque celer uenias, uirides Nereidas oro,
  scilicet ut uenias in mea damna celer.

34 mutati *PEG*ω: mutari ς   44–5 *del. Merkel*   44 pudendus *P²EG*ω:
pigendus *P*   45 flentis *E²G*ω: flentes *P²E*ς: flente *P*

uotis ergo meis alii rediture redisti?
  ei mihi, pro dira paelice blanda fui!   60
aspicit immensum moles natiua profundum;
  mons fuit: aequoreis illa resistit aquis.
hinc ego uela tuae cognoui prima carinae,
  et mihi per fluctus impetus ire fuit.
dum moror, in summa fulsit mihi purpura prora.   65
  pertimui: cultus non erat ille tuus.
fit propior terrasque cita ratis attigit aura;
  femineas uidi corde tremente genas.
non satis id fuerat? quid enim furiosa morabar?
  haerebat gremio turpis amica tuo!   70
tum uero rupique sinus et pectora planxi
  et secui madidas ungue rigente genas,
impleuique sacram querulis ululatibus Iden.
  illuc has lacrimas in mea saxa tuli.
sic Helene doleat defectaque coniuge ploret,   75
  quaeque prior nobis intulit, ipsa ferat.
nunc tibi conueniunt, quae te per aperta sequantur
  aequora, legitimos destituantque uiros;
at cum pauper eras armentaque pastor agebas,
  nulla nisi Oenone pauperis uxor erat.   80
non ego miror opes, nec me tua regia tangit,
  nec de tot Priami dicar ut una nurus.
non tamen ut Priamus nymphae socer esse recuset
  aut Hecubae fuerim dissimulanda nurus;
dignaque sum fieri rerum matrona potentis;   85
  sunt mihi, quas possint sceptra decere, manus.
nec me, faginea quod tecum fronde iacebam,
  despice; purpureo sum magis apta toro.
denique tutus amor meus est; ibi nulla parantur
  bella, nec ultrices aduehit unda rates.   90

---

60 ei mihi ς: et mihi *PG*ς: et tibi *E*ς   75 defectaque *P*: desertaque *EG*ω
78 uiros *PEG*ω: thoros ς   85 fieri rerum *Housman*: et cupio fieri *PEG*ω
86 quas *P²EG*ω: qua *P*: quae ς   89 ibi *Bentley*: tibi *codd.*

Tyndaris infestis fugitiua reposcitur armis;
  hac uenit in thalamos dote superba tuos.
quae si sit Danais reddenda, uel Hectora fratrem
  uel cum Deiphobo Pulydamanta roga.
quid grauis Antenor, Priamus quid suadeat ipse,   95
  consule, quis aetas longa magistra fuit.
turpe rudimentum, patriae praeponere raptam.
  causa pudenda tua est; iusta uir arma mouet.
nec tibi, si sapias, fidam promitte Lacaenam,
  quae sit in amplexus tam cito uersa tuos.   100
ut minor Atrides temerati foedera lecti
  clamat et externo laesus amore dolet,
tu quoque clamabis. nulla reparabilis arte
  laesa pudicitia est; deperit illa semel.
ardet amore tui? sic et Menelaon amauit.   105
  nunc iacet in uiduo credulus ille toro.
felix Andromache, certo bene nupta marito!
  uxor ad exemplum fratris habenda fui.
tu leuior foliis, tum cum sine pondere suci
  mobilibus uentis arida facta uolant;   110
et minus est in te quam summa pondus arista,
  quae leuis assiduis solibus usta riget.
hoc tua (nam recolo) quondam germana canebat,
  sic mihi diffusis uaticinata comis:
'quid facis, Oenone? quid harenae semina mandas?   115
  non profecturis litora bubus aras!
Graia iuuenca uenit, quae te patriamque domumque
  perdat! io prohibe: Graia iuuenca uenit!
dum licet, obscenam ponto demergite puppim!
  heu, quantum Phrygii sanguinis illa uehit!'   120
uox erat in cursu: famulae rapuere furentem;
  at mihi flauentes deriguere comae.

97 – VI 49 *desiderantur in* P   119 demergite *G*ω: di(i) mergite *E*ς: dimergite
ς   121 uox erat ς: dixerat *EG*ω

a, nimium miserae uates mihi uera fuisti:
  possidet en saltus illa iuuenca meos!
sit facie quamuis insignis, adultera certe est;   125
  deseruit socios hospite capta deos.
illam de patria Theseus, nisi nomine fallor,
  nescioquis Theseus abstulit ante sua.
a iuuene et cupido credatur reddita uirgo?
  unde hoc compererim tam bene quaeris? amo.   130
uim licet appelles et culpam nomine ueles;
  quae totiens rapta est, praebuit ipsa rapi.
at manet Oenone fallenti casta marito,
  et poteras falli legibus ipse tuis.
me Satyri celeres (siluis ego tecta latebam)   135
  quaesierunt rapido, turba proterua, pede
cornigerumque caput pinu praecinctus acuta
  Faunus, in immensis qua tumet Ida iugis.
me fide conspicuus Troiae munitor amauit:
  ille meae spolium uirginitatis habet,   140
id quoque luctando. rupi tamen ungue capillos,
  oraque sunt digitis aspera facta meis.
nec pretium stupri gemmas aurumque poposci:
  turpiter ingenuum munera corpus emunt.
ipse ratus dignam medicas mihi tradidit artes   145
  admisitque meas ad sua dona manus.
quaecumque herba potens ad opem radixque medenti
  utilis in toto nascitur orbe, mea est.
me miseram, quod amor non est medicabilis herbis!
  deficior prudens artis ab arte mea.   150
[ipse repertor opis uaccas pauisse Pheraeas
  fertur et e nostro saucius igne fuit.]
quod nec graminibus tellus fecunda creandis
  nec deus, auxilium tu mihi ferre potes.

124 illa *Eω Plan.*: graia *Gς*   130 hoc *ς*: h(a)ec *EGς*   140–5 *del. Merkel*
141 tamen *codd.*: prius *Bentley*   147 medenti *Heinsius*: medendi *codd.*   151–2
del. Merkel   153 nec *Gς*: neque *Eω*

et potes et merui: dignae miserere puellae!   155
  non ego cum Danais arma cruenta fero,
sed tua sum tecumque fui puerilibus annis
  et tua, quod superest temporis, esse precor.

VI
HYPSIPYLE IASONI

Litora Thessaliae reduci tetigisse carina
  diceris auratae uellere diues ouis.
gratulor incolumi, quantum sinis; hoc tamen ipsum
  debueram scripto certior esse tuo.
nam ne pacta tibi praeter mea regna redires,   5
  cum cuperes, uentos non habuisse potes;
quamlibet aduerso signatur epistula uento.
  Hypsipyle missa digna salute fui.
cur mihi fama prior quam littera nuntia uenit,
  isse sacros Marti sub iuga panda boues,   10
seminibus iactis segetes adolesse uirorum
  inque necem dextra non eguisse tua,
peruigilem spolium pecudis seruasse draconem,
  rapta tamen forti uellera fulua manu?
o ego si possem timide credentibus ista   15
  'ipse mihi scripsit' dicere, quanta forem!
quid queror officium lenti cessasse mariti?
  obsequium, maneo si tua, grande tuli.
barbara narratur uenisse uenefica tecum,
  in mihi promissi parte recepta tori.   20
credula res amor est. utinam temeraria dicar
  criminibus falsis insimulasse uirum!

---

ante VI 1 lempnias ysiphile bachi genus esone nato | dicit et in uerbis pars
quota mentis erat *E*: om. *G*ω   3 ipsum *Plan.* ς: ipso *EG*ω: ipsa *Heinsius*   7
quamlibet ς: quemlibet *G*: quaelibet *E*ω   signatur ς: signetur *EG*ω   9 quam
littera nuntia *E*ς: quam nuntia littera ς: de te quam littera *G*ς   10 Marti
Heinsius: Martis *codd.*   15 o *Heinsius*: hoc *G*ς: haec *E*ς

nuper ab Haemoniis hospes mihi Thessalus oris
  uenerat et tactum uix bene limen erat,
'Aesonides', dixi, 'quid agit meus?' ille pudore   25
  haesit in opposita lumina fixus humo.
protinus exsilui tunicisque a pectore ruptis
  'uiuit? an', exclamo, 'me quoque fata uocant?'
'uiuit', ait timidus; timidum iurare coegi.
  uix mihi teste deo credita uita tua est.   30
ut rediit animus, tua facta requirere coepi:
  narrat et aeripedes Martis arasse boues,
uipereos dentes in humum pro semine iactos,
  et subito natos arma tulisse uiros;
terrigenas populos ciuili Marte peremptos   35
  implesse aetatis fata diurna suae.
[deuictus serpens. iterum, si uiuat Iason,
  quaerimus; alternant spesque timorque uices.]
singula dum narrat, studio cursuque loquendi
  detegit ingenio uulnera nostra suo.   40
heu, ubi pacta fides? ubi conubialia iura
  faxque sub arsuros dignior ire rogos?
non ego sum furto tibi cognita; pronuba Iuno
  adfuit et sertis tempora uinctus Hymen.
an mihi nec Iuno, nec Hymen, sed tristis Erinys   45
  praetulit infaustas sanguinolenta faces?
quid mihi cum Minyis? quid cum Tritonide pinu?
  quid tibi cum patria, nauita Tiphy, mea?
non erat hic aries uillo spectabilis aureo,
  nec senis Aeetae regia Lemnos erat.   50

24 uenerat et *codd.*: uenit et ut *Bentley*   28 uocant *Gꜱ*: trahunt *Eω*   29
timidus timidum *Heinsius*: timidum quod amat *E*: timidum quod ait *ω*: timi-
dumque mihi *Gꜱ*   31 ut rediit animus *ꜱ*: utque animus rediit *EGꜱ*: utque
rediit animus *ꜱ*   32 et (*om. Gꜱ*) aeripedes *codd.*: aenipedes *Heinsius*   37–8
del. Housman   38 *post* 62 *E*   uices *Palmer*: uicem *Bentley*: fidem *codd.*   41
heu *ꜱ*: heus *EGꜱ*   45 an *Postgate*: at *codd.*   47 Tritonide *EGω*: Dodonide
Plan.   50 *denuo incipit P*

certa fui primo (sed me mea fata trahebant)
    hospita feminea pellere castra manu;
Lemniadesque uiros nimium quoque uincere norunt.
    milite tam forti fama tuenda fuit.
urbe uirum uidua tectoque animoque recepi.   55
    hic tibi bisque aestas bisque cucurrit hiems.
tertia messis erat, cum tu dare uela coactus
    implesti lacrimis talia uerba suis:
'abstrahor, Hypsipyle; sed dent modo fata recursus,
    uir tuus hinc abeo, uir tibi semper ero.   60
quod tamen e nobis grauida celatur in aluo,
    uiuat, et eiusdem simus uterque parens.'
hactenus, et lacrimis in falsa cadentibus ora
    cetera te memini non potuisse loqui.
ultimus e sociis sacram conscendis in Argo.   65
    illa uolat; uento concaua uela tument.
caerula propulsae subducitur unda carinae;
    terra tibi, nobis aspiciuntur aquae.
in latus omne patens turris circumspicit undas;
    huc feror, et lacrimis osque sinusque madent.   70
per lacrimas specto, cupidaeque fauentia menti
    longius assueto lumina nostra uident.
adde preces castas immixtaque uota timori,
    nunc quoque te saluo persoluenda mihi.
uota ego persoluam? uotis Medea fruatur?   75
    cor dolet, atque ira mixtus abundat amor.
dona feram templis, uiuum quod Iasona perdo?
    hostia pro damnis concidat icta meis?
non equidem secura fui, semperque uerebar
    ne pater Argolica sumeret urbe nurum.   80

---

51 mea *Eω*: mala *PG*ς   54 forti fama *Delz*: forti uita *P²EGω*: forti ripa ς:
fortuna *P*   55 uidua *Heinsius*: uidi *PEGω*: iuui ς   58 suis *Heinsius*: tuis
codd.   66 uento ... tument *Francius*: uentus ... tenet *codd.*   75 fruatur
Heinsius: fruetur *codd.*   78 concidat *P*ς: concidet *EGω*

Argolidas timui: nocuit mihi barbara paelex!
    non exspectata uulnus ab hoste tuli.
nec facie meritisque placet, sed carmina nouit
    diraque cantata pabula falce metit.
illa reluctantem cursu deducere lunam   85
    nititur et tenebris abdere solis equos;
illa refrenat aquas obliquaque flumina sistit;
    illa loco siluas uiuaque saxa mouet.
per tumulos errat passis discincta capillis
    certaque de tepidis colligit ossa rogis.   90
deuouet absentes simulacraque cerea figit
    et miserum tenuis in iecur urget acus,
et quae nescierim melius. male quaeritur herbis
    moribus et forma conciliandus amor.
hanc potes amplecti thalamoque relictus in uno   95
    impauidus somno nocte silente frui?
scilicet ut tauros, ita te iuga ferre coegit,
    quaque feros anguis, te quoque mulcet ope.
adde quod ascribi factis procerumque tuisque
    se iubet et titulo coniugis uxor obest.   100
atque aliquis Peliae de partibus acta uenenis
    imputat et populum, qui sibi credat, habet:
'non haec Aesonides, sed Phasias Aeetine
    aurea Phrixeae terga reuellit ouis.'
non probat Alcimede mater tua (consule matrem),   105
    non pater, a gelido cui uenit axe nurus.
illa sibi Tanai Scythiaeque paludibus udae
    quaerat et a patria Phasidos usque uirum!
mobilis Aesonide uernaque incertior aura,
    cur tua polliciti pondere uerba carent?   110

---

82 expectata *P*: expectato *P²EGω*   85 cursu *PEGω*: curru ς   91 figit
P: fingit *EGω*   93 male ς: mage *PEGω*   100 iubet *Koch*: fauet *PG*ς: facit
P²Eω: uolet *G²*ς: πείθει *Plan.*   103 Phasias Aeetine *Salmasius*: fil/////// *P*:
filia ph(f)asias (o)ete *P²EG*ς   104 reuellit *PEGω*: reuulsit ς   107 tanai
ς: tanais *PEGω*: a thanais ς   108 patria *P²EGω*: patrio *P*: ripa *Bentley*
110 polliciti *PGω*: pollicito *E*ς

uir meus hinc ieras; cur non meus inde redisti?
  sim reducis coniunx, sicut euntis eram.
si te nobilitas generosaque nomina tangunt,
  en ego Minoo nata Thoante feror!
[Bacchus auus; Bacchi coniunx redimita Corona   115
  praeradiat stellis signa minora suis.]
dos tibi Lemnos erit, terra ingeniosa colenti;
  me quoque dotales inter habere potes.
nunc etiam peperi; gratare ambobus, Iason.
  dulce mihi grauidae fecerat auctor onus.   120
felix in numero quoque sum prolemque gemellam,
  pignora Lucina bina fauente, dedi.
si quaeris, cui sint similes, cognosceris illis.
  fallere non norunt; cetera patris habent.
legatos quos paene dedi pro matre ferendos;   125
  sed tenuit coeptas saeua nouerca uias.
Medeam timui: plus est Medea nouerca;
  Medeae faciunt ad scelus omne manus.
spargere quae fratris potuit lacerata per agros
  corpora, pignoribus parceret illa meis?   130
hanc tamen, o demens Colchisque ablate uenenis,
  diceris Hypsipyles praeposuisse toro.
turpiter illa uirum cognouit adultera uirgo;
  me tibi teque mihi taeda pudica dedit.
prodidit illa patrem; rapui de caede Thoanta.   135
  deseruit Colchos; me mea Lemnos habet.
quid refert, scelerata piam si uincit et ipso
  crimine dotata est emeruitque uirum?
[Lemniadum facinus culpo, non miror, Iason;
  quamlibet ignauis iste dat arma dolor.]   140

---

111 cur ω: uir *PEG*ς   115–16 *delendos censeo*   118 dotales *Salmasius*: q/////is
P: quod tales *G*ς: res tales *E*ς   130 corpora *codd.*: uiscera *Bentley*   131
hanc tamen o *EGω*: hanc o *P*: hanc o tu *P²*ς   137 uincit *E*ς: uincet *PG*ς:
uincat ς: uicit *Kenney*   139–40 *del. Peters*   140 quamlibet *P*: quodlibet
*EG*ς: quolibet *P²*   ignauis *Housman*: iratis *P²*ς: ad facinus *EG*ς: *om. P*ς   iste
Madvig: ipse *codd.*

dic age, si uentis, ut oportuit, actus iniquis
  intrasses portus tuque comesque meos,
obuiaque exissem fetu comitante gemello
  (hiscere nempe tibi terra roganda fuit),
quo uultu natos, quo me scelerate uideres?   145
  perfidiae pretio qua nece dignus eras?
ipse quidem per me tutus sospesque fuisses,
  non quia tu dignus, sed quia mitis ego.
paelicis ipsa meos implessem sanguine uultus,
  quosque ueneficiis abstulit illa tuos.   150
Medeae Medea forem! quod si quid ab alto
  iustus adest uotis Iuppiter ille meis,
quod gemit Hypsipyle, lecti quoque subnuba nostri
  maereat et leges sentiat ipsa suas;
utque ego destituor coniunx materque duorum,   155
  cum totidem natis orba sit illa uiro.
nec male parta diu teneat peiusque relinquat:
  exulet et toto quaerat in orbe fugam.
quam fratri germana fuit miseroque parenti
  filia, tam natis, tam sit acerba uiro.   160
cum mare, cum terras consumpserit, aera temptet;
  erret inops, exspes, caede cruenta sua!
haec ego, coniugio fraudata Thoantias, oro.
  uiuite deuoto nuptaque uirque toro!

---

150 tuos *Bentley*: suis *codd.*   152 ille *Heinsius*: ipse *codd.*   156 cum ς: a
*PEG*ω   illa *PG*ω: atque *E*ς: aque *Burman*

VII
DIDO AENEAE

Sic ubi fata uocant, udis abiectus in herbis
  ad uada Maeandri concinit albus olor.
nec quia te nostra sperem prece posse moueri,
  alloquor (aduerso mouimus ista deo);
sed merita et famam corpusque animumque pudicum   5
  cum male perdiderim, perdere uerba leue est.
certus es ire tamen miseramque relinquere Dido,
  atque idem uenti uela fidemque ferent?
certus es, Aenea, cum foedere soluere naues,
  quaeque ubi sint nescis, Itala regna sequi?   10
nec noua Carthago nec te surgentia tangunt
  moenia nec sceptro tradita summa tuo?
facta fugis, facienda petis; quaerenda per orbem
  altera, quaesita est altera terra tibi.
ut terram inuenias, quis eam tibi tradet habendam?   15
  quis sua non notis arua tenenda dabit?
scilicet alter amor tibi restat et altera Dido,
  quamque iterum fallas, altera danda fides.
quando erit ut condas instar Carthaginis urbem
  et uideas populos altus ab arce tuos?   20
omnia ut eueniant, nec di tua uota morentur,
  unde tibi, quae te sic amet, uxor erit?
uror ut inducto ceratae sulpure taedae,
  ut pia fumosis addita tura focis.
Aeneas oculis uigilantis semper inhaeret,   25
  Aenean animo noxque quiesque refert.

---

ante VII 1 accipe, Dardanide, moriturae carmen Elissae; | quae legis a nobis
ultima uerba legis *E*ς: om. *PG*ω   4 aduerso *codd.*: auerso *Heinsius*   5 merita
et *Heinsius*: merite *P*: meriti *P²EG*ω   11 surgentia *E*ς: crescentia *PG*ω   17
scilicet alter amor tibi restat *Diggle*: alter amor tibi est habendus *P*: a. a. t. et
extat habendus *EG*ς: a. a. t. restat habendus ς   21 di *Van Lennep*: te *codd.*
24-5 *habent* ς: om. *PE*ς   focis ς: rogis ς   26 quiesque *Housman*: diesque *codd.*

ille quidem male gratus et ad mea munera surdus,
    et quo, si non sim stulta, carere uelim;
non tamen Aenean, quamuis male cogitat, odi,
    sed queror infidum questaque peius amo.   30
parce, Venus, nurui, durumque amplectere fratrem,
    frater Amor; castris militet ille tuis!
aut ego, quae coepi (neque enim dedignor), amorem,
    materiam curae praebeat ille meae!
fallor, et ista mihi falsae iactatur imago: 35
    matris ab ingenio dissidet ille suae.
te lapis et montes innataque rupibus altis
    robora, te saeuae progenuere ferae,
aut mare, quale uides agitari nunc quoque uentis,
    qua tamen aduersis fluctibus ire paras.   40
quo fugis? obstat hiems: hiemis mihi gratia prosit.
    aspice, ut euersas concitet Eurus aquas.
quod tibi malueram, sine me debere procellis.
    iustior est animo uentus et unda tuo.
non ego sum tanti (numquid censeris inique?)   45
    ut pereas, dum me per freta longa fugis.
exerces pretiosa odia et constantia magno,
    si, dum me careas, est tibi uile mori.
iam uenti ponent, strataque aequaliter unda
    caeruleis Triton per mare curret equis.   50
tu quoque cum uentis utinam mutabilis esses !
    et, nisi duritia robora uincis, eris.
quid, quasi nescires, insana quid aequora possint,
    expertae totiens tam male credis aquae?

---

33 quae *PEGω*: quem ς   amorem *Madvig*: amare *codd*.   35 falsae *Heinsius*: falso *codd*.   40 qua ς: quo *PEGω*   43 malueram *PEGω*: -erim ς   45 numquid censeris *Shackleton Bailey*: quid non censeris ς: quid non c////ris *P(ut uid.)*: quod non censeris *P²GP²ς*: quod non meditaris ς: quam tu dimittis *Eς*: quamuis merearis ς   53 quasi *Bentley*: si *codd*.   possint *Eς*: possent ς: possunt *PGς*

ut, pelago suadente uiam, retinacula soluas,   55
    multa tamen latus tristia pontus habet.
nec uiolasse fidem temptantibus aequora prodest;
    perfidiae poenas exigit ille locus,
praecipue cum laesus Amor, quia mater Amorum
    nuda Cytheriacis edita fertur aquis.   60
perdita ne perdam timeo, noceamue nocenti,
    neu bibat aequoreas naufragus hostis aquas.
uiue, precor! sic te melius quam funere perdam;
    tu potius leti causa ferere mei.
finge, age, te rapido (nullum sit in omine pondus!)   65
    turbine deprendi: quid tibi mentis erit?
protinus occurrent falsae periuria linguae
    et Phrygia Dido fraude coacta mori.
coniugis ante oculos deceptae stabit imago
    tristis et effusis sanguinolenta comis.   70
quid tanti est ut tum 'merui, concedite!' dicas
    quaeque cadent, in te fulmina missa putes?
da breue saeuitiae spatium pelagique tuaeque;
    grande morae pretium tuta futura uia est.
haec minus ut cures, puero parcatur Iulo!   75
    te satis est titulum mortis habere meae.
quid puer Ascanius, quid commeruere Penates?
    ignibus ereptos obruet unda deos?
sed neque fers tecum, nec, quae mihi, perfide, iactas,
    presserunt umeros sacra paterque tuos.   80
omnia mentiris; neque enim tua fallere lingua
    incipit a nobis, primaque plector ego.
si quaeras, ubi sit formosi mater Iuli,
    occidit a duro sola relicta uiro.

---

55 uiam *Bentley*: etiam *codd.*   71 quid tanti est *PG*ς: quidquid id est *E*: quid-
quid id est ω   ut tum *Madvig*: tutum *P*: totum *P²E²G*ω: tu *E*   75 haec
minus ut cures *Housman*: nec mihi tu curae *PE²G*ς: nec tibi sum curae *E*ς:
nec mihi tu parcas ω   77 quid commeruere *Palmer*: quid meruere *P*ς: quid
di meruere *P²EG*ω: uel quid meruere ς

haec mihi narraras et me mouere. merentem   85
  ure: minor culpa poena futura mea est.
nec mihi mens dubia est, quin te tua numina damnent:
  per mare, per terras septima iactat hiems.
fluctibus eiectum tuta statione recepi
  uixque bene audito nomine regna dedi.   90
his tamen officiis utinam contenta fuissem,
  nec mea concubitu fama sepulta foret!
illa dies nocuit, qua nos decliue sub antrum
  caeruleus subitis compulit imber aquis.
audieram uocem: nymphas ululasse putaui;   95
  Eumenides fati signa dedere mei.
exige, laese pudor, poenas, uiolataque lecti
  iura nec ad cineres fama retenta meos,   97a
uosque, mei manes, animaeque cinisque Sychaei   97b
  ad quem, me miseram, plena pudoris eo.
est mihi marmorea sacratus in aede Sychaeus;
  appositae frondes uelleraque alba tegunt.   100
hinc ego me sensi noto quater ore citari;
  ipse sono tenui dixit 'Elissa, ueni!'
nulla mora est, uenio, uenio tibi debita coniunx;
  sum tamen admissi tarda pudore mei.
da ueniam culpae: decepit idoneus auctor;   105
  inuidiam noxae detrahit ille meae.
diua parens seniorque pater, pia sarcina nati,
  spem mihi mansuri rite dedere uiri.
si fuit errandum, causas habet error honestas;
  adde fidem, nulla parte pigendus erit.   110

---

85 et *Diggle*: at *P²Gω*: an *E*: a/ *P*   mouere *Pς*: nouere *EGω*   86 ure *P*: inde
Gς: illa *P²Eς*   92 nec ... concubitu *Werfer*: et ... concubitus *codd.*   mea
Kenney: mihi *codd.*   95 uocem *PGς*: uoces *Eω*   96 fati ... mei *Van Lennep*:
fatis ... meis *codd.*   97 uiolataque lecti ς: uiolate sicheu *P²Eω*: uiolate
sichei *Gς*: uiolente siceo *P*: umbraeque Sychaei *Merkel*   97a–b habent ς:
om. *PEGω*   97b cinisque ς: umbraeque *Bentley*   98 quem ς: quas *PEGω*
100 appositae ς: opp- *PEGω*   103 debita *Gς*: dedita *PEς*   104 admissi ς:
amissi *Pς*: amisso *EGς*   mei *Pς*: meo *EG*

durat in extremum uitaeque nouissima nostrae
  prosequitur fati, qui fuit ante, tenor.
occidit internas coniunx mactatus ad aras
  et sceleris tanti praemia frater habet.
exul agor, cineresque uiri patriamque relinquo,   115
  et feror in dubias hoste sequente uias.
applicor his oris, fratrique elapsa fretoque
  quod tibi donaui, perfide, litus emo.
urbem constitui lateque patentia fixi
  moenia finitimis inuidiosa locis.   120
bella tument; bellis peregrina et femina temptor
  uixque rudis portas urbis et arma paro.
mille procis placui, qui me coiere querentes
  nescioquem thalamis praeposuisse suis.
quid dubitas uinctam Gaetulo tradere Iarbae?   125
  praebuerim sceleri bracchia nostra tuo.
est etiam frater, cuius manus impia poscit
  respergi nostro, sparsa cruore uiri.
pone deos et quae tangendo sacra profanas:
  non bene caelestes impia dextra colit.   130
si tu cultor eras elapsis igne futurus,
  paenitet elapsos ignibus esse deos.
forsitan et grauidam Dido, scelerate, relinquas
  parsque tui lateat corpore clausa meo.
accedet fatis matris miserabilis infans,   135
  et nondum nato funeris auctor eris,
cumque parente sua frater morietur Iuli,
  poenaque conexos auferet una duos.
'sed iubet ire deus.' uellem uetuisset adire,
  Punica nec Teucris pressa fuisset humus!   140

---

113 internas ς: in terras *PEGω*: in terris ς: Hercaeas *Heinsius*   116 dubias
ς: duras *PEGω*   117 his oris *Heinsius*: ignotis *codd.*   119 fixi *P²EGω*: finxi
*P*ς: feci ς   122 rudis *PE*ς: rudes *P²Gω*   127 poscit ς: possit *PEGω*: posset
ς   133 dido *P*: didon *EGω*   136 nato *Plan. (ut uid.) Slichtenhorst Heinsius*:
nati *PEGω*

hoc duce nempe deo uentis agitaris iniquis
  et teris in rabido tempora longa freto?
Pergama uix tanto tibi erant repetenda labore,
  Hectore si uiuo quanta fuere forent.
non patrium Simoenta petis, sed Thybridis undas: 145
  nempe ut peruenias quo cupis, hospes eris.
utque latet uitatque tuas abstrusa carinas,
  uix tibi continget terra petita seni.
hos potius populos in dotem, ambage remissa,
  accipe et aduectas Pygmalionis opes.   150
Ilion in Tyriam transfer felicius urbem
  resque loco regis sceptraque sacra tene!
si tibi mens auida est belli, si quaerit Iulus,
  unde suo partus Marte triumphus eat,
quem superet, ne quid desit, praebebimus hostem.   155
  hic pacis leges, hic locus arma capit.
tu modo, per matrem fraternaque tela, sagittas,
  perque fugae comites, Dardana sacra, deos,
(sic superent, quoscumque tua de gente reportat
  Mars ferus, et damni sit modus ille tui,   160
Ascaniusque suos feliciter impleat annos
  et senis Anchisae molliter ossa cubent!)
parce, precor, domui, quae se tibi tradit habendam.
  quod crimen dicis praeter amasse meum?
non ego sum Pthia magnisue oriunda Mycenis,   165
  nec steterunt in te uirque paterque meus.
si pudet uxoris, non nupta, sed hospita dicar;
  dum tua sit Dido, quidlibet esse feret.

---

142 rabido *E*ς: rapido *PG*ω   145 petis *P²E*ω: bibis *G*   147 utque latet
uitatque tuas abstrusa (obstrusa *G*ς) carinas *PG*ς: utque iuuent uentusque tuas
remusque carinas *E*ω   150 aduectas *codd.*: auectas *Heinsius*   152 resque
loco *Palmer*: inque loco *P²EG*ω: inque locum ς: sisque loco *Shuckburgh* scep-
traque sacra *P*ω: regia sceptra *EG*ς: sceptra sacrata *P²*   155 quem superet
*G*ω: quod superest *PE*ς   157 matrem *E*ς: patrem *PG*ω   159 reportat
Madvig: reportas *codd. post* 159 *desinit E*   165 Pthia *edd. uett.*: phthia ς: pytia
G: phithias *P²* magnisue *Burman*: magnisque *PG*ω: magnis ς

nota mihi freta sunt Afrum plangentia litus;
    temporibus certis dantque negantque uiam.   170
cum dabit aura uiam, praebebis carbasa uentis;
    nunc leuis eiectam continet alga ratem.
tempus ut obseruem, manda mihi: certior ibis,
    nec te, si cupies, ipsa manere sinam.
et socii requiem poscunt, laniataque classis   175
    postulat exiguas semirefecta moras.
pro meritis et siqua tibi praebebimus ultra,
    non spe coniugii tempora parua peto,
dum freta mitescunt et amor, dum tempore et usu
    fortiter edisco tristia posse pati.   180
si minus, est animus nobis effundere uitam;
    in me crudelis non potes esse diu.
aspicias utinam quae sit scribentis imago!
    scribimus, et gremio Troicus ensis adest,
perque genas lacrimae strictum labuntur in ensem,   185
    qui iam pro lacrimis sanguine tinctus erit.
quam bene conueniunt fato tua munera nostro!
    instruis impensa nostra sepulcra breui.
nec mea nunc primum feriuntur pectora telo;
    ille locus saeui uulnus Amoris habet.   190
Anna soror, soror Anna, meae male conscia culpae,
    iam dabis in cineres ultima dona meos.
nec consumpta rogis inscribar Elissa Sychaei.
    hoc tantum in tumuli marmore carmen erit:
PRAEBVIT AENEAS ET CAVSAM MORTIS ET ENSEM   195
IPSA SVA DIDO CONCIDIT VSA MANV.

---

169 plangentia *Heinsius*: frangentia *codd.*   173 certior *scripsi*: certius ς:
serius *PGω*   174 ipsa *Pω*: ipse *Gς*   177 praebebimus *Burman*: debebimus
codd.   178 non *Hall*: pro *codd.*   179 mitescunt *Pς*: mitescant *Gς* tem-
pore et usu *Salmasius*: tempter & //// *P*: temperet usum *P²ω*: forte tepescat *Gς*
180 edisco *Pς*: ediscam *Gς*   181 si *P²Gω*: sin *P(ut uid.)* ς   187 fato ς:
facto *PGω*   194 tantum *Housman*: tamen *codd.*   196 usa *PGω*: icta ς

X
ARIADNE THESEO

Mitius inueni quam te genus omne ferarum;
    credita non ulli quam tibi peius eram.
quae legis, ex illo, Theseu, tibi litore mitto,
    unde tuam sine me uela tulere ratem.
in quo me somnusque meus male prodidit et tu,   5
    per facinus somnis insidiate meis.
tempus erat, uitrea quo primum terra pruina
    spargitur et tectae fronde queruntur aues.
incertum uigilans ac somno languida moui
    Thesea prensuras semisupina manus.   10
nullus erat! referoque manus iterumque retempto,
    perque torum moueo bracchia: nullus erat!
excussere metus somnum; conterrita surgo,
    membraque sunt uiduo praecipitata toro.
protinus adductis sonuerunt pectora palmis,   15
    utque erat e somno turbida, rupta coma est.
luna fuit; specto, si quid nisi litora cernam.
    quod uideant oculi, nil nisi litus habent.
nunc huc, nunc illuc, et utroque sine ordine, curro;
    alta puellares tardat harena pedes.   20
interea toto clamanti litore 'Theseu!'
    reddebant nomen concaua saxa tuum,
et quotiens ego te, totiens locus ipse uocabat:
    ipse locus miserae ferre uolebat opem.
mons fuit: apparent frutices in uertice rari;   25
    hinc scopulus raucis pendet adesus aquis.

---

ante x 1 illa relicta feris etiam nunc, improbe Theseu, | uiuit. et haec aequa
mente tulisse uelis? *edd. Veneta 1474 et Parmensis 1477: om. codd.*   1–2 *post* 6 *G:*
del. Francius   3 quae *PG*ς: quam ω   9 ac *Heinsius:* a *PG*ως: an ς   10
semisupina *Heinsius:* semisopita *codd.*   16 e *P*ς: a *G*ω   rupta ς: rapta *PG*ω
21 clamanti *P*²ς: clamanti in *G*ς: clamaui ς: *de P incert.*   26 hinc *G*ς: nunc
*P*ς: hic ς

ascendo (uires animus dabat) atque ita late
  aequora prospectu metior alta meo.
inde ego (nam uentis quoque sum crudelibus usa)
  uidi praecipiti carbasa tenta Noto. 30
ut uidi indignam quae me uidisse putarem,
  frigidior glacie semianimisque fui.
nec languere diu patitur dolor; excitor illo,
  excitor et summa Thesea uoce uoco.
'quo fugis?' exclamo; 'scelerate reuertere Theseu! 35
  flecte ratem! numerum non habet illa suum!'
haec ego: quod uoci deerat, plangore replebam.
  uerbera cum uerbis mixta fuere meis.
si non audires, ut saltem cernere posses,
  iactatae late signa dedere manus; 40
candidaque imposui longae uelamina uirgae,
  scilicet oblitos admonitura mei.
iamque oculis ereptus eras: tum denique fleui.
  torpuerant molles ante dolore genae.
quid potius facerent, quam me mea lumina flerent, 45
  postquam desieram uela uidere tua?
aut ego diffusis erraui sola capillis,
  qualis ab Ogygio concita Baccha deo;
aut mare prospiciens in saxo frigida sedi,
  quamque lapis sedes, tam lapis ipsa fui. 50
saepe torum repeto, qui nos acceperat ambos,
  sed non acceptos exhibiturus erat,
et tua, quae possum, pro te uestigia tango
  strataque quae membris intepuere tuis.
incumbo, lacrimisque toro manante profusis 55
  'pressimus', exclamo, 'te duo: redde duos!

31 ut *Bentley*: aut *codd.* indignam quae me *Housman*: a//uamque me *P*: aut
tamquam que me *G*: aut etiam cum me ω: aut fuerant quae me ς   46
desieram *P*ς: desierat *G*: desierant ω   53 quae *PG*ω: qua ς

uenimus huc ambo; cur non discedimus ambo?
  perfide, pars nostri, lectule, maior ubi est?'
quid faciam? quo sola ferar? uacat insula cultu.
  non hominum uideo, non ego facta boum.   60
omne latus terrae cingit mare; nauita nusquam,
  nulla per ambiguas puppis itura uias.
finge dari comitesque mihi uentosque ratemque:
  quid sequar? accessus terra paterna negat.
ut rate felici pacata per aequora labar,   65
  temperet ut uentos Aeolus, exul ero.
non ego te, Crete centum digesta per urbes,
  aspiciam, puero cognita terra Ioui.
et pater et tellus iusto regnata parenti
  prodita sunt facto, nomina cara, meo.   70
cum tibi, ne uictor tecto morerere recuruo,
  quae regerent passus, pro duce fila dedi,
tum mihi dicebas: 'per ego ipsa pericula iuro,
  te fore, dum nostrum uiuet uterque, meam.'
uiuimus, et non sum, Theseu, tua, si modo uiuit   75
  femina periuri fraude sepulta uiri.
me quoque, qua fratrem, mactasses, improbe, claua:
  esset, quam dederas, morte soluta fides.
[nunc ego non tantum quae sum passura recordor,
  sed quaecumque potest ulla relicta pati.]   80
occurrunt animo pereundi mille figurae,
  morsque minus poenae quam mora mortis habet.
iam iam uenturos aut hac aut suspicor illac,
  qui lanient auido uiscera dente, lupos.
forsitan et fuluos tellus alat ista leones.   85
  quis scit an et saeua tigride Dia uacet?

---

69 et ς: at *PG*: nam ω   71 uictor *P*: uictus *P²Gω*   73 tum ς: cum
PGω   75 uiuit ς: uiuis *PGω*: uiuo *Bentley*   79–80 *del. Palmer*   85–6 *del.*
Bentley 85 forsitan *codd.*: quis scit an *Housman*   alat *Pς*: alit *Gω*   86 quis (qui
Pς) scit an *codd.*: forsitan *Housman*   et saeua tigride Dia uacet *Heinsius*: et haec
trigides insula habent *P*: haec saeuas tigridas insula habet *Gς*

et freta dicuntur magnas expellere phocas!
  quid uetat et gladios per latus ire meum?
tantum ne religer dura captiua catena,
  neue traham serua grandia pensa manu,   90
cui pater est Minos, cui mater filia Phoebi,
  quodque magis memini, quae tibi pacta fui!
si mare, si terras porrectaque litora uidi,
  multa mihi terrae, multa minantur aquae.
caelum restabat: timeo simulacra deorum.   95
  destituor rabidis praeda cibusque feris.
siue colunt habitantque uiri, diffidimus illis:
  externos didici laesa timere uiros.
uiueret Androgeos utinam! nec facta luisses
  impia funeribus, Cecropi terra, tuis;   100
nec tua mactasset nodoso stipite, Theseu,
  ardua parte uirum dextera, parte bouem;
nec tibi quae reditus monstrarent, fila dedissem,
  fila per adductas saepe relecta manus.
non equidem miror, si stat Victoria tecum   105
  strataque Cretaeam belua planxit humum.
non poterant figi praecordia ferrea cornu;
  ut te non tegeres, pectore tutus eras.
illic tu silices, illic adamanta tulisti,
  illic qui silices Thesea uincat habes.   110
nec pater est Aegeus, nec tu Pittheidos Aethrae   131
  filius; auctores saxa fretumque tui!   132
crudeles somni, quid me tenuistis inertem?
  at semel aeterna nocte premenda fui.
uos quoque crudeles, uenti, nimiumque parati
  flaminaque in lacrimas officiosa meas.
dextera crudelis, quae me fratremque necauit,   115
  et data poscenti, nomen inane, fides.

88 quid *Heinsius*: quis *codd.*   96 rabidis *Gς*: rapidis *Pω*   104 relecta *Heinsius*: recepta *codd.*   106 planxit *Heinsius*: texit *Gς*: tinxit *ς*: strauit *P²G²ς*: pressit *ς*: *de P incert.*   131–2 *post* 110 *transposuit Birt*   112 at *Gω*: aut *P*

in me iurarunt somnus uentusque fidesque;
    prodita sum causis una puella tribus.
ergo ego nec lacrimas matris moritura uidebo,
    nec, mea qui digitis lumina condat, erit?   120
spiritus infelix peregrinas ibit in auras,
    nec positos artus unguet amica manus?
ossa superstabunt uolucres inhumata marinae?
    haec sunt officiis digna sepulcra meis?
ibis Cecropios portus, patriaque receptus,   125
    cum steteris turbae celsus in ore tuae
et bene narraris letum taurique uirique
    sectaque per dubias saxea tecta uias,
me quoque narrato sola tellure relictam:
    non ego sum titulis subripienda tuis.   130
di facerent ut me summa de puppe uideres!   133
    mouisset uultus maesta figura tuos.
nunc quoque non oculis, sed, qua potes, aspice mente   135
    haerentem scopulo, quem uaga pulsat aqua.
aspice demissos lugentis more capillos
    et tunicas lacrimis sicut ab imbre grauis.
corpus, ut impulsae segetes aquilonibus, horret,
    litteraque articulo pressa tremente labat.   140
non te per meritum, quoniam male cessit, adoro:
    debita sit facto gratia nulla meo,
sed ne poena quidem. si non ego causa salutis,
    non tamen est cur sis tu mihi causa necis.
has tibi plangendo lugubria pectora lassas   145
    infelix tendo trans freta longa manus.
hos tibi, qui superant, ostendo maesta capillos.
    per lacrimas oro, quas tua facta mouent,
flecte ratem, Theseu, uersoque relabere uelo!
    si prius occidero, tu tamen ossa feres.   150

126 turbae *G*ω: turbes *P*: urbis *P²*ς   in ore *G*ς: in aure *P*: in orbe ς: in arce
*P²*ς: honore *G²*ς   127 narraris *P*ς: narrabis *G*ω   129 sola ς: solam *PG*ω
149 uelo *Burman*: uento *codd.*

XI
CANACE MACAREO

Siqua tamen caecis errabunt scripta lituris,
  oblitus a dominae caede libellus erit.
dextra tenet calamum, strictum tenet altera ferrum,
  et iacet in gremio charta soluta meo.
haec est Aeolidos fratri scribentis imago;   5
  sic uideor duro posse placere patri.
ipse necis cuperem nostrae spectator adesset,
  auctorisque oculis exigeretur opus.
ut ferus est multoque suis truculentior Euris,
  spectasset siccis uulnera nostra genis.   10
scilicet est aliquid, cum saeuis uiuere uentis:
  ingenio populi conuenit ille sui.
ille Noto Zephyroque et Sithonio Aquiloni
  imperat et pinnis, Eure proterue, tuis.
imperat, heu, uentis, tumidae non imperat irae!   15
  possidet et uitiis regna minora suis.
quid iuuat admotam per auorum nomina caelo
  inter cognatos posse referre Iouem?
num minus infestum, funebria munera, ferrum
  feminea teneo, non mea tela, manu?   20
o utinam, Macareu, quae nos commisit in unum,
  uenisset leto serior hora meo!
cur umquam plus me, frater, quam frater amasti,
  et tibi, non debet quod soror esse, fui?
ipsa quoque incalui, qualemque audire solebam,   25
  nescio quem sensi corde tepente deum.
fugerat ore color, macies adduxerat artus,
  sumebant minimos ora coacta cibos.

---

ante xi 1 Aeolis Aeolidae quam non habet ipsa salutem | mittit et armata uerba notata manu ς: *om. PG*ω   10 spectasset *G*ω: spectat sed *P*: spectaret ς
19 num *PG*ς: non ς   27 adduxerat *PG*ω: abduxerat *G*ς: obduxerat ς

nec somni faciles et nox erat annua nobis,
    et gemitum nullo laesa dolore dabam.   30
nec, cur haec facerem, poteram mihi reddere causam,
    nec noram, quid amans esset; at illud eram.
prima malum nutrix animo praesensit anili;
    prima mihi nutrix 'Aeoli,' dixit 'amas!'
erubui, gremioque pudor deiecit ocellos: 35
    haec satis in tacita signa fatentis erant.
iamque tumescebant uitiati pondera uentris,
    aegraque furtiuum membra grauabat onus.
quas mihi non herbas, quae non medicamina nutrix
    attulit, audaci supposuitque manu,   40
ut penitus nostris (hoc te celauimus unum)
    uisceribus crescens excuteretur onus?
a, nimium uiuax admotis restitit infans
    artibus et tecto tutus ab hoste fuit!
iam nouiens erat orta soror pulcherrima Phoebi,   45
    et noua luciferos Luna mouebat equos.
nescia quae faceret subitos mihi causa dolores,
    et rudis ad partus et noua miles eram.
nec tenui uocem. 'quid,' ait, 'tua crimina prodis?'
    oraque clamantis conscia pressit anus.   50
quid faciam infelix? gemitus dolor edere cogit,
    sed timor et nutrix et pudor ipse uetant.
contineo gemitus elapsaque uerba reprendo
    et cogor lacrimas combibere ipsa meas.
mors erat ante oculos et opem Lucina negabat   55
    (et graue, si morerer, mors quoque crimen erat),
cum super incumbens scissa tunicaque comaque
    pressa refouisti pectora nostra tuis;
et mihi 'uiue soror, soror o carissima' dixti,
    'uiue nec unius corpore perde duos!   60

44 tecto *P*ς: tectis *G*: tectus ω   46 et noua *Housman*: nonaque *P*ς: denaque *G*ω: pronaque *Bentley*   53 contineo ς: continuo *PG*ω   56 morerer ω: mrcor *P(ut uid.)*: morior *P*²*G*ς: moriar ς   59 dixti ω: aisti *PG*ς

spes bona det uires: fratri nam nupta futura es.
  illius, de quo mater, et uxor eris.'
mortua, crede mihi, tamen ad tua uerba reuixi;
  et positum est uteri crimen onusque mei.
quid tibi grataris? media sedet Aeolus aula: 65
  crimina sunt oculis subripienda patris.
frugibus infantem ramisque albentis oliuae
  et leuibus uittis sedula celat anus,
fictaque sacra facit dicitque precantia uerba;
  dat populus sacris, dat pater ipse uiam.   70
iam prope limen erat: patrias uagitus ad aures
  uenit, et indicio proditur ipse suo.
eripit infantem mentitaque sacra reuelat
  Aeolus. insana regia uoce sonat.
ut mare fit tremulum, tenui cum stringitur aura,   75
  ut quatitur tepido fraxinus icta Noto,
sic mea uibrari pallentis membra uideres;
  quassus ab imposito corpore lectus erat.
irruit et nostrum uulgat clamore pudorem,
  et uix a misero continet ore manus.   80
ipsa nihil praeter lacrimas pudibunda profudi;
  torpuerat gelido lingua retenta metu.
iamque dari paruum canibusque auibusque nepotem
  iusserat, in solis destituique locis:
uagitus dedit ille miser (sensisse putares),   85
  quaque suum poterat uoce rogabat auum.
quid mihi tunc animi credis, germane, fuisse
  (nam potes ex animo colligere ipse tuo),
cum mea me coram siluas inimicus in altas
  uiscera montanis ferret edenda lupis?   90

---

61 fratri(-tris P^2ς) nam nupta futura es $PG\omega$: nam fratri n. f. e. ς: germani
n. f. e. ς   62 et $PG\omega$: es ς   67 frugibus Pς: frondibus $G\omega$ 72 ipse Gς:
ille $P\omega$ 76 tepido $PG\omega$: trepido ς   fraxinus icta *Palmer*: fraxina uirga
$P^2G\omega$: fraxincies P 77 pallentis *Heinsius*: pallentia *codd.*   89 inimicus
codd.: immitis *Bentley*

exierat thalamo: tum demum pectora plangi
  contigit inque meas unguibus ire genas.
interea patrius uultu maerente satelles
  uenit et indignos edidit ore sonos:
'Aeolus hunc ensem mittit tibi' (tradidit ensem):   95
  'et iubet ex merito scire, quid iste uelit.'
scimus, et utemur uiolento fortiter ense;
  pectoribus condam dona paterna meis.
his mea muneribus, genitor, conubia donas?
  hac tua dote, pater, filia diues erit?   100
tolle procul, decepte, faces, Hymenaee, maritas
  et fuge turbato tecta nefanda pede!
ferte faces in me quas fertis, Erinyes, atras,
  et meus ex isto luceat igne rogus!
nubite felices Parca meliore, sorores,   105
  amissae memores sed tamen este mei.
quid puer admisit tam paucis editus horis?
  quo laesit facto uix bene natus auum?
si potuit meruisse necem, meruisse putetur.
  a, miser admisso plectitur ille meo!   110
nate, dolor matris, rabidarum praeda ferarum,
  ei mihi, natali dilacerate tuo,
nate, parum fausti miserabile pignus amoris,
  haec tibi prima dies, haec tibi summa fuit!
non mihi te licuit lacrimis perfundere iustis,   115
  in tua non tonsas ferre sepulcra comas.
non super incubui, non oscula frigida carpsi:
  diripiunt auidae uiscera nostra ferae.
ipsa quoque infantes cum uulnere prosequar umbras,
  nec mater fuero dicta nec orba diu.   120
tu tamen, o frustra miserae sperate sorori,
  sparsa, precor, nati collige membra tui

---

91 plangi *P*ς: planxi *G*ω   92 genas *P²*ς: comas *PG*ς   103 atras *Burman*:
atrae *codd.*   104 et *G*ς: at *P*: ut ς   106 amissae *PG*ς: amissi ς: admissi ς
111 rabidarum ς (*'quidam' Burmanni*) *Plan.*: rapidarum *PG*ω

et refer ad matrem socioque impone sepulcro
   urnaque nos habeat quamlibet arta duos.
uiue memor nostri, lacrimasque in uulnera funde,   125
   neue reformida corpus amantis amans.
tu, rogo, dilectae nimium mandata sororis
   perfice; mandatis obsequar ipsa patris.

125 uulnera *P*ϛ: uulnere ω: fulnere *G*: funere *G*²ϛ   127 dilectae *PG*ϛ: pro-
iectae *P*²ω   128 perfice ϛ: perfer *PG*ω   obsequar *Housman*: persequar *P*:
perfruar *G*ω

INCERTI AVCTORIS
EPISTVLA SAPPHVS AD PHAONEM

Ecquid, ut aspecta est studiosae littera dextrae,
    protinus est oculis cognita nostra tuis?
an, nisi legisses auctoris nomina Sapphus,
    hoc breue nescires unde ueniret opus?
forsitan et quare mea sint alterna requiras   5
    carmina, cum lyricis sim magis apta modis.
flendus amor meus est: elegia flebile carmen.
    non facit ad lacrimas barbitos illa meas.
uror ut, indomitis ignem exercentibus Euris,
    fertilis accensis messibus ardet ager.   10
arua, Phaon, celebras diuersa Typhoidos Aetnae;
    me calor Aetnaeo non minor igne tenet.
nec mihi, dispositis quae iungam carmina neruis,
    proueniunt: uacuae carmina mentis opus.
nec me Pyrrhiades Methymniadesue puellae,   15
    nec me Lesbiadum cetera turba iuuant.
uilis Anactorie, uilis, mihi crede, Gyrinno,
    non oculis grata est Atthis, ut ante, meis,
atque aliae centum, quas non sine crimine amaui.
    improbe, multarum quod fuit, unus habes.   20
est in te facies, sunt apti lusibus anni.
    o facies oculis insidiosa meis!
sume fidem et pharetram: fies manifestus Apollo.
    accedant capiti cornua: Bacchus eris.
et Phoebus Daphnen, et Cnosida Bacchus amauit,   25
    nec norat lyricos illa uel illa modos.

---

4 ueniret *Fϛ*: mouetur ω   7 elegia ϛ: elegi quoque *Fϛ*: elegi ω   8 illa
Bentley: ulla *codd.*   11 celebras *Bentley*: celebrat *codd.*   17 crede Gyrinno
Bentley: candida Cydro *codd.*   19 non *F*: hic ω: nec *Burman*   23 pharetras
F: -am ω

at mihi Pegasides blandissima carmina dictant,
   iam canitur toto nomen in orbe meum;
nec plus Alcaeus, consors patriaeque lyraeque,
   laudis habet, quamuis grandius ille sonet.   30
si mihi difficilis formam natura negauit,
   ingenio formae damna rependo meae.
sum breuis, at nomen, quod terras impleat omnes,
   est mihi; mensuram nominis ipsa fero.
candida si non sum, placuit Cepheia Perseo   35
   Andromede, patriae fusca colore suae.
et uariis albae iunguntur saepe columbae
   et niger a uiridi turtur amatur aue.
si, nisi quae facie poterit te digna uideri,
   nulla futura tua est, nulla futura tua est.   40
at me cum legeres, etiam formosa uidebar;
   unam iurabas usque decere loqui.
cantabam, memini (meminerunt omnia amantes);
   oscula cantanti tu mihi rapta dabas.
haec quoque laudabas, omnique a parte placebam,   45
   sed tum praecipue, cum fit amoris opus.
tum te plus solito lasciuia nostra iuuabat,
   crebraque mobilitas aptaque uerba ioco,
quique, ubi iam amborum fuerat confusa uoluptas,
   plurimus in lasso corpore languor erat.   50
nunc tibi Sicelides ueniunt, noua praeda, puellae.
   quid mihi cum Lesbo? Sicelis esse uolo.
o uos erronem tellure remittite uestra,
   Nisiades matres Nisiadesque nurus!

---

32 rependo *codd.*: repende *Bentley*   33–4 *sic F*ς: nec me despicias si sum
tibi corpore parua | mensuramque breuis nominis ipsa fero ω   33 sum
codd.: sim *Bentley*   41 me ω: mea *F*ς legeres *codd.*: legerem *Wakker* etiam
codd.: sat iam *Housman*   45 haec ς: hoc *F*ω: me ς omnique a ω: omni
tibi ς   46 tum ς: tunc *F*ω   49 quique ubi iam *Heinsius*: ecquid ubi *F*:
et quod ubi ς: atque ubi iam ς   53 o *F*ς: nec ς: at ς: aut *Bentley* uestra
Micyllus: nostrum *F*ω

nec uos decipiant blandae mendacia linguae: 55
   quae uobis dicit, dixerat ante mihi.
tu quoque, quae montes celebras, Erycina, Sicanos,
   (nam tua sum) uati consule, diua, tuae.
an grauis inceptum peragit fortuna tenorem
   et manet in cursu semper acerba suo?   60
sex mihi natales ierant, cum lecta parentis
   ante diem lacrimas ossa bibere meas.
carpsit opes frater meretricis captus amore
   mixtaque cum turpi damna pudore tulit;
factus inops agili peragit freta caerula remo,   65
   quasque male amisit, nunc male quaerit opes.
me quoque, quod monui bene multa fideliter, odit;
   hoc mihi libertas, hoc pia lingua dedit.
et tamquam desint, quae me sine fine fatigent,
   accumulat curas filia parua meas.   70
ultima tu nostris accedis causa querelis:
   non agitur uento nostra carina suo.
ecce, iacent collo sparsi sine lege capilli,
   nec premit articulos lucida gemma meos.
ueste tegor uili, nullum est in crinibus aurum,   75
   non Arabum noster dona capillus habet.
cui colar infelix, aut cui placuisse laborem?
   ille mei cultus unicus auctor abes.
molle meum leuibusque cor est uiolabile telis,
   et semper causa est, cur ego semper amem,   80
siue ita nascenti legem dixere Sorores
   nec data sunt uitae fila seuera meae,
siue abeunt studia in mores artisque magistra
   ingenium nobis molle Thalea facit.
quid mirum, si me primae lanuginis aetas   85
   abstulit, atque anni quos uir amare potest?

63 carpsit opes *Bentley*: arsit inops *codd.*: arsit iners *Oudendorp*   69 desint
... fatigent ω: desit ... fatiget *F*ς   sine fine ω: hac sine cura *F*   78 abes
Heinsius: abest *codd.*   83 artisque magistra *Heinsius*: artesque magistras *codd.*

hunc ne pro Cephalo raperes, Aurora, timebam;
  et faceres, sed te prima rapina tenet.
hunc si conspicias, quae conspicis omnia, Phoebe,
  iussus erit somnos continuare Phaon.   90
hunc Venus in caelum curru uexisset eburno,
  sed uidet et Marti posse placere suo.
o nec adhuc iuuenis, nec iam puer, utilis aetas!
  o decus atque aeui gloria magna tui!
huc ades inque sinus, formose, relabere nostros.   95
  non ut ames oro, uerum ut amere sinas.
scribimus, et lacrimis oculi rorantur obortis;
  aspice, quam sit in hoc multa litura loco.
si tam certus eras hinc ire, modestius isses,
  et modo dixisses 'Lesbi puella, uale!'   100
non tecum lacrimas, non oscula nostra tulisti.
  denique non timui, quod dolitura fui.
nil de te mecum est nisi tantum iniuria; nec tu
  admoneat quod te pignus amantis habes.
non mandata dedi, neque enim mandata dedissem   105
  ulla, nisi ut nolles immemor esse mei.
per tibi, qui numquam longe discedat, Amorem,
  perque nouem iuro, numina nostra, deas,
cum mihi nescio quis 'fugiunt tua gaudia' dixit,
  nec me flere diu nec potuisse loqui.   110
et lacrimae deerant oculis et uerba palato,
  astrictum gelido frigore pectus erat.
postquam se dolor inuenit, nec pectora plangi
  nec puduit scissis exululare comis,
non aliter quam si nati pia mater adempti   115
  portet ad exstructos corpus inane rogos.

---

89 conspicias ς: -iat *F*ω   conspicis ς: -it *F*ω   96 uerum ut *F*: sed te ut ς:
sed quod ς: sed ut ς: me sed *Heinsius* amere *de Vries*: amare *codd.*   100
et modo ω: et mihi *F*: si modo ς   103 nec tu *Burman*: nec te *codd.*   104 te
Burman: tu *codd.* pignus ς: munus *F*ω   107 discedat ω: discedit *F*ς   113
inuenit *F*ω: imminuit ς

gaudet et e nostro crescit maerore Charaxus
    frater, et ante oculos itque reditque meos,
utque pudenda mei uideatur causa doloris,
    'quid dolet haec? certe filia uiuit' ait.   120
non ueniunt in idem pudor atque amor. omne uidebat
    uulgus: eram lacero pectus aperta sinu.
tu mihi cura, Phaon; te somnia nostra reducunt,
    somnia formoso candidiora die.
illic te inuenio, quamuis regionibus absis;   125
    sed non longa satis gaudia somnus habet.
saepe tuos nostra ceruice onerare lacertos,
    saepe tuae uideor supposuisse meos.
oscula cognosco, quae tu committere lingua
    aptaque consueras accipere, apta dare.   130
blandior interdum uerisque simillima uerba
    eloquor, et uigilant sensibus ora meis.
ulteriora pudet narrare, sed omnia fiunt:
    et iuuat et siccae non licet esse mihi.
at cum se Titan ostendit et omnia secum,   135
    tam cito me somnos destituisse queror.
antra nemusque peto, tamquam nemus antraque prosint:
    conscia deliciis illa fuere meis.
illuc mentis inops, ut quam furialis Enyo
    attigit, in collo crine iacente feror.   140
antra uident oculi scabro pendentia tofo,
    quae mihi Mygdonii marmoris instar erant.
inuenio siluam, quae saepe cubilia nobis
    praebuit et multa texit opaca coma;
at non inuenio dominum siluaeque meumque.   145
    uile solum locus est; dos erat ille loci.
cognoui pressas noti mihi caespitis herbas;
    de nostro curuum pondere gramen erat.

129 lingua *F*: linguae ω   134 siccae *F*: sine te ω

incubui tetigique locum, qua parte fuisti;
  grata prius lacrimas combibit herba meas.   150
quin etiam rami positis lugere uidentur
  frondibus, et nullae dulce queruntur aues.
sola uirum non ulta pie maestissima mater
  concinit Ismarium Daulias ales Ityn.
ales Ityn, Sappho desertos cantat amores.   155
  hactenus; ut media cetera nocte silent.
est nitidus uitroque magis perlucidus omni
  fons sacer (hunc multi numen habere putant),
quem supra ramos expandit aquatica lotos,
  una nemus; tenero caespite terra uiret.   160
hic ego cum lassos posuissem flebilis artus,
  constitit ante oculos Naias una meos.
constitit et dixit: 'quoniam non ignibus aequis
  ureris, Ambracia est terra petenda tibi.
Phoebus ab excelso quantum patet aspicit aequor: 165
  Actiacum populi Leucadiumque uocant.
hinc se Deucalion Pyrrhae succensus amore
  misit, et illaeso corpore pressit aquas.
nec mora, uersus Amor fugit lentissima mersi
  pectora; Deucalion igne leuatus erat.   170
hanc legem locus ille tenet. pete protinus altam
  Leucada nec saxo desiluisse time.'
ut monuit, cum uoce abiit; ego frigida surgo,
  nec lacrimas oculi continuere mei.
ibimus, o nymphe, monstrataque saxa petemus;   175
  sit procul insano uictus amore timor.
quidquid erit, melius quam nunc erit. aura, subito
  et mea non magnum corpora pondus habe.

153 pie *F*ς: prius ω   157 uitroque ς: uitreoque *F*ω omni *Bentley*: amni
*F*ς: amne ω   169 fugit *F*ς: figit ς: tetigit ω mersi *F*: pirr(h)e ω   173 fri-
gida *F*ω: territa ς   174 nec lacrimas oculi continuere mei *F*: nec grauidae
lacrimas continuere genae ω   178 habe *Damsté*: habent *codd.*

tu quoque, mollis Amor, pennas suppone cadenti,
    ne sim Leucadiae mortua crimen aquae.   180
inde chelyn Phoebo, communia munera, ponam,
    et sub ea uersus unus et alter erunt:
GRATA LYRAM POSVI TIBI PHOEBE POETRIA SAPPHO
    CONVENIT ILLA MIHI CONVENIT ILLA TIBI.
cur tamen Actiacas miseram me mittis ad oras,   185
    cum profugum possis ipse referre pedem?
tu mihi Leucadia potes esse salubrior unda;
    et forma et meritis tu mihi Phoebus eris.
an potes, o scopulis undaque ferocior omni,
    si moriar, titulum mortis habere meae?   190
at quanto melius tecum mea pectora iungi,
    quam poterant saxis praecipitanda dari!
haec sunt illa, Phaon, quae tu laudare solebas,
    uisaque sunt totiens ingeniosa tibi.
nunc uellem facunda forem: dolor artibus obstat   195
    ingeniumque meis substitit omne malis.
non mihi respondent ueteres in carmina uires;
    plectra dolore tacent, muta dolore lyra est.
Lesbides aequoreae, nupturaque nuptaque proles,
    Lesbides, Aeolia nomina dicta lyra,   200
Lesbides, infamem quae me fecistis amatae,
    desinite ad citharas turba uenire meas!
abstulit omne Phaon, quod uobis ante placebat.
    me miseram, dixi quam modo paene 'meus'!
efficite ut redeat, uates quoque uestra redibit.   205
    ingenio uires ille dat, ille rapit.
ecquid ago precibus pectusue agreste mouetur?
    an riget, et Zephyri uerba caduca ferunt?

---

189 omni *F*: illa ω   tecum … iungi *F*: iungi … tecum ω   192 poterant
saxis ω: saxis poterant *F*   198 tacent *F*ω: iacent ς   201 amatae *F*:
amare ω   202 citharae uerba uenire meae *Bentley*   meas *codd.*: mea *Housman*   207 pectusue ς: pectusque *F*ς: pectusne ς   208 riget ω: piget *F*

qui mea uerba ferunt, uellem tua uela referrent;
   hoc te, si saperes, lente, decebat opus.   210
siue redis, puppique tuae uotiua parantur
   munera, quid laceras pectora nostra mora?
solue ratem! Venus orta mari mare praestat amanti.
   aura dabit cursum; tu modo solue ratem!
ipse gubernabit residens in puppe Cupido;   215
   ipse dabit tenera uela legetque manu.
siue iuuat longe fugisse Pelasgida Sappho
   (non tamen inuenies, cur ego digna fugi),
hoc saltem miserae crudelis epistula dicat,
   ut mihi Leucadiae fata petantur aquae.   220

211 parantur ς: paramus *F*ω   212 laceras ω: cruciatur *F*: crucias *Bentley*
215 gubernabit ω: gubernator *F*   217 iuuat ω: iuuet *F*ς   218 non ω:
nec *F*   fugi *de Vries*: fuge *codd.*   219–20 *del. Bentley*

COMMENTARY

I Penelope Vlixi

The first of the *Heroides* serves as an introduction to the entire collection, illustrating by example both the major themes of the following epistles and the manner of treatment. Its primary reference is to a single literary model, Homer's *Odyssey*, and O.'s selection of Homeric epic for eroticized treatment in the introductory elegy should be regarded as an implied statement of his own literary principles. O.'s epistle is the earliest surviving example of a trend towards romanticizing the story of Ulysses' return to Penelope (Stanford (1963) 143); but he was surely not the first poet in antiquity to read the *Odyssey* as a love story, as he himself characterized it several years later in a defence of his poetry to Augustus: *Trist.* 2.375–6 *aut quid Odyssea est nisi femina propter amorem, | dum uir abest, multis una petita procis?* Poets for centuries had treated Penelope as an *exemplum pudicitiae* (*RE* xix 483–4), but there are traces of a reaction against this tendency in Horace's suggestion of an erotic treatment of the *Odyssey* as a subject for a music girl in an invitation to a symposium: Hor. *Carm.* 1.17.17–20 *hic in reducta ualle Caniculae | uitabis aestus et fide Teia | dices laborantes in uno | Penelopen uitreamque Circen.* Prose summaries by the Greek poet Parthenius of two stories of the amorous escapades of Odysseus with Polymele (*Erot.* 2) and Euippe (*Erot.* 3) offer further evidence of an inclination by Hellenistic Greek writers to focus upon the erotic conquests of the Homeric hero. An interesting twist is provided later by Lucian, who produces the text of an epistle from Odysseus to Calypso (*Ver. hist.* 2.35) expressing regret for his decision to leave her for Penelope. Our evidence for the role of Penelope in post-Homeric accounts of the story is scanty (Jacobson (1974) 245–6), but it seems clear that it was O. who took the imaginative step of representing the events of the *Odyssey* from her point of view. In so doing, he has taken her character far beyond the traditional role of a paradigm of fidelity.

Penelope's epistle is not simply a prolonged lament for her unfortunate position; more than in any of the other poems O. sustains the fiction that this is a real letter. Penelope aims at persuading

Ulysses to return, with the implied reproach that return lies within his power if only he wishes it (1, 7–10, 81–96nn.). This tone is sustained by the sophisticated interplay of references to the text of the *Odyssey*, against which O.'s reader will test the 'facts' as presented by Penelope. The imagined time of composition is fixed within very narrow limits by references to events described by Homer. The opening section of the poem makes it clear that Penelope writes after the fall of Troy and the return of the Greeks, but three references to Telemachus' mission to Pylos and Sparta (37–8, 63–5, 99–100) place the epistle after her interview with Telemachus, which in the *Odyssey* (17.107–65) takes place the day before the suitors are killed. The epistle's many ironic references to the text of the *Odyssey* are further emphasized, as Kennedy (1984) 417–18 suggests, by the fact that the intended carrier of the letter would therefore be none other than Ulysses himself, recently arrived in Ithaca in the guise of a Cretan stranger. Thus conceived, O.'s epistle of Penelope is not simply a rhetorical reworking of a Homeric theme, but a masterly exploration of character, making new the material of the oldest literary tradition available to him.

1–22 Penelope follows the salutation of the opening line with a recapitulation of all her former fears for Ulysses while he was fighting at Troy. This part of the epistle avoids any overt note of reproach, although it contains some hints of her present state of mind; e.g. the suggestion that her fears were worse than the reality (11 *grauiora pericula ueris*) or the coy description of herself at the loom with no mention of the celebrated ruse used to put off the suitors. As a whole this section serves to evoke the atmosphere of the Trojan war, the epic backdrop against which this domestic drama is played.

1 Haec: sc. *uerba*, as in 10.3 *quae legis*; cf. *Pont.* 4.14.1 *haec tibi mittuntur*, 2.10.2 *haec … scribere uerba*, 3.4.1 *haec … uerba.* Palmer's correction of *hanc*, the reading of the MSS, removes the awkward ellipse of *epistulam* or *salutem* postulated by editors. Such an ellipse is too harsh for O. and it is not defended by Cic. *Att.* 15.20.4, where modern editors read *haec putaui mea manu scribenda*, referring not to the entire letter but only to the preceding passage. In Cicero's letters ellipse of *litterae* is common (see Shackleton Bailey on *Att.* 13.12.1), but there is only one example of ellipse of *epistula*, and none of *salutem*. The error perhaps arose through a scribe's recollection of other Ovidian epistolary openings such as *Trist.* 5.13.1 *hanc ... salutem, Pont.* 1.3.1 *hanc ... salutem.*

lento: not simply 'slow', but 'tarrying'. The adjective forms a standard component in the elegists' arsenal of reproachful epithets for the less amorous partner in a love affair. Numerous examples in Pichon (1902) 186; cf. 2.23, 6.17, 19.70. Here it introduces the theme, elaborated throughout the epistle (cf. 66), that Ulysses' absence is not entirely involuntary.

Vlixē: vocative. This form is supported by Priscian (*GLK* II 277 and 288), although it is anomalous in the Latinized name of Odysseus, which draws its forms from the fifth and later the third declensions; see Leumann (1977) 458 and Housman (1910) 259–60 (= *Class. pap.* 834–5). Some MSS read *Vlixes*, the regular vocative in early Latin, as in Pacuvius, *trag.* 256; cf. *Met.* 13.83 where some MSS also have *-es*, and for further details, see N–W I 447–9.

2 nil ... attinet 'it is no good your writing me a reply': the subjunctive *rescribas* should be construed with *attinet*, a unique example of this construction that may be explained by analogy with *oportet*, *necesse est*, and *opus est*. *attinet* is not found in any MSS of the *Heroides*, the majority of which offer *attamen* or *sed tamen* here, but the verse is quoted four times in this form in the fourth-century metrical treatise of Aelius Festus Apthonius, *GLK* VI 109.3 and VI 111.24. As Housman (1922) 88–91 (= *Class. pap.* 1052–4) demonstrates, this must have been what stood in the text known to the grammarian and *attinet* is thus attested by a witness at least seven centuries older than E or G.

3 iacet 'is fallen': no special point is intended by the repetition of the verb in 7 *iacuisset.* Such casual iteration is more common in Latin poetry than critics are often prepared to admit. As Housman notes in the preface to *Lucan*, p. xxxiii: 'Each author has his own principles and practice. Horace was as sensitive to iteration as any modern ... Virgil was less sensitive, Ovid much less; Lucan was almost insensible.' For further discussion, see Austin on Virg. *Aen.* 2.505, Shackleton Bailey (1956) 9, and, with special reference to O., Kenney (1959) 248. Examples of repetition without point in this poem are 12 *timoris ...* 16 *timoris*; 40 *dolo ...* 42 *dolo* (but see 40n.).

certe 'to be sure', anticipating the pentameter.

Danais 'Greek': cf. 21 *Achiuis,* 25 *Argolici.*

puellis includes, presumably, Penelope herself, now some 20 years older than when Ulysses left for the Trojan War. Although Penelope takes pains in this letter to portray herself as a desirable young woman, she is none the less conscious of the passage of time, as indicated by the pointed contrast in the final couplet of the poem (see 115–16n.).

4 uix ... tanti ... fuit 'Priam and all of Troy were hardly worth so great a cost': i.e. your long absence. *tanti* is genitive of price; cf. *Am.* 3.6.37–8 *nec tanti Calydon nec tota Aetolia tanti, | una tamen tanti Deianira fuit*, Prop. 3.20.4 *tantine, ut lacrimes, Africa tota fuit?* The pentameter restates and amplifies the idea expressed in the hexameter, a common manner of exposition in elegy.

5–6 A wistful complaint, framed as a wish in highly stylized language. Penelope's complaints against Paris are the subject of a fragment (1st cent. BC) of Greek hexameter verse (*SH* 952). O. may be reworking a familiar topos.

5 o utinam: a poetic combination for introducing a wish; cf. *Am.* 2.5.7, Hor. *Carm.* 4.5.37. Likewise, *tum cum* is a combination of particles largely limited to poetry (H–S 619); cf. 3.23, 5.109. Because they are taken closely together, they can stand before the third-foot caesura, where O. otherwise avoids a monosyllable; cf. *Fast.* 5.625 *fama uetus, tum cum Saturnia terra uocata est.* The hiatus after *o* and other interjections is very common in elegy; cf. Platnauer (1951) 57.

Lacedaemona: the Greek form of the accusative singular is regular in proper names. In the *Her.* we find: *Thesea* (2.13), *Demophoonta* (2.98), *Phyllida* (2.105, 2.147), *Agamemnona* (3.83), *Briseida* (3.137), *Troezena* (4.107), *Hectora* (5.93), *Iasona* (6.77), *Simoenta* (7.145), *Phasida* (16.345, 19.176), *Cnosida* (*ES* 25).

6 insanis: not simply a reference to the conventional wildness of the elements (for which cf. 7.53 *insana ... aequora*, 18.28 *insani ... freti*), but suggestive of the madness of Paris and his enterprise.

adulter is a commonplace word, avoided by Tibullus and Propertius, who prefer the more discreet *amans* or *amator*. O., however, is less circumspect in his portrayal of illicit affairs and employs it often in his elegies. In the high style it refers almost exclusively to the celebrated miscreants of mythology: it is found only twice in the *Aeneid*, of Paris (10.92) and Aegisthus (11.268); so, too, of Paris in the only occurrence in Propertius (2.34.7). In Helen's epistle to Paris the subject of adultery is much on her mind and the word is often used: cf. 17.18, 17.46, 17.217.

7-10 Penelope's complaint that she must sleep alone and pass the night in weaving echoes Cynthia's complaint in a particularly well-known Propertian elegy: 1.3.41 *nam modo purpureo fallebam stamine somnum*. O. neatly reverses a common motif in Hellenistic epigram where the male lover, alone at night, laments the faithlessness of his mistress; cf. e.g. Meleager, *AP* 5.191 (= *HE* 4378). For Horace this theme is a commonplace: *Epist.* 1.1.20 *nox longa quibus mentitur amica*. The note of reproach in *deserto* (7) is reiterated in *relicta* (8) and *uiduas* (10).

7-8 O. recasts in elegiac terms as a complaint the description given by Homer's Penelope of her days and nights in her secret interview with the disguised Odysseus (*Od.* 19.513-17): 'The day times I indulge in lamentation, mourning | as I look to my own tasks and those of my maids in the palace. | But after the night comes and sleep has taken all others, | I lie on my bed, and the sharp anxieties swarming | thick and fast on my beating heart torment my sorrowing self' (Lattimore).

7 deserto ... lecto: perhaps an unconscious reminiscence of Cat. 68.29 *frigida deserto tepefactet membra cubili*; cf. 81 below, 5.106, and *Met.* 7.710 *primaque deserti referebam foedera lecti*.

frigida frequently refers to 'one who spends the night alone, abandoned by her lover' (Pichon (1902) 156), but it is also a term for the chilling of affections; cf. *Am.* 2.1.5, 2.7.9, *Rem.* 492.

8 quererer: the switch to the imperfect tense implies that the complaint is continual. The theme of complaint, signalled by *queri*, *querela*, *et sim.*, is a leitmotiv of the *Her.*, especially appropriate in light of the ancient view that elegy originated in lamentation; cf. *ES* 7n.

9-10 O.'s reader has heard of Penelope's weaving before, but in a different context. In the *Odyssey* one of the suitors complains (2.93-110) about the ruse that she had used to put them off, when she claimed that she could not remarry until she had woven a funeral shroud for her husband's father, Laertes. In the daytime she worked at her loom, at night she secretly unravelled what she had done. Penelope later describes this trick to Odysseus in his disguise as a beggar (19.137–55). There is only the faintest allusion to this scene here, and as Barchiesi (1992) 24 notes, the absence of a reference to this deception at a point where it would be appropriate is deliberate. A Roman sensibility would instantly have responded to this depiction of a faithful wife at her loom, a scene which typified for them all the essential feminine virtues; see Ogilvie's comments on Livy's portrayal of Lucretia at 1.57.7.

9 spatiosam fallere noctem 'to beguile the spacious night': the adjective *spatiosus* is a favourite with O., who introduced a great many such formations in *-osus* into Latin poetic diction (Knox (1986b) 99–101). Its application to time is O.'s innovation: cf. *Am.* 1.8.81, *Met.* 8.530, 12.186, 13.206, 15.623. With *fallere* (*TLL* s.v.188.1ff.) it makes a striking phrase, but one that is an easy step from Propertius' *purpureo fallebam stamine somnum* (1.3.41): with *fallere noctem*, i.e. to make the night seem less long, cf. *Trist.* 4.1.13–14 *cantantis pariter, pariter data pensa trahentis,* | *fallitur ancillae decipiturque labor.* There is perhaps also a touch of irony by O. in using this verb: Penelope's weaving is still a trick, but one used only to while away the time.

10 lassaret ... manus 'nor would the hanging web continually [imperfect] wear out my widowed hands': O. perhaps hints at other associations as well; in Greek epigram weaving is often portrayed as a concomitant of unwanted chastity: cf. Nicarchus, *A.P.* 6.285 (= *HE* 2737), Anon. *A.P.* 6.48 (= *HE* 3812), 6.283 (= *HE* 3818), 6.284 (= *HE* 3822), and in Latin poetry, 19.16, *Am.* 1.13.24, *Ars* 1.689, 2.219, *Med.* 14, Tib. 1.3.85–92, Prop. 3.6.9–14. The homely image is further enhanced by the use of *lassare*, apparently, like the adjective *lassus*, a word of colloquial tone (10.145n.). *delassare* is attested in Plautus, but the simplex is first found in Tib. 1.9.55, and is much favoured by O., who uses it almost as often as the synonymous *fatigare* (14:16). From O. the word spread to later poetry and after the elder Seneca to prose.

uiduas agrees grammatically with *manus* though in sense it refers to *mihi*, a trick of style known as enallage or a 'transferred epithet'. It is quite common in Latin poetry: cf. Bell (1923) 319, H–S 159–60.

pendula tela: on the ancient loom, the warp (*tela*) hung down from a cross-beam.

11 grauiora pericula ueris implies at least that Penelope's fears were out of proportion to reality and suggests another note of reproach: perhaps Penelope suffered more than Ulysses; cf. Jacobson (1974) 251.

12 res est: an idiomatic phrase, favoured by O. in the more conversational style of the poetic epistle: cf. 6.21 *credula res amor est*, *Pont.* 2.7.37, 2.9.11, 3.9.23, 4.15.31.

13 in te ... ituros: sc. with hostile intent, a common usage of *eo* with this prepositional phrase.

Troăs: a Greek form of the accusative plural.

14 nomine in Hectoreo 'at the mention of Hector's name': cf. *Am.* 2.1.5 *in sponsi facie* 'at the sight of her betrothed's face', Goold (1965) 30. The personal adjective takes the place of a genitive, a common feature of Latin poetic style, developed partly in imitation of Greek epic and tragic diction, but chiefly representing a development of an early feature of the Latin language by writers, including prose authors (K–S 1 209–12) seeking to avoid the more familiar usage: cf. Löfstedt (1942) 107–24, Austin on *Aen.* 2.543, H–S 60–1. The possessive *Hectoreus* is first attested in a fragment of Cicero's verse (*Hom. fr.* III.2 Soubiran) translated from Greek.

semper should be construed (ἀπὸ κοινοῦ) with both *fingebam* and *pallida eram*.

15 ab hoste reuictum 'laid low by the enemy': i.e. Memnon, leader of the Ethiopian allies of Troy and slayer of Antilochus, the son of Nestor (*Od.* 4.187, 11.52). The MSS are unanimous in offering a reading, *ab Hectore uictum*, which contradicts this well-established tradition. It is highly unlikely that O. is relying upon a variant unknown to us. Hyg. *Fab.* 113, which refers to Hector as his slayer, is probably corrupt, but in any event, since O. is one of his sources, may only show that the corruption in this passage is ancient. Nor is it probable that O. deliberately portrays Penelope in error on this trivial point. The corruption is also betrayed by the feeble repetition of *nomine in Hectoreo ... Hectore*. Housman (1897) 102–3 (= *Class. pap.* 381–2) restores the sense of the passage, if not perhaps O.'s exact words. The three examples cited by Penelope in 15–20 thus refer to the three great champions of Troy: Memnon, Hector, Sarpedon.

17 Menoetiaden: Patroclus, son of Menoetius.

falsis 'deceptive', not simply = *alienis*. Patroclus led the Greeks into battle wearing the armour of Achilles in order to deceive the Trojans into believing that Achilles himself had returned to the fight, and was in that sense a 'false Achilles'. O.'s transference of the epithet is bold; the line was subsequently reinterpreted by Seneca in imitation at *Ag.* 618 where Patroclus is called *falsus Achilles*.

18 posse carere dolos: indirect statement dependent upon *flere*, a construction limited to poetry; cf. *TLL* s.v. 900.57–8. For Ulysses these words carry a special meaning, since *dolus* was a fixed feature in the characterization of Odysseus as a wily trickster in literature, although δόλος is not a pejorative word in Homer; cf. Stanford (1963) 249 n.17. In Hor. *Serm.* 2.5.3 the epithet *dolosus* is used alone to identify Ulysses.

19 Tlepolemus: a son of Heracles, slain by Sarpedon, king of Lycia (*Lyciam ... hastam*), who fought for the Trojans (*Il.* 5.627–62).

sanguine ... tepefecerat: the periphrasis gives the line a heroic tone; cf. Virg. *Aen.* 9.418–19 *hasta ... haesit tepefacta cerebro*, 9.701, 10.570, adapting a Homeric phrase (*Il.* 16.333, etc.).

21 denique 'in sum'.

quisquis erat ... iugulatus 'whoever had had his throat slit': *iugulare* is a harsh word, avoided by the poets and in prose by the historians (*TLL* s.v. 634.75). It is found at *Am.* 3.8.21, where O. uses it with deliberate crudeness to refer to a competitor: *forsitan et quotiens hominem iugulauerit ille | indicet*. In his other works it occurs only once in 14.11, five times in the *Met.*, and once in the *Ibis* .

22 frigidius glacie: the result of fear; cf. 10.32.

23–56 O.'s Penelope now passes to the immediate aftermath of the war and the return of the Greeks, a happy theme that she uses to point the contrast between her circumstances and the fortunate women whose men have already come home.

23 bene ... amori 'a sympathetic god took good care of my chaste love': the dative *amori* should be construed with both *consuluit* and *aequus*, a usage known as amphibole (Bell (1923) 293–303), which is often impossible to render succinctly into English. *bene* is redundant with *consulere*, a colloquial combination found in O. otherwise only at *Pont.* 2.9.34. In *casto ... amori* O.'s Penelope perhaps points a contrast between herself and Helen who was punished for her adulterous love.

24 cinerem: most MSS have the plural. In this idiom (*in cinerem uertere*), the singular seems to have been preferred; cf. *Met.* 2.216, Tib. 1.9.12, Hor. *Epist.* 1.15.39. It is likely that O. would avoid *cineres* before a word beginning with *s*-, while it is only at *Trist.* 5.12.68 that we find *cineres* before a vowel to avoid elision; cf. Maas (1902) 518–20, 525.

sospite ... uiro: ablative absolute.

26 ponitur ad patrios ... deos: i.e. is hung up in the temples of the gods. *ponere* is the proper word for a dedication.

barbara: Trojan, from Penelope's point of view.

27 grata ... dona 'thank-offerings'.

nuptae: restored by conjecture for *nymphae* in the MSS, a Graecism occasionally found in Latin verse with the meaning 'young women', e.g. 9.50 *Ormeni nympha* (Astydamia), 9.103 *nympha ... Iardani* (Omphale), *Ciris* 435. That sense is not appropriate here for the wives of the Greek warriors, nor is a different meaning 'wife' supported by 16.128, where Paris pays Helen a compliment by calling her a Spartan nymph. Heinsius' conjecture has indirect MS support in the translation by Planudes, who has αἱ γυναῖκες here, his regular rendering of *nuptae*, although in one instance (12.207) he does translate *nuptam* by νύμφην. In some MSS of the *Fasti* at 2.605 and 5.205 *nymphae* also appears in error for *nuptae*.

28 uicta suis Troica fata 'the fate of Troy has yielded to their own', a bold phrase: *fata uincere* usually has a different meaning, as at Virg. *Aen.* 11.160 *uiuendo uici mea fata*, with Servius' comment: *id est naturalem ordinem uita longiore superaui.* This use is well-attested (*TLL* s.v. *fatum* 364.76–9), but by saying that one nation's fate has overcome another's, O. extends the idea inherent in Virgil's conception of opposing fates of two peoples as expressed at *Aen.* 7.293–4 *fatis contraria nostris | fata Phrygum.* O.'s bold usage is in turn imitated by Manilius 1.512 *fatis Asiae iam Graecia pressa est,* itself a daring expression for the conquest of Greece by Troy (by way of Rome).

29 iustique: the epithet is conventional for elders, from whom the magistrates of the city would be drawn; cf. *Fast.* 4.524, *Met.* 8.704.

-que ... -que: polysyndetic -*que* was a native feature of the Latin language (H–S 515), but it is never used in classical prose, and its use in poetry from Ennius on is probably due to imitation of Homeric τε ... τε and Greek usage. It is always more common in epic than in other genres (see Smith on Tib. 1.1.33), but, interestingly, it is completely avoided by Propertius in his first book, nor is it favoured by

Horace. By O.'s time it was a standard element in the poetic language.

30 narrantis ... pendet ab ore uiri 'hangs upon the lips of her husband as he tells his tale': a clear reminiscence of *Aen.* 4.79 *pendet ... narrantis ab ore,* of Dido in her eagerness to hear the tale of Troy again from Aeneas. O.'s imitations of the *Aeneid* in this epistle evoke the epic background with which Penelope's domestic situation makes a sharp contrast.

coniunx: the epic word for 'wife' (Axelson (1945) 57–8), found 19 times in the single epistles. In the epistles from heroines of epic (1, 3, 6, 7) it is decisively the preferred term, with 11 occurrences compared with four of the everyday *uxor*; but in the remaining poems the choice is almost evenly balanced (8:9), and in each case is determined by the tone O. is trying to effect: see Lyne (1989) 43–8, 60–2.

31–2 O.'s description of returning husbands outlining their campaigns on the table-top (*mensa ... posita*) lends a touch of realism to this scene. Tibullus had already described such a vignette in brief: 1.10.29–32 *alius sit fortis in armis | ... ut mihi potanti possit sua dicere facta | miles et in mensa pingere castra mero.* In a later imitation of this passage, O. adapts it to a different but appropriate context to show Ulysses diagramming his battles in the sand by the seashore as he tells his story to Calypso: *Ars* 2.133–6 *'haec' inquit 'Troia est' (muros in litore fecit), | 'hic tibi sit Simois; haec mea castra puta. | campus erat' (campumque facit), 'quem caede Dolonis | sparsimus.'* The ironies of O.'s imitation of Penelope's envious recounting of the stories heard by other Greek women will not be lost on the reader of the *Ars*.

32 et: postponed: a neoteric mannerism (Norden (1927) 402–4 and Ross (1969) 67–9) especially common with this conjunction: in the single *Her.* it occurs at 9.118, 11.16.

exiguo ... mero: the word-order, with noun and epithet enclosing the direct object *Pergama*, reflects the sense, showing Troy entirely (*tota*) encompassed 'in a drop of wine'. *Pergama* (always plural, *metri causa*), the citadel of Troy, is often a synonym for the city.

33–6 These verses echo somewhat ironically the most celebrated after-dinner conversation in Roman poetry: Aeneas describing the Trojans' inspection of the deserted battlefield before Troy: Virg. *Aen.* 2.29–30 *hic Dolopum manus, hic saeuus tendebat Achilles; | classibus hic locus, hic acie certare solebant.* The Trojan war is evoked by reference to the literary landscape, with which O.'s readers would have an easy familiarity.

33 Sigeia tellus: i.e. the land of Troy, so called after the promontory Sigeum, the burial place of Achilles and Patroclus; cf. Virg. *Aen.* 7.294 *Sigeis ... campis.* The periphrasis with *tellus* adds a bit of epic colour: in O. it occurs only once in the *Amores* (3.9.47), but in the *Met.* and *Fasti* it is found 12 times. The more common form of the adjective is *Sigeus*; the four-syllable form is found only in O., here and at *Met.* 13.3. Such variation in proper adjectives is frequent in O.; see Bömer on *Met.* 12.9.

34 steterat: the pluperfect is used in place of the imperfect or perfect to denote remote time with considerable freedom by the elegists (H–S 320, Platnauer (1951) 112–15). The change of tenses, *ibat ... est ... steterat ... tendebat ... terruit,* vividly renders the course of the impromptu dinner-table campaign.

Priami ... senis 'old Priam', his standard sobriquet in Latin poetry since Ennius, *Ann.* 14 Sk. *ueter ... Priamus.* Cf. Hom. *Il.* 13.368, 21.526.

35 Aeacides: Achilles, grandson of Aeacus.

tendebat 'used to pitch his tent': an elliptical usage common in military language, but an anachronism in referring to the huts of the heroic age; cf. Virg. *Aen.* 2.29 *hic saeuus tendebat Achilles.*

36 hic ... equos 'Hector's mangled corpse terrified the horses into headlong gallop': *admissos* has predicative force. The line refers to the desecration of Hector's body as Achilles dragged it behind his chariot; cf. *Epiced. Drusi* 319–20 *uir religatus ad axem | terruit admissos sanguinolentus equos.* After Achilles killed Hector and stripped him of his armour, the Greeks mutilated his corpse (*Il.* 22.367–75) and Achilles then dragged it behind his chariot around the walls of Troy. Attention is focused on the graphic scene in a patterned line (p. 33).

37–8 Penelope appears to be taking credit for Telemachus' mission to Pylos, although the *Odyssey* tells us that he went without his mother's knowledge. Strictly interpreted her words *te quaerere misso* are not false, since he was indeed sent to seek word of his father, but by Athena, not her. In the *Odyssey* Penelope never learns of Athena's role, and many readers have been disturbed by what appears to be a deliberate lie by O.'s character. But O. found a precedent in his reading of Homer for a cunning Penelope willing to stretch the truth: at *Od.* 18.257–73 Penelope is lying when she reports Odysseus' injunction to her to marry; cf. Büchner (1940), Winkler (1990) 129–61.

37 namque: postponed (cf. 32n.) *namque* is not commonly found in this position: this is the earliest example in O.'s poetry and the only one in the *Her.*: cf. *Fast.* 1.129, *Met.* 2.474, 8.273, 10.515, 14.312, *Trist.* 1.10.47, *Pont.* 3.3.99. O. blends formal stylistic features with the conversational tone of Penelope's epistle. For this type of parenthesis, explaining why Penelope knows something she might be expected not to know, cf. 4.51–2 *namque mihi referunt, cum se furor ille remisit,* | *omnia,* where Phaedra explains her knowledge of the Bacchic revels.

senior: emphasized by its separation from *Nestor,* the noun it modifies: Nestor's great age was proverbial. The comparative *senior* is a metrically convenient substitute for *senex.*

te quaerere misso: the infinitive after a verb of motion to indicate purpose is not used in classical prose (K–S 1 680–81, H–S 344–45), but is found occasionally in poetry as an archaism; cf. Tränkle (1960) 14–15. This instance is unique in O.

38 nato: Telemachus.

39–46 The expedition of Diomedes and Ulysses to the camp of Rhesus, king of the Thracians, is related in *Il.* 10.331–502. The Trojan spy Dolon was met by the heroes on their way; before being killed he informed them of the location of Rhesus' camp. The Thracian king was surprised in his sleep and slain along with twelve of his men.

39–40 Many critics have suspected *dolo* in 40. Although O. is tolerant of iteration (3n.), the repeated *dolo* at the end of successive pentameters is rhetorically emphatic but without point, and that is not O.'s manner. As Bentley saw, the couplet should be athetized, although 37–8, which he would also delete, should probably be retained. The interpolation provides an identification of the *Doloneia* alluded to in the following couplets. The interpolator was knowledgeable: he imitates Virg. *Aen.* 1.469–70 *Rhesi ... tentoria ... prodita somno,* and makes the etymological link between Dolon and *dolus,* a word often associated with Ulysses (18n.), as by O. in 42. But the clumsy transition *rettulerat ... rettulit et* and the repetition of *dolo* give him away. For a similar interpolation glossing a name only alluded

to, cf. *Met.* 8.317, which is followed in some MSS by a line naming
Atalanta.

40 hic ... ille refer to the further (Rhesus) and nearer (Dolon)
objects respectively; for this reversal of the usual order, cf. *Met.*
3.205, *Fast.* 1.674, *Trist.* 1.2.24, and see Shackleton Bailey (1956) 259,
H–S 182, *TLL* s.v. *hic* 2715.40ff.

41 o: the interjection adds a note of pathos to these lines (41–6)
in which Penelope knowingly misrepresents Ulysses' role in the ex-
pedition: most of the hard work was done by Diomedes.

nimium nimiumque: expressive gemination is a feature of col-
loquial speech rarely found in classical verse (Hofmann (1951) 58–60,
H–S 808–9) except in the more common *iam iam*. The only other
example of this combination is [Tib.] 3.6.21, an imitation of this
passage. Elsewhere O. has *iterumque iterumque* (*Ars* 2.127), *minimum min-
imumque* (*Trist.* 5.6.35); cf. 2.129n. As she expands upon her fears
about this adventure, O.'s Penelope slips into less elevated style.

42 nocturno ... dolo: O. cleverly reverses the more familiar
associations of this phrase, which is used by Propertius (2.9.6) and
O. (*Am.* 3.9.30) to refer to Penelope's weaving. *tangere castra = perue-
nire in castra*; cf. *Met.* 4.779 *Gorgoneas tetigisse domos*, *Trist.* 3.2.18 *poenae
tellus est mihi tacta meae*.

43 totque: thirteen, including Rhesus (Hom. *Il.* 10.483–9), but
the killing was done by Diomedes, while Ulysses only dragged the
bodies out of the way and secured the horses.

mactare 'to slaughter', a very strong word, transferred from the
vocabulary of sacrifice and rarely found in this secular context: it is
so used only twice in the *Aeneid* (2.667, 10.413). In O.'s verse, with the
exception of the *Met.* and *Fasti*, it occurs only three more times in
the *Heroides* (7.113, 10.77, 10.101). Its use here may be ironic, since
Penelope's exaggeration of Ulysses' role in the expedition appears to
be deliberate.

adiutus ab uno: sc. Diomedes.

44 bene cautus 'very cautious': this use of a qualifying adverb
with an adjective or another adverb is colloquial; cf. *ES* 67 *bene multa*,
Trist. 1.7.15, Hofmann (1951) 70–5, H–S 163. The irony of this line is
biting, as O. plays upon the reader's familiarity with the events de-
scribed in the *Iliad*.

45 usque ... dum 'until': the perfect indicative is unusual in this contruction (H–S 615); O. has only one other example (*Met.* 3.91) and there are few other examples in classical Latin.

metu micuere sinus 'my heart fluttered with fear': a successful phrase varied at 5.37 *attoniti micuere sinus*; cf. *Ars* 3.722, *Fast.* 3.36, 3.331, 6.338.

45–6 amicum | ... per agmen: the Greek camp.

46 Ismariis: i.e. Thracian, identified by Mt Ismarus.

47 uestris 'yours and your comrades''.

disiecta = 'sic evertere et destruere, ut in diversas partes tamquam iactum frangatur' (Loers); cf. Virg. *Aen.* 8.290 *disiecit urbes*.

lacertis 'strength'.

48 Ilios: Greek form of the nominative.

murus ... solum 'that what once was wall is now level ground': the accusative and infinitive construction is coordinate with *Ilios* as subject of *prodest*. O. reworks *Aen.* 10.59–60 *non satius cineres patriae insedisse supremos | atque solum quo Troia fuit*.

50 uirque ... carendus abest 'and I must forever submit to my husband's absence': the regular construction is impersonal, as in *Trist.* 1.5.83 *mihi ... patria tellure carendum est*. This is the only attested instance of a personal passive of *careo*; since it is found as a transitive verb with accusative object in comedy and post-classical prose (*TLL* s.v. 454.67–455.9) this should perhaps be considered a colloquial usage. The phrase *dempto fine* = *sine fine* recurs at *Trist.* 3.11.2; cf. *Am.* 1.9.10 *exempto fine*.

51 diruta sunt aliis ... Pergama: O.'s Penelope ironically echoes the words of Diomedes to the Rutulian ambassadors who ask his help against Aeneas: Virg. *Aen.* 11.279–80 *nec mihi cum Teucris ullum post diruta bellum | Pergama*.

uni ... restant: O. himself reworks this passage in a later poem in a characteristically clever self-imitation, referring to the same circumstances from the very different point of view of Hecuba: *Met.* 13.507 *soli mihi Pergama restant*.

52 incola ... uictor: a deliberate anachronism, for the Greeks did not stay to colonize the Troad. O. is thinking of the Roman practice of settling colonists in conquered territories, which he uses here as a background against which to present the exaggerated picture of the devastated site of Troy.

53–6 A vivid picture of the site of Troy that is again anachronistic: although ten years have passed since the Greek victory, it is still too early to speak of crops growing on the site of the city and of farmers coming unexpectedly upon the bones of fallen warriors. The image gains resonance from recognition of the context of the passage in Virgil's *Georgics* that O. here imitates: 1.491–7 *nec fuit indignum superis bis sanguine nostro | Emathiam et latos Haemi pinguescere campos. | scilicet et tempus ueniet, cum finibus illis | agricola incuruo terram molitus aratro | exesa inueniet scabra robigine pila, | aut grauibus rastris galeas pulsabit inanis | grandiaque effossis mirabitur ossa sepulcris.* Virgil writes of the battles of Pharsalus (48 BC) and Philippi (42 BC), perhaps twelve years after the event and tells of a time far in the future when the farmer will unwittingly till the battlefield. O.'s Penelope writes as if that time has already come for Troy, a pathetic exaggeration made plausible only because it comes from a disheartened spouse.

53 resecandaque ... humus 'fertilized with Phrygian blood, the overgrown soil awaits the sickle': there is a note of irony in these lines because the soil of Asia Minor, which was proverbially rich (cf. Nisbet–Hubbard on Hor. *Carm.* 2.12.22), is here said to be rich with the blood of the Trojan War. *humum resecare* is a striking phrase.

54 luxuriat: the proper term for abundant vegetation; cf. *Ars* 1.360 *ut seges in pingui luxuriabit humo.*

55 semisepulta: a striking word, attested only here, to render Virgil's *effossis ... ossa sepulcris.* O. is fond of such compounds in *semi-*: while the other elegists avoid them entirely, O. uses a number of them, including in the *Her. semianimis, semideus, semirefectus, semisupinus, semiuir*; cf. Linse (1891) 47, 51.

uirum: genitive plural, an archaic form familiar in epic verse: Virgil uses genitive *uirum* 34 times in the *Aeneid*. Its use is severely restricted by O., who has the very common form *deum* only at *Am.* 1.13.45, *Met.* 2.280, 2.848, 4.574, 10.686, *Trist.* 1.5.70, 2.37, *Pont.* 2.8.58, *diuum* at *Met.* 6.542, 12.561, *Graium* at *Met.* 13.281. This is O.'s only example of *uirum*, which is common in all the epic poets except Lucan: for the details see N–W I 176.

56 ossa: enjambment with a sense pause after the 'first trochee' in the pentameter, even a light pause as here, is rare in Propertius, Tibullus, and O.'s early elegies. It becomes a mannerism in O.'s later elegiac verse; cf. Platnauer (1951) 25–6.

57–80 Penelope describes her attempts to secure information about Ulysses' whereabouts, which are always without success. This leads easily to an expression of vague fears about the unknown, and an interesting digression on her worst fear, that Ulysses' absence is deliberate because he has abandoned her for another woman.

57 uictor 'though victorious', concessive.

58 in quo ... orbe 'in what part of the world'.

ferreus 'with a heart of steel': a common epithet in elegy for one immune to love (Pichon (1902) 146): cf. 3.138, 4.14, 10.107.

59-62 In *Od.* 19 Penelope does in fact question a newly arrived stranger (Odysseus in disguise) about her absent spouse. O. deftly incorporates the ironies implicit in the Homeric scene into his own account, adding a further twist: in 61-2 Penelope outlines her practice of giving each departing sailor a letter to transmit to Ulysses in the event their paths should cross. If she adheres to this policy, we may infer from the dramatic date of this epistle (see introd. note) that the next visitor to receive such an epistle, the very one she is now writing, will be Ulysses himself in disguise; cf. Kennedy (1984) 417-18. O.'s Penelope is represented as a figure not unlike Propertius, as he describes himself when his mistress is travelling overseas: 1.8a.23-4 *nec me deficiet nautas rogitare citatos | 'dicite, quo portu clausa puella mea est?'*

59 quisquis ... peregrinam ... puppim: an easy enallage (1.10n.) for *quisquis peregrinus. puppim* does not here stand for *nauis* by synechdoche: the phrase *uertere puppim* refers to landing a ship stern first.

60 multa: 'retained' accusative; the regular construction with the active verb is with two accusative objects, of the person questioned and the thing asked.

60-2 ille ... huic refer to the same person.

61 reddat: the subj. indicates purpose.

62 charta 'a letter': from Greek χάρτης, the papyrus roll containing Penelope's complaint; cf. *Pont.* 4.3.26 *uerbis charta notata tribus.*

63-4 Pylon ... | misimus 'I have sent to Pylos': the ellipse of direct object is common with this verb (*TLL* s.v. 1184.80ff.), but in this case the ambiguity is more deliberate. There is no explicit reference to Telemachus' journey, although it is the most obvious reference for the reader familiar with the *Odyssey*. After the fact Penelope implies that *she* (emphatic *nos*) was behind Telemachus' mission.

63 antiqui: he had outlived three generations of men (*Il.* 1.250).

Neleia ... arua: the line imitates in rhythm and articulation *Od.* 3.4–5 οἱ δὲ Πύλον, Νηλῆος ἐϋκτίμενον πτολίεθρον, | ἷξον 'they came to Pylos, Neleus' strong-founded citadel'. The epithet Νηλήϊος, which O. introduces here to Latin verse, is found only once each in the *Odyssey* (4.639) and *Iliad* (11.682) as an epithet of Pylos. The accusative without preposition to indicate place to which is a common poeticism: cf. Virg. *Aen.* 1.2–3 *Lauiniaque uenit | litora.*

64 incerta ... fama: on the morning of the day before the suitors are killed, Telemachus reports to his mother (*Od.* 17.108–17) what he learned from Nestor, saying simply that Nestor had no news of Odysseus at all.

65 et is emphatic, 'Sparta too'. The Greek form of the name is preferred in the nominative and accusative by poets after Propertius and is the only form used by O.; cf. N–W 1 78.

nescia ueri: O.'s Penelope is being disingenuous: in *Od.* 17.118–49 Telemachus repeats substantial parts of Menelaus' words to him, enough to inform Penelope that Ulysses is being kept captive by Calypso.

66 quas ... abes: Penelope now turns abruptly to address Ulysses again.

lentus: in.

67 utilius starent 'it would be more to my advantage if they stood' (Housman).

moenia Phoebi: the walls of Troy, so called because they were built by Apollo and Neptune; cf. 16.182 *moenia, Phoebeae structa canore lyrae.*

68 leuis 'inconstant': because she would have prayed for the fall of Troy (*uotis ... meis*) for many years.

69 scirem: sc. 'if Troy still stood', a condition implied by 67 *starent.*

70 multis = *cum querelis multarum mulierum*, by brachylogy.

querela: 8n.

71 timeam ... timeo: the repetition here is emphatic, playing perhaps upon the maxim offered in 12. The expression is proverbial: cf. Kenney on Apul. *Met.* 5.4.2.

72 area lata 'broad scope': the metaphor for a field of endeavour is a favourite of Ovid's: e.g. *Trist.* 4.3.84 *et patet in laudes area* *lata tuas*, *Am.* 3.1.26, *Fast.* 4.10. Penelope's meaning is explained in the following couplet.

73 quaecumque aequor habet: the object *pericula* must be supplied from the following clause, an example of the ἀπὸ κοινοῦ construction, in this case made easier by the anaphoric repetition of the relative pronoun. Likewise, the verb *habet* must be supplied in the second clause.

75 metuo: after suggesting in the previous couplet that she fears only the dangers of a hazardous voyage, Penelope changes direction. Her resentment is now in the open, and as it gets the better of her, her language becomes more familiar: *stulte* and its related forms (*stultus, stultitia*) are avoided in the high style (Axelson (1945) 100), where synonyms such as *furor, insania, demens* are preferred. They are common in amatory elegy, but 7.28 *stulta* is the only other example in the single *Her.*

quae uestra libido est 'knowing you men and your lust': this type of loosely connected relative clause may be colloquial. The earliest example is in Cicero, *Verr.* 2.1.105 *qua est ipse sagacitate in his rebus*, but it is frequent only in his letters (e.g. *Fam.* 7.2.1, 4.5.6). It is not common in prose; and in O. the only other examples occur in 17.29 *quae tua nequitia est*, *Met.* 5.373, *Pont.* 1.7.59, 2.2.2; cf. *OLD* s.v. *qui* 12a, K–S II 314, H–S 565. *uestra* is a generalizing plural: O. puts into Penelope's mouth the accusation levelled at Propertius: 3.19.1–2 *obicitur totiens a te mihi nostra libido:* | *crede mihi, uobis imperat ista magis.* Cf. *Ars* 1.281 *parcior in nobis nec tam furiosa libido*, *Ars* 1.341–2 *omnia feminea sunt ista libidine mota;* | *acrior est nostra plusque furoris habet.*

76 peregrino ... amore: i.e. *amore peregrinae mulieris.* At the time when Penelope is writing this epistle she has already heard from Telemachus that Ulysses is being detained by Calypso. Hellenistic Greek writers may well have focused on Ulysses' amorous adventures. Parthenius, *Erot.* 2 provides a sketch of his love affair with Polymele, the daughter of Aeolus, and a scholiast notes that this story was touched upon by the influential poet-scholar Philetas in his *Hermes* (*CA*, p. 91). Ulysses' affair with Euippe in Epirus after the murder of the suitors, also summarized by Parthenius (*Erot.* 3), may have figured in a tragedy by Sophocles (fr. 205 Radt). In referring to Ulysses as a wandering philanderer, O.'s Penelope gains credibility from the non-Homeric tradition.

77–8 Again a note of irony is introduced by the reference to a scene known to readers of the *Odyssey* (5.214–20) but not to 'Penelope', in which, as Jacobson (1974) 268 notes, Ulysses does tell Calypso about his wife: 'circumspect Penelope | can never match the impression you make for beauty and stature ...' (Lattimore). The portrait that he paints, of a plain and ordinary woman, although not intended as criticism in a comparison with the goddess Calypso, is far from flattering.

77 rustica 'provincial', O.'s favourite epithet for describing the lack of sophistication that he especially criticizes in women: e.g. 4.102, 16.287, 17.12, 17.13, *Am.* 2.4.13, 2.8.3, 3.10.18, *Ars* 2.566, *Rem.* 329–30. The same idea is played on in *rudes* in the pentameter.

78 quae tantum ... sinat 'the sort of wife who objects to coarseness only in wool': the subjunctive *sinat* is generic. The adjective *rudis*, while properly referring to the unworked wool, also connotes lack of refinement. The plural *lanas* is not introduced out of metrical necessity, but possibly by analogy with the Greek word for wool (ἔρια), which is commonly found in the plural; cf. Maas (1902) 494.

79 tenues uanescat in auras: a proverbial expression; cf. *Am.* 2.14.41 *ista sed aetherias uanescant dicta per auras*, Otto (1890) 364.

80 reuertendi liber 'free to return': the construction with the defining genitive (or genitive of respect) is unique. More regular would be the impersonal *alicui liberum esse* with an infinitive (e.g. Cic. *Phil.* 1.12). A similar use is found at Luc. 6.106 *liber terrae ... hostis*, Sil. 2.441 *it liber campi pastor*. It should not be confused (as it is at *TLL* s.v. *liber* 1286.24) with the separative genitive used by analogy with Greek. The extension of such genitives is a feature of the poetic language (H–S 77–8) and O. would have been emboldened by the example of such experiments as Virgil's description of Aeneas as *certus eundi* (*Aen.* 4.554).

81–96 Events in Ithaca during Ulysses' absence are briefly sketched to point the contrast between Penelope's steadfast fidelity, in the face of pressure from her father as well as the suitors, and the frivolous affairs in which she fears Ulysses may be indulging. Penelope's illustrations of her difficulties are clearly intended to persuade Ulysses to return: some criticism of him is thus implied since it is thereby suggested that he needs to be persuaded.

81–4 In the *Odyssey* (15.16–17), Athena reports to Telemachus the growing pressures on Penelope in order to speed his return to Ithaca: 'now her father and her brother are urgent with her | to marry Eurymachus' (Lattimore). No incident in the text indicates that this pressure is real, but Penelope makes the same claim in her private interview with the beggar who is Odysseus in disguise (*Od.* 19.158–9). Her emphasis on the point in this epistle is designed to impart a sense of urgency, but her insistence on her determination to wait for him in 83–4 represents a significant departure from events in the *Odyssey*, where Penelope determines to settle the issue immediately by marrying the man who can successfully string Odysseus' bow. Some critics have taken these lines as a straightforward representation of Penelope as a paradigm of fidelity and suggested that lines 85–6 be deleted and this couplet be transposed to follow 114 (Sedlmayer (1880) 6–7). But at the end of the poem the couplet makes a false climax; indeed, as Jacobson (1974) 260 notes, 'the language is rather stiff, formal, impassive, almost cold'.

81 Icarius: father of Penelope.

uiduo ... lecto 'a deserted bed', as in 5.106, 10.14, 16.318, *Trist.* 5.5.48, Prop. 2.9.16.

82 cogit: conative present, 'tries to force me'; cf. *Od.* 15.16 κέλονται 'urge' (above 81–4n.).

immensas ... moras 'my endless delaying': i.e. in remarrying.

83 increpet usque: the repetition (epanalepsis) suggests indignation.

oportet: a prosaic word; that is to say, although metrically convenient, it is rare in hexameters. It occurs once in Virgil in the *Eclogues* (6.5) and four times in Propertius (2.4.1, 2.8.25, 3.7.72, 4.1.70) and only ten times in O.'s works, including this instance and 6.141; cf. Axelson (1945) 13–14, Clausen on Virg. *Ecl.* 6.5. Perhaps the shift to less 'poetic' diction underlines the rising indignation of Penelope.

85–6 pietate ... frangitur 'he is moved by my sense of duty': cf. *Met.* 8.508 *nunc animum pietas maternaque nomina frangunt. pietas* is rarely used to characterize the relationship between husband and wife; but cf. Prop. 3.13.23–4 *hic nulla puella | nec fida Euadne, nec pia Penelope.*

pudicis = Greek σώφρων 'self-controlled', which became a byword for Penelope in post-Homeric literature; cf. Aristoph. *Thesm.* 547, Eur. *Tro.* 422, Hor. *Serm.* 2.5.77 *pudica.*

86 uires ... suas: cf. *Pont.* 3.6.24 *uires temperat ille suas.*

87–90 In the first book of the *Odyssey* (245–51 = 16.122–8), Tele-machus complains about the suitors: 'For all the greatest men who have power in the islands, | in Doulichion and Same and in wooded Zakynthos, | and all who in rocky Ithaka are holders of lordship, | all these are after my mother for marriage and wear my house out | ... and these eating up my substance | waste it away; and soon they will break me myself to pieces' (Lattimore). O.'s Penelope means to worry Ulysses, not only about the damage being done to his pos-sessions, but about the existence of powerful rivals, a tactic advo-cated for women in *Am.* 1.8.95–100 and *Ars* 3.593–6.

87 alta Zacynthos: a short open vowel is not normally allowed to stand before initial *sc-, sm-, sp-, st-,* or *z-,* but O. allows exceptions to the rule here and at *Am.* 2.6.21 *hebetare zmaragdos,* in order to in-troduce foreign words into the line. Propertius was much freer in this respect: cf. Platnauer (1951) 62. O. reproduces as precisely as Latin permits *Od.* 1.246 (= 16.123, 19.131) Δουλιχίωι τε Σάμηι τε καὶ ὑλήεντι Ζακύνθωι. Zacynthos is incorporated into the relative clause for metrical reasons: *Zacynthii* cannot be made to scan. Virgil also imitates the line at *Aen.* 3.270–1 with altered wording: *iam medio appa-ret fluctu nemorosa Zacynthos | Dulichiumque Sameque et Neritos ardua saxis.*

88 turba ... luxuriosa: construe in apposition to *proci.*

ruunt in me 'descend upon me': as of a hostile attack, with per-haps some suggestion of sexual aggression (Jacobson (1974) 269); cf. Hor. *Carm.* 2.5.3–4 *ruentis | in uenerem*; Plaut. *Cas.* 890 *libet in Casinam irruere.*

89 inque tua regnant ... aula 'play the king in your castle': a paradox.

90 uiscera nostra 'our vitals': the metaphor is not uncommonly applied to the resources of a state (e.g. Cic. *Dom.* 23, 124 *uisceribus aerarii, Pis.* 28 *rei publicae uisceribus*) or of a household (e.g. *Q. fr.* 1.3.7 *cum de uisceribus tuis et fili tui satis facturus sis quibus debes*); cf. *Trist.* 1.7.19–20 *libellos | imposui rapidis, uiscera nostra, rogis,* where the apposi-tion follows the object, the more usual order.

dilacerantur 'are being torn apart': the verb is literally appro-priate to the appositive *uiscera* and metaphorically to the subject *opes*; cf. Plaut. *Capt.* 670–2 *me meamque rem ... dilacerasti, TLL* s.v. 1159.82ff. O.'s Penelope renders *Od.* 16.315 'they overbearingly consume our goods, and spare nothing', where the Greek verb δαρδάπτουσιν, which properly refers to the actions of a wild beast, is itself a powerful metaphor.

91 Medontaque dirum: in the *Odyssey* Medon is the herald of Odysseus, not a suitor, and is generally portrayed as loyal to Penelope, although he is mentioned in the company of the suitors at 16.252 and 17.172–3. Perhaps, as Jacobson (1974) 260 suggests, O.'s Penelope exaggerates deliberately, but it is perhaps more likely that O. is drawing on another tradition. In *Od.* 16.247–51 Homer gives 108 as the number of Penelope's suitors, but we learn the names of only 14 of them from him. Scholars in antiquity eagerly supplied the gap, and in one list of 129 names found in Apollodorus, *Epit.* 7.27–30 the name of Medon from Dulichium appears. Pisander and Polybus are mentioned at *Od.* 22.243. The epithet *dirum* applies to them as well, since it need only agree with the nearest noun.

92 Eurymachique auidas Antinoique manus: the two chief suitors. Noun (*manus*) and epithet (*auidas*) are distributed over two parts of the phrase and should be construed with each, a form of artful word patterning with which we may compare *Am.* 1.11.1 *colligere incertos et in ordine ponere crines*, 3.9.21 and other examples collected by Housman in his note on Manil. 1.269–70. For the enallage, *auidas ... manus*, cf. 1.10n.

93 turpiter 'to your disgrace' may be construed with *absens* or *alis*.

94 tuo partis sanguine rebus 'with the goods won at the cost of your blood': the interlocking word-order (abAB) underlines Penelope's indignation, while *sanguine* is deliberate exaggeration: Penelope refers to Ulysses' labours before the Trojan war. *partis* is ablative of the past participle of *pario*.

95 The rhythm of this line is unusual: the trochaic caesura in the third foot is followed by a quadrisyllabic word which coincides with the end of the fourth foot ('bucolic' diaeresis). There is only one other such line in O.'s elegiacs (*Fast.* 3.863). O. has the trochaic caesura in approximately 1 out of 11 hexameters in the single *Her.*, compared with a rate of *c.* 1 in 25 in his later elegies and the double epistles.

Irus egens renders Homer's Ἶρος ἀλήτης (*Od.* 18.25), the beggar who fought with the disguised Ulysses.

Melanthius: the goatherd of Ulysses.

actor = *pastor*, a unique attestation of the word in this sense. As noted by Barchiesi (1984) 159–60, O.'s periphrasis does not simply reproduce the description of Melanthius as αἰπόλος αἰγῶν in the *Od*yssey (17.247), but recalls those passages in which he is represented as driving the flocks of Odysseus for the suitors to dine on, especially his first mention in the *Odyssey* (17.212–14): 'there Melanthios, son of Dolios, came upon them | as he drove his goats (αἶγας ἄγων), the ones that were finest among his goatflocks, | for the suitors' dinner' (Lattimore). Cf. also *Od*. 22.198–9 'when you drive (ἀγινεῖς) the goats'.

96 ultimus ... pudor 'as the crowning disgrace': predicative with *accedunt*. By its position at the end of the line and separation from its epithet, *pudor* has climactic effect.

accedunt in tua damna 'are added to your losses': that his servants should conduct themselves in such a manner is a disgrace to be calculated in addition to the financial losses Ulysses has already suffered. *damnum* is properly a legal term (*TLL* s.v. 22.54ff.): it is not common in Latin poetry, and is not found at all, for example, in Catullus, Lucretius, Virgil or Tibullus. In contrast, *damnum* is found 75 times in O.'s verse. It owes its frequent appearance in O.'s lexicon to his readiness to incorporate legal language into poetry: Kenney (1969).

97–116 In the final section of the epistle, Penelope emphasizes her isolation and the precarious position of Ulysses' household. The sequence of thought here is confused and several editors have suggested rearrangement of couplets in order to smooth the argument. The most likely candidate for transposition is 103–4 (to follow 96), where the mention of the three faithful servants intrudes awkwardly into a passage otherwise devoted to members of Ulysses' family; but if it follows 96, the reference in *hac* (see 103n.) points to the suitors. It is likely that the disorganized sequence of thought is intended to re-flect Penelope's state of distress, culminating in her despairing reference to her own old age.

97–8 The couplet echoes *Od*. 14.173–4 where Eumaeus enumerates the faithful members of Ulysses' household, with an especially close imitation in the pentameter of 173 Λαέρτης θ' ὁ γέρων καὶ Τηλέμαχος θεοειδής 'Laertes the old man and godlike Telemachus'.

97 sine uiribus = *inualida*; adnominal prepositional phrases with *sine* often take the place of adjectives formed with privative *in-*; cf. H–S 428, Bömer on *Met.* 3.250.

uxor: three times before in this epistle Penelope has referred to herself as *coniunx* (30n.); now she uses the everyday word, as she tries to elicit sympathy.

98 puer: he is twenty when the *Odyssey* begins, but Penelope wants to emphasize his youth; cf. 107–8.

99–100 Penelope's assertion here that the suitors plotted to ambush Telemachus while he was making preparations for his departure to Pylos is at odds with *Od.* 4.701 where Penelope learns from the herald Medon that the trap is to be sprung upon him on his homeward voyage (οἴκαδε νισσόμενον). Her account of Telemachus' mission is becoming muddled as she now appears to suggest, contradicting the claim made in 63–5, that he went on his own initiative (*inuitis omnibus* = *Od.* 4.665 τόσσων ... ἀέκητι).

101 euntibus ordine fatis: the fates proceed in order when parents die before their children: cf. Tac. *Ann.* 16.11 *seruauitque ordinem fortuna ac seniores prius, tum cui proxima aetas exstinguuntur.*

102 comprimat: i.e. close the eyes, like *condas* below (113).

103 hac faciunt 'are on our side': for the use of *hac*, cf. Enn. *Ann.* 232 Skutsch *Iuppiter hac stat* (= Virg. *Aen.* 12.565). This use of *facere* is colloquial, being largely confined to Cicero's letters, the continuators of Caesar, etc. (*TLL* s.v. 121.30ff.); cf. *Am.* 1.3.11–12 *at Phoebus comitesque nouem uitisque repertor | hac faciunt*, where MSS read *haec* as here.

custosque boum: a periphrasis for *armentarius* or *pastor*, the ordinary words, to characterize the loyal cowherd, Philoetius.

longaeuaque nutrix: Eurykleia, the faithful nurse who recognized her master through his disguise when she bathed his feet. She is dignified by the epic epithet *longaeua*, a compound coined by Virgil on the model of Greek μακραίων; cf. Norden (1927) 177, Tränkle (1960) 42. Such forms are used sparingly by O.; this one recurs at 5.40, *Fast.* 3.68, *Met.* 10.462. On *-que ... -que*, cf. 29n.

104 immundae cura fidelis harae 'faithful warden of the unclean sty': a somewhat grandiose periphrasis for *subulcus*. In Hom. *Od.* 13.404–6 Eumaeus is characterized by Athena to Odysseus as 'the swineherd who is in charge of your pigs, but always his thoughts are kindly and he is a friend to your son and to circumspect Penelope'. *cura* = *curator*, anticipating the much later use of *cura* in official terminology (*TLL* s.v. 1469.57ff.) for a public functionary.

105 ut qui sit: causal, a prosaic construction (K–S II 293, H–S 560). The only other example in classical verse is *Met.* 1.605–6 *ut quae ... nosset.*

inutilis armis 'of no use in fighting': a common expression for those unfit for military service; cf. Caes. *BG* 7.78.1 *ei qui ualetudine aut aetate inutiles sunt bello, TLL* s.v. *inutilis* 277.62ff.

107 uiuat modo 'only let him live': with something of the force of a conditional clause; cf. Prop. 1.7.3–4 *primo contendis Homero | (sint modo fata tuis mollia carminibus).*

108 erat ... tuenda: the indicative mood is regular when the suggestion of potential is carried by the gerundive. By analogy with the subjunctive the imperfect tense is used for present potential; cf. 112, K–S I 173, H–S 328.

illa: his present age.

109 pellere: for the infinitive dependent upon the noun *uires*, cf. H–S 351.

110 citius 'quickly': the comparative of *cito* is early used in the same sense as the positive, like *ocius*, especially in colloquial Latin (H–S 168–9).

portus et ara tuis 'safe harbour and sanctuary': a familiar pairing; cf. *Trist.* 4.5.2 *unica fortunis ara reperta meis, Pont.* 2.8.68 *portus et ara fugae,* Cic. *Verr.* 2.5.48 *hic locus est unus quo perfugiant, hic portus, haec arx, haec ara sociorum.*

111 sitque precor 'and I pray you may have still': the subjunctive in parataxis without a subordinating *ut* or *ne* is common with verbs of wishing, etc.; cf. *Fast.* 6.219, *Trist.* 1.10.1, *Epiced. Drusi* 471, Mart. 1.108.1.

112 in patrias artes erudiendus erat 'ought to have been trained in his father's ways': the more common idiom is with *ad* (*TLL* s.v. *erudio* 829.75ff.).

113 respice 'have a thought for'.

tu: the pronoun emphasizes that Laertes wants Ulysses and no other to perform this final service of closing his eyes for burial; cf. Austin and Reeve (1970) 5.

sua: the reflexive refers to the subject (*ille*) of the main clause.

114 extremum fati sustinet ... diem 'puts off the final day of fate': a regular use of *sustineo* in prose (*OLD* s.v. 8b). For the periphrasis for 'dying day', cf. Val. Max. 7.2 *ad ultimum usque fati diem*.

115–16 certe ego: a rare instance in the *Her.* of a long open vowel elided before a short; elsewhere we find only 12.91 *uidi etiam*, 19.81 *certe ego*, 20.178 and 21.211; cf. Platnauer (1951) 74–5.

puella ... anus stand in pointed contrast at line-end. The cheated expectations of lovers long separated is a theme that O. later adapts to his own situation in an epistle addressed to his wife: *Pont.* 1.4.47–8 *te quoque, quam iuuenem discedens urbe reliqui,* | *credibile est nostris insenuisse malis.* In the *Odyssey* Penelope is portrayed as still youthfully beautiful (18.187–213), although she herself denies this (18.251–3, 19.124–6). As O.'s Penelope turns to contemplate her own position in the final couplet, she laments the wasted years of waiting and thinks of herself as an old woman.

115 fueram: pluperfect for imperfect (34n.); cf. *Trist.* 3.11.25 *non sum ego quod fueram*, Prop. 1.12.11 *non sum ego qui fueram*.

116 protinus ut redeas 'though you return immediately': concessive *ut,* though common in prose, is relatively rare in Augustan poets other than O.: cf. 2.137, 3.134, 7.15, 7.21, 7.55, 10.65, 17.121, H–S 647.

facta ... anus: an ironic reference to Prop. 2.9.8 *illum expectando facta remansit anus*, an approving comment on Penelope as an example of fidelity.

II Phyllis Demophoonti

Phyllis' epistle to Demophoon represents a variation on a theme often developed in Hellenistic narrative, the foreign princess seduced by a travelling hero, who (sometimes) marries her but inevitably leaves her. In its broad outlines the story is summarized by a late mythographer (Apollod. *Epit.* 6.16–17): 'Demophoon put in to the land of the Thracian Bisaltians with a few ships; and there Phyllis, the king's daughter, fell in love with him and was given to him in marriage with the kingdom for her dowry. But he wished to depart to his own country, and after many entreaties and swearing to return, he did depart. Phyllis accompanied him as far as the place called the "Nine Roads", and she gave him a casket, telling him that it contained a sacrament of Mother Rhea, and that he was not to open it until he had abandoned all hope of returning to her. Demophoon went to Cyprus and settled there. And when the appointed time passed, Phyllis called down curses on Demophoon and killed herself; Demophoon opened the casket, and, struck with fear, mounted his horse and galloped off wildly to meet his end; for his horse stumbled, he was thrown and fell on his sword.' No earlier narrative of the story survives in Greek, but we can be certain that the story was known to O. from a version by Callimachus. A partial line, often quoted by Greek grammarians, is all that remains of what was apparently a celebrated piece: fr. 556 Pfeiffer νυμφίε Δημοφόων, ἄδικε ξένε 'bridegroom Demophoon, unjust guest'. Attempts to reconstruct the details of Callimachus' narrative are misguided, but a summary account of the story provided by the sixth-century epistolographer Procopius of Gaza (*Epist.* 47 Garzya–Loenertz = 86 Hercher), who quotes this very line, is probably owed to Callimachus. O. also quotes Callimachus in a brief narrative of Phyllis' story incorporated into his *Remedia amoris* as an *exemplum* of the dangers of solitude when one is in love (597–8): *'perfide Demophoon' surdas clamabat ad undas,* | *ruptaque singultu uerba loquentis erant.* In view of O.'s many other references to the story (*Ars* 2.353, 3.38, 3.460, *Rem.* 55), as well as the caustic comment by Persius about poems on this subject (1.34 *Phyllidas, Hypsipylas, uatum et plorabile siquid*), a wide circulation for Callimachus' account may be postulated. We may even suspect its influence on other literary heroines in similar straits, for example Dido in Virgil's *Aeneid*; cf. Heinze (1915) 134 n. 2. That tradition is subsumed by O. in his portrayal of Phyllis in this poem. In addition, he rings some important changes upon the mythographical background: Demophoon comes to Thrace not quite by chance, but is forced to land because of damage to his ship (45n.); Phyllis, not her father, chooses Demophoon as her husband and offers her kingdom as dowry (111n.); and Phyllis does not rush to the shore and hang herself in immediate despair as is told elsewhere (5n.), but waits a long time before giving up hope of Demophoon's return (7–8n.). The practical purpose of this epistle is quickly forgotten; O.'s Phyllis makes little attempt to persuade Demophoon, and a happy outcome to the affair is precluded by her determination to commit suicide. Phyllis' epistle is an exploration of the process of despair that led to that act. Callimachus' half-line was for O. only the beginning of the story.

1–6 The first line has the appearance of an epistolary salutation, naming both recipient and sender; but in the pentameter the tone immediately shifts to complaint as Phyllis gives details about the length of Demophoon's absence.

1 Hospita is emphasized by its position. Phyllis refers to herself only as Demophoon's hostess, a sad suggestion that she now means no more to him than when he first arrived in Thrace. In the only fragment of Callimachus' account, Phyllis levels her accusation against Demophoon as a faithless guest, a theme that Callimachus may well have developed at great length, for it is consistently recalled by the Roman poets. In a brief catalogue of faithless lovers, Propertius includes Theseus and his son Demophoon (2.24.43–4): *paruo dilexit spatio Minoida Theseus, | Phyllida Demophoon, hospes uterque malus.* Demophoon's father Theseus, who abandoned Ariadne and is an obvious companion for his son in such a list, can only be termed *hospes malus* by a kind of mythographical zeugma. What unites father and son is the trait of infidelity, but only Demophoon can be said to have violated the bonds of guest and host(ess). By shifting the focus from the treacherous *hospes* to the betrayed *hospita*, O. fixes our perspective upon her feelings of indignation at the perfidy of her lover.

hospita ... tua ... Rhodopeia Phyllis: the adjectives belong to both nouns by amphibole (Bell (1923) 293–303).

Rhodopeia: i.e. Thracian, from Rhodope, a mountain range in western Thrace.

2 queror: a note struck often in this epistle in particular; cf. 8 *querela,* 26 *queror,* 1.8n.

3 cornua ... coissent: lit. 'once the horns of the moon had met to form a full circle', i.e. after one month; cf. *Met.* 2.344 *luna quater iunctis implerat cornibus orbem,* 7.530, *Fast.* 2.175. *pleno ... orbe* (cf. *toto orbe,* 5) is ablative of result (H–S 127), a development of the instrumental ablative that may be illustrated by Lucr. 2.98 *interuallis magnis resultant* 'they rebound to create large spaces' or *Met.* 10.494 *duratur cortice pellis* 'the skin hardens to bark'. The construction is used freely in poetry and is amply illustrated in O.'s works: cf. *Met.* 4.397, 6.115, 9.81.

4 'It was agreed that you would drop anchor on our shores.' The tone is formal and restrained, but the language is suggestive: *pacta*, from *pacisco*, is also the proper term for betrothal, a usage in which it is regularly construed with the dative (6.5n.), viz. 'your anchor was plighted to our shores'. By a common anachronism *ancora* is used for a ship of the heroic age when weighted stones, not anchors, were used to moor ships.

5 quater: four months have elapsed since Demophoon's departure. The repetition of *quater* with a different verb emphasizes the passage of time: Phyllis wishes to illustrate her restraint. In contrast, Hyginus (*Fab.* 59) reports that when Demophoon did not arrive on the appointed day, Phyllis immediately (*eo die*) rushed to the shore nine times (121–48n.) and committed suicide.

6 nec: with adversative sense, a common usage , 'but ... not'; cf. H–S 481.

Actaeas: i.e. Athenian, from Ἀκτή, an ancient name for Attica (Strab. 9.391; Plin. *Nat.* 4.7). The adjective Ἀκταῖος is not attested in Greek poetry before Callimachus, where it appears in the opening line of the *Hecale*; see Hollis *ad loc.*

Sithonis: also 'Thracian', from Sithonia, the central of the three peninsulas of Chalcidice, named after a Thracian king Sithon. The adjective is not a patronymic, although the fact that Phyllis herself is addressed as *Sithonis* at *Rem.* 605 misled Servius (on *Ecl.* 10.66) to identify her as Sithon's daughter. It is true that O. is fond of coining such Greek feminine adjectives (cf. Bömer on *Met.* 5.303), but even though this is the first attestation of *Sithonis*, its appearance in later Greek verse (e.g. Nonnus, *Dion.* 48.113) strongly suggests that O. found the word in an earlier Greek source; cf. Clausen on Virg. *Ecl.* 10.66 *Sithonias*.

7–22 Phyllis develops the twin themes suggested in the opening address, her patience in waiting so long for Demophoon's return and her *naïveté* in believing his promises. During his absence she had imagined any number of excuses for the delay and feared that he had suffered some disaster. These fears are elaborated to emphasize by contrast his deliberate lying.

7–8 'If you were to add up the days, as we who are in love do with care (*bene*), my complaint does not come before its appointed (*suam*) time': *diem* (fem.) is regularly used to indicate the expiration of a defined period of time; cf. Fraenkel (1964) I 27–72.

querela: 2n.

9 spes quoque lenta fuit 'my hope too has been slow', sc. like Demophoon who has been slow (*lentus*, 23) to return; cf. 17.108 *spes tua lenta fuit.*

9–10 tarde ... | credimus: this remark explains in a vague and general way the preceding assertion. There is a slight suggestion of sarcasm in the word-play *credita ... credimus*, as Phyllis inverts a commonplace idea that people are eager to believe what they wish to be true.; cf. Caes. *BG* 3.18.2 *fere libenter homines quod uolunt credunt*, Otto (1890) 97.

10 inuita nunc es amante nocens: the sense is clear though the text is uncertain: 'your lover is reluctant to believe you guilty now'. Most MSS read *inuita nunc et amante noces*, but the participle *nocens* used adjectivally (= 'guilty') makes for better sense than the finite verb 'injure' without an object.

11 saepe ... saepe: rhetorically effective repetition, enhanced by the sense pause after the fourth foot ('bucolic' diaeresis).

12 alba ... uela: the epithet is conventional, but in the context may suggest the story of Theseus, Demophoon's father, whose successful return to Athens was to have been heralded by hoisting white sails: like his father, Demophoon disappoints the hopes of those who wait for him.

procellosos ... Notos: the south wind (Gk Νότος, in prose *Auster*), which would bring Demophoon back to Thrace from Athens, was notoriously stormy, especially in the months from November to March. Hence the familiar word-play in Greek νότιος ('wet') / Νότος is reproduced in O.'s choice of epithet; cf. *Am.* 2.6.44 *uota procelloso per mare rapta Noto.*

13–14 'I cursed Theseus thinking that he would not let you go, but (*nec*, 6n.) perhaps it was not he who detained your sailing.' The subjunctive *nollet* indicates an unconfirmed allegation.

13 Thesea: accusative, 1.5n.

deuoui: a strong word, 'not merely "execrated" but consigned to perdition by magical arts' (Palmer); cf. *CIL* xi 1823 *hunc ego aput uostrum numen demando, deuoueo, desacrifico.* Phyllis' assertion that she cursed Theseus underlines O.'s rejection of the prevailing tradition that it was Demophoon whom she cursed before she died: Apollod. *Epit.* 6.16 (introd. n.).

14 tenuit 'detained': in prose we would expect *detinuit*. The usual meaning of *cursum tenere* is 'to hold to a course', but the simple form commonly appears in place of the compound in poetry (Bell (1923) 330–9). The plural *cursus* avoids the rhyme *cursum . . . tuum.*

forsitan: the usual view that O. uses the subjunctive and indicative indifferently with this particle (H–S 334) requires modification. In the *Her.* the only instances of the indicative are in this epistle (cf. 104), but in both cases *forsitan* follows the verb and its force is thus rather adverbial. (The text at 10.86 is too corrupt to base conclusions upon.) At *Am.* 3.6.100 the indicative is due to brachylogy, while at 3.8.21 *forsitan* introduces a future condition. This leaves *Am.* 1.6.45 as the only instance of the indicative in O.'s early poetry: his indifference to the mood is a feature of his later style and characteristic of general relaxation among other writers on this point.

15–20 Phyllis feared shipwreck, a reasonable enough concern in the circumstances of sea travel in the ancient world; and Demophoon had already suffered one mishap at sea that brought him to her shores in the first place (45n.).

15 uada . . . ad Hebri: not specifically 'shallows', but more generally the 'waters' of the Hebrus (mod. Maritza), one of the two principal rivers of Thrace. The word-order noun–preposition–genitive is not uncommon; in O.: e.g. 21.172 *face pro thalami*, *Ars* 3.805, *Fast.* 3.733, *Trist.* 1.9.11, 4.7.13, *Pont.* 2.9.2. But there is no precise parallel for this word-order with separation of the preposition from the noun it governs, a stylistic liberty with which O. was particularly free in other combinations; cf. Platnauer (1951) 97–103. There are a few comparable cases in O.'s exile poetry: *Trist.* 1.10.15 *Aeoliae mare . . . in Helles*, 5.2.75 *rapidae flammis . . . in Aetnae.*

16 cana 'foaming': cf. 3.65, 5.54.

naufraga is proleptic with *mersa*, 'drowned in shipwreck'.

17–20 In most MSS this passage is transmitted without lines 18–19, leaving *deos* without a governing verb. Sense is not restored by attempts to rescue the grammar by reading *deo* (Palmer), with *supplex* governing the following *ut* clause, and thereby collapsing Phyllis' prayer to a god and her self-address into a single act. Four later MSS and the first Aldine edition (1502) supply lines 18–19 with some variation. As Housman comments in his lectures, 'these variants are token of a long history and a remote origin, not of a recent concoction'. Even if they were not written by O., at least two lines of similar content would have to be posited as a supplement for the lacuna between 17 and 20. Accordingly, they might as well stand in the text, especially since, as Housman (1897) 202 (= *Class. pap.* 391) argues, they are entirely Ovidian in diction and sense. Their loss could well be explained by the homoearchon, 17 *saepe* ... 19 *saepe*.

18 turicremis: a poetic compound coined by Lucretius (2.353), used once by Virgil at *Aen.* 4.453 and by O. at *Ars* 3.393.

cum prece ... sum uenerata 'I begged the gods as I prayed': the verb *ueneror* regularly governs a subjunctive clause (*OLD* s.v. 1b) in the sense 'to beseech'. The combination with *cum prece* produces a tautology of the type common in religious formulae, e.g. Liv. 8.9.7 *Di ... Manes, uos precor ueneror ... uti ... prosperetis*. One late MS and the Aldine edition read *sum ... deuenerata*, a verb that is attested once in Tib. 1.5.14 in the sense 'to avert by supplication', which is difficult to accommodate in this passage.

19 uentos ... fauentes: cf. *Met.* 15.49. *caelo pelagoque* are locative ablatives, with *uidens*.

21–2 Phyllis sums up her attempts at self-delusion: *denique* (1.21n.) 'in a word' marks the final entry in this catalogue of possible excuses for Demophoon's absence before the transition to a new topic.

22 et ad causas ingeniosa fui 'and I was good at making excuses': cf. *Met.* 11.313 *nascitur Autolycus furtum ingeniosus ad omne*, *Trist.* 2.288 *in culpam ... ingeniosa*, 2.343 *in ... poenas ingeniosus*, *Ib.* 188 .

23–62 The transition to a new train of thought is marked by the abrupt *at* and the change to present tenses. Phyllis contrasts her present conviction that Demophoon has broken faith with her earlier *naïveté*, and stresses the injustice of his treatment of her. The focus of her address now moves back in time to the days when Demophoon arrived in Thrace as Phyllis recalls her benefactions to him.

23 lentus abes: 1.1n.

23–4 iurata ... | numina 'the oaths you swore by the gods': this passive sense of *iuratus* originates with O.; cf. *Met.* 2.46 *dis iuranda palus*, Sen. *Ag.* 792 *iurata superis unda*, Sil. 13.747 *diuos iuratos*. It is an extension of the construction of *iurare* with the accusative, a Graecism increasingly common in the late Republic (Norden (1927) 226).

24 nostro motus amore 'moved by any love for me': the possessive adjective *nostro* is used for the objective genitive.

25 uentis et uerba et uela dedisti 'the winds carried off your words and your sails' (sc. when you left me), a striking formulation. By the figure of syllepsis *dedisti* must be understood in a different sense with each object (p. 30). The alliteration lends emphasis: cf. 7.8, *ES* 209, *Am.* 1.7.16, *Rem.* 286, *Met.* 8.134, *Trist.* 1.2.18.

26 The pentameter restates and amplifies the hexameter, repeating the two objects *uela* and *uerba* in inverse order (chiasmus). The line is articulated into two object clauses in asyndeton, with the verb *carere* to be taken with both (ἀπὸ κοινοῦ): 'I lament the fact that your sails have not returned and your words were not spoken in good faith.'

27–30 Before she goes into the details of Demophoon's breach of faith, Phyllis protests her own innocence: she did not commit any crime and did not deserve to be treated so by Demophoon. The second couplet (29–30) does not simply repeat the idea of the first (27–8), but reformulates with rhetorical point the earlier outburst.

27 dic mihi: emphatic and colloquial, in parataxis with the interrogative *quid feci*; cf. Virg. *Ecl.* 3.1 *dic mihi, Damoeta, cuium pecus?*, *TLL* s.v. *dico* 982.33ff.

nisi ... amaui 'but loved unwisely', a commonplace: cf. Calp. Flacc. *Decl.* 2 *miraris, si aliquis non sapienter amat, cum incipere amare non est sapientis?* Elsewhere O. cites Phyllis as an example of *naïveté* in love: *Rem.* 55 *uixisset Phyllis, si me foret usa magistro*, *Ars.* 3.37–42. *nisi* is regular following interrogatives and negative expressions (K–S II 413–14).

non sapienter = *insipienter*, the latter being a form attested only in comedy and Cicero's letters.

28 crimine ... meo 'by my very fault I might well have won you for my own': Phyllis employs lovers' logic: her only fault (*crimine*, cf. 7.164) consisted in loving Demophoon, a fault which might have been expected to win his loyalty. The perfect indicative *potui* is regular in the past potential of this verb. The perfect infinitive is used where the present might be expected for its metrical shape and does not indicate any temporal priority to *potui*; cf. Prop. 1.1.15 *potuit domuisse*, Platnauer (1951) 109–12, H–S 351–3. *demeruisse* is an intensive compound, 'thoroughly to deserve you'. The word, previously attested only rarely in comedy and prose, was introduced to serious poetry by O., who was fond of such colloquial compounds; cf. Knox (1986a) 40–1.

29 in me: ablative, 'in my case'.

scelus is not noticeably different in meaning from *crimine* above, an instance of *variatio*. The word-play with *scelerate* has the effect of emphasizing the magnitude of Demophoon's fault: her *scelus*, as defined in *recepi*, consisted in observing the obligations of a host, while he is truly criminal. *scelerate* is a gloss on Callimachus' ἄδικε (fr. 556 Pfeiffer; cf. introd. n.).

30 pondus et instar 'equal weight'; by hendiadys.

31 pacta fides ubi nunc 'Where now is your promise of faith?': the first member of a rising tricolon, developed and expanded in the last two members. The reading transmitted by the MSS obscures the sense and rhetorical articulation by the intrusion of *iura* in uncomfortable asyndeton, probably from a reader's gloss. In this context *iura* must refer to the bonds of social or familial obligation, a sense in which O. never uses it without qualification; cf. 6.41 *conubialia iura*, 9.159 *iura sacerrima lecti*, 16.286, 21.140, *Am.* 3.6.82, *Met.* 6.536, 7.715. Moreover, the point of this couplet is more specific: it is not a generalized absence of good faith that Phyllis laments, but the promise that Demophoon made, in token of which he gave his hand and swore by the gods. The formulation recalls Euripides' description of Medea's complaints against Jason, another famous oath-breaker (*Med.* 21–2): 'she cries out his oaths, she invokes the pledge he gave with his right hand, and calls the gods to witness'.

commissaque dextera dextrae: as a token of good faith (*fides*); the juxtaposition of variant forms of the same word with different metrical values is a common device in O.: cf. Hopkinson (1982) 174.

32 deus: sc. Amor, often associated with Hymenaeus; e.g. *Met.* 1.480, 4.758. Phyllis is now referring to his oath to return.

in falso plurimus ore 'ever on your lying lips': the adverbial use of *plurimus*, *multus*, *paucus* and the like was branded by the author of the *Rhet. Her.* 4.45 as colloquial. However, the idiom is common in poetry; cf. *Met.* 11.562–3 *sed plurima nantis in ore est* | *Alcyone coniunx*, H–S 161–2, *TLL* s.v. *multus* 1608.83ff.

33 promissus socios … in annos 'promised for years of life together' (Showerman): the regular expression for betrothal is *promittere in matrimonium* (*TLL* s.v. *matrimonium* 478.53ff.). O. creates a new phrase by substituting the periphrasis *socios annos*: as Heinsius notes (on *Am.* 1.9.6), *socius* and related words are often used by O. to describe marriage in a usage peculiar to him. Here the wedding-god *Hymenaeus* stands by metonymy for the bond of marriage.

34 coniugii: one of only two examples in the certainly genuine *Heroides* of a genitive in *-ii* in a choriambic word (the simple *-i* being excluded by the metre), the other is at 7.178. There are only 3 examples in the *Amores* (1.9.32, 1.15.2 *ingenii*; 1.12.28 *auspicii*); cf. Maas (1902) 512n., N–W I 146.

sponsor 'guarantor': a legal term for the third party to a transaction (*sponsio*) who formally pledges the good faith of another; in 16.116 Aphrodite is described as *sponsor coniugii*. Hymenaeus, having been invoked by Demophoon, becomes now for Phyllis the guarantor of the marriage contract. The word is rare in poetry: it is found twice in Hor. (*Serm.* 2.6.23, *Epist.* 1.16.43), but not in Virgil, Propertius, or Tibullus. For O.'s use of legal terminology, cf. 1.96n.

obses: not simply 'hostage', but one who is held as a pledge that faith will be kept in a private transaction (*TLL* s.v. 218.15ff.). In this broader sense, cf. Cic. *Cluent.* 188 *nihil de alteris Oppianici nuptiis queror, quarum ille cum obsides filios ab eo mortuos accepisset*. It appears in combination with *sponsor* at Liv. 9.5.3.

35–44 Phyllis returns now to the oath by which Demophoon swore to return to her and relentlessly catalogues the deities that he invoked. This list is carefully constructed as a rising tricolon, giving first the sea (35–6), next Neptune in a couplet (37–8) that provides the predicate *iurasti*, and finally, in two couplets (39–42) tacked on in asyndeton, a succession of goddesses. Within this artful structure the first member itself consists of a tricolon, articulated by the repetition of *quod*, while throughout there is a note of insistence in the repeated *per*.

35 totiens emphasizes the changeableness of the sea, which thus makes an ironic oath for Demophoon to swear by.

36 nempe: an emphatic colloquial particle (K–S I 807) used sparingly by the poets, among whom O. is a significant exception, for he uses it freely in his elegiac verse; cf. 6.144, 7.141, 7.146, 9.61, 9.70, 16.292, 17.223, 20.70, 20.94, 20.191, Knox (1986a) 38–9. It appears here as a conjecture by Bentley for *saepe* of the MSS. The two words are often confused by scribes and *saepe* makes no sense in this context: Demophoon arrived in Thrace only once.

ieras: sc. when he arrived in Thrace.

37 The line lacks a caesura in the third foot, one of only eight non-caesural hexameters in O.'s elegies; cf. Platnauer (1951) 6–7. The unusual rhythm lends emphasis to *iurasti*, a molossus (– – –) occupying the central position between supporting caesurae; cf. *ES* 113.

fictus: i.e. *falsus*.

37–8 tuum ... auum: i.e. Neptune. Neptune and Theseus' mortal father Aegeus both had intercourse with Aethra, Demophoon's grandmother, on the night his father Theseus was conceived; thus the god can be called his grandfather (Apollod. *Bibl.* 3.7, Hygin. *Fab.* 37). Epithet (*tuum*) and noun (*auum*) enclose and complete a syntactical unit, a type of word-order favoured in Latin poetry; cf. Pearce (1966).

38 mulcet: cf. *Met.* 1.331 *mulcet aquas rector pelagi*, Virg. *Aen.* 1.65–6, of Aeolus, *tibi diuum pater atque hominum rex | et mulcere dedit fluctus et tollere uento*.

39 nimiumque mihi facientia tela 'the weapons that are all too well fitted to wound me': this intransitive use of *facere* is largely restricted to prose (*TLL* s.v. 122.42ff.); but cf. *Am.* 2.9b.36 *hic tua dextra facit*, *Ars* 3.57 *dum facit ingenium*. The more common construction is with *ad* (6.128n.), and the dative is attested before late Latin only once in Prop. 3.1.20 *non faciet capiti dura corona meo*, cf. Tränkle (1960) 65.

40 arcus ... faces 'one weapon the bow, the other the torch': referring to Cupid's standard armament, as at *Pont.* 3.3.67 *per mea tela, faces, et per mea tela, sagittas*. The plural *arcus* prevents an elision here, but perhaps also = 'bow and arrows', by analogy with the Greek plural τόξα (LSJ s.v. II); cf. *Ars* 3.29 *femina nec flammas nec saeuos discutit arcus*.

41 'And Juno, who graciously presides over the marriage couch': *alma* is adverbial. This is the only example of this epithet applied to Juno in surviving literature; cf. Traina (1991) 4–5.

42 taediferae ... deae: the 'torch-bearing goddess' is Demeter, so called because according to myth she searched the world for her lost daughter Persephone with a torch in each hand. The epithet *taedifer*, which occurs only here and at *Fast.* 3.786 *taedifera dea*, is O.'s translation of the Greek δαιδοφόρος, attested only as an epithet of Hecate (Bacch. 23.1) or the Furies (*SH* 1154). The 'secret rites' (*mystica sacra*) refer to the Eleusinian mysteries of Demeter, a common Greek oath, especially appropriate for an Athenian like Demophoon.

43-4 'If each of the many gods you have wronged should avenge himself, you by yourself would not satisfy the penalty.' Phyllis ends her list of deities by whom Demophoon swore his false oath with a conceit, but its purpose is not simply rhetorical: Phyllis pointedly leaves his punishment to the gods. This attitude stands in stark contrast with the tradition found elsewhere (introd n.) that Phyllis cursed Demophoon and brought about his death. O. courts the reader's sympathy for Phyllis by suppressing this detail of the myth.

44 uindicet ... eris: the mixed condition is of a type avoided in classical prose before Tacitus. *uindicare* is a legal term, used often by O., who has a similar predilection for the cognates *uindex* and *uindicta*; cf. Kenney (1969) 253.

in poenas 'to pay the penalty'.

45 'Moreover I was actually mad enough to repair your shattered ships': no other account of the story describes Demophoon as shipwrecked. O. seems to have developed this theme from Virgil's Dido and Aeneas; cf. 55, 103-4nn; Jacobson (1974) 60. It is highly likely that Virgil's portrayal of Dido as an abandoned heroine was influenced by narratives such as Callimachus' lost account of Phyllis. O.'s incorporation of Virgilian elements in his portrayal of Phyllis may therefore be read as a form of commentary on his predecessor and as testimony to a common tradition. O.'s Phyllis gains in sympathy from having been betrayed, like Dido, by the man she restored from destitution.

at marks an additional consideration in Phyllis' ironic bill of indictment against herself, continuing the line of reasoning developed in 27-30.

furiosa 'in my madness': the theme of love as madness was a favourite with O. and his neoteric predecessors; cf. 5.69, *Am.* 2.2.13, Knox (1986a) 20-1.

46 qua desererer 'by which I might be abandoned': the subjunctive is final.

47 remigiumque: although commonly used for a crew of rowers, here, as at Virg. *Aen.* 8.80 *remigioque aptat*, it means the oars themselves. Demophoon, we must assume, was not the only survivor of the wreck.

quo me fugiturus abires 'by which you were to leave, intending to run away from me': Phyllis, of course, is not incensed over helping him to leave, as she knew all along he would, but because it now seems that he did not intend to return. The reading of PGS *quod . . . haberes* is banal.

48 patior . . . meis: a proverbial expression; cf. Tib. 1.6.10 *heu heu, nunc premor arte mea*, Otto (1890) s.v. *telum* 1.

49 blandis . . . uerbis: the blandishments of the elegiac lover; cf. Cat. 64.139-40 *at non haec quondam blanda promissa dedisti | uoce mihi*.

50 generi nominibusque tuis: the nouns combine to express a single idea (hendiadys), 'your distinguished ancestry': cf. 17.51 *sed genus et proauos et regia nomina iactas*, Hor. *Carm.* 1.14.13 *iactes et genus et nomen inutile*.

51 Phyllis now suspects Demophoon of being a complete fraud, adopting the strategy described by O. in the *Ars* (1.659-62): *et lacrimae prosunt; lacrimis adamanta mouebis: | fac madidas uideat, si potes, illa genas. | si lacrimae, neque enim ueniunt in tempore semper, | deficient, uncta lumina tange manu*. The practice is also recommended for women (*Ars* 3.291-2), and the topos of tears simulated for amatory purposes is common; cf. McKeown on *Am.* 1.8.83-4.

52 quaque: sc. *uia*. The point is perhaps better made if we adopt Slichtenhorst's suggestion *cumque* 'on command'.

53-4 The two previous couplets form a tricolon with anaphora, this one recapitulates the points made there. The reading of the MSS in the first part of 53 forms an ineffective appendix (*quoque*) to the preceding lines by taking up the idea already treated fully in 31-44 that Phyllis was taken in by Demophoon's false oaths, when the subject now is his personal pleading. In addition, *dis* would have to mean not the 'gods' but 'your oaths to the gods'; the text here prints a correction suggested by E. J. Kenney *per litteras*.

53 quo iam tot pignora nobis? 'Why make all those pledges to me?': the verb is often omitted in this colloquial idiom; cf. *Am.* 2.19.7 *quo mihi fortunam . . . ?*, 3.4.41, Hor. *Epist.* 1.5.12.

54 inde: i.e. *ex eis,* partitive with *parte,* referring to *pignoribus*; one pledge would have sufficed for her deception.

capi 'be deceived'

55 nec moueor 'but I am not upset': for adversative *nec,* cf. 6n.

te iuui portuque locoque: for the construction, cf. *Met.* 11.281–2 *urbe uel agro | se iuuet,* Virg. *Aen.* 1.571 *opibusque iuuabo,* Juv. 3.211. *locus* means 'a place to stay', as at *Met.* 8.628 *mille domos adiere locum requiemque petentes.*

56 'This ought to have formed the limit of my kindness.' The demonstrative *haec* is attracted to the gender of the predicate; cf. 66, 3.8 *haec quoque culpa tua est.*

57–8 'I regret the disgrace of having crowned my act of hospitality by marrying you'; *iugali* occurs in poetry for *coniugali* (*TLL* s.v. 624.12ff.). The phrase *lectum iugale* is attested only once before O. at *Aen.* 4.496, where Dido is giving instructions for her funeral pyre.

58 lateri conseruisse latus: the disgrace of having been taken in by Demophoon and marrying him seems the more grievous as she recalls sleeping with him. O. varies a phrase of Tibullus (1.8.26) *femori conseruisse femur,* a familiar euphemism for sexual intercourse in Greek as well; cf. 19.138 *molle latus lateri composuisse tuo, Am.* 1.4.43, 3.7.10, 3.14.22, *Ars* 1.140, 1.496, Soph. *Trach.* 938–9 πλευρόθεν | πλευράν.

59–60 'I could wish that the previous night had been my last, when I could have died in possession of my good name.' The use of the proper name in referring to herself lends a tone of dignity; cf. 5.80n. The sentiment is weakly echoed in 12.5 *tum potui Medea mori bene.*

61–2 Phyllis concludes her recollection of Demophoon's sojourn in Thrace with a flat assertion of the merit of her case, rephrased in the form of a general maxim in the pentameter: *spes* and *merito* correspond in chiasmus to *meruisse* and *speraui* in the hexameter, while *uenit* is repeated for rhetorical emphasis, the second instance, *aequa uenit,* being equivalent to *est,* 'is just'; cf. 5.8, Prop. 2.25.28 *si qua uenit sero, magna ruina uenit. ex merito* 'deservedly' is an adverbial phrase with the participle as substantive, a common usage in O.: cf. 2.62, *Am.* 1.15.40, *Met.* 5.200; H–S 266.

63–90 Phyllis returns to the theme of her own *naïveté* in a section designed to shame Demophoon by a series of invidious comparisons to his famous father. She likens herself to the victims of Theseus, whose conquests she lists in a familiar catalogue (67–72). For the most part O. reproduces the canonical list of Theseus' exploits found, e.g., at Soph. fr. 730c Radt or *Met.* 7.433–50, but he appends as a final entry (75–8) the abandonment of Ariadne. The contrast of Demophoon with Theseus is harshly critical, for Phyllis is his only triumph, which can only be compared with the one act of which Theseus is ashamed.

63–4 non est operosa ... | gloria: by its position at the beginning of the pentameter in enjambment and followed by a strong pause, *gloria* is emphasized ironically, 'it is a cheaply earned reputation'.

64 simplicitas 'guilelessness': for O. this is a quality to be desired in a lover; cf. *Am.* 1.3.14, 1.10.13, 2.4.18. The word is otherwise rare in poetry.

65–6 'I was deceived by your words, because I was in love and because I am a woman. May the gods grant that this be the sum total of your praise!' Phyllis now coldly states what she sees is the truth of the matter. The pair of nouns in apposition is predicative, highlighted by the enclosing word order, *tuis ... uerbis.* Together they convey the conventional notion that a woman in love is easy prey. For the construction cf. 7.121, *Met.* 6.524–5 *fassusque nefas et uirginem et unam | ui superat.*

faciant ... sit: the subjunctive without a subordinating particle *ut* (parataxis) is a colloquial construction frequent in comedy and Cicero's letters, but used sparingly in poetry; cf. 98, 13.92, 13.144, *Am.* 1.4.56, H–S 530. The pentameter ironically echoes 56.

67 inter ... Aegidas: i.e. among other statues of the descendants of Aegeus, who was the father of Theseus and thus grandfather of Demophoon.

statuaris 'let a statue of yourself be set up': cf. Tac. *Dial.* 13.6 *statuar ... non maestus et atrox, sed hilaris et coronatus.*

68 magnificus titulis ... suis 'resplendent in his titles'. The grandiloquent adjective, a rarity in Augustan verse, points the contrast between father and son. *titulis* refers to the inscriptions on the base of the statue.

69 Sciron lectus 'when the name of Sciron has been read': he was a notorious robber slain by Theseus on the road near Megara.

Procrustes: a son of Poseidon who killed his victims by lopping off the legs of those too tall to fit his bed and stretching those too short for it; he, too, was killed by Theseus.

70 Sinis: another villain slain by Theseus. His preferred method of disposing of his captives was to bend down two pine trees and tie one leg to each before releasing the trees. Hence his epithet πιτυοκάμπτης 'pine-bender'.

et tauri mixtaque forma uiri: i.e. *tauri uirique mixta forma*, the Minotaur; cf. 10.127n. Descriptions of the monster naturally stress the unnatural combination of man and bull, which O. reflects in the involved word-order; cf. Virg. *Aen.* 6.25–6 *mixtumque genus prolesque biformis | Minotaurus*; Eur. fr. 996 Nauck σύμμικτον εἶδος. The displacement of *-que* is a characteristic feature of the style of Tibullus (see Smith on 1.1.40), enthusiastically adopted by O. but infrequently found in other poets; cf. Platnauer (1951) 91–2.

71 domitae bello Thebae: Theseus led a campaign against Creon, king of Thebes, when he refused burial to the Argives who had died in the campaign of the Seven against Thebes.

bimembres: the Centaurs, who are so styled at 9.99–100 *confisum pedibus formaque bimembri ... agmen*; *Met.* 12.240, 12.494, 15.283. Theseus overwhelmed them at the wedding feast of Pirithous.

72 pulsata: Theseus 'pounded on the doors' of the palace of Pluto to demand Persephone as bride for his friend Pirithous.

nigri regia ... dei: cf. *Met.* 4.438 *nigri fera regia Ditis*.

73 illos: sc. *titulos*, the inscriptions on the statue. Demophoon will also be commemorated in an inscription there for betraying Phyllis. For the motif of incorporating inscriptions into elegy, cf. 147–8n.

75 de tanta rerum turba factisque: construe *tanta* with *factis* (ἀπὸ κοινοῦ), 'of the multitude of great deeds of your father'. *res* and *facta* are indistinguishable in meaning, but the pleonasm is appropriate as Phyllis stresses the single bad example.

76 sedit 'deeply impressed itself': cf. *Rem.* 108, 268.

Cressa relicta: the jilted Cretan (antonomasia) is Ariadne; cf. *Am.* 1.7.15–16 *talis periuri promissaque uelaque Thesei | fleuit praecipites Cressa tulisse Notos*, Prop. 1.3.2 *languida desertis Cnosia litoribus*.

77 'The only act that he tries to excuse is the only one that you admire in him'; the repetition of *solum* is for rhetorical effect.

78 heredem patriae ... fraudis: O. formulates the notion of inherited character flaws in legal terminology: *heres* is found 16 times in O.'s poetry, but is otherwise common only in Horace. O. recalls this passage at *Ars* 3.459 *Demophoon, Thesei criminis heres*.

perfide: in O.'s choice of epithet we may hear an echo of Phyllis' imprecation of Demophoon as reported by Callimachus, fr. 556 Pfeiffer νυμφίε Δημοφόων, ἄδικε ξένε (introd. n.); for this is the word he uses to render it at *Rem.* 597 *'perfide Demophoon' surdas clamabat ad undas*. But O. also evokes other heroines in Roman poetry who had been portrayed in the same manner: in the first instance, Ariadne, who is on Phyllis' mind here, as shown in Cat. 64.132–3 *'sicine me patriis auectam, perfide, ab aris, | perfide, deserto liquisti in litore, Theseu?'* The same tradition of lament by an abandoned heroine may be detected in the prosecutorial tone of Dido, another queen deserted by a foreign prince who broke his promise: *Aen.* 4.305–6 *dissimulare etiam sperasti, perfide, tantum | posse nefas tacitusque mea decedere terra?* See Clausen (1987) 47.

agis 'you act the part': cf. 8.41–2 *quas egerat olim | Dardanius partis aduena, Pyrrhus agit, Ars* 1.611 *est tibi agendus amans*.

79 illa: sc. Ariadne.

nec inuideo: a parenthetical insertion that O. uses elsewhere in his less formal or epistolary style; cf. *Trist.* 1.1.1 *parue (nec inuideo) sine me, liber, ibis in urbem, Pont.* 1.8.8 *tuta (neque inuideo) cetera turba latet*.

meliore marito: sc. than Theseus. In erotic or amatory contexts *fruor* is a common euphemism for sexual relations (*TLL* s.v. 1424.22ff.), especially in elegy (Pichon (1902) 156).

80 capistratis 'haltered': a technical word attested only here in classical verse; Phyllis imagines Ariadne riding on the chariot of her divine husband Bacchus drawn by harnessed tigers. *tigribus* stands for the whole vehicle like *equi* in similar contexts, e.g. Virg. *Geo.* 3.358.

81–6 O. develops a theme to which Virgil's Dido insistently returns in her condemnation of Aeneas, namely that no other man will now be interested in marrying her: *Aen.* 4.534–6 *en quid ago? rursusne procos inrisa priores | experiar, Nomadumque petam conubia supplex, | quos ego sim totiens iam dedignata maritos?*; cf. 4.36–8, 320–1. Once again, Phyllis' isolation and bereavement are emphasized through the extended reminiscence of Virgil's heroine; cf. Jacobson (1974) 62.

81–2 'But the Thracians whom I rejected refuse to marry me on the grounds that I am rumoured to have preferred a foreigner to my own people': the subjunctive *ferar* is somewhat illogical, but can be explained by analogy: without the verb of saying, *praeposuisse* would stand in the subjunctive since Phyllis is repeating the reasons alleged by the Thracians. This extension of the subjunctive in subordinate clauses is quite common: K–S II 200–1.

81 despecti ... Thraces: cf. Virg. *Aen.* 4.36–7 *despectus Iarbas,* | *ductoresque alii.* A patterned line (p. 33).

conubia: this word occurs only four times in elegy (here, II.99, *Am.* 2.7.21, and *Fast.* 3.195), although this is perhaps not surprising since in elegy the subject rarely turns to marriage. Still, the distribution of the word in Latin poetry strongly suggests some hesitancy over its scansion that may have led the poets to prefer synonyms like *coniugium.* The second syllable is short by nature, and the nominative and accusative plural can only be admitted to hexameter and elegy if the *-u-* is lengthened artificially. Beginning with Catullus, it is lengthened to accommodate the nominative and accusative plural, by analogy with the verb *nubere,* where the first syllable is long, and perhaps in imitation of a familiar practice in Greek prosody that allowed words containing a run of three short syllables to fit into the hexameter; cf. Leumann (1977) 115, Austin on *Aen.* 4.126.

83 iam nunc: the pleonasm is emphatic: 'right now'.

doctas ... Athenas: the epithet is conventional of Athens as a centre of learning; cf. Prop. 1.6.13, 3.21.1. But in a poem set in the heroic age *doctas* is an anachronism, imported in order to highlight the contempt of the imagined Thracian interlocutor for the sophisticated foreigner Phyllis fell for.

84 armiferam is an epic compound apparently coined by O., who introduced several such forms in *-fer* and *-ger* to Latin verse; cf. Linse (1891) 37–9. The subjunctive *regat* is final, 'to rule'.

Thracen: accusative, a Greek form.

85 exitus acta probat: Phyllis' imagined critic ends with a moralizing maxim: 'The outcome is the measure of our actions.' Cf. Cic. *Rab. Post.* 1.1 *hoc plerumque facimus, ut consilia euentis ponderemus, et, cui bene quid processerit, multum illum prouidisse, cui secus, nihil sensisse dicamus, Att.* 9.7a.1, Otto (1890) 126–7.

86 ab euentu ... notanda 'are to be branded in accordance with their results'.

87–8 'And yet if our seas should foam beneath your oars, then they would say that I counselled well both for myself and for my people.' The hexameter takes the form of a patterned line (p. 33).

spumescant: the inceptive form of *spumo*, attested only here. The instrumental ablative *remo* is a 'poetic singular' to avoid the cacophonous effect of sigmatism; cf. 3.65 *Pthiis canescant aequora remis.*

89–90 'But I did not, nor will the thought of my palace affect you, and you will not bathe your weary limbs in the waters of Thrace.' Phyllis punctuates her series of reflections contrasting her reputation and Demophoon's with a couplet consisting of an elegant tricolon, whose third member occupies the pentameter in a 'patterned' line. In diction, too, the tone here shifts to a higher level.

89 te ... tanget: i.e. 'non curabis regiam meam' (Ruhnken); cf. 5.81 *non ego miror opes, nec me tua regia tangit.* The sentiment is like that of 7.11–12: like Dido, Phyllis has offered the kingship to a foreigner and he is apparently unmoved. Some editors attempt to construe by an impossible enallage *tu regiam meam tanges.*

90 fessaque: *fessus* is an 'epic word', rare in elegy compared to its metrically equivalent synonym *lassus*; cf. Axelson (1945) 29–30. It recurs at 4.90, while *lassus* is attested but once in the certainly genuine epistles (10.145n.). *-que* continues the negation, a relatively rare combination (H–S 517).

Bistonia: i.e. Thracian, after a local people. The elaborate periphrasis 'bathe in the waters of Thrace' stands for 'come to Thrace'; cf. Virg. *Ecl.* 1.63 *bibere Ararim* for 'live in Gaul'.

91–120 Phyllis' admission to herself that Demophoon has abandoned her leads to a melancholy recollection of the day of departure and their tearful farewell at the harbour. She no longer pretends to persuade Demophoon to return: the epistle has become an undisguised monologue.

91 oculis ... abeuntis inhaeret: cf. 7.25 *Aeneas oculis semper uigilantis inhaeret, Trist.* 4.3.19.

92 premeret portus 'crowded the harbour'.

93 ausus es implies not daring but callousness, 'you had the nerve'.

colloque infusus amantis 'hanging on your lover's neck': an unusual and graphic expression, perhaps suggested by Virg. *Aen.* 8.406 *coniugis infusus gremio*, where Venus is seducing Vulcan. It is adopted by O. only here and at *Met.* 11.386, and rarely recurs in later poetry.

94 oscula ... moras 'to kiss me close and long': a patterned line (p. 33) to focus attention on the image. The details of the scene matter to Phyllis, for they underscore the depth of Demophoon's betrayal; for the expression cf. Mart. 6.34.1 *basia da nobis ... pressa.*

95 tuis ... nostras: again, a patterned line with chiastic word order (aABb) that seemingly reflects the sense, 'mingle my tears with yours'.

96 foret: subjunctive because the causal clause reports the thoughts of someone (Demophoon) other than the speaker (Phyllis). *queri* ironically picks up the note repeatedly struck by Phyllis in the opening of the poem (2n.), for Demophoon's complaint, she now realizes, was feigned.

98 fac exspectes: 66n.

Demophoonta: accusative, a Greek form; cf. 1.5n.

99–101 exspectem ... | exspectem ... exspecto: Phyllis ironically repeats Demophoon's own expression to introduce what the reader begins to think is a threefold repetition (rising tricolon); but this expectation is defeated in the final couplet when Phyllis breaks off her complaint to confess that she has not yet given up hope.

99 qui ... abisti: the expression is condensed, with the antecedent of the relative clause (*te*) unexpressed and the future participle *uisurus* supplying the sense of a final clause: 'with no intention of ever seeing me again'.

100 pelago uela negata meo 'sails denied return to my sea'.

101 serus: the adjective has concessive force, 'though late'; take *modo* with *redeas.*

102 sit solo tempore lapsa fides: the verb has the effect of further softening the accusation: Demophoon will have kept his promise, slipping only in respect (ablative) of its timing.

103 infelix: a constant epithet of Dido in the *Aeneid,* which is much on O.'s mind in this epistle.

altera coniunx: the same fear of another woman is expressed by Penelope at 1.75–6. In the pentameter *alter* must be supplied from *altera* with *Amor,* cf. 12.205, 20.35.

104 forsitan: 14n.

Amor: not simply the emotion: in a text that did not distinguish upper- and lower-case letters, an ancient reader would detect a reference to the god also, who has not shown her favour.

105–16 Phyllis expresses her fear that Demophoon has even forgotten who she is and therefore reminds him in a series of indignant relative clauses. But, as Housman (1897) 103–4 (= *Class. pap.* 383) remarks, 'into the midst of these relatives relating to Phyllis there intrudes the preposterous distich 109 sq., with "cuius" and "cui" relating not to Phyllis but to Demophoon; and then after "quae" for Phyllis in 111 you slip back again to "cui" for Demophoon in 115'. A number of remedies have been proposed, the most plausible of which involves placing 109–10 after 114 with repunctuation (Madvig). Housman adopts this transposition and emends *cui* (115) to *huic*. Against this transposition it may be objected that the couplet with relative *qua* (113–14) tacked on to 111–12 is an acceptable parallel for the loosely attached couplet 109–10 in its original position. Since this leaves the couplet 115–16 in a position which is impossibly distant from the antecedent *tibi*, we must suppose the loss of a third couplet beginning with *quae*, omitted before it by homoearchon. The third member of the tricolon would have been a suitable place to remind Demophoon that she gave him her love and he abused it.

105 iamque: introduces the conclusion to Phyllis' agitated musings about another woman: now Demophoon has completely forgotten her. The correction of MS *utque* by Housman (1899) 175–6 (= *Class. pap.* 476) seems indispensable. *nullam = non*, an idiom that is apparently colloquial; cf. 10.11, Cat. 8.14, [Virg.] *Ciris* 177, H–S 205, Hofmann (1951) 80.

tibi excidimus 'you have forgotten me': cf. 12.71 *an exciderunt mecum loca?*, Tib. 3.1.20, Sen. *Med.* 561–2.

puto: a parenthetical insertion, colloquial in tone, as indicated by the shortened -*o*; cf. Bömer on *Met.* 3.266, Hartenberger (1911) 50–7. This use of *puto* is common in O.'s other elegies, although this is the only occurrence in *Her.*; cf. Knox (1986a) 61.

106 ei mihi: an expressive interjection of pain found also in the higher genres (Hofmann (1951) 13).

quae ... et unde: cf. *Pont.* 4.5.11 *si quis, ut in populo qui sitis et unde requiret*, Livy 23.34.4 *cum quaereret qui et unde.* The combination is old:

e.g. Hom. *Od.* 1.170 τίς πόθεν εἶς ἀνδρῶν 'What man are you and whence?'

107–8 'I am she, Demophoon, who, when you had been driven far in wanderings, gave you access to the harbours of Thrace and offered you welcome as a guest.' The verb *dedi* is to be taken by syllepsis (25n.) with both *portus* and *hospitium*.

longis erroribus acto: O. diverges from the tradition that makes Thrace Demophoon's first stop on his homeward journey. His Phyllis is perhaps simply exaggerating, but O. is also incorporating details more appropriate to the story of Dido, who received Aeneas after much wandering; cf. *Aen.* 1.755 *erroresque tuos.*

109 cuius opes auxere meae: sc. *opes*, by brachylogy. The pointed juxtaposition of words of contrasting meaning at line-end (*diues egenti*) emphasizes Phyllis' indignation, further underscored by the alliteration with anaphora in the pentameter.

egenti: echoes the lament of Dido, *Aen.* 4.373–4 *egentem | excepi et regni demens in parte locaui.*

111 subieci: O. deviates slightly, but significantly, from the story as attested in Greek mythographical sources (Apollod. *Epit.* 6.16, Tzetzes ad Lycoph. *Alex.* 496), where it is Phyllis' father who gives his daughter to Demophoon with the kingdom as her dowry. The effect of the alteration by O. is to lend emphasis to her feelings of guilt: in this, as in many other details, he may well have been influenced by Virgil's Dido (45, 81–6, 107–8, 117nn.); cf. Jacobson (1974) 60.

regna Lycurgi: Thrace. In myth Lycurgus was a king of Thrace who resisted the worship of Dionysus and was punished by the god with death. For the periphrasis, cf. Virg. *Aen.* 3.14 *acri quondam regnata Lycurgo.*

112 nomine femineo: not a periphrasis for *femina* as ablative of agent without preposition, but an extension of the use of the instrumental ablative *nomine* in legal phrases, 'in the name of' (*OLD* s.v. 14). The adjective *femineus* stands, as often (1.14n.) for the genitive; cf. Sil. 14.70 *Aeolio regnatas nomine terras.* In this case the use is also a metrical convenience, since *femina* cannot appear in elegiacs in the oblique cases.

uix satis apta regi 'scarcely capable of being ruled': construe *satis* closely with the participle with some depreciatory force: Phyllis has, after all, ruled Thrace up to this point. The construction of *aptus* with the infinitive is found only in poetry; cf. 9.116 *ferre ... uix satis apta*.

113–14 Both the hexameter and pentameter exhibit 'patterning' in an elaborate periphrasis for 'all Thrace', signified by distinctive place names: Rhodope (1n.), a spur of the Balkans extending to the south-east, Haemus, the northern branch of the same range, and the river Hebrus (15n.). The river is *sacer* perhaps because of its associations with Dionysiac cult, but the epithet is common with rivers: e.g. Hom. *Od.* 10.351 ἱερῶν ποταμῶν, Stat. *Silv.* 1.6.77 *Nilus sacer*.

114 admissas 'headlong': a metaphor from driving chariots as in 1.36; cf. *Am.* 3.6.86 *nec capit admissas alueus altus aquas*.

115 For the lacuna preceding this couplet, cf. 105–16n.

libata 'was offered up': a striking metaphor, since *libo* is properly applied to pouring a libation, and thus by extension to other offerings to the gods; cf. 4.27 *tu noua seruatae carpes libamina famae*, 16.161 *uel mihi uirginitas esset libata*. The sacral imagery is sustained in *auibus ... sinistris*, refering to ill omens observed in the flight of birds. *cui* is indirect object, not instrumental dative.

116 fallaci: only here in the single *Her.* Adjectives in -*ax* are formed from verbs and indicate tendencies, often with a pejorative sense; cf. Leumann (1977) 376, Austin on Virg. *Aen.* 6.3.

zona: a girdle, Greek ζώνη; its removal signifies loss of virginity; cf. Cat. 67.28 *zonam soluere uirgineam*, Barchiesi (1992) 160. The importance of the symbol is emphasized in a patterned line. In the *Remedia amoris* (602) a glance at her girdle sets the stage for Phyllis' suicide, for which it becomes the instrument.

117 pronuba Tisiphone: the matron who conducted the bride to her wedding in a Roman marriage ceremony was known as the *pronuba*. Phyllis here attributes that function to Tisiphone, one of the three Furies, thus asserting that her 'marriage' to Demophoon was doomed from the start. O. assimilates the story to the sequence of events in book 4 of the *Aeneid* (166), where Earth (*Tellus*) and Juno (*pronuba Iuno*) attend the union of Dido and Aeneas. The idea of one of the Furies acting as *pronuba* probably derives from Juno's curse on Aeneas' wedding to Lavinia, *Aen.* 7.319 *Bellona manet te pronuba*.

ululauit: an onomatopoeic verb, not ordinarily associated with the wedding ceremony; again, O. recalls the eerie accompaniment of nymphs at the wedding of Aeneas and Dido: *Aen.* 4.168 *summoque ulularunt uertice Nymphae.*

118 deuia 'haunting remote spots' (Housman): the bird that shuns humans in the daytime is the screech-owl (*bubo*), whose call is a sign of ill omen; cf. *Met.* 10.452–3 *ter omen | funereus bubo letali carmine fecit,* Plin. *Nat.* 10.34–5.

119 Allecto: another of the three Furies, who participated (*adfuit*) in the ceremony. Serpents are a frequent accompaniment of the Furies in their capacity as avenging demons in Roman poetry, often pictured entwined in their hair (e.g. Virg. *Geo.* 4.482–3, Tib. 1.3.69–70). The tiny serpents coiled round Allecto's neck like a collar (*torquata*) are a novel touch by O.

120 mota 'kindled' (Housman): cf. *Met.* 3.464 *flammas moueo, Ars* 2.301, *Am.* 2.16.12. These torches carried in the wedding procession were taken from a funeral, another ill omen; cf. *Met.* 6.430 *Eumenides tenuere faces de funere raptas,* Prop. 4.3.13–14 *quae mihi deductae fax omen praetulit illa | traxit ab euerso lumina nigra rogo.* The adjective *sepulcralis* is attested in poetry only here and at *Met.* 8.480.

face: the short open vowel at the end of the pentameter is rare in O. compared with the other elegists; cf. Platnauer (1951) 64–6. Examples in the single *Her.* are 5.30, 5.54, 5.136, 6.98, 6.148.

121–48 Phyllis describes the anxious days watching by the sea for the sight of Demophoon's ship. This scene was famous, to judge from a reference by Procopius (*Epist.* 47 Garzya–Loenertz = 86 Hercher; see introd. note), in which he describes himself anxiously watching for delivery of a letter from his brother: 'I look out to sea just like Phyllis ... who wept as she looked out over the ocean and noted every merchantman, in case one of them might be bringing back Demophoon.' How much of this scene is owed to Callimachus, we cannot say, but some of the topographical details may derive from him, since it was presumably the setting for this scene that motivated his interest in the story. The name of the place was Ἐννέα Ὁδοί 'Nine Roads', later Amphipolis, on the Strymon in Thrace. No extant Greek source connects the original name with Phyllis, but Antipater of Thessalonica, a contemporary of O., mentions Amphipolis as the location of her burial mound (*AP* 7.705). O. in the *Ars* is the earliest authority for associating the name with nine trips made by Phyllis to the shore: 3.37–8 *quaere, Nouem cur una Viae dicatur,* *et audi | depositis siluas Phyllida flesse comis.* And he refers to the name again in *Rem.* 601, where he is certainly reflecting Callimachus. We may speculate, however, that the psychological elaboration of the moment and, in particular, the prolonged reflection on suicide, which is the logical result of her steady deterioration, are the product of O.'s own imagination.

121 tamen should be construed closely with the verb *calco* as adversative to the concession implied in the adjective *maesta* : 'though unhappy, still I walk the shores'; cf. Tib. 1.9.4 *sera tamen tacitis poena uenit pedibus,* Virg. *Ecl.* 1.27.

fruticosaque 'covered with thickets': an adjective found only here and at *Met.* 6.344 in poetry, but common in the elder Pliny's *Natural history.* Such adjectives in *-osus* are common in Latin agricultural prose and are used by the poets sparingly to add a touch of realism (Knox (1986b)); cf. 10.25 *frutices in uertice rari.*

122 'Where the sea opens far and wide before my eyes': Phyllis means that, like Ariadne (10.26–30), she walks both along the beach and on the hills above the shore to scan the horizon; O. describes this also at *Rem.* 595 *qua poterat, longum spectabat in aequor.* Most MSS read *quaque ... litora,* an impossibly weak repetition after *litora* in the hexameter, made all the more unlikely by our expectation that Phyllis has her gaze fixed upon the sea not the shore. The reading *aequora,* found in two later MSS, was printed by Aldus. The pentameter should be construed with *prospicio* in 124.

123 laxatur 'is thawed,' after the evening's frost.

123–4 frigida ... sidera: even at night, when the stars may be said to be cold by an easy enallage (1.10n.) because they bring the chill, Phyllis watches the direction of the wind to see if it might bring a ship north from Athens.

125 lintea: originally simply a piece of cloth, but by O.'s time a common poetic expression for 'a ship's sail'. Phyllis' words in the pentameter refer to Demophoon as the answer to her prayers to the gods, echoing O.'s own words as he awaits the return of Corinna: *Am.* 2.11.43–4 *primus ego aspiciam notam de litore puppim | et dicam 'nostros aduehit illa deos.'*

127–8 'Scarcely restrained by the waves, I run ahead into the sea, where the shifting sea first extends its waters.' Phyllis means that she runs out into the shallow waters, where the waves break and then are dissipated over the sand, an image fixed in the patterned pentameter; cf. Cat. 64.128.

129 minus et minus: understand correlative *eo*, omitted by ellipse as at 4.19 *uenit amor grauius, quo serior*. The expressive gemination *minus et minus* is characteristic of everyday speech; cf. 1.41n. In the *Met*. O. alludes to this complaint of Phyllis by the seashore in his description of Alcyone as she sees the corpse of Ceyx carried closer to the shore: *Met*. 11.722–3 *quod quo magis illa tuetur,* | *hoc minus et minus est mentis*.

utilis 'capable of standing': for the sense, cf. Plin. *Nat*. 7.104 *ter et uiciens uulneratus est, ob id neutra manu, neutro pede satis utilis*.

130 linquor 'I faint away': a striking use of the passive for the usual construction *animus relinquit aliquem*. Later authors who employ this phrase add the specifying ablative *animo*, e.g. Sen. *Dial*. 3.12.1, Suet. *Iul*. 45.1, Tac. *Ann*. 3.46 *quasi exanimes linquebantur*.

ancillis excipienda cado: in pointed contrast to the situation as described in *Rem*. 591–2, where Phyllis is alone, *quid nisi secretae laeserunt Phyllida siluae?* | *certa necis causa est: incomitata fuit*. The everyday words for 'slave', *seruus* and *ancilla*, which were generally avoided by the other Augustan poets, are rather common in O.; cf. McKeown on *Am*. 1.8.87.

131–48 Phyllis closes the epistle by describing her contemplation of suicide, an act which of course is accomplished afterwards; but at this point Phyllis takes over so completely the role of narrator that one almost expects a description of her hanging. She begins with an excursus describing the place where the thought of death occurred to her: the break with the preceding narrative is marked by the lack of grammatical connection (asyndeton) and a distinctive phrase to mark this as a digression, e.g., *est locus*. O. makes considerable use of this mannerism, especially in the *Met*.; cf. Bömer on *Met*. 11.229, Austin on Virg. *Aen*. 1.12, Williams (1968) 639–41. The literary purpose of this pause in the 'action' is to raise the level of suspense while the scene is being set: the return to the narrative is usually marked by some form of demonstrative, in this case *hinc* (133). But here the reader's expectations of narrative to follow are cheated because the actual suicide cannot be depicted. Contrast the capsule narrative of her death in the *Rem*., which begins *limes erat tenuis* ... (599).

131 'There is a bay curving gently into the shape of a drawn bow' (Palmer): this description is echoed by O. in another excursus in the *Metamorphoses*: 11.229 *est sinus Haemoniae curuos falcatus in arcus,* the only other instance in Latin in which *falcatus* is used in a topographical description. The plural *arcus* is poetic, 40n. O. doubtless has in mind the many sickle-shaped promontories of the eastern Mediterranean called Δρέπανον.

132 ultima ... cornua: the furthest points of the promontory; *cornu* is the proper term for a projecting headland and, as Housman notes, it also 'keeps up the figure of *arcus*'.

praerupta ... mole rigent 'rise stiffly in a precipitous crag': the ablative is descriptive. The verb *rigeo* in such descriptions is uniquely Ovidian; cf. *Met.* 11.150–1 *late riget arduus alto | Tmolus in ascensu.*

133 hinc: 131–48n.

immittere corpus: i.e. to throw herself; *corpus* is virtually equivalent to the reflexive pronoun (*TLL* s.v. 1012.41ff.). On the bolder usages of poets in this regard, see Housman on Manil. 1.539, Shackleton Bailey (1956) 33–4, Fedeli on Prop. 1.11.11.

134 mens fuit 'I intended': the construction with the infinitive is first attested here and limited to poetry; similar locutions in prose govern a subordinate clause with *ut.*

pergis 'persevere'.

135–6 Phyllis' wish to have her unburied corpse carried out to sea to Demophoon plays off the familiar topos of a person drowning at sea who wishes his body carried to shore for burial, e.g. 18.197–9 (Leander to Hero) *optabo tamen ut partes expellar in illas | et teneant portus naufraga membra tuos. | flebis enim tactuque meum dignabere corpus, Met.* 11.564–5. These lines form the protasis to a condition completed by *dices* in 138, 'if the waves carry me to you ... then you will say'. The juxtaposition *tua me* is pointed and emphatic.

135 proiectam: the proper word for a corpse cast out without burial (*OLD* s.v. 7a).

136 intumulatus: only attested here (*hapax legomenon*), coined by O. for *insepultus,* which will not scan in hexameters.

137 ut: concessive; cf. 1.116n. The elision before a monosyllable standing before the third-foot caesura is extremely rare in O.; cf. Platnauer (1951) 82.

teque 'harder than iron, steel ... and you': the climax is un-expected, reversing the usually complimentary sense of the hyper-bole; cf. Cic. *Fam.* 5.12.7 *tu fac in augenda gloria te ipsum uincas*, Plin. *Nat.* 36.5 *Praxiteles marmoris gloria superauit etiam semet.* See 10.110n.

139–42 Poison, the sword, and the noose (in a rising tricolon) would be welcome forms of death. The language is graphic and luxuriant: Phyllis craves (139 *sitis*) poison, and the thought of a bloody death (139–40 *cruenta ... morte*) is pleasing (140 *iuuat*); while she lingers expansively on the embrace of the noose (141–2). The repeti-tion of *iuuat* in 142 is not elegant, but cf. 4.84–7, *Am.* 2.19.59–60.

140 gladio: the everyday word for 'sword' in the Roman army is usually avoided in poetry in favour of *ensis* (Axelson (1945) 51); in the *Am.* and the certainly genuine *Her. gladius* is found only here and at 10.88 against 14 occurrences of *ensis*. O.'s Phyllis makes the idea of falling on her sword especially vivid for a Roman reader by using the more familiar word.

141–2 'My neck too, because it yielded to the embrace of your faithless arms, I would gladly entangle in a noose.' Phyllis' deliber-ation over the form of her suicide is a familiar motif in tragedy (Fraenkel (1964) 1 465–7, Zwierlein (1986) 117–18), taken to an ex-treme here; cf. Barchiesi *ad loc.*

141 nectenda: ordinarily 'to bind', as of the act of tying a noose around the neck (cf. *Met.* 10.378 *laqueoque innectere fauces*), but here transferred to the embrace. So, too, 142 *implicuisse*, a word with erotic overtones in O.'s verse (cf. *Am.* 2.18.9 *implicuitque suos circum mea colla lacertos*, and see Bömer on *Met.* 3.343) is shifted to a new context. By this double enallage (1.10n.) Phyllis' identification of the embrace of Demophoon with the tightening of the noose is reflected in the language.

142 praebuerunt: the scansion with a short *-e-* (also at *Am.* 1.14.25) probably reflects popular pronunciation of the preferred ending in the literary language with a long *-e-*; cf. 5.136, 7.166, 12.71, 14.72, Leumann (1977) 607–8. This prosody is an occasional metrical convenience that also allows some words that would not be possible in elegiacs with conventional scansion; for the practice of the ele-gists, cf. Platnauer (1951) 53–4. For the construction *praebere nectenda*, cf. 13.31 *pectendos ... praebere capillos.* For the perfect infinitive *impli-cuisse* where we expect the present, cf. 28n.

143 stat 'I am determined': for the construction with infinitive, see Austin on Virg. *Aen.* 2.750.

tenerum pensare ... pudorem 'to atone for modesty which proved frail' (Housman): the slight oddity of the expression is the result of the rhetorical opposition *matura tenerum*.

144 in necis electu 'in choosing the manner of my death': the noun *electus*, attested only here in classical Latin, is a coinage of a type familiar in O.; cf. Linse (1891) 28–9.

futura ... est = *erit*, a periphrasis for the future that becomes increasingly common in the post-classical period (H–S 312); cf. 7.86.

145 inscribende 'your name will have to be inscribed'. For similar vocatives, cf. *Am.* 2.9.1 *indignande* (Madvig), *Fast.* 3.344, *Trist.* 1.5.1, *Pont.* 4.13.1.

inuidiosa 'calculated to draw hatred upon you' (Shuckburgh): a favourite adjective with O.; cf. Knox (1986b) 97–101.

146 aut hoc aut simili carmine: a realistic touch that catches the reader off guard: Phyllis does not expect to be able to dictate the text of the epitaph (*carmine*, as at 7.194 and often) on her tomb.

147–8 To provide a version of one's own epitaph is a characteristic topos of elegy; the motif is found at Tib. 1.3.55–6, [3.2.29–30], Prop. 2.13.35–6, 4.7.85–6. O. uses the motif in Dido's epistle, 7.195–6, and elsewhere at *Am.* 2.6.61–2, *Trist.* 3.3.73–6.

147 PHYLLIDA DEMOPHOON: the hemistich is an echo of Prop. 2.24.43–4 *paruo dilexit spatio Minoida Theseus, | Phyllida Demophoon, hospes uterque malus*, repeated by O. at *Ars* 2.353. The pointed juxtaposition of personal names is mirrored (chiasmus) at line-end in *hospes amantem*.

LETO DEDIT: an archaic phrase, found elsewhere in O. only at 20.104. This is the only use permitted in classical prose of the otherwise poetic *letum* (*TLL* s.v. 1189.26ff.). The Roman poets responded to the age-old creative challenge of rendering 'to kill' with a wealth of periphrases, discussed by Axelson (1945) 67–8.

148 NECIS CAVSAM: O. changes his mind on this in *Rem.* 592: *certa necis causa est: incomitata fuit. nex* belongs to the high style: it is not found in Catullus, Propertius, or the *Amores*.

MANVM: the point is scored in the pentameter by construing both *causam* and *manum* with *praebuit* (ἀπὸ κοινοῦ). The absence of punctuation in contemporary texts and inscriptions would make the effect more obvious: a modern reader is apt to mark a pause after *causam* or *praebuit*. The brachylogy is combined with syllepsis: 'he provided the cause [abstract object], *I* (*ipsa*) the hand [concrete] to do it.'

V Oenone Paridi

Helen was not the first woman taken to wife by Paris, a detail that we do not learn from the epic tradition. The story of Oenone, his first love, is not attested by Homer or the tragedians who treated episodes of the Trojan War. Although the Judgement of Paris is widely attested in classical Greek literature – Euripides, in particular, often touches on the theme – we do not learn of Oenone in extant sources until the Hellenistic period. Her tale is first alluded to by Lycophron (3rd cent. BC) at *Alex.* 57–68 and Bion 2.11 (2nd cent. BC), and it was also mentioned briefly by Hellanicus, *FGrH* 4 F 29; see Stinton (1965) 40–50 (= *Collected papers* 47–56). The outlines of the story are given in a summary by Parthenius (1st cent. BC) in his *Erotica pathemata* 4: 'When Alexander, the son of Priam, was tending flocks on Mt Ida, he fell in love with Oenone the daughter of Cebren [a river-god]. It is said that because she had been possessed by some divinity she could tell the future, and she was generally renowned for her wisdom. Alexander took her away from her father to Ida, where his pastures were, and lived with her there as his wife. He was so much in love with her that he swore he would never desert her. But she said that she understood that he was much in love with her for the present, but that there would come a time when he would leave her and cross over to Europe. There he would become infatuated with a woman and bring war to his people. She also told him that it was fated that he would be wounded in the war, and that only she would be able to cure him. Alexander always stopped her when she spoke of these matters.' Parthenius goes on to describe the fulfilment of this prophecy and the suicide of Oenone, who at first refused to heal Paris, but repented only to arrive at Troy to find him already dead.

This narrative coincides with those found in other mythographers (Apollod. *Bibl.* 3.12.6 and Conon, *Narr.* 23), with some variation in the manner of Oenone's suicide and other details, but it is not clear where Parthenius and the other mythographers found it. A commentator on Parthenius mentions two earlier prose works, Nicander's *On poets* and the *Troica* of Cephalon of Gergis (a pseudonym for Hegesianax), but these are not necessarily indications of Parthenius' sources. The existence of a Hellenistic narrative poem on Paris and Oenone has long been suspected, based on analysis of the lengthy narrative of the death of Paris in Quintus of Smyrna's *Posthomerica* 10; cf. Rohde (1913) 118–19, Vian (1969) 7–12, *RE* xxiv 1284–6. This evidence for a Hellenistic model for this episode is not very convincing, depending for the most part on subjective assessments of the bucolic setting of Paris' deathbed entreaty to Oenone and the pathetic strain of narrative, a type that is readily attributed to Hellenistic tastes. The bucolic strand in the tradition surrounding Paris' life before Troy is not peculiar to Hellenistic taste; it runs throughout the tradition even when Oenone is not included; cf. Stinton (1965) 16 (= *Collected papers* 29). But the suspicion that there was an influential literary account of Oenone is warranted. Certainly, if we may judge by O.'s practice in the other *Heroides*, it is highly likely that in Oenone's epistle his audience was hearing from a figure already known to them from poetry. O. refers to Oenone rather obliquely at *Rem.* 457, and the story was well-known in the first century AD: it was performed as a mime in Domitian's reign (Suet. *Dom.* 10.4) and there are several representations in decorative art (Roscher III 786–91). In this connection it might be worth mentioning that Euphorion (2nd cent. BC) wrote an *Alexander* (*CA*, p. 29), although its contents are not known.

O.'s treatment of the story adopts a very different focus from the other accounts known to us: theirs is on the death of Paris and Oenone's rejection of him, the central episode in all other extant narratives. In this epistle O. takes up the story at an unusual point: the letter that Oenone writes is set well before the final drama takes place, just after she has seen Paris bringing his new bride to Troy. O.'s epistle thus plays upon the reader's familiarity with Paris' tragic end, an ironic twist emphasized by O.'s rejection of the traditional attribution to Oenone of the power of prophecy (39n.). As she writes, she is as unaware of the future as Paris.

1–4 The poem opens abruptly with a question, not a formal salutation, which is postponed to the second couplet, a circumstance favourable to the introduction, from a marginal note, of a more suitable epistolary opening concocted by a medieval reader (p. 36). Oenone imagines that Helen, his new bride (*coniunx . . . noua*), will not allow Paris to open the letter which she knows is from her rival Oenone, while Paris is imagined as reacting with fear to any epistle since it might contain a challenge from Agamemnon.

1 Perlegis: the verb is rare in Augustan poetry (see McKeown on *Am.* 1.11.19), but occurs 11 times in O.'s epistolary verse (*Her.*, *Trist.*, *Pont.*)

2 ista: an emphatic demonstrative (Knox (1986a) 56–7), leaving the impression that another letter might come, this time written in a Greek hand.

Mycenaea: the epithet refers to Agamemnon, king of Mycenae and leader of the Greek expedition now gathering against Troy; cf. 3.109, *Am.* 2.8.12. Paris need not worry that the letter is from him.

littera 'writing' (not 'epistle') done in a Greek hand, here refers anachronistically to the form of the Greek alphabet since Homeric heroes do not write. O.'s play on the linguistic setting of his characters is similar to the opening of Briseis' epistle to Achilles (3.2), where she complains of the difficulties of writing in Greek, *uix bene barbarica Graeca notata manu,* another witty anachronism.

3 Pegasis 'fountain nymph' from Greek πηγή has aroused suspicion as an epithet for Oenone, but the word is too rare to have occurred to a scribe as a correction. In Latin poetry it is used as an epithet for the Hippocrene, the spring on Parnassus derived from Pegasus (cf. *Trist.* 3.7.15 *Pegasides undae*, Mart. 9.58.6, [Mosch.] 3.78 Παγασὶς κράνα, Nonn. *Dion.* 7.234), or as a name for the Muses associated with that spring (cf. *ES* 27, Prop. 3.1.19, [Virg.] *Catal.* 9.2). But O. may be drawing on material lost to us: Quintus of Smyrna (3.300–1) gives Pegasis as the name of a fountain nymph of the Troad, whose son was slain by Odysseus, and the name was common in the region (Robert (1960) 220–6). Admittedly, it is an odd way to refer to the daughter of a river-god. The river Cebren was a small stream, named from an obscure town in the Troad on the banks of the river Satriois. But *Pegasis* at least provides a context for her claim to be *celeberrima siluis*, where nymphs abide, which Micyllus' *Pedasis* does not.

4 laesa 'injured', in the figurative sense, having been betrayed by her lover, as often in elegy (Pichon (1902) 102). But as Oenone strikes

the familiar note of complaint in *queror* (1.8n.), there is also a sugges-
tion of more formal legal imagery: *laedere* is the proper judicial term
for damage done to the interests of another (Berger (1953) s.v.), while
queror may also be used of lodging a formal complaint in a court of
law (*OLD* s.v. 1e) .

si sinis ipse: not 'if you will let me complain', but 'if you will
allow yourself to be called mine'. *ipsa*, the reading of some MSS,
misplaces the point: only Paris can allow Oenone to claim him as
her own, while we have no reason to suppose that anyone other than
Oenone would complain on her behalf. Like the English possessive,
meus, tuus, etc. are used familiarly as terms of endearment.

5–32 Oenone laments the change in her fortune and recalls the
time when she and Paris lived together, drawing a picture of an
idyllic life in the country. This passage draws heavily on Hellenistic
motifs already developed by the elegists. There is considerable irony
in O.'s application of the picture of pastoral bliss in love to a pair of
shepherds; the usual form of this topos is an impossible wish by the
unhappy (urban) love-poet.

5 quis deus: Oenone's first suspicion is that she has fallen foul
of some divinity; cf. *Am.* 3.12.4 *quosue deos in me bella mouere querar?*,
Prop. 1.12.9, 3.18.8. This thought is quickly followed up in the pen-
tameter by the worry that she may unwittingly have committed some
crime, a sequence of thought imitated in 8.87–8 *quae mea caelestis in-
iuria fecit iniquos,* | *quod mihi (uae miserae!) sidus obesse querar?*

7–8 This couplet rounds off Oenone's expression of concern with
a general maxim. The thought that one must bear the inescapable is
a common topic of consolation literature: cf. *Am.* 1.2.10 *leue fit, quod
bene fertur, onus*, 2.7.11–12, Nisbet–Hubbard on Hor. *Carm.* 1.24.19,
Otto (1890) 134. That commonplace is subjected to a rational analy-
sis by Oenone, with the pentameter containing the conclusion that
an unjust burden need not be borne silently.

7 patiare: the present subjunctive is regular with the generaliz-
ing second person (H–S 419).

8 indigno: a dative of 'disadvantage'; the gender is masculine
because the statement is gnomic, not specific to Oenone (K–S 1 61).
For the articulation of the line with repetition of the verb, cf. 2.62.

9 nondum tantus eras 'you were not yet so important': Paris
had not yet been recognized as the son of Priam.

10 edita de magno flumine nympha: the participle has concessive force: 'though a nymph born of a great river'. Oenone was the daughter of the river-god Cebren (Parthenius, *Erot.* 4, Apollod. *Bibl.* 3.12.5). She inflates her status by not naming the river, which was in no way 'great'.

11 qui nunc Priamides: sc. *es*. Once acknowledged as Priam's son, Paris acquires a new patronymic, used here with exquisite irony by Oenone. The first syllable, short by nature, is lengthened for metrical convenience by Homer.

absit reuerentia uero 'let no deference to rank keep back the truth': a somewhat prosaic aside. *reuerentia* is found only at Prop. 3.13.13 among other Augustan poets, but was incorporated into the poetic language by O. (13 occurrences). The ablative *uero* is separative.

12 seruus ... seruo: the repetition of *seruus* in a different case (polyptoton, cf. H–S 707–8) underlines the harshness of Oenone's position; for slavery was not an idea treated lightly in ancient literature and Agelaus, to whom Priam gave Paris as a baby, was a slave. The words *seruus* and *ancilla* are rare in Augustan poetry (cf. McKeown on *Am.* 1.8.87) in spite of the wide use of slavery as a metaphor in love affairs by the elegists; cf. Lyne (1979). O. introduces an anachronistic note here: a contemporary would of course immediately assume that a shepherd would be a slave. In Roman law there was no such thing as a slave marriage, but an Augustan law of 18 BC, the *Lex Iulia de maritandis ordinibus*, legitimized marriage between slave-born and *ingenui*, while strictly barring such unions among the senatorial class; cf. *OCD*² s.v. 'marriage'.

nympha 'though a nymph': the noun has the force of a concessive participial phrase, but O. also plays on the meaning of Greek νύμφη 'bride'.

tuli with the infinitive (= *sustinui* 'deigned') is a rare construction, modelled on Greek ἔτλην; cf. *Fast.* 4.177–8 *spectare ruinas | non tulit*, *Met.* 2.628, Shackleton Bailey (1956) 153.

13–32 Oenone's description of her days with Paris is a compilation of topics from pastoral and elegiac verse. Shaded and grassy places are standard features of lovers' rendezvous; cf. Nisbet–Hubbard (1978) 52–3, Bömer on *Fast.* 2.315. In such a setting Tibullus imagines himself tending flocks, sharing his life with Delia: 1.1.27–8

sed Canis aestiuos ortus uitare sub umbra | arboris ad riuos praetereuntis aquae.
And in the later pastoral romance of *Daphnis and Chloe*, the two
young lovers share the shade of an oak as they watch their flocks
(Longus 1.13). Propertius depicts Aphrodite and Anchises in the same
setting on Mt Ida: *quamuis Ida Phrygem pastorem dicat amasse | atque inter
pecudes accubuisse deam*, 2.32.35–6. So celebrated had the story of Paris
and Oenone become in antiquity that a reader of Propertius under-
stood these lines as a reference to Paris, and his name has ousted
Phrygem (or its equivalent) from all the medieval MSS. Depictions of
Paris and Oenone in art regularly adopt this setting; for examples,
cf. Roscher III 786–91. O. perhaps also recalls Propertius' idyllic
description of love in a pastoral setting in the time before the
Trojan War: 3.13.35–8 *hinnulei pellis totos operibat amantis, | altaque
natiuo creuerat herba toro, | pinus et incumbens lentas circumdabat umbras; |
nec fuerat nudas poena uidere deas.*

13 requieuimus: cf. *Met.* 10.556–7, Aphrodite to Adonis point-
ing out a shady spot, *'libet hac requiescere tecum' | (et requieuit) 'humo'.*

arbore tecti: the verb *tegere* properly refers to the cover provided
by a roof; the image is thus one of dense shade. O. probably had in
mind such phrases as Virg. *Ecl.* 1.1 *Tityre, tu patulae recubans sub tegmine
fagi.*

14 praebuit herba torum: the phrasing is adopted from Greek
pastoral; cf. Theocr. 5.33–4 ὧδε πεφύκει ποία, | χά στιβάς ἆδε 'here
is grass and a couch'. O.'s usage made it into common poetic idiom:
cf. 4.98 *sustinuit positos quaelibet herba duos, Met.* 10.556 *datque torum
caespes.*

15 super stramen faenoque 'on straw and in a deep bed of
hay': with studied variation of the construction; cf. Hor. *Serm.* 1.4.26
ob auaritiam aut misera ambitione. The accommodations are an emblem
of rustic simplicity: cf. *Fast.* 1.205–6 on the early Romans, *nec pudor in
stipula placidam cepisse quietem | et faenum capiti supposuisse fuit.*

16 humili ... casa: not a picturesque cottage, but the simple
hut of a herdsman; cf. Virg. *Ecl.* 2.29 *humilis ... casas,* Tib. 2.5.26. To
endure such a life was a token of great love: cf. Tib. 2.3.27–8 *Delos
ubi nunc, Phoebe, tua est, ubi Delphica Pytho? | nempe Amor in parua te iubet
esse casa.*

defensa est 'was kept off'.

17–20 Oenone recalls how she accompanied Paris on the hunt as

a show of her devotion. This motif is a constant theme in elegy,
developed at length in one poem by Propertius (2.19.17–26) in
which the poet ironically asserts his courage to follow his mistress
anywhere, even if she chooses to go hunting. This theme is further
highlighted in elegy by the prominence accorded to one version of
the myth of the huntress Atalanta, according to which she was won
by the persistence of Milanion, who performed menial tasks for her
during the chase. This story forms an exemplum as the centrepiece
of the programmatic introduction to Propertius' first book (1.1.9–16)
and O. makes similar use of the myth at 4.99–100 and *Ars* 2.185–92.
It is not unreasonable to suppose that the prominence of this story
and its related motifs in the work of the surviving elegists is owed to
their predecessor, Cornelius Gallus, in whose poetry the story may
have figured prominently: cf. Ross (1975) 61–5. Oenone is constantly
portrayed by O. as the betrayed lover of elegy, and the reversal of
the standard roles of male and female is thereby emphasized by ref-
erence to the literary tradition.

17 saltus 'defiles': cf. *Met.* 2.498, 5.578.

18 The wild beast hides her cubs in the involved word-order: sc.
qua rupe suos catulos fera tegeret.

19 retia ... tetendi: handling the nets was a tedious and menial
chore undertaken by the lover as a sign of devotion; cf. *Ars* 2.189,
Met. 10.171, Virg. *Ecl.* 3.74–5, Tib. 1.4.49–50, [Tib.] 4.3.11–14.

comes 'as your attendant': cf. 4.103 *ipsa comes ueniam.*

maculis 'meshes': O.'s terminology is correct; cf. Var. *R.* 3.11.3
saeptum totum rete grandibus maculis integitur.

20 egi refers not to the leading of hounds on a leash, but driving
them before in pursuit of the prey; cf. Gratt. 214 *te siluis egit*, ad-
dressed to a hound.

iuga longa: the epithet, though conventional (Prop. 3.14.16), is
topographically correct here, since Mt Ida consists of a chain of
ridges; cf. 16.110 *longa ... Ida.*

21–30 Oenone now recalls with some bitterness how Paris had
carved her name on the beech trees and inscribed a dedication of his
love for her. O. adapts a celebrated motif of Hellenistic poetry: in
his narrative of the love-story of Acontius and Cydippe, Callimachus
included such a moment: fr. 73 Pfeiffer ἀλλ' ἐνὶ δὴ φλοιοῖσι κεκομ-
μένα τόσσα φέροιτε | γράμματα, Κυδίππην ὅσσ' ἐρέουσι καλήν 'but

on your bark may you bear so many carved letters as will say Cydippe is beautiful'. Although the practice is commonly referred to elsewhere, Propertius' adaptation in a poem in which he casts himself in the role of Acontius (1.18.22) is an indication of the celebrity that attached to Callimachus' amatory narrative. So, too, the appearance of this vignette in Gallus' lament in the tenth Eclogue (53) strongly suggests that he preceded Propertius in adapting this motif of Greek amatory verse to a Roman context (Ross (1975) 73). But O. is not simply exploiting an elegiac motif to portray Oenone as a lost lover; as often, he looks beyond his immediate model to an earlier source to incorporate a broader range of reference into the interpretative pattern. Readers familiar with the epithalamium composed by Theocritus for Helen and Menelaus will notice the irony in recalling that her companions will inscribe a tree in Helen's honour: 18.47 γράμματα δ' ἐν φλοιῶι γεγράψεται 'letters will be written on bark'.

21 incisae seruant a te: the prepositional phrase should be construed with *incisae*.

fagi: the beech tree is among those mentioned by Propertius that carry his inscription for Cynthia: 1.18.19–20 *uos eritis testes, si quos habet arbor amores,* | *fagus et Arcadio pinus amica deo.*

22 legor Oenone: the beech is inscribed simply with her name; cf. Prop. 1.18.22 *scribitur et uestris 'Cynthia' corticibus.*

23–4 This couplet follows v. 22 in most MSS, but is omitted in *P* and *G*, and may be suspected as an interpolation on two grounds. First, the line-ending *fluuiali consita riuo* anticipates the sense of 27 *consita margine ripae.* One of these phrases is likely to be an imitation of the other, and v. 23 is condemned by the tautology in *fluuiali . . . riuo* (Dörrie (1960a) 202–3) and the clumsy expression, which tells us that the tree was 'planted *in* the stream'. Second, the scansion of *littera* with a short open vowel before the consonant cluster *scr-* has no parallel in O.'s verse; cf. Platnauer (1951) 62–3. The interpolated couplet may have originated as a marginal annotation, which was inserted into the text by a reader who found the transition too abrupt from the beech trees that carry Oenone's name in 21–2 to the inscription on the poplar in 27–8.

25 crescunt: the conceit that carvings will grow in size as the trees grow is developed from Virg. *Ecl.* 10.53–4 *tenerisque meos incidere* *amores | arboribus, crescent illae, crescetis, amores.* But the articulation of O.'s line (*quantum … tantum*) recalls the original in Callimachus, *Aet.* fr. 73 Pf. τόσσα φέροιτε … ὅσσ' ἐρέουσι.

26 in titulos surgite recta meos 'grow straight to become my memorial': the use of *in* to denote the end or object was exploited by the poets, sometimes in quite novel ways; cf. 4.16 *figat sic animos in mea uota tuos*, H–S 274. *recta* would more properly refer to the inscription: the epithet is transferred (enallage, 1.10n.) to *nomina*.

28 rugoso: to describe bark, cf. *Met.* 7.627, Plin. *Nat.* 16.31. The adjective is rare in poets other than O.; for the form, cf. 1.9n.

carmen 'inscription': cf. 2.146, 7.194.

29–30 The 'text' of Paris' inscription is his oath to remain faithful to Oenone. It takes the form of the impossible conditions (*adynata*) that will have to occur before Paris breaks his vow. Such expressions are proverbial in both Greek and Latin (Otto (1890) 139), and were often used in literature; cf. Dutoit (1936). The *adynaton* of 29 is from the celebrated ode in Euripides' *Medea* (410) ἄνω ποταμῶν ἱερῶν χωροῦσι παγαί 'the springs of the sacred rivers go backwards'. For the use of *adynata* in lovers' oaths, O. might have thought of Prop. 1.15.29–30 *multa prius retro labentur flumina ponto, | annus et inuersas duxerit ante uices, | quam tua sub nostro mutetur pectore cura.* Other examples of the topos in O. are found at *Am.* 2.1.26, *Met.* 13.324, 14.38, *Trist.* 1.8.1, *Pont.* 4.6.45.

29 PARIS OENONE: the juxtaposition is pointed, and prepares for the poignant repetition in 32. O. uses the ablative in *-e* for this name since Greek does not have this case; cf. the Greek form of the accusative *Oenonen* in 32.

30 XANTHI: with the Simois, one of the two rivers designating the land of Troy; cf. Virg. *Aen.* 5.634 *Hectoreos amnis, Xanthum et Simoenta.*

VERSA RECURRET AQVA: this half-line is repeated in the present tense at *Am.* 2.1.26.

31 lymphae: for water, a poetic word otherwise reserved by O. for the *Met.* (9 occurrences); in his elegies it is used only here and *Med. fac.* 99.

32 sustinet: first attested with the infinitive in O. Such extensions of the use of the complementary infinitive are characteristic of poetry; cf. K–S I 675 and above 12n. The perfect *deseruisse* is not here simply equivalent to the present (aoristic): 'he has deserted her and endures it'.

33–40 Oenone traces her misfortune to the Judgement, when Paris was arbiter in a dispute among Athena, Hera, and Aphrodite over who was the most beautiful. The story was told in the *Cypria*, which formed part of the epic cycle attributed to Homer and dealt with events of the Trojan war before the point where the *Iliad* begins. Paris' award of the prize to Aphrodite, who induced him to steal Helen for his wife, was reckoned as the cause of the Trojan war (*Il.* 24.25–30); against this tradition Oenone views events from a personal perspective. A number of details are left out of Oenone's summary, partly because she only learned of the story from Paris. The Judgement of Paris was an important theme in Greek tragedy and was also commonly portrayed in art; cf. Stinton (1965), Clairmont (1951).

33 illa dies traces the evil to a specific moment, as in 7.93.

fatum ... dixit 'pronounced my fate': the expression has a formal and austere note; cf. *ES* 81 *legem dixere Sorores*, Hor. *Carm.* 3.3.57–8 *fata Quiritibus | hac lege dico*. The sense-pause after *dixit* in the fifth foot is uncommon in the hexameter of O.'s elegies (Platnauer (1951) 25), and lends emphasis to the repetition of *illa*.

34 pessima mutati ... amoris hiemps: a striking and original metaphor for the cooling of passion, 'the awful storm of changed love'; cf. *Rhet. Her.* 4.61 *hiemem fortunae*. The image is frozen in the patterned line (p. 33).

35 sumptisque decentior armis: the adjective and the ablative absolute take the place of an unreal condition, 'who would have been more lovely if she had put on armour'. A witty commentary by a Roman of Augustan times on a venerable Greek myth; the insult to Athena also suits Oenone's bitter tone.

36 arbitrium: a legal term for the settlement of a dispute, rare elsewhere in poetry, but occurring 23 times in O., though only here in the *Her.* The phrase *in arbitrium uenire* 'come under arbitration' is attested in Sen. *Dial.* 6.26.3, *Epist.* 13.1, Ulp. *Dig.* 21.1.31.13.

nuda applies to all three goddesses. Aphrodite's nudity during the Judgement was part of the tradition as early as Sophocles' satyr play Κρίσις 'The Judgement'. The notion that all three goddesses bared themselves for Paris may be first attested in Prop. 3.13.38 *nec fuerat nudas poena uidere deas* (see Fedeli *ad loc.*), but it was doubtless an earlier Hellenistic refinement of the myth; cf. 17.15–16 *et in altae uallibus Idae | tres tibi se nudas exhibuere deae*, *Ars* 1.247–8, Prop. 2.2.13–14, Lucian, *Dear. iud.* 9–10.

37 attoniti micuere sinus 'my heart fluttered in astonishment': 1.45n.

37–8 gelidusque cucurrit, | . . . tremor: a variation of a Virgilian phrase for 'cold fear', *Aen.* 2.120–1 *gelidusque per ima cucurrit | ossa tremor*, 6.54–5, 12.447–8.

38 narrasti: a syncopated form with a colloquial tone, as Cicero remarks in *Orat.* 157, but common in poetry; cf. Leumann (1977) 598–9, N–W III 478–500.

39 neque . . . modice: the understatement (litotes) is not uncommon in prose (*TLL* VIII 1236.79ff.), but is found only here in poetry.

consului: in most accounts of her story, Oenone is said to have had the power of prophecy and to have foretold Paris' disaster; e.g. Parthenius, *Erot.* 4.4, Apollod. *Bibl.* 3.12.6. This feature of the myth was surely traditional, but O. has eliminated it in order to portray Oenone as a woman reacting out of fear and jealousy; and so she consults sorceresses (*anus*) and seers (*senes*) to help her make sense of what has happened.

40 longaeuosque: 1.103n.

constitit esse nefas 'they all agreed that it was an evil portent'.

41–76 Oenone recounts her parting from Paris (41–60) at the dockside, and his return from Greece with Helen (61–76) in two carefully balanced and symmetrical vignettes. As Paris takes leave of her the two lovers dissolve in tears, a moment which is echoed ironically in 71–4 as Oenone retreats alone to the mountains to cry over her lost lover: cf. Jacobson (1974) 192–3. O. follows the outline of events in the *Cypria*, where the building of a fleet and Paris' journey follows immediately upon the Judgement. This accords with traditional accounts of Aphrodite's promise of Helen as bride in exchange for awarding her the prize. Here Oenone's leave-taking from Paris is depicted without any mention of Helen or of Aphrodite's bribe. No motive is assigned for his journey. O. means to portray

Paris as outrageously callous, concealing from Oenone the true rea-
son for his departure.

41–2 The building of the fleet is described in a fast-moving cou-
plet, with ellipse of the auxiliary verbs, culminating in a patterned
line representing the finished ship at sea awaiting the departure. The
building of the fleet figured prominently in the *Cypria*, and in the
Iliad the death of Phereklos, said to have been the craftsman who
fashioned Paris' ships (*Il.* 5.62–3 νῆας ... | ἀρχεκάκους 'the ships that
started the evil'), receives special notice. The identity of the ship-
builder was the subject of scholarly controversy in antiquity: O.
himself names Phereklos at 16.22, but sidesteps the issue here with
the passive verbs.

41 caesa abies traces the origins of Oenone's misfortune as far
back as the felling of trees on Ida for timber, a theme also found at
Euripides' *Medea* (3–4) where the nurse refers to the felling of trees
on Mt Pelion to make the *Argo*.

42 ceratas 'caulked' with wax. In antiquity wax was used to
water-proof ships' timbers; cf. D–S 1 2.1019. The unglamorous epithet
describes ships elsewhere only at *Rem.* 447 *non satis una tenet ceratas
ancora puppes*. The patterned line marks a pause as the scene is now
set for the farewell.

43 flesti: a syncopated perfect, 38n.

parce negare: a poetic equivalent for the prohibition with *noli*,
which is rarely attested in verse: Axelson (1945) 135, H–S 337.

44 'Your present love [for Helen] is the one to make you blush
rather than your past love [for me].' The implied connection with
the previous verse is that he denied crying at his separation from
Oenone out of embarrassment. This verse and the following hexa-
meter were deleted as spurious by Merkel, followed by Palmer 'on
account of epanalepsis and ineptitude'. But the verses are unobjec-
tionable in diction and metre, and the repetition (epanalepsis) of
flesti is not without rhetorical point: Oenone imagines that Paris
denies having been affected by their separation and she wishes to
emphasize the fact that he did cry.

iste pudendus amor: cf. *Fast.* 3.500 *ille pudendus amor*.

45 flentis: construe the genitive with *nostros* (= *meos*). The plural
possessive is unusual in this idiom, but cf. Cic. *Fam.* 2.11.1 *totum nego-*

tium non est dignum uiribus nostris, qui ... soleam. In the singular it is quite common: cf. *Am.* 1.8.108 *ut mea defunctae molliter ossa cubent;* K–S I 245.

ocellos: the diminutive is increasingly infrequent in Augustan elegy. This form is found 10 times in the *Amores*, but only here and 11.35 in the *Her.*, as opposed to 48 instances of *oculus;* cf. Axelson (1945) 42–3, Tränkle (1960) 28–9.

46 miscuimus lacrimas: a novel expression for mutual weeping; cf. Sen. *Ag.* 664 *lacrimas lacrimis miscere iuuat.*

47 uincitur uitibus ulmus: the 'binding' of vines to the supporting elm is a familiar motif in amatory poetry and epithalamia; cf. *Am.* 2.16.41 *ulmus amat uitem, uitis non deserit ulmum: | separor a domina cur ego saepe mea?,* Cat. 61.102–5, Hor. *Epist.* 1.16.3.

48 nexa: 2.141–2n.

collo: dative.

49 a quotiens: the combination is characteristic of elegy since Prop. 1.18.21, and often used by O., usually for pathetic effect, which is heightened here by the anaphora of *quotiens* in 51; cf. 16.241–3, *Am.* 1.13.27–8, 2.19.11–13. *a* is by itself a plaintive interjection of soft colouring. It is never used by the epic poets, but much affected by the neoterics and their elegiac successors; cf. Ross (1969) 51–3.

quererere teneri: a cacophonous complaint.

51 'How often did you send me away and then call me back for another kiss.' *repetere* may also have some of its proper legal sense of 'reclaiming' something lost; cf. *OLD* s.v. 9.

dimissae: a harsh word in this context, suggesting not only Paris' attempts to send Oenone away from the ship, but his desertion of her: *dimittere* is the regular word for divorcing a wife; cf. *Ars* 3.33 *Phasida iam matrem fallax dimisit Iason,* TLL s.v. 1210.69ff.

52 uix sustinuit dicere lingua 'uale': a standard component in departure scenes; cf. 13.14 *uix illud potui dicere triste 'uale'.* O. later reworks the motif in describing his own departure from Rome for exile: *Trist.* 1.3.57–8 *saepe 'uale' dicto rursus sum multa locutus, | et quasi discedens oscula summa dedi.*

53 lintea: 2.125n.

54 remis eruta 'churned by the oars': the metaphor, as Ruhnken (1831) 35 notes, is drawn from digging the earth; cf. *Am.* 3.8.43 *non freta demisso uerrebant eruta remo.*

canet: a poetic equivalent for *canescit,* coined by Virgil; in prose it is attested only in Tacitus; cf. 3.65 *canescant aequora remis.*

55 prosequor: the verb properly refers to escorting someone on a journey, with *oculis* forming a pathetic image less appropriately imitated at 12.55 *oculis abeuntem prosequor udis* as Medea watches Jason leave the room; cf. [Quint.] *Decl.* 12.6 *inde fugientia uela longo uisu prosecuti.*

56 qua licet 'as long as I can', referring to opportunity rather than distance; cf. *Pont.* 2.8.55 *nos quoque uestra iuuat quod, qua licet, ora uidemus.*

lacrimis umet harena: hyperbole, since we might expect the strand to be moist already. The verb *umere* belongs to the higher stylistic registers: it occurs only once in Tibullus among the other elegists and is elsewhere almost exclusively found in epic; cf. McKeown on *Am.* 1.14.34.

57 uirides: the sea-nymphs, like their father Nereus and other sea deities, take their epithet from the colour of the sea; cf. 9.14 *Nereus caeruleus, Trist.* 1.2.59, Hor. *Carm.* 3.28.10. Oenone, as the daughter of a river-god and thus a nymph herself, addresses her prayers to sympathetic divinities. *Nereidas,* with a short final syllable, is the Greek form of the accusative.

58 scilicet: searingly ironic. Her prayers for Paris' safety have availed another; the motif recurs in Hypsipyle's complaint, 6.75–8.

in mea damna 'to my loss': for this expression with *in* and the accusative of the object attained, cf. *Am.* 3.11.22, *Pont.* 1.2.44. At 1.96 the preposition has a different force (see n.). *damnum* is a legal term, 1.96n.

59 ergo: the particle conveys something of the indignation of Oenone by suggesting a long train of complaints which is left unexpressed. This rhetorical technique was adapted by the Roman poets from Greek predecessors, and Propertius and Ovid will open elegies with this or an equivalent expression, e.g. *igitur,* or *et merito;* cf. Norden (1927) 253, H–S 511. The short *o* is found in post-Augustan poets, but perhaps here first; cf. *Trist.* 1.1.87, Hartenberger (1911) 53.

alii rediture redisti: take *redisti* with *alii* and *rediture* with *uotis,* 'expected to return in answer to my vows, have you returned for the sake of another?' (Goold) The dative *alii* is very rare in non-dramatic verse; cf. Hor. *Carm.* 3.29.52, *Serm.* 2.2.135, 2.7.81, N–W II

535. O. sacrifices logic for the sake of the word-play. The attributive use of the future participle is cultivated for its brevity by the poets and by prose stylists of the Silver Age under the influence of poetic usage (H–S 390). Here it appears in the vocative in agreement with the addressee in the second person.

60 ei mihi: 2.106n.

dira 'dreadful', but suggesting also 'ill-omened', as Oenone recalls her initial apprehensions. *paelex* is a well-established Graecism (παλλακίς).

blanda 'persuasive': the topos recurs at [Sen.] *HO* 292–3 *uota, quae superis tuli,* | *cessere captae, paelici felix fui.*

61 aspicit 'faces': cf. 6.69 *circumspicit.*

moles natiua: a naturally formed breakwater, which, as the parenthesis explains, had been a crag (*mons*); cf. *Fast.* 5.149–50 *est moles natiua loco* ... | ... *pars bona montis ea est* and Caesar's description of the harbour at Oricum, *BC* 3.40.2 *ex altera parte* molem *tenuit* naturalem *obiectam, quae paene insulam oppidum effecerat.*

62 aequoreis: a poetic coinage, like many formations in *-eus* (Norden (1927) 218, Ross (1969) 60–3); O. found the phrase with *aqua* convenient: it occurs 20 times in his works.

63 prima: construe with *uela*, 'I recognized the sails first'.

64 mihi ... impetus ... fuit 'I had an impulse': with the infinitive, a construction apparently coined by O.; cf. 4.38 *est mihi ... impetus ire, Am.* 2.5.46, *TLL* s.v. *impetus* 610.5–9.

per fluctus ... ire: like Phyllis, 2.127.

65 fulsit mihi purpura 'a gleam of purple caught my eye'.

66 cultus non erat ille tuus: Oenone still thinks of Paris as a shepherd, and therefore not suited to the purple, the dress of royalty. Her fear, therefore, is at first only vague: she knows that Paris' ship carries another, she does not yet know whom.

67–8 fit propior ... uidi: the heightened tension in Oenone's recollection is conveyed by the parataxis in place of a subordinate temporal clause. When the ship finally reached shore (*terras ... attigit*), Oenone saw clearly that the stranger was a woman.

68 femineas: for the metrically impossible *feminae.* The use of an adjective in such instances is a feature of poetic style (Ross (1969) 60–3) even when metre permits the genitive (1.14n). The use of *genas* for 'face' is a unique extension of the meaning.

69 non satis id fuerat? 'was that not enough?': pluperfect for the imperfect, 1.34n. Most forms of the pronoun *is* are rare in poetry, 7.15n.

quid enim ... morabar: an aside that picks up 65 *dum moror*, 'Why indeed was I hanging about to see this?' *enim* is asseverative.

furiosa: 2.45n.

70 haerebat gremio ... tuo 'was clinging to your breast': their intimacy gives the game away; cf. Prop. 3.8.32 *ille* [sc. Paris] *Helenae in gremio maxima bella gerit.*

amica: a colloquial use for 'girl-friend' common in elegy; cf. 3.114, 3.150, 9.110, Reitzenstein (1912) 16n. 23. Here, it is uttered with a note of reprobation in the epithet; cf. 13.133 also of Helen, *turpis adultera.*

71–2 rupique sinus 'I tore my dress': a gesture of wild grief; cf. 6.27 *tunicis a pectore ruptis, Ars* 3.707–8. The use of *rumpere* in this sense appears to be O.'s innovation; cf. *OLD* s.v. 6c.

-que ... et ... | et: the polysyndetic combination suits the extravagant description of Oenone's reaction; cf. 10.5n.

pectora planxi: an alliterative combination favoured by O.; cf. 10.145, 11.91, 12.153, *ES* 113. The description is echoed, with similar articulation, in the mock tragic *Am.* 2.6.3–4 *plangite pectora pinnis | et rigido teneras ungue notate genas.* Beating the breast and scratching the cheeks were extravagant gestures of grief usually accompanying a funeral; see the passages collected by Pease on *Aen.* 4.673.

73–4 Oenone returns to Mt Ida, where she had lived with Paris and where the Judgement took place. There she fills the mountain, called holy (*sacram*) because it was home to a cult of Cybele, with cries of complaint. The excessive emotion is suggested by the associations of the mountain in cult, in which the ecstatic cries of female worshippers (*ululatus*) figure prominently: Cat. 63.24 *ubi sacra sancta acutis ululatibus agitant.*

73 Iden: accusative, a Greek form.

74 has lacrimas: the lamentations she has just described.

mea saxa: as a local nymph Oenone of course has a proprietary interest in the mountain, but the possessive pronoun also associates the landscape with her grief.

75 sic Helene doleat: imprecations against Helen by both Trojans and Greeks abound in Greek tragedy. In these cases she represents the cause of the war (Heinze (1915) 50); Oenone reduces this motif to a strictly personal level.

defectaque 'abandoned': for the construction with the simple ablative, cf. *Pont.* 3.4.37 *his ego defectus*, *TLL* s.v. 325.26ff.

77–98 Oenone compares herself to Helen: she was a better wife for Paris when he was only a shepherd, and she would make a better wife for him as a prince. For the first time, too, since the thinly veiled allusion at the opening of the epistle (1–2n.), she refers to the Greek expedition. She speaks of Hector as still alive and refers to the demand for Helen's return (91) in terms that suggest a setting before the actual outbreak of fighting, many years before Paris' death.

77–8 'The sort of women who would follow you across the open sea suit your taste': the plurals *quae* and *uiros* are generalizing, and so too is the subjunctive, although Oenone is of course referring only to Helen.

78 legitimos ... uiros 'lawfully-wedded husbands': a technical description; cf. 16. 285–6 *an pudet et metuis Venerem temerare maritam | castaque legitimi fallere iura tori?* The adjective *legitimus* is introduced to poetry by O., who uses it 16 times, another indication of his fondness for legal terminology; cf. Kenney (1969) 253. There is a pause after *aequora* in the pentameter, with the enclitic conjunction *-que* postponed to the second place in the new clause, a common affectation in O.'s elegiac style; cf. Platnauer (1951) 91–2.

79 pastor 'herdsman': not specifically a shepherd, and here it is a herd of cattle (*armenta*) Paris is said to tend. In appropriate contexts the noun by itself suffices to identify Paris; cf. Nisbet–Hubbard on Hor. *Carm.* 1.15.1.

80 Oenone: the name is used in place of the pronoun for pathos, a rhetorical device adapted to epic narrative by Virgil but at home in a variety of genres: cf. Norden (1927) 266. The repetition of *pauper* (polyptoton, 12n.) suits the note of indignation.

81–2 A rising tricolon in which each member repeats the simple notion that Oenone is not interested in Paris for his money by adding some detail. The repetition of the pronouns *ego ... me* is emphatic. In the pentameter, the *ut* clause comes with easy ellipse of a verb to be supplied from the context suggested by *miror ... tangit*.

81 tangit: cf. 2.89n.

tot: sc. *nuribus*. In the *Iliad* (24.493) Priam speaks of 50 sons, but the number was variously calculated in antiquity as mythographers eagerly hunted out the names of offspring not attested by Homer (Roscher III 2937–40). Virgil speaks vaguely of Priam's *centum* ... *nurus* (*Aen.* 2.501).

83–6 In an aside Oenone hastens to add that the status she rejects would not be out of proportion to her natural station.

83 non tamen ut 'not that': *ut* does not depend on *tangit* in 81, but on *non tamen*, and introduces a limiting clause; cf. Prop. 2.19.21 *non tamen ut uastos ausim temptare leones*, Cic. *Att.* 11.15.3 *non ut queas*, 14.17.4 *non ut deliberarem*.

84 aut Hecubae fuerim dissimulanda nurus 'or that I should have been ignored as a daughter-in-law by Hecuba': for this sense of *dissimulare*, cf. *Pont.* 1.2.145–6 *coniunx mea sarcina uestra est:* | *non potes hanc salua dissimulare fide.* The repetition of *nurus* from 82 is weak.

85–6 'And I am worthy of becoming a great lord's wife; my hands might well adorn a sceptre': providing the positive counterpart to the negative assertion in the previous couplet. Not only would Oenone not shame her parents-in-law, she would be an adornment as queen. Certainly Housman was right to reject the reading of the MSS (see app. crit.) here, which makes Oenone assert that she 'wants to marry a person of importance' only five lines after she has declared *non ego miror opes, nec me tua regia tangit*. A reader must have inserted the words *et cupio* to mend the text after the loss of a word, and Housman's *rerum* is the most plausible supplement. For the phrase, cf. *Fast.* 1.88 *populo rerum ... potente*, Lucr. 2.50 *reges rerumque potentes.* Oenone's phrasing is formal and stately: *matrona* in the sense of 'wife' is rare; cf. Hor. *Carm.* 3.2.7 *matrona tyranni.* In O.'s works it recurs only in the *Met.* and *Fast.* For the subjunctive in the pentameter, cf. 3.70 *est mihi, quae lanas molliat, apta manus.*

87 faginea ... fronde 'a bed of beech-leaves': the adjective *fagineus* is not 'poetic' like some other adjectives in *-eus* (62n.). It belongs to the agricultural lexicon (Cat. *Agr.* 21.5) and O. is the only poet who uses it; cf. Cato, *Agr.* 5.8 *frondem populneam, ulmeam, querneam caedito.* A bed of leaves is another rustic touch: Virg. *Ecl.* 1.79–80 *requiescere noctem* | *fronde super uiridi.*

tecum ... iacebam: a common euphemism for sexual intercourse; cf. Adams (1982) 177.

88 despice: Oenone asserts her worth in spite of the im-
poverished circumstances in which she lived with Paris, a moral
commonplace inverted by O. in the advice given by the bawd to
Corinna: *Am.* 1.8.63–4 *nec tu, siquis erit capitis mercede redemptus,* | *despice.*

purpureo … toro: i.e. a royal bed.

89 denique 'in short'.

tutus amor 'a risk-free affair', with the literal sense present also,
since Paris risks his life by his affair with Helen.

ibi 'therein': an idiomatic usage; cf. *TLL* s.v. 146.71ff.

90 bella: for the pause after an opening trochaic word, 1.56n.
bellum parare is a regular prose expression, but occurs first here in
poetry; cf. *Rem.* 2, *Met.* 7.456. It then passes into the standard
vocabulary of Silver Latin (Lucan, Statius, Silius).

91 Tyndaris … fugitiua reposcitur 'the daughter of Tyn-
dareus is reclaimed as a runaway': the patronymic, used for Helen
since Euripides, forms a memorable counterpoint to the contemp-
tuous *fugitiua*. This adjective, which is attested only here in Latin
poetry, is the proper legal term for runaway slaves; cf. *TLL* s.v.
1494.78ff. The patterned line (p. 33) lends emphasis to the point.

92 hac … dote: with heavy irony. Helen brought war as her
dowry, a topos exploited since Aeschylus, who characterized her (*Ag.*
406) as ἄγουσά τ' ἀντίφερνον Ἰλίωι φθοράν 'bringing destruction
to Troy as her dowry'. O. uses the topos again in Canace's epistle
(11.100n.); cf. *Ars* 2.155, *Met.* 5.15. Oenone sees herself supplanted by
an arrogant new mistress; *superbia* is a standard feature in the char-
acter of the elegiac mistress; cf. Knox (1986a) 21.

93–6 Oenone suggests that Paris consult the leaders of Troy
about the return of Helen. Each of those named here has been se-
lected by O. because of his hostility to Helen either in the Homeric
poems or in later traditions about the Trojan War. Details may have
been given in the *Cypria* during the embassy of the Greeks (Ἑλένης
ἀπαίτησις) following the landing as described by Proclus. In the
summary of the *Cypria* (*EGF* p. 32, 72–3) we learn of an embassy of
Greeks to Troy 'demanding the return of Helen and her posses-
sions'. O. seems to refer to this tradition in the *Met.* when he repre-
sents Odysseus debating with Ajax for the arms of Achilles: 13.200–1
accusoque Parin praedamque Helenamque reposco | *et moueo Priamum Priamo-
que Antenora iunctum*; cf. *Ars* 3.439–40 *Troia maneret,* | *praeceptis Priami si*

foret usa sui. This tradition of an embassy is acknowledged in the *Iliad*: 3.205–24, 11.139–40.

93 si sit ... reddenda: for the indirect question introduced by *si*, cf. 6.37, K–S II 426.

Hectora: mentioned first, both because he is Paris' eldest brother and because his fate is so intimately connected with his city's. No surviving tradition connects him with the demands for the return of Helen, but O. may have inferred his attitude from the reproachful words (αἰσχροῖς ἐπέεσσι) addressed to Paris by him in *Il.* 3.38–57 and 6.325–31. For the form of the accusative, 1.5n.

94 Deiphobo: Hector's favorite brother (*Il.* 22.233) and, according to post-Homeric tradition, Helen's husband after the death of Paris. Nothing in the tradition suggests that he ever proposed Helen's return, but O. may be hinting at the tradition followed by Virgil at *Aen.* 6.494–534, according to which Helen shared in the plot to take Troy and betrayed Deiphobus to Menelaus; cf. Austin on *Aen.* 6.518. Virgil represents a bitter and angry Deiphobus in the Underworld.

Pulydamanta: the son of Panthous, a priest of Apollo, born on the same day as Hector: *Il.*18.252 'but he was better in words, the other with the spear far better'. According to a post-Homeric tradition, represented by Q.S. 2.43–62 and Dares 27, and probably known to O., he also advocated the return of Helen. The first syllable of the name is long, reflecting the Homeric form Πουλυδάμας.

95 grauis Antenor: the 'Trojan Nestor' (cf. Eur. fr. 899 Nauck, Plato, *Symp.* 221c); in the *Iliad* he urges the return of Helen and the goods stolen with her (7.347–50).

Priamus: no testimony survives of Priam's counsel about demands for the return of Helen; indeed his name does not appear in summaries of the *Cypria*, although he can hardly have been denied a role in the negotiations. In Homer's account of the watch from the walls (*Teichoskopia*), Priam offers friendly words to Helen while the old men talk about her return (*Il.* 3.159–60).

96 quis = *quibus*, an archaism (Fedeli (1980) 228) used by O. in his amatory elegies only here and at *Ars* 3.342. The form was kept alive by poets and archaizing prose stylists; cf. N–W II 469.

aetas longa magistra: a variation on the proverb *usus magister est optimus*; cf. Otto (1890) 359.

97 rudimentum 'first essay': in pointed contrast with *magistra* in the preceding line. The word is rare in Augustan poetry, attested only once in Virgil (*Aen.* 11.157) and once more in O. (*Ars* 1.193).

98 arma mouet: a poetic equivalent for *bellum mouere* 'to start a war'; cf. Bömer on *Met.* 5.197. The expression *iusta arma* seems also to be based on the more common phrase *bellum iustum*, defined by Cicero (*Off.* 1.36) as war waged after a formal demand for restoration of damages has been made.

uir: her husband, Menelaus.

99–134 This section of the epistle takes the form of a denunciation (*psogos*) of Helen.

99 nec tibi, si sapias, fidam promitte 'and, take my advice, don't count on her fidelity': as Oenone grows more agitated, the language becomes less formal: *si sapias* (also found with indicative) is a colloquial phrase in strong assertions (Hofmann (1951) 134, 200); cf. 20.174, *Am.* 2.2.9, *Ars* 1.643, *Rem.* 372, 477, *Met.* 14.675, Prop. 2.16.7, *Copa* 29, Hor. *Serm.* 1.9.34. *sibi promittere* is also idiomatic: cf. *Met.* 11.576 *reditusque sibi promittit inanes*, 11.662.

Lacaenam 'the Spartan woman': a contemptuous mode of reference to Helen since Euripides, *Andr.* 486; cf. Norden (1927) 266.

100 sit ... uersa: the subjunctive is causal, suggesting that since Helen left Menelaus so quickly for Paris, he might suffer the same fate.

101 minor Atrides: Menelaus, the younger son of Atreus.

temerati foedera lecti 'the violation of the bond of marriage': a transferred epithet (enallage, 1.10n.). *temerare* is a strong word, defined (Paul. *Fest.* p. 201 Lindsay) as *uiolare sacra et contaminare*; in earlier poetry there is only an isolated occurrence in Virgil, but it is often used by O. of the violation of marriage; cf. 16.285 (Paris to Helen) *metuis Venerem temerare maritam*. The metaphor of marriage as a *foedus* is common in Roman erotic poetry; cf. Reitzenstein (1912) 9–36.

102 clamat: with the accusative almost 'to complain about', a usage familiar from comedy (see the examples collected at *TLL* s.v. 1252.76ff.), suggested also by the context, in which Menelaus plays the duped husband.

externo: not simply 'foreign' but 'of an interloper' as at 17.96, Prop. 1.3.44, 2.19.16; contrast Prop. 2.32.31 of Helen and Paris, *Tyndaris externo patriam mutauit amore.*

laesus: cf. *Ars* 1.687 *laesi . . . mariti.*

103–4 nulla reparabilis arte | laesa pudicitia est: Oenone formulates her warning in a gnomic statement, a variation of such proverbial expressions as *praeterita mutare non possumus* (Otto (1890) 286).

laesa pudicitia: a variation of more familiar expressions for the loss of virginity, this combination was apparently coined by O.; cf. Sen. *Con.* 1.2.18, and see 7.97n.

semel 'once and for all': cf. Hor. *Carm.* 3.5.29–30 *nec uera uirtus cum semel excidit | curat reponi.*

105 ardet amore tui: the metaphor of the fire of love (7.23n.) might by O.'s time seem trite, and so it is in Oenone's sarcastic question.

Menelaon: the Greek form of the accusative avoids an elision; cf. 17.249.

106 in uiduo . . . toro: 1.81n.

credulus: the gullibility of lovers was a commonplace in Roman love poetry; cf. Hor. *Carm.* 1.5.9 *qui nunc te fruitur credulus,* Prop. 2.25.21–2 *tu quoque qui pleno fastus assumis amore, | credule, nulla diu femina pondus habet,* and see 6.21n.

107 felix Andromache: the moving portrayal of her farewell to Hector at *Il.* 6.370–493 contributed much toward the making of Hector and Andromache into a model of conjugal affection.

certo . . . marito 'a faithful husband': the epithet is common in elegy; cf. Fedeli (1980) 303.

108 uxor . . . habenda fui 'I should have been married': a variation of the formula *uxorem ducere*; cf. *TLL* s.v. *habeo* 2408.53ff.

ad exemplum 'on the model of': a prosaic phrase, used once more by O. at *Pont.* 4.7.49, but not elsewhere in poetry (*TLL* s.v. *exemplum* 1347.47ff.).

109 leuior foliis: the phrase is proverbial (Otto (1890) 140) in this brief form, but is here treated to an Ovidian expansion in the pentameter; cf. *Am.* 2.16.45 *uerba puellarum foliis leuiora caducis.*

tum cum: 1.5n.

111 minus est in te . . . pondus 'there is less substance in you': the play on *pondus* echoes *pondere* in the preceding couplet.

summa . . . arista: the preposition is to be construed ἀπὸ κοινοῦ from *in te* preceding. In this line O. plays on the ancient etymo-

logy of *arista*, which is also suggested by *arida* in 110: Varr. *RR* 1.48.2
arista dicta, quod arescit prima.

112 leuis: the adjective is predicative with *riget*, 'becomes light as
it dries'.

  assiduis solibus usta: cf. Lucr. 5.251–2 *perusta | solibus assiduis*;
the expression is elsewhere found only in prose (and once in Persius)
in the singular. The plural is probably not simply poetic, but sug-
gests the effect of repeated days of sunshine.

113 nam recolo: cf.16.279, echoing the couplet's content and
articulation, *hoc mihi (nam repeto ...) ... | ... erat uerax uaticinata soror.*

  quondam: the occasion of this personal prophecy, not attested
elsewhere, is left vague. Since O. is apparently conflating material
from more than one source in his portrayal of Cassandra (*germana*),
this incident is perhaps his own addition to the story, although *recolo*
could signal allusion to a (lost) text.

  canebat: frequently used of prophetic utterance.

114 diffusis ... comis: the characteristic coiffure of a prophet-
ess; cf. Virg. *Aen.* 6.48 (the Sibyl) *non comptae mansere comae.*

  uaticinata: not entirely synonymous with *canebat*, for the word
might also suggest the wilder ravings of a *uates*; cf. Cic. *Sest.* 23 *eos ...
uaticinari atque insanire dicebat.*

115 The prophecy was presumably set in a time when Oenone
was still married to Paris and devoting herself to him (*quid facis?*), but
before Paris had set out on his expedition. It begins with everyday
aphorisms, but switches to the wilder oracular style in 117–20.

  quid harenae semina mandas?: a proverbial expression (Otto
(1890) 159), repeated with variation in the pentameter, for which cf.
17.139 *proscindere litus aratro*, *Trist.* 5.4.48, *Pont.* 4.2.16, Prop. 2.11.2,
Juv. 7.48.

116 non: construe with *profecturis*; cf. *Met.* 13.411 *non profecturas ten-
debat ad aethera palmas*, with Bömer's note. For the attributive use of
the future participle, cf. 59n.

117–18 Graia iuuenca uenit ... Graia iuuenca uenit: an
example of the so-called *versus serpentinus*, a couplet in which the first
hemistich of the hexameter is repeated as the second of the penta-
meter, a stylistic affectation illustrated by the opening of *Amores* 1.9,
*militat omnis amans, et habet sua castra Cupido: | Attice, crede mihi, militat
omnis amans.* O. is fond of this trick; cf. *Am.* 3.2.27–8, 3.6.61–2, *Rem.*

385–6, *Fast.* 4.365–6, McKeown on *Am.* 1.9.1–2, *ES* 213–14. Such repetitions need not be exact in order to achieve the desired emphasis, e.g. *Am.* 3.2.43–4 *sed iam pompa uenit, linguis animisque fauete;* | *tempus adest plausus: aurea pompa uenit, Ars* 1.699–700. In later Latin the trick becomes a mannerism: all six couplets of Mart. 9.97 are so constructed, and the *Latin Anthology* contains a series of 44 epigrams (25–68 SB) that employ this device.

117 Graia: the form is poetic; *Graecus* never occurs in epic and O. avoids it in the *Met.*; cf. Austin on *Aen.* 2.148.

iuuenca: the metaphorical use as a reference to young girls is found already in Hor. *Carm.* 2.5.5–6, where, however, it is easily suggested by the context: *circa uirentes est animus tuae* | *campos iuuencae.* O.'s Cassandra perhaps borrows this metaphor from Lycophron 102, where Cassandra refers prophetically to Paris as the 'wolf who seized the unwed heifer'. On the tendency of oracular language to represent human beings as animals, cf. Aesch. *Ag.* 1125–6, as Cassandra prophesies the murder of Agamemnon by Clytemnestra, ἄπεχε τῆς βοὸς | τὸν ταῦρον 'keep the bull from the cow'.

perdat: the subjunctive is final, 'to destroy'.

io: a ritual exclamation, only here in the *Her.*, uttered by Cassandra now under the influence of Apollo.

119 obscenam: O. mimics oracular language in playing off the two associations of the word, first 'ill-omened' (cf. Paul. *Fest.* p. 201 Lindsay *obscena dicta … quae mali ominis habebantur*), because it brings destruction to Troy, and second, 'immoral' because it carries the adulteress Helen. The plural *demergite* is addressed to no one in particular, and the Trojans in general.

121 uox erat in cursu 'she was still speaking': the half-line is repeated from *Am.* 1.8.109, and is found again at *Fast.* 5.245. The idiomatic phrase *in (medio) cursu* recurs at *Rem.* 119, 430, *Fast.* 6.362, *Met.* 10.401, 13.508, *Pont.* 4.11.18; cf. *OLD* s.v. 8b. The urgency of the moment is conveyed by the parataxis. Most MSS read *dixerat in cursu*, which Heinsius corrected without knowing of the reading of a late MS, Florentinus Riccardianus 489.

122 mihi 'for my part': the so-called 'ethic' dative.

deriguere 'stood on end': cf. *Fast.* 3.332 *hirsutae deriguere comae.*

123 a: 49n.

nimium: construe with *uera*, recalling Cassandra's own words in the *Agamemnon* of Aeschylus (1240–1): 'and you shall very soon call me too true a prophet (ἄγαν ἀληθόμαντιν)'.

124 saltus 'pastures': Oenone demonstrates that she has unravelled the riddle by returning to the animal imagery.

125 sit facie quamuis insignis 'no matter how lovely she is': construe *quamuis* with the adjective *insignis*; the subjunctive *sit* alone makes the concession.

adultera: like the masculine form (1.6n.) this word is avoided by the other elegists, but O. is not shy: he uses it 11 times while in the other Augustan poets it occurs only at Hor. *Carm.* 3.3.25, also of Helen, *Lacaenae . . . adulterae.* Oenone does not mince words.

126 socios ... deos: marriage gods; cf. *Am.* 2.11.7 *ecce fugit notumque torum sociosque Penates.*

hospite capta 'smitten with her guest': Paris was a guest in the house of Menelaus when he seduced Helen, a situation which O. makes much of in *Her.* 16–17. The ablative is instrumental; cf. 4.64 *capta parente soror,* 19.102, *Rem.* 554, *Fast.* 1.416.

127–32 According to an ancient tradition, before her marriage to Menelaus Helen was abducted by Theseus with the help of his friend Pirithous. He hid her at Aphidnae in Attica, but she was rescued by her brothers, the Dioscuri, who laid siege to the town during Theseus' absence. The story is widely attested, with much variation in detail: cf. *RE* Suppl. XIII 1162–73. O. mentions it often: in Paris' epistle to Helen (16.149–52) he represents Theseus as falling in love with Helen as she exercised in the nude in accordance with Spartan custom.

127 nisi nomine fallor: O., mindful of his characterization, makes the Phrygian Oenone hesitate over the details of Greek mythology; thus the hero of Athens becomes 'some fellow' (*nescioquis*) named Theseus. The aside has a conversational tone; cf. Cic. *Att.* 4.19.1 *nisi fallor.*

129 a iuuene et cupido 'from a man both young and eager': according to the prevailing account Theseus was about fifty (Plut. *Thes.* 31.32), but Oenone is drawing her own inference about his age.

uirgo: in epic verse *uirgo* is often only a synonym for *puella*, but in the single *Her.*, where it occurs four times (6.133, 12.83, 14.55), it always means 'virgin'. Most accounts of the myth make Helen out to be very young, seven years old (Hellanicus) or ten (Diodorus), apparently to counter allegations that Theseus raped her. A lively academic controversy developed over this question in antiquity among apologists for Helen, such as Isocrates. O.'s Oenone bases her argument only on probability and presses a charge denied by Helen in her reply to Paris' epistle: 17.25–6 *non tamen e facto fructum tulit ille petitum;* | *excepto redii passa timore nihil.*

130 amo: the unusual sense pause in the last foot of the pentameter (Platnauer (1951) 27) lends emphasis to the reply.

131–2 Oenone plays upon Paris' suspicions by voicing a sentiment likely to be shared by a man. Helen makes a more plausible case in her own defence: 17.21–4 *an, quia uim nobis Neptunius attulit heros,* | *rapta semel uideor bis quoque digna rapi?* | *crimen erat nostrum, si delenita fuissem;* | *cum sim rapta, meum quid nisi nolle fuit?*

131 uim licet appelles: O. repeats the half-line later, when he approaches the subject of rape from a straightforwardly male point of view in *Ars* 1.673–6 *uim licet appelles: grata est uis ista puellis;* | *quod iuuat, inuitae saepe dedisse uolunt.* | *quaecumque est Veneris subita uiolata rapina,* | *gaudet, et improbitas muneris instar habet.*

culpam nomine ueles: an echo, with deliberate irony, of *Aen.* 4.172 *coniugium uocat, hoc praetexit nomine culpam.*

132 totiens: twice, actually.

praebuit ipsa rapi 'of her own accord (*ipsa*) exposed herself to rape': the infinitive is prolative, an unusual construction found only in poetry; cf. Pers. 2.28 *praebet tibi uellere barbam*, Sil. 10.465. The expression here is condensed: the usual idiom would be *se rapiendam ipsa praebuit.*

133–46 Oenone's denunciation of Helen accomplishes two rhetorical objectives. First, it is likely to play upon Paris' suspicions (if he has any) about Helen's character. Oenone's explanation suggests to Paris that, far from obtaining the ideal marriage that motivated him to go to Sparta, he has fallen into the trap, familiar in elegiac verse, of a hopeless passion for a faithless mistress. The second major rhetorical objective then follows naturally; for Oenone then proceeds to highlight her own fidelity to their idealized relationship by cataloguing a number of would-be lovers whom she rejected before she met Paris, implying that she could have been unfaithful but chose not to be.

133–4 fallenti ... falli: the implication to be drawn from the word-play is that it would have been acceptable to cheat on a cheating husband, which O. positively asserts, again from the man's perspective, at *Ars* 1.645 *fallite fallentes*.

casta: with the dative almost = *fida*.

134 et 'and yet'.

legibus ... tuis 'on the terms you set': cf. 6.154.

135 Satyri: the nymph Oenone is pursued by woodland divinities, the Satyrs, who were associated with Pan, and portrayed as goat-like creatures; hence the epithet *celeres* because of their hooves.

136 quaesierunt: for the prosody, cf. 2.142n.

turba proterua: cf. Hes. fr. 123.2 M–W γένος οὐτιδανῶν Σατύρων καὶ ἀμηχανοεργῶν 'the race of worthless and unfit Satyrs', Nemes. 3.46 *cohors lasciua*.

137 cornigerumque: a poetic compound (2.84), describing the appearance of Faunus, an Italian woodland deity assimilated to the Greek god Pan; cf. 4.49 *Faunique bicornes*. For the accusative *caput*, 6.44n.

pinu: Pan has the same headgear at *Met.* 1.699 *pinuque caput praecinctus acuta*.

138 in immensis ... tumet ... iugis: an unusual locution, but topographically correct (20n.); cf. [Sen.] *HO* 775 *Euboica tellus uertice immenso tumens* and Lucan 4.11.

Ida: O.'s MSS usually have the Greek form of the nominative *Ide*, but the Latin form is required by the metre here and at 16.110.

139–46 Although all accounts of Oenone's story attribute to her the unique ability to heal Paris, no other source attributes this power to a gift from Apollo or refers to his rape of Oenone. If this episode was O.'s innovation, it derives from a familiar model. In Greek mythology compensation for lost virginity regularly follows rape by a god and it may take many forms: at *Met.* 14.133 the Cumaean Sibyl describes Apollo's offer of eternal youth and beauty. The graphic description of the rape has disturbed readers and editors, many of whom have followed Merkel in deleting 140–5, 'quorum iactura levis est, praesertim pueris' (Shuckburgh). But the resulting couplet 139/ 46 is unsatisfactory on a number of grounds, especially because it too casually dismisses the god's infatuation with Oenone, when O is at pains to show that she rejected all advances.

139 fide conspicuus 'resplendent with his lyre': for the construction of *conspicuus* with the ablative, of which O. is fond, cf. *TLL* s.v. 499.23ff.

Troiae munitor: Apollo; 1.67n. The noun *munitor* is not attested before Livy and occurs only here in poetry.

140 Palmer objects (in his note on 135) that this line directly contradicts 133, but Apollo's rape occurred before she married Paris.

spolium uirginitatis: a defining genitive (H–S 62–3); cf. 17.114 *spolium nostri ... pudoris.*

141 id quoque luctando 'and that too by a struggle': a very prosaic-sounding phrase for the addition of an attribute with emphasis, normally taking the form of *et is, atque is,* etc. (K–S I 619). For the infrequency of forms of *is* in poetry, cf. 7.15n.

rupi ... capillos: an Ovidian phrase for tearing hair; cf. 3.15 *rupique capillos,* 10.16, *Met.* 10.722–3. It is Apollo's hair that is referred to, and in the next line his face (*ora*) that is scratched; cf. 20.81–2.

142 aspera 'wounded': from the scratching; cf. 20.82 *oraque sint digitis liuida nostra tuis.*

143 stupri: originally a word meaning 'disgrace' in general, *stuprum* came to have a specialized reference to an illicit sexual act. In law it referred to illicit intercourse with an unmarried woman and was thus distinguished from adultery: *Dig.* 48.5.6.1 *proprie adulterium in nupta committitur ... stuprum uero in uirginem uiduamue committitur.* It is often used of a forcible violation, although not exclusively; see Adams (1982) 200–1. Oenone refers bluntly to sex in terms usually avoided in Roman poetry: *stuprum* occurs only four times in O.'s works, and is not otherwise common in Augustan verse.

gemmas aurumque: cf. Plaut. *Most.* 286 *amator meretricis mores sibi emit auro et purpura.*

144 turpiter ... emunt 'it is shameful to purchase': for the idiom, see 7.151n.

ingenuum ... corpus: the expression has a legal flavour; cf. *TLL* s.v. *ingenuus* 1546.24ff. Illicit sex with a free-born woman was very severely frowned upon: *Rhet. Her.* 2.30.49 *maius esse maleficium ingenuam stuprare quam sacrum legere.*

145 ratus dignam: sc. *me.*

medicas ... artes: cf. *Met.* 2.618 *medicas exercet artes,* 8.526, 15.629.

146 sua dona: the father of medicine was Paean (Hom. *Il.* 5.401, 5.899, Solon, fr. 13.57 West), whose functions were later absorbed by Apollo.

147 potens ad opem 'capable of helping': the construction with a preposition and noun is unusual, and is not attested again until late antiquity. It is a development of the more common usage *potens* with *ad* and the gerundive, for which see *TLL* s.v 286.6off., and may be paralleled by the unique instance with *in* at Petr. 89.14 *mens semper in damnum potens.*

medenti = *medico* ; cf. 21.14 *adiuuor et nulla fessa medentis ope.*

149–50 The topos of love as an incurable disease is first found in Latin poetry in Propertius 2.1.57–8, but it is far older than that, for it is attested in Theocritus (11.1–3) and in Greek Romance, drawing on earlier pastoral, as in Longus 2.7.7. O. gives the topic a new twist here in that Oenone has real medical powers. He uses the same approach in portraying Apollo as the healer unable to treat his passion for Daphne in *Met.* 1.523–4 *ei mihi, quod nullis amor est sanabilis herbis | nec prosunt domino, quae prosunt omnibus, artes.*

149 me miseram: accusative of exclamation, a colloquial construction much employed by O.; cf. 7.98, 17.182, 19.65, 19.121, 19.187, 20.133, *ES* 204, Knox (1986a) 56.

medicabilis: a rare word, attested only in O. (*Rem.* 135, *Pont.* 1.3.25) and few isolated occurrences until later antiquity. On O.'s fondness for new adjectives in *-bilis*, cf. McKeown on *Am.* 1.6.59, Linse (1891) 42–5.

150 deficior ... ab arte: the usual construction is with the simple ablative, but cf. *Fast.* 3.321 *perductus ab arte*, Caes. *BC* 3.64.3 *a uiribus deficeretur.*

prudens = *peritus*: cf. Nep. *Con.* 1 *prudens rei militaris* (= *peritus*), Phaedr. 1.14.11 *non artis ulla medicae prudentia.* The adjective has concessive force here, 'though skilled'.

151–2 The story of Apollo's infatuation with Admetus is adduced as a parallel for Oenone's helplessness before the power of love. According to the earliest versions, Apollo was made to serve as his slave for one year as punishment for killing the Cyclopes (Hesiod) or the sons of the Cyclopes (Pherecydes), but an erotic motivation is attested in Callimachus' *Hymn to Apollo* 48–9 'ever since the time when by Amphrysus he tended the yoked mares, fired with love (ὑπ' ἔρωτι κεκαυμένος) for young Admetus'. The story may well have had wider circulation in Hellenistic literature, and it is a familiar exemplum for the power of love in Latin elegy; cf. Solimano (1970). Tibullus retells the story at considerable length (2.3.11–30), and adds the comment, *fabula nunc ille est*; cf. *Ars* 2.239–40, *Met.* 2.679–85, [Tib.] 3.4.67–72. It is doubtful, however, that the exemplum is apposite here. The reference to Admetus as an example of the power of love over Apollo is hard to credit after Oenone has already cited herself in 139, and it breaks the train of logic that runs smoothly from 150 to 153. Accordingly, the couplet was deleted by Merkel. The interpolation probably had its origin in a marginal note, perhaps a quotation from another poet; it seems to have been composed under the influence of *Ars* 2.239–40 *Cynthius Admeti uaccas pauisse Pheraei | fertur et in parua delituisse casa.*

151 repertor opis: the inventor of the skill was Apollo (146n.), but *opis* is a difficult way to refer to medicine without further qualification, as above in 147.

Pheraeas: Thessalian, from the city Pherae.

152 fertur suggests a reference to a literary tradition; cf. Norden (1927) 123–4.

e nostro saucius igne: the metaphor of the fire of love is conventional (7.23n.), but the prepositional phrase for the instrumental ablative is anomalous; and *noster ignis* for 'the fire I now feel' is difficult.

154 deus: sc. Apollo.

auxilium 'cure': as often in the lexicon of medical terminology; cf. *OLD* s.v. 6. There is an ironic hint of Paris' fated death when only Oenone could have cured him, but the irony is O.'s not Oenone's, since O. does not follow the tradition that she had the gift of prophecy.

156 non ego cum Danais arma cruenta fero 'I do not bring a bloody war with the Greeks': a final ominous reference to the impending invasion of the Greeks; for the sentiment, cf. 89–90. O. perhaps hints at the version of the story attested in Lycophron, *Alex.* 58–60 in which Oenone sends her son Corythus to guide the Greeks to Troy. Here O. causes her to echo the last appeal of Dido to Aeneas carried by her sister Anna at Virg. *Aen.* 4.425–6: cf. 7.166n.

158 temporis: partitive genitive.

precor: the construction with the infinitive is rare; cf. 19.82, *Pont.* 1.7.6, Tib. 2.5.4, Val. Fl. 7.353, Plin. *Nat.* 18.131. The wish is also attributed to Oenone by Quintus of Smyrna: 10.425–7 'I had hoped to reach the celebrated threshold of life with him, worn with age but in eternal harmony.'

VI Hypsipyle Iasoni

The setting for O.'s letter from Hypsipyle to Jason is formed by the Argonauts' visit to the island of Lemnos, a story often retold in ancient mythographical sources (e.g. Apollod. *Bibl.* 1.9.17, Hyg. *Fab.* 15, 254). On their outbound voyage Jason and his crew landed at Lemnos, where the queen Hypsipyle ruled over a population composed entirely of women. Some time before, Aphrodite had punished the women of the island for their neglect of her cult by causing their husbands to reject them in favour of Thracian women captured from the mainland. In revenge the Lemnian women murdered the entire male population together with their foreign concubines. Hypsipyle alone saved her father Thoas, a fact not known to her subjects when the Argonauts arrived. The Argonauts stayed long enough to mix with the local female population, and Jason had an affair with the queen before departing to complete the retrieval of the Golden Fleece. O.'s epistle is set in the immediate aftermath of Jason's return to Greece with Medea as his bride; the character of Hypsipyle he draws from Apollonius.

A tradition associating Jason with Hypsipyle is known to Homer, who refers to Euneos as king of Lemnos and calls him the son of Jason and Hypsipyle (*Il.* 7.467–71). The story of the Argonauts' visit to Lemnos was also the subject of tragedies by Aeschylus (frr. 247–8 Radt) and Sophocles (frr. 384–9 Radt), but we know nothing of how they treated the story. Substantial portions of Euripides' *Hypsipyle* survive, but this play treats the adventures of the Lemnian queen well after her affair with Jason, when her fellow countrywomen discover that she did not actually kill her father in the mass execution of males. O.'s epistle clearly is based on the account of the myth given by Apollonius of Rhodes in the first book of his *Argonautica* (609–909). In particular, O. plays off the parting scene of Jason and

Hypsipyle: several reminiscences in the text are developed to under-
score the ironies in Jason's promises of fidelity (e.g. 59n.). Readers
will note also some significant departures from the outlines of the
story as set out by Apollonius (56–7, 59–60, 61–2 nn.). In some in-
stances O. may be drawing on alternative traditions about Jason's
visit to Lemnos which have left traces elsewhere in the literary
record; cf. *RE* IX 437–9. It is also possible that O. was drawing on
the extremely influential Latin version of the *Argonautica* by Varro of
Atax, which may have diverged from Apollonius on some points (*Am.*
1.15.21–2, *Ars* 3.335, *Trist.* 2.439). But in one important respect O. is
plainly pursuing his own course by insisting throughout the epistle
that Jason was married to Hypsipyle (41–6n.). In Apollonius' ac-
count they were never married, although marriage is *implied* at some
places in the text of the *Argonautica* and it is also suggested elsewhere
in the tradition. That was enough for O., who developed these sug-
gestions into a basis for portraying Hypsipyle as another manifes-
tation of a strong-willed woman undone by her infatuation for an
unworthy hero.

1–8 The first four couplets form the salutation, naming recipient
and sender. The identification of Jason in the first couplet is oblique:
he is the gentleman who returned to Thessaly with the Golden
Fleece. The salutation is not complete until line 8 when Hypsipyle
names herself, although her identity could already be guessed in 5.

1 reduci ... carina 'your ship safely returned': by the familiar
poetic synecdoche of *carina* 'keel' for *nauis* 'ship', O. renders the pro-
saic idiom found at, e.g., Livy 21.50.6 *una tantum perforata naui sed ea
quoque ipsa reduce*, 22.60.13.

2 diceris: emphasized by its position at the beginning of the
pentameter, where it completes the predicate constituted by the
hexameter. The tone thus achieved by the *passive* verb is scathing:
Hypsipyle has heard the news of Jason's return from somebody else.

uellere diues 'enriched by the fleece': the construction with the
ablative is common in poetry, but infrequent in prose.

ouis: the creature that carried Phrixus to Colchis was a ram (cf.
49 *aries*), but it is often called by the generic term 'sheep': e.g. 12.8
Phrixeam ... ouem, Am. 2.11.4, Prop. 2.26.6.

3 gratulor incolumi: the adjective is proleptic, 'I congratulate you on your safe return', expressing a familiar sentiment in a welcome-home note: cf. the opening of Cic. *Fam.* 13.73.1 *gratulor tibi quod ex prouincia saluum te ad tuos recepisti.*

quantum sinis: 'i.e. you keep me so much in the dark ... that you seem unwilling even to allow me to congratulate you' (Palmer).

3–4 hoc tamen ipsum | debueram ... certior esse 'yet I ought to have been informed of this very thing': the construction *hoc certior esse* = *hoc scire* might be explained by analogy with expressions like *auctor sum* = *suadeo*, governing an accusative at Cic. *Att.* 13.402, *Fam.* 6.8.2, as suggested by Housman (1899) 174 (= *Class. pap.* 473). But it seems more likely that *certior esse* = *certior fieri* and the accusative *hoc* is retained as an abbreviated form of the regular construction with the accusative and infinitive. In poetry the positive form *certus* is more common than the comparative (e.g. Prop. 1.6.36, Val. Fl. 1.58, Sil. Ital. 11.57, Virg. *Aen.* 3.179), but O. does use the more prosaic *certior* in works of epistolary nature: cf. *Trist.* 3.14.44, *Pont.* 1.2.6.

5 pacta tibi 'pledged to you as my marriage portion' (Palmer): 2.4n.; cf. Virg. *Aen.* 10.649 *thalamos pactos.* In the *Argonautica* of Apollonius, Hypsipyle offers the kingship of Lemnos to Jason at their first meeting without any mention of marriage (1.827–9) as part of a strategy to protect the island; but when she later reiterates her offer (1.890–4) at the moment of parting, it is clear that she means it as an offer to marry, which Jason tacitly declines.

praeter suggests that while she did not expect him to stay, a stop at Lemnos on the homeward voyage would have been in order.

6 uentos non habuisse potes: sc. *secundos* : 'you may not have had fair winds'.

7 quamlibet: concessive with the adjective *aduerso* in ablative absolute: 'however adverse the wind may be'.

signatur properly refers to the seal affixed to a letter, not the writing of one.

8 Hypsipyle: naming herself explicitly for pathos; 5.80n.

missa ... salute 'the sending of a greeting': the so-called '*ab urbe condita* construction' in which a participial phrase takes the place of a verbal noun. For details, see H–S 393–4, K–S 1 766–8.

9–54 Hypsipyle reveals how she learned of Jason's return to Iolcos from a third party. She had already heard reports of his succesful exploits in Colchis and so might have expected him to return to Lemnos, even though she has also heard rumours of his intended marriage to Medea, rumours which she did not credit. Her fears, however, are confirmed by the chance arrival of one of Jason's countrymen, who unwittingly divulges the crucial information – and provokes this epistle. This portion of the poem is skilfully designed to evoke the narrative background of the Argonauts' adventure and offers a fresh development of the character drawn from the Apollonian tradition: without yet altering any of the details, O. represents Hypsipyle as a woman deeply affected by her encounter with the visiting hero. The suggestions in Apollonius' narrative that this was a true love affair are made explicit, at least from Hypsipyle's point of view.

9 nuntia uenit: the adjective is predicative, 'came with word'.

10 isse: this and the following infinitives (11 *adolesse*, 12 *eguisse*, 13 *seruasse*, 14 *rapta esse*) are governed by the implied indirect statement following 10 *fama … uenit*. Hypsipyle now recounts the three tasks completed by Jason in Colchis for Aeetes, while pointedly understating his role in accomplishing them.

Marti … boues: the fire-breathing bulls, which Jason had to use to plough the field. No source records that the bulls were sacred to Mars, though that might be inferred from A.R. 3.409, where they are said to inhabit the Plain of Mars. According to Apollod. *Bibl.* 1.9.23 they were a gift from Hephaestus.

panda: i.e. *curua*. O. repeats the second half of the line from *Am.* 1.13.16, which is in turn a variation of Tib. 1.10.46 *duxit araturos sub iuga curua boues*.

11–12 Jason's second trial required him to sow the freshly ploughed field with the teeth of a dragon. The tradition prevailing since the fifth-century BC logographer Pherecydes (*FGrH* 3 F 22), and followed by Apollonius (3.1183–90), was that Athena gave to Aeetes half of the teeth of the dragon slain by Cadmus at Thebes. From these teeth there grew immediately a crop of armed men, whom Jason tricked into killing one another by the same device as Cadmus, tossing a stone in their midst.

11 segetes … uirorum 'crops of men': at line-end, *uirorum* comes as something of a paradox, for the language up to that point is strictly appropriate to agriculture (cf. Virg. *Geo.* 1.104 *iacto …*

semine), but this 'harvest' is of men. An unattributed fragment of a Latin tragedian quoted by Charisius (*GLK* I 284.19, 286.7) is generally assigned to Ennius' *Medea Exul* (*Sc.* frr. 274–5 Vahlen², cf. Jocelyn, p. 350) *non commemoro quod draconis saeui sopiui impetum,* | *non quod domui uim taurorum et segetis armatae manus.* This must have been spoken by Medea with an eye on Eur. *Med.* 476 θανάσιμον γύην. O. reuses the phrase in a different setting in his story of Cadmus, *Met.* 3.110 *crescit . . . seges clipeata uirorum.*

adolesse 'reached maturity': a syncopated perfect infinitive (5.38n.) from *adolesco*, sometimes used metaphorically for plant growth, employed here with light verbal humour.

12 inque necem 'for their slaughter' (*OLD* s.v. *in* 21c).

13–14 The climax of the expedition was the theft of the Fleece, which was accomplished when Medea charmed the guardian serpent to sleep. Hypsipyle's summary of the events gives only the barest details, leaving the reader unclear at this point whether she suppresses or is ignorant of the role played by Medea in Jason's feats. We learn more about what Hypsipyle has heard in 97–104.

13 peruigilem ... draconem: the enclosing word-order reflects the sense, as the serpent protects the fleece. The adjective *peruigil* occurs first in this passage and is later limited almost exclusively to poetry; it may be an Ovidian coinage: cf. *Met.* 7.149 *peruigilem superest herbis sopire draconem.*

spolium 'hide': the original sense of the word (cf. Ernout–Meillet (1960) s.v.), attested primarily in poetry; cf. 4.100 *ferae spolium*, 9.113 *spolia . . . leonis*, Lucr. 5.954 *spoliis . . . ferarum.*

14 uellera fulua 'the Golden Fleece': cf. *Am.* 2.11.4 *conspicuam fuluo uellere . . . ouem*, *Ars* 3.335–6 *fuluis insignia uillis* | *uellera.*

15 o ego: although the poetic combination *o ego* is generally rare, it is fairly common in O.'s verse; cf. *Met.* 8.51–2, where it also introduces a conditional clause expressing a wish, *o ego ter felix, si . . . possem*, Bömer on *Met.* 2.520. The MSS divide between *haec* and *hoc* in place of *o*, which is Heinsius' conjecture; but both of the transmitted readings pose difficulties since a line bracketed by two demonstrative pronouns referring to the same object is impossibly awkward for O. The hiatus after *o* is common; cf. 1.5n.

timide credentibus ista 'those who hesitate to believe these things': cf. *Ars* 2.143 *timide confide figurae.*

16 quanta forem 'how grand I should be.'

17–18 'Why do I complain that as my reluctant husband you have failed to perform your duty? I have received a great indulgence if only I remain yours.' The contrast between the marital obligations (*officium*) due to her but unfulfilled and a lover's attentions (*obsequium*) is pointed and heavily ironic. Since O. ignores the tradition that Jason did not marry Hypsipyle, the question arises what his obligation as a husband was. Of course, it is implied here that Jason had an obligation to write, but in the context of marriage, *officium*, a rare word in Augustan poetry (see McKeown on *Am.* 1.9.9), refers to the legal obligation of intercourse and procreation (*TLL* s.v. 520.30ff.). In the pentameter Hypsipyle uses the less forceful *obsequium*, a stock term in the vocabulary of the elegists for the indulgences freely granted by a lover: cf. Smith on Tib. 1.4.40 *obsequio plurima uincit amor.* Hypsipyle is willing to discount Jason's dereliction if he still regards her as his lover.

lenti: 1.1n.

19 barbara ... uenefica 'a foreign sorceress', as O. refers to her elsewhere: *Am.* 3.7.79 *Aeaea uenefica, Met.* 7.316. *ueneficus* and *ueneficium* (150n.) refer to any form of witchcraft, not just poisoning.

narratur 'there is talk': the passive construction is deliberately vague: Hypsipyle has only heard rumours.

20 in ... parte recepta tori 'admitted to a share of the bed promised to me': we would expect *in* and the accusative, but the ablative here is sanctioned by the analogy of Virg. *Aen.* 4.374 *regni ... in parte locaui*; cf. *Ars* 1.566 *erit in socii femina parte tori.* The word-order is of a type not uncommon in O.: e.g. *Rem.* 610 *inque suae portu ... salutis, Trist.* 2.295 *in magni templum ... Martis*; cf. Platnauer (1951) 102.

promissi: promised when they married; once again O. stresses a point not recorded elsewhere in the tradition.

21 credula res amor est: lovers are quick to credit malicious gossip out of jealousy, a common theme in amatory verse, for which O. cites as example in the *Ars Amatoria* (3.684–6) the story of Cephalus and Procris: *nec sis audita paelice mentis inops, | nec cito credideris: quantum cito credere laedat, | exemplum uobis non leue Procris erit.* At *Met.* 7.826, where O. relates that story in full, he repeats the present half-line verbatim. The phrasing is a familiar idiom, perhaps colloquial: cf. 1.12n. and the examples collected at *OLD* s.v. *res* 2a.

22 insimulasse: a legal term (Paul. *Fest.* p. 111 Lindsay '*insimulare*' *crimen in aliquem confingere*), used only by O. among poets after Lucilius, attested here and *Am.* 2.7.13 *nunc temere insimulas.*

23–5 The sentence is arranged in parataxis, 'scarcely had he arrived (*uenerat*) when …' This construction is known to the grammars (H–S 623–4) as *cum inversum*, in which the principal idea is carried by a temporal *cum* clause after a main clause with a pluperfect or imperfect indicative. O. makes particular use of it in fast-paced narrative, often while suppressing the subordinating conjunction *cum*, as he does here: cf. Haupt–Ewald on *Met.* 8.83.

23 Haemoniis: i.e. Thessalian. Properly Haemonia designates only a part of the country, otherwise known as Pelasgiotis (*RE* VII 2219ff.), but in Roman poetry it is simply a synonym of Thessalia.

24 uix bene means little more than *uix*, and the combination is virtually unique to O. (*TLL* s.v. *bonus* 2125.29ff.). He uses it often to introduce the so-called *cum inversum* construction.

25 dixi: where *cum dixi* might be expected; cf. *Fast.* 5.278, *uix bene desieram, rettulit ille mihi,* 6.513, *Met.* 2.47, 3.14–15, 11.260, 14.753–4.

25–6 ille … humo: the demeanour of the Thessalian visitor (*Thessalus hospes*, which might well describe Jason) is described in terms that evoke Apollonius' description of Jason on his way to meet Hypsipyle for the first time: A.R. 1.784 ὁ δ᾿ ἐπὶ χθονὸς ὄμματ᾿ ἐρείσας 'with his eyes fixed on the ground'.

25 Aesonides: Jason, the son of Aeson.

quid agit: a conversational expression for 'How is he?'; cf. Plaut. *Trin.* 51, Hor. *Serm.* 1.9.4, among many examples at *TLL* s.v. *ago* 1380.21ff. Initially at least, Hypsipyle feigns casualness, but the reluctance of the stranger to speak then provokes a passionate outburst.

26 haesit 'hesitated'.

opposita … humo 'the ground in front of him': cf. *Met.* 13.541 *aduersa figit modo lumina terra.*

lumina fixus: cf. Virg. *Aen.* 11.507 *oculos horrenda in uirgine fixus,* *Am.* 3.6.67 *oculos in humum deiecta modestos.* The accusative is direct object after a 'middle' participle, i.e. one which indicates an action performed upon the subject. This native Latin construction is sometimes confused with the true accusative of respect ('Greek' accusative) with passive constructions. See H–S 36–8, K–S I 291, Löfstedt (1933) 421–2.

27 exsilui 'I sprang up': indicating violent emotion; cf. *Ars* 1.115 *protinus exsiliunt animum clamore fatentes.*

tunicisque a pectore ruptis: 5.71n.

28 fata uocant: a Virgilian phrase; cf. *Aen.* 10.471–2 *etiam sua Turnum | fata uocant.* The expression is only found in poetry, and at *Phaed.* 115a Plato refers to the equivalent phrase in Greek (ὅταν ἡ εἱμαρμένη καλῆι) as an example of tragic diction. It suits Hypsipyle's sense for the melodramatic in this epistle.

29 timidus; timidum: the repetition at the beginning of a new clause of the same word that concludes the preceding clause (anastrophe) is a favourite figure in O.; cf. McKeown on *Am.* 1.2.41. The stranger speaks timidly, without looking her in the eye (25–6), so Hypsipyle forces him to swear to it. The reading of E, *timidum quod amat*, is adopted by some editors, who interpret 'a lover is a timid thing' (Shuckburgh) and compare the sentiment uttered by Penelope at 1.14. The thought would be apt here, but though *quod amas* and the like for 'beloved' are common, it is incredible that O., or any other Roman writer, should understand *quod amat = amator*. It is preferable to accept Heinsius' explanation that *timidum* was omitted because of the repetition (haplography).

31 ut rediit animus 'when my composure was restored': cf. 13.29, *Ars* 3.707, *Fast.* 3.333, 5.515. The final syllable of *rediit* is scanned long, reflecting the earlier quantity of the vowel in the 3rd person singular of the perfect, obsolete by Augustan times. In his elegiac verse O. strictly limits this licence to verbs that form their perfect in -*i(u)i*, such as compounds of *eo* or *peto*; cf. Platnauer (1951) 60–1. An apparent exception to this practice is 9.141 *occubuit*: if that poem is not by O., its author perhaps did not feel bound by O.'s self-imposed restraint.

32–8 O. has already given us a summary of the labours of Jason in 10–14, but the repetition (if it may be so called) is not out of place: by recreating the excited account of Jason's heroics by the stranger, O.'s Hypsipyle is able to juxtapose her own distress, *uulnera nostra* (40), with Jason's successes.

32 et = *etiam*, qualifying *arasse.*

aeripedes: cf. 12.93, *Met.* 7.105, Val. Fl. 7.545. The compound reproduces the Greek χαλκόπους 'with feet of bronze', used as an epithet for the bulls in Apollonius' *Argonautica* (3.410, 3.496). According to traditions found in Pherecydes (*FGrH* 3 F 112) and Pindar (*Pyth.* 4.225–6), the bulls of Aeetes had hooves of bronze and breathed fire. That the bulls were actually fashioned of bronze by Hephaestus for Aeetes appears to be an innovation added by Apollonius (3.230). In the Homeric epics the epithet χαλκόπους is a figurative description of an animal's hooves; it is this usage that is reflected in Virgil's description of the hind of Cerynaia, *aeripedem ceruam* (*Aen.* 6.802), copied by Silius Italicus 3.39.

33 uipereos: a poetic formation for the regular (unmetrical) prose form *uiperinus*, which cannot scan in elegiacs; cf. Norden (1927) 218. The extension of the adjective to apply to dragons in addition to ordinary snakes is O.'s innovation; cf. *Met.* 3.102–3 *iubet supponere terrae* | *uipereos dentes, populi incrementa futuri*, 4.573 on Cadmus' dragon, and *Met.* 7.122 on Jason's.

34 subito: construe with *natos*, 'and men suddenly sprung forth'.

35 terrigenas populos: the adjective is a poetic compound, first attested in Lucretius, and used by O. especially to refer to the men sprung from the teeth of Cadmus' or Jason's dragon; cf. 12.99, *Met.* 3.118, 7.36, 7.141.

ciuili Marte 'civil war', because the earth-born men all have the same parent; cf. *Met.* 7.142 *ciuilique cadunt acie*.

36 implesse ... suae 'fulfilled the fates of their lives in a day': an interesting phrase. *diurnus* 'lasting a single day' is unusual but paralleled by Cicero (*Tusc.* 3.65) *luctum lacrimis finire diurnis*, translating Hom. *Il.* 19.229 ἐπ' ἤματα δακρύσαντας, and Man. 1.184. For *fata implere* 'to complete one's allotted span of life', cf. *Trist.* 4.10.77 *complerat genitor sua fata*.

37–8 These lines follow awkwardly on the previous couplets and most editors would agree with the substance of the characterization by Housman (1897) 105 (= *Class. pap.* 385) of lines 37–8 as 'a shameful interpolation, ungrammatical in language, inept in sense, and destructive of coherency'. His admiration for 35–6, 'no better written couplet in all his works', is perhaps a bit excessive, but there is no good reason to consider it or any preceding couplets as part of the interpolation as some editors have. O. breaks off the narration at this point, leaving the reader to infer the missing details from *singula dum narrat*.

37 deuictus serpens: a fragment of a more complete phrase.

38 alternant ... uices 'change places': the reading of the MSS, *fidem*, produces a meaningless phrase which should probably not be attributed even to an interpolator. Bentley restored *uicem*, but the idiom requires the plural: cf. *Met.* 15.409 *alternare uices*, [Virg.] *Moret.* 29 *alternatque uices*.

39 studio cursuque 'in the rush of his excitement': hendiadys.

40 ingenio ... suo 'unconsciously': i.e. *sponte*, an older use, as we learn from Nonius 323.1 *'ingenio' ueteres dixerunt et sua sponte uel natura*.

uulnera nostra 'the wounds I suffer': the possessive pronoun functions like an objective genitive. The metaphor of the 'wounds of love' is as old as love poetry, with examples from the earliest Greek lyric; cf. Lucke on *Rem.* 623. Hysipyle returns to it in v. 82.

41–6 Earlier in the epistle Hypsipyle's remarks could have been construed as only a promise of marriage (5, 20nn.); she now asserts that they were in fact already married, a position she maintains through the remainder of the letter (60, 111–12, 134, 163). This contrasts starkly with the tradition found in Apollonius, where Hypsipyle's offers of kingship and, by implication, marriage (1.827–9, 888–98) are declined. By making Hypsipyle insist upon this liaison as a marriage, O. places Jason in a harsh light: the relatively calm departure depicted by Apollonius is transformed by O. into a betrayal of trust, a recurring pattern in these epistles whose heroines in turn betray no sympathy for the hero's traditional values.

41 heu, ubi pacta fides?: 2.31n. For the hiatus, cf. 1.5n.

conubialia: the adjective appears for the first time here in Latin and is not used again by O. If it is an Ovidian coinage, its failure to win acceptance (it is attested only rarely in Latin verse, never in prose) may be due to hesitation over the scansion: 2.81n. The metrical difficulties posed by this and other synonymous forms (e.g. *coniugalis*) perhaps led to O.'s experimentation with *socius* and *socialis* (2.33n.) to deal with the subject of marriage.

42 faxque ... rogos: 2.120n. The contrast between wedding and funeral torches is a commonplace: cf. *Rem.* 38, referring to Cupid's torch, *non tua fax auidos digna subire rogos*, Prop. 4.11.46, Erinna, *AP* 7.712.

43 non ego sum furto tibi cognita 'I was not your clandestine lover': *furtum* is a metaphor especially common in poetry for illicit sexual intercourse (Adams (1982) 167–8), while *cognosco* is a well-established Latin euphemism for carnal knowledge (Adams (1982) 190); cf. *Am.* 2.8.3 *mihi iucundo non rustica cognita furto.* Hypsipyle's statement here accords with the 'facts' of the tradition: the Argonauts were welcomed by the Lemnian women, but in the traditional world of myth such conduct did not necessarily require marriage.

pronuba: at first Hypsipyle thinks of a marriage attended by Juno, who presided over weddings, but like Phyllis (2.117n.) she realizes now that it was one of the Furies who came.

44 Hymen: personified as a god of marriage, from the Greek Ὑμήν, originally a wedding refrain of uncertain meaning.

sertis tempora uinctus 'his brows bound with wreaths': cf. Cat. 61.6, addressed to Hymen, *cinge tempora floribus.* The retained accusative with a perfect passive participle is a poetic usage, extended to prose of the Augustan period (H–S 36–8).

45 nec Iuno: introduces the topos of the ill-omened wedding (2.117n.), with a list of gods who did *not* attend the wedding. This formulation is repeated in O.'s description of the wedding of Procne and Tereus at *Met.* 6.428–30: *non pronuba Iuno, | non Hymenaeus adest, | non illi Gratia lecto. | Eumenides tenuere faces de funere raptas.* The theme of an ill-omened wedding is found in a fragment of Euphorion (*CA*, p. 29, fr. 4), but a closer parallel is found in the *Hero and Leander* of the fifth-century poet Musaeus, where the thought is similarly articulated (275–9): 'none glorified Hera the union-maker (οὐ ζυγίην Ἥρην) in song, | nor did the attendant gleam of torches (οὐ δαΐδων) flash on the bed | nor (οὐδὲ) was there any who gambolled and sprang in leaping dance, | nor (οὐχ) did father or mother intone the wedding song, but (ἀλλὰ) ...' It is possible that both O. and Musaeus (who did not read O.) were familiar with a Hellenistic poem now lost that developed this theme; cf. Kost (1971) 483.

47–8 Hypsipyle waxes indignant in an elegant rising tricolon with anaphora. The form of the question, *quid mihi cum*, has a colloquial flavour, 'What have they got to do with me?'; cf., e.g., 14.65, *Am.* 1.7.27, 2.19.57, 3.6.87, *Trist.* 3.11.55, Plaut. *Curc.* 688 *quid mecum est tibi?*, Cic. *Fam.* 15.10.2 *si mihi tecum minus esset.*

47 Minyis: the descendants of Minyas, a Boeotian hero to whom no myth attaches. The name is applied to the Argonauts at an early stage and there is abundant evidence of ancient scholarly speculation about its origin (cf. Roscher II 3016–22). Apollonius, for example, offers three different but not mutually exclusive explanations in his *Argonautica*; cf. Vian (1976) 10–12.

Tritonide pinu: sc. the *Argo*, from a cult title of Athena (cf. Austin on Virg. *Aen.* 2.171), who aided in its construction; cf. *Met.* 2.794 (of Athens) *Tritonida ... arcem. pinu* is used for 'ship' by metonymy, a poeticism found only sparingly before O. (Virg. *Ecl.* 4.38, *Aen.* 10.206, Hor. *Epod.* 16.57), but made into a feature of the standard poetic idiom by him. Here it is especially appropriate as the wood from which the *Argo* was made (e.g. Eur. *Med.* 1–4). The variant *Dodonide*, found in Planudes' translation, is probably a learned slip, involving a recollection of A.R. 1.527 Δωδωνίδος ... φηγοῦ, referring to the beam from an oak tree of Dodona incorporated into the ship.

48 Tiphy: a Greek vocative. The apostrophe conveys a formal note of indignation; it also serves a more mundane purpose of allowing O. to vary the construction and thus escape the problem of construing a Greek word (which would have no ablative) with the preposition *cum. nauita*, found only here and at 10.61 in the *Heroides*, is an archaic and poetic alternative for *nauta*; cf. Bömer on *Met.* 1.133. Tiphys was the helmsman of the *Argo* who, in the account of Apollonius (2.854) died on the outward voyage after having negotiated the greatest perils; but this did not occur until after the visit to Lemnos and so Hypsipyle need not have learned of his death.

49–50 The imprecisions of these lines betray Hypsipyle's distress. She speaks of the ram when she means the fleece, and refers to Aeetes as *senex*, quite at variance with Apollonius' portrayal of Aeetes as a man in the prime of life.

49 spectabilis 'remarkable': 'the word is commonly found in Ovid, more rarely in other poets of the classical period' (Ruhnken (1831) 42). It occurs 12 times in O.'s verse, and may well have been coined by him (cf. Ciceronian *aspectabilis*); after O. it is attested in both prose and verse. On such neologisms see 5.149n.

aureo: scanned as a spondee by the coalescence of the last two vowels (synizesis); cf. *Am.* 1.8.59 *aurea*, 2.13.9 *alueo*, 3.9.21 *Orpheo*, *Ars* 3.457 *Theseo*, *Met.* 7.151 *aureae*, *ES* 35 *Perseo*. This device allows the use of words which would not otherwise scan in elegiac or hexameter verse; see Norden (1927) 217–18, Platnauer (1951) 68.

50 regia: not 'palace' but 'royal seat'; cf. Hor. *Epist.* 1.11.2 *Croesi regia Sardis*, Plin. *Nat.* 5.2.1 *Caesarea, Iubae regia*.

Lemnos: with a short final syllable, the Greek form of the name.

51 O. follows the account of Apollonius, who describes how the Lemnian women prepared to repel the Argonauts, thinking them to be Thracians, but were dissuaded from the attempt by Aethalides, the herald of the Argonauts (*Arg.* 1.640–52). Other accounts, e.g. Sophocles in his *Lemniai*, told of a great battle between the Lemnians and Jason's crew.

certa fui: with the infinitive, *pellere* (7.7n.).

me mea fata trahebant: Hypsipyle interrupts herself to express a familiar Stoic sentiment that each person has a destiny that he must follow; cf. Sen. *Epist.* 107.11 *ducunt uolentem fata, nolentem trahunt*. Hypsipyle's resistance to this destiny is futile. The phrase recurs at 12.35, *Met.* 7.816, *Trist.* 2.341.

52 hospita … castra for 'visiting troops' is an oxymoron, since a military force would not be regarded as 'guests'.

feminea: 5.62n.

53–4 'The women of Lesbos know only too well how to defeat men.' Hypsipyle's first reference to the crime of the Lemnian women (see introd. note) is only thinly veiled. In the narrative of Apollonius (*Arg.* 1.793–833), she concocts an elaborate story to conceal the fate of the men of Lemnos. O.'s Jason is apparently unaware of earlier events, and these lines would be understood by him as something of empty bluster: the irony is for third parties to this correspondence.

53 Lemniades: a Greek feminine adjective, found before O. only in Apollonius (1.653, 2.32, 3.1205). Roman poets made a practice of utilizing the exotic names that they found in Hellenistic authors.

nimium quoque 'even too much': a somewhat unusual phrase, found only in O., who uses it also at *Ars* 1.587, *Fast.* 1.437, *Trist.* 4.10.99, *Pont.* 3.9.49.

54 milite tam forti: collective singular, 'so bold a troop', as often with military expressions, e.g. *eques, pedes, remex*; cf. K–S I 67. The free use of the instrumental ablative is a poeticism, adopted by post-Augustan prose stylists; but cf. 5.150n. A reader might suspect that the gender of *milite* here is feminine (11.48n.); O. was the only writer to treat *miles* this way (*TLL* s.v. 939.68ff., Bömer on *Met.* 2.415).

fama tuenda fuit: like others among O.'s heroines, Hypsipyle feels the loss of her good name as a result of her abandonment by Jason. For *fama* most MSS read *uita*, which makes little sense since Hypsipyle's life was never threatened by Jason. P, the oldest MS, originally read *fortuna* before it was corrected to *forti uita*. This is probably due to a misreading of its exemplar which had *forti* followed by a trochaic word. Editors have offered a number of suggestions (e.g. *causa, zona, porta, terra, nonne . . . fui*) but *fama*, proposed by Delz (1986) 82, best suits the context.

55–74 Hypsipyle now expands on the reasons for her resentment: the fact that she welcomed Jason into her land, that he remained of his own choice, and departed only reluctantly and with a promise to return. After worrying for so long about him, she now finds that he has come home safely, but not to her.

55 urbe ... uidua 'our city, devoid of men': *uidua* is nicely expressive, for the women of Lemnos were indeed widows as a result of their actions. The text printed here is Heinsius'; the MSS offer *uidi*, which makes no point at all, while Palmer emended to *iuui*, a reading that later turned up in some MSS. *iuui* has some merit, and the resulting expression could be compared with 2.55.

urbe ... tectoque animoque recepi 'I took you into my city, my home, and my heart': by syllepsis (p. 30) the verb is construed with the three ablatives in a slightly different sense, although it is semantically proper to each; cf. *Met.* 14.78 *excipit Aenean illic animoque domoque.*

56 bisque aestas bisque ... hiems: the seasons indicate the passage of years, a familiar poetic device; cf. Cat. 95.2–3 *nonam post denique messem | ... nonamque edita post hiemem,* Liv. 5.22.8 *decem aestates hiemesque continuas circumsessa.* Hypsipyle emphasizes the length of Jason's stay to highlight his perfidy.

cucurrit: an unusual metaphor; cf. Prop. 3.10.21 *nox ... currat,* Hor. *Carm.* 2.5.13–14 *currit ... aetas.*

57 tertia messis: i.e. Jason left during the summer, the time of the harvest, after a stay of two years (by inclusive reckoning). O.'s chronology diverges sharply from Apollonius' account, which implies a stay of only a few days: 1.861–2 'the sailing was put off from one day to the next'. The possibility that O. is following some other (lost) source cannot be discounted, but a more likely explanation is that this represents a deliberate innovation to legitimize the bitterness of Hypsipyle's complaint. Again, the passage of time is stressed, here by the *cum inversum* construction (23–5n.).

coactus: by Hercules, who in the account of Apollonius remained with the ship and refused to join the other members of the expedition in the company of the women of Lemnos, finally persuading them to set sail by threatening to abandon the expedition (A.R. 1.862–74). In O.'s chronology, Heracles would have had to be extraordinarily patient and uncharacteristically continent.

58 'Your eyes filled with suitable (*suis*) tears when you spoke these words': a bold expression, combining two ideas *lacrimis oculos implere* and *uerba dicere*. The use of the reflexive adjective is idiomatic (*ES* 72n.) and especially characteristic of O.'s style: cf. 14.67 *lacrimae sua uerba sequuntur* (= *Epiced. Drusi* 165), 20.76, *Fast.* 2.542, *Met.* 10.506, *Trist.* 1.3.80. *talia* looks forward to the report of Jason's farewell.

59 abstrahor, Hyspipyle: Jason's words to Hypsipyle stand in pointed contrast with his farewell in Apollonius (1.900–1), which follows a short speech by Hypsipyle in which she raises the question of his future return and possible offspring. Jason's reply, which also begins with an address to her by name, is non-committal: 'Hypsipyle, I hope that all these things may be accomplished by the gods', or in other words, 'whatever will be will be'. He goes on to deal at greater length with what we might call 'custody arrangements' in the event that Hypsipyle should give birth. The bland portrayal of Jason by Apollonius is devastating, but O. paints an even more explicit portrait of his betrayal by depicting an emotional parting: *abstrahor* is a strong word, connoting forcible removal.

recursus 'return': a poeticism introduced by O. from the familiar metaphorical use of *currere* of sailing; for the plural, cf. 2.14n.

60 uir 'husband': emphasized by the repetition and the fact that these are reported as Jason's own words.

61–2 As O. portrays Jason in Hypsipyle's account, he is considerably more interested in becoming a parent than the figure depicted at *Arg.* 1.901–9. There Jason reassures Hypsipyle, in response to her inquiry, that he has no interest in taking her child from her; but also asks that she send this child (or children) to his parents as consolation in the event that he is unable to return home. As

Burman notes, Apollonius' Jason is not portrayed as a romantic hero ('minus certe amatorie').

61 quod: the neuter is regular for the unborn embryo, cf. Plaut. *Amph.* 501 *quod erit natum tollito,* Cic. *Cluent.* 33 *id quod conceperat seruare.*

e nobis 'by me': the regular expression for agency in conception (*TLL* s.v. *ex* 1105.62ff.), to be taken with *grauida*; cf. *Am.* 2.13.5 *ex me conceperat,* Plaut. *Amph.* 111 *utrimque est grauida, et ex uiro et ex summo Ioue.*

grauida ... in aluo: Jason borrows a heroic tag to describe pregnancy; cf. Acc. fr. 1 Ribbeck *Maia nemus retinens grauido concepit in aluo,* Calvus, fr. 14 Buechner. O. adopts the phrase, but alters the gender; cf. *Am.* 2.14.17 *si Venus Aenean grauida temerasset in aluo.*

celatur 'lies hidden': cf. Hor. *Carm.* 4.6.19–20 *latentem | matris in aluo.*

62 eiusdem almost = 'also', introducing a further point that restates the hexameter from a different perspective: 'and let us also both be its parents'.

63 hactenus et 'so much you said, and ...': a formulaic transition in O.; cf. 17.265, *ES* 156, Bömer on *Fast.* 5.661.

64 cetera: sc. his actual farewell to Hypsipyle.

65 ultimus: another pointed divergence from the *Argonautica,* where he is the first (1.910 παροίτατος). On this point O. is followed by Valerius Flaccus (2.425), who is influenced by O. in his portrayal of a more romantic Jason.

sacram: because Athena had a hand ι ιts construction.

Argo: accusative, a Greek form regular in Augustan verse; cf. 7.7 *Dido,* *Am.* 2.2.45 and 2.19.29 *Io,* 2.16.31 *Hero,* Virg. *Aen.* 7.324 *Allecto*; and see N-W 1 481.

66 uento concaua uela tument 'the billowing sails swell before the wind': the alliteration is perhaps expressive of the swiftness of the ship. The reading of the MSS *uentus ... tenet* is flat and without parallel; the correction was suggested by Francius (reported by Burman), who adduced *Ars* 2.432 *saepe tument Zephyro lintea saepe Noto.* Cf. too Front. *Str.* 2.13.11 *quae [uela] cum ... tumentia et flatu plena uidisset,* and *tumidus* as an epithet of sails at Hor. *Epist.* 2.2.201, Sil. 1.575, 7.242–3.

67 'The dark blue wave is churned up from beneath the keel as it is driven along': the separative dative (in place of the ablative) with *subduco* is a poetic licence later adopted by Silver prose authors, especially Tacitus. It is first found with this verb in Virg. *Aen.* 6.524 *capiti subduxerat ensem,* where the dative avoids a run of three short syllables (cf. Norden (1927) 232); but O. greatly extends its use: cf. Bednara (1906) 570. The couplet is artfully composed: the hexameter is a patterned line (p. 33), while the pentameter is arranged chiastically with an ἀπὸ κοινοῦ construction.

69 in latus omne: construe with *patens,* 'exposed on every side'; cf. Livy 44.7.1 *patere omnia in omnis partes.*

turris: a lighthouse perhaps, like the 'tower of Hero' from which she watched for Leander.

circumspicit 'surveys': a personification; cf. *Trist.* 1.5.69–70 *quae de septem totum circumspicit orbem* | *montibus,* 5.61n.

70 feror: indicates wild movement, as in a fragment of an unidentified tragedy by Pacuvius (393 Ribbeck) *alcyonis ritu litus peruolgans feror,* or O.'s own tragedy, *Medea* (fr. 2) *feror huc illuc, ut plena deo.*

osque sinusque: 1.29n.

71 -que continues with a slightly adversative sense: 'I watch through tears and yet . . .'; for other examples in poetry see Fraenkel (1957) 219 n. 4.

cupidaeque . . . menti: a Catullan phrase for a heart in love; cf. 64.147 *cupidae mentis . . . libido.*

72 longius assueto: this form of brachylogy, in which the participle is treated as a noun in the ablative of comparison, is a poetic innovation that becomes common in O.; cf. *Am.* 1.13.48, *Ars* 2.411, *Met.* 7.84, *ES* 47, K–S II 470–1, H–S 108–9. It is a nice conceit to imagine that Hypsipyle's eyesight has improved.

73 adde 'consider also': a familiar rhetorical injunction in enumerating an argument, found often in Lucretius, but in Virgil, for example, only in the *Georgics,* 2.155 *adde tot egregias urbes*; cf. 99n.

74 nunc quoque: i.e. although I have been deserted.

persoluenda scans as five syllables by treating the -*u*- as a vowel, a diaeresis not uncommon with *soluo* and its compounds in the pentameter; cf. 9.86 *inuoluisse,* 12.4 *euoluisse, Fast.* 5.330 *persoluere,* Platnauer (1951) 71. In the following line *persoluam* does not require a diaeresis.

75–108 Mention of the vows made by Hypsipyle for Jason's safe return leads to her resentment at the thought that another woman will enjoy their fulfilment – Medea, who is mentioned here for the first time. The remainder of Hypsipyle's epistle is dominated by her fear and resentment of Jason's new bride. The character of Medea fascinated O., who also wrote a tragedy, now lost, about her and related her story in *Met.* 7. If *Her.* 12 is not by O. (see p. 7), the second half of this epistle probably represents O.'s earliest large-scale treatment of her character.

75 uota ego persoluam?: this motif is repeated at *Her.* 5.59; cf. Tib. 1.5.17–18 *omnia persolui: fruitur nunc alter amore, | et precibus felix utitur ille meis.*

76 ira mixtus ... amor 'mingled wrath and joy': the ablative is regular with *miscere.*

abundat: not a common word in poetry (avoided by Cat., Prop., Virg. (2), Hor. only in the *Satires*), used only twice by O. of excessive passion; cf. *Ars* 2.552 *barbaria noster abundat amor.*

77 dona: the offerings she vowed in return for his safety.

uiuum ... perdo: a paradox, since *perdere* suggests loss by death (*OLD* s.v. 3c).

Iasona: accusative, a Greek form.

78 damnis: 1.96n.

79 equidem 'to be sure': an emphatic particle, used in classical Latin with the first person and representing a more elevated expression than *ego quidem*; cf. H–S 174. *-que* expands upon the previous statement (*OLD* s.v. 6a), 'to be precise, I was afraid'.

80 Argolica: used for mainland Greece without specific reference to the Argolis, like *Argolidas* 'mainland girls' in the following verse.

81 paelex: since Hypsipyle considers herself Jason's legitimate wife, she refers to Medea as a concubine, 5.60n.

82 non expectata ... ab hoste: for *hostis* used of a rival in love, part of a familiar military metaphor, cf. 12.182, *Am.* 1.9.18, 1.9.26, 2.12.3, Prop. 1.11.7. Naturally, the circumstances require the gender to be feminine (*TLL* s.v. 3062.69ff.); cf. *Ars* 2.461.

83–94 In the depiction of Medea as a witch the streams of myth and popular religion converge; for while Medea's power over nature was apparently a consistent feature of the tradition, the details of Hypsipyle's depiction reflect widely held beliefs in magic, which were not limited to the illiterate; cf. Hunter on A.R. 3.531–3. The

detail lavished on enumerating Medea's powers is not simply deco-
rative: Hypsipyle does not yet say that Medea has bewitched Jason,
but her words (83, 93–4) make it very easy to draw that inference.
Since so much of ancient magic had to do with love charms and the
like (Fauth (1980)), it is easy for Hypsipyle to plant this suggestion,
and she eventually (97–8) gives way to the force of her own logic to
assert that Jason must have been won by magic. Valerius Flaccus
seems to have known a tradition that Medea bewitched Jason
(7.488–9), but, curiously, there was also a tradition that it was he
who bewitched her: see Jacobson (1974) 99 n. 12. Accounts of magic
and witchcraft are common in Roman poetry, and Hypsipyle's por-
trayal of Medea draws on a number of conventional themes; cf.
Eitrem (1941), Luck (1962), and Tupet (1976). In O.'s poetry, *Am.* 1.8
and *Met.* 7.179–293 are the most conspicuous examples of this fasci-
nation with the supernatural.

83 carmina 'spells' need only refer to the incantations that
Medea employed to lull to sleep the dragon that guarded the Golden
Fleece. Similarly, the dangerous herbs (*dira pabula*, 84) recall in the
first instance the drugs that she gave Jason to protect him from
Aeetes' fire-breathing bulls. But both incantations and philtres
played a role in aphrodisiac magic and Hypsipyle is building up to
her claim that Jason was bewitched. The rest of the description is
simply an elaboration of Medea's powers as a witch, without specific
reference to Jason, but intended to paint a terrifying portrait of his
new lover.

84 diraque: 'dreadful', because the herbs are used in magic
rituals. An epithet is required because *herba*, not *pabula*, is the reg-
ular word for magical herbs (*TLL* s.v. *herba* 2618.30ff.): cf. *Rem.* 249
mala pabula, *Met.* 13.943, 14.43.

cantata ... falce: i.e. *incantata* ; cf. *Am.* 1.14.39 *non te cantatae lae-
serunt paelicis herbae*, Prop. 4.5.13 *audax cantatae leges imponere lunae*, *TLL*
s.v. *canto* 291.21ff.

85 deducere: the 'drawing down of the moon' (i.e. producing
an eclipse) was a power often attributed to witches (*Am.* 2.1.23, Fedeli
on Prop. 1.1.19) and was especially a feature of aphrodisiac magic;
cf. A.R. 3.533 'she bound (ἐπέδησε) the stars and the paths of the
moon'. The solar eclipse is on occasion an additional feature; cf. *Am.*
2.1.24.

87 obliquaque flumina sistit: another familiar component in the repertoire of powers ascribed to witches; cf. A.R. 3.532 'and she stops the loud-rushing rivers', Fedeli on Prop. 1.1.23-4. The epithet *obliqua* 'sloping' suggests their steady flow, which Medea can halt; cf. *Met.* 9.18 *cursibus obliquis inter tua regna fluentem,* Hor. *Carm.* 2.3.11-12.

88 loco ... mouet 'dislodges': a prosaic expression, to judge from the examples given at *OLD* s.v. 7a; cf. *Met.* 5.498 *mota loco cur sim* of the spring Arethusa. The power to move rocks and trees by song is most commonly associated with Orpheus (*RE* xviii 1248ff.), but O. also assigns this power to Medea at *Met.* 7.204-5 *uiuaque saxa sua conuulsaque robora terra | et siluas moueo.*

uiua: the epithet can be used of rocks in their natural state (cf. Austin on *Aen.* 1.167), but O. surely plays on the idea that the sorceress stirs the trees and rocks to life.

89-90 Human bones were much prized in witchcraft. The elder Pliny describes a number of magical cures effected by parts of the human body in book 24 of the *Natural history,* e.g. *ulcera non serpere osse hominis circumscripta.* Popular superstitions about the use of corpses are reflected in the witch stories of Petronius (*Sat.* 63) and Apuleius (*Met.* 2.21), and perhaps in the Law of the Twelve Tables which prohibited tampering with a dead body (*FIRA* I, p. 67), *homini mortuo ne ossa legito, quo post funus faciat.* Hence the common portrait in literature of wiches slinking about in graveyards, as in the grotesque depiction of the witch Erictho in Luc. 6.533-7: *fumantis iuuenum cineres ardentiaque ossa | e mediis rapit illa rogis ipsamque parentes | quam tenuere facem, nigroque uolantia fumo | feralis fragmenta tori uestesque fluentes | colligit in cineres et olentis membra fauillas.* Cf. Hor. *Serm.* 1.8.22, Tib. 1.2.48, Stat. *Theb.* 4.508.

89 passis discincta capillis 'with her dress untied and her hair flowing loose': in performing a magic ritual it is important that the witch who wishes to bind another must herself be unbound, so all knots in clothing, hair and the like must be eliminated. Compare O.'s description of Medea about to perform a ritual in *Met.* 7.182-3: *egreditur tectis uestes induta recinctas, | nuda pedem, nudos umeris infusa capillos.*

90 certaque: Medea is no run-of-the-mill witch; she takes only specific items.

91 The practice of sympathetic magic on a figurine intended to represent the victim is widely attested, both in papyri bearing magical texts and in archaeological finds, including specimens of the art dating perhaps to the 5th century BC; cf. Faraone (1991) 4–7. O. provides the only literary references to the practice of inserting pins into such a figurine, a procedure reminiscent of the voodoo dolls of current-day Haiti. But the action reported here is probably not intended as harmful, but rather an erotic operation. Instructions for making a wax figurine are preserved in the so-called 'Paris magical papyrus' (*PGM* IV 296–466), together with instructions to 'take thirteen copper needles and stick one in the brain ... stick two in the ears and two in the eyes ...' (trans. Betz (1986) 44). O. describes a similar procedure with a doll and wax tablet at *Am.* 3.7.29–30 *sagaue poenicea defixit nomina cera | et medium tenuis in iecur egit acus.*

deuouet 'curses': the verb belongs to the lexicon of magic (2.13n.); cf. *CIL* XI 1823 (= Audollent (1904) no. 129) *hunc ego aput uostrum numen demando deuoueo desacrifico.*

figit: i.e. *defigit* 'binds with a spell' = Greek καταδέω, a standard term in magic, as in *Am.* 3.7.29 *defixit nomina cera.* The force of the omitted prefix *de-* is carried over from the preceding *deuouet*, a process often noted in both Latin and Greek: Clausen (1955) 50–1, Watkins (1966), Renehan (1977).

93 et quae nescierim melius 'and things which it might be better for me not to know': the perfect subjunctive is used in cautious assertion (K–S I 176–80).

93–4 male quaeritur herbis | ... amor 'it is wrong for love to be sought by drugs when it ought to be won by character and beauty': Hyspipyle expresses her view in the form of a generalizing *sententia*, but she is referring only to her specific case; cf. *Ars* 2.105–8, Tib. 1.8.24 *forma nihil magicis utitur auxiliis*, Prop. 3.6.25, 4.7.72.

95 potes 'can you endure?' Cf. *Am.* 3.8.11 *hunc potes amplecti?*

relictus 'is expressive of the terror Jason should feel at being *left alone* in the same bedroom with such a fearful creature' (Palmer).

96 somno ... frui 'sleep peacefully': cf. *Met.* 2.779, *Pont.* 2.2.64, Mart. 12.18.13. O. is fond of such periphrases with *fruor*; see Bömer on *Met.* 1.487.

97 scilicet signals the sarcasm of Hypsipyle at this point, 'I suppose'.

tauros: apparently the fire-breathing bulls of Aeetes, whom

Medea did not yoke, though she did make it possible for Jason to harness them by protecting him from their flames. O. is more interested in equipping Hypsipyle with a rhetorical point than in mythographical precision. *iugum ferre* is a common metaphor for marriage (Lilja (1965) 85), but here sounds paradoxical: in ancient poetry it is usually the woman who is said to be yoked by the man; cf. Nisbet–Hubbard on Hor. *Carm.* 2.5.1.

ita: a prosaic word increasingly avoided by poets of the Augustan period. O. has the adverb 30 times in the *Met.* in phrases that echo Virgil's use of the word in the *Aeneid*. In O.'s elegiacs it occurs rarely: 4 times each in *Am.* and *Ars.* In the single *Her.* it is found elsewhere only at 10.27, *ES* 81. The frequency of *ita* in *Trist.* (18) and *Pont.* (19) cuts against the trend discernible in other poets: see Axelson (1945) 121–2, Ross (1969) 72–4.

98 quaque ... mulcet ope: Hypsipyle's reference to the charming of the serpent is suitably vague: she has not heard exactly how Medea did it. In the *Argonautica* (4.145–61) Medea first soothes (*mulcet*) it with an incantation and then puts it to sleep by sprinkling a drug over its eyes.

anguis: Hypsipyle apparently has in mind the serpent that guarded the fleece, but the plural, perhaps suggested by *tauros* above, is generalizing.

99 adde quod 'add to that the further consideration that': the expression marks a transition in the argument; it is not found in epic but is used freely by Horace and Lucretius; cf. McKeown on *Am.* 1.14.13, Nisbet–Hubbard on Hor. *Carm.* 2.18.17, *TLL* s.v. *addo* 591.56ff.

ascribi factis: the metaphor is not legal as Palmer suggests, but drawn from inscriptional monuments, to which Medea wants her name added; likewise *titulo* in the pentameter is used figuratively for 'glory'; cf. *OLD* s.v. 7.

procerumque: the Argonauts.

100 iubet 'demands': Hypsipyle represents that Medea is trying to 'steal Jason's thunder'. The MSS reading *se fauet* cannot be Ovidian, since *fauere* does not govern an accusative and infinitive in classical Latin. Attempts at improvement are found in some MSS (*se facit* and *se uolet*) and continue to be offered by critics: e.g. *sese auet* (Madvig), *spem fouet* (Watt), *sustinet* (Diggle). Most of these are ob-

jectionable on metrical or grammatical grounds. The emendation
iubet (Koch) captures the spirit, if not perhaps the letter, of what O.
wrote, for the insistent *obest* requires a more urgent sense than that
offered by most proposals. And it may have indirect MS support in
Planudes, who translates πείθει 'urges'. In MSS *iubet* is frequently
corrupted to *iuuet*, which may in turn have produced *fauet*.

101 Peliae de partibus 'from Pelias' faction': the language sug-
gests a political dispute between supporters of Jason and Pelias (cf.
OLD s.v. *pars* 16b) over Jason's *acta*.

102 imputat: an accounting term, 'to charge to', used figura-
tively among the poets only by O. who is fond of such everyday
words; cf. *Met.* 2.400, 15.470.

populum, qui sibi credat, habet 'he has a following that be-
lieves him': for this sense of *populus*, cf. Sen. *Con.* 10 pr. 2 *quamuis
aliquo tempore suum populum habuerit*. The subjunctive in the relative
clause is generic.

103–4 Hypsipyle quotes the taunt of an imagined detractor.

103 Phasias Aeetine 'the Phasian daughter of Aeetes': cf. *Met.*
8.528 *matres Calydonides Eueninae*. The line ends with a spondee in the
fifth foot, a rhythm generally avoided by the Roman elegists (Plat-
nauer (1951) 38–9), except when needed to accommodate a Greek
proper name: e.g. *Am.* 1.6.53 *Orithyiae*, 2.13.21 *Ilithyia*, *Ars* 3.147 *Cyl-
lenaea*. The epithet *Phasias*, from the river Phasis, is not attested in
Greek until late antiquity (Agathias, *AP* 4.3.62), but it is likely that
O. found it in a lost Greek poem. The same can be said for the
patronymic *Aeetine*, restored by Salmasius, though it is first found in
Dionysius Periegetes 490.

non haec: sc. *egit*, 'Jason did not do these things', from *acta*
above.

104 Phrixeae … ouis: cf. 12.8 *Phrixeam … ouem*, of the ram
which carried Phrixus to Colchis (2n.): the grammatical gender of
ouis does not necessarily coincide with sex.

reuellit 'tore down': from the tree in the precinct of Mars, where
Phrixus dedicated the fleece to the god; cf. Stat. *Theb.* 12.699–700
patriis modo fixa reuellunt | arma deis, Livy 45.28.3. For the form of the
perfect, cf. N–W III 418–19.

105 Alcimede: Jason's mother according to the genealogy of
Apollonius (1.47), and traditional since Pherecydes (*FGrH* 3 F 104),

although she was also known by other names: Polymele in the Hes-
iodic *Catalogue of women* (fr. 38; 43a.1 M–W), Polyphane in Herodorus
(*FGrH* 31 F 40). O. is probably not following the tradition attested
in Apollod. *Bibl.* 1.9.27 that she hanged herself in despair before
Jason's return. Of course, O.'s Hypsipyle is not in a position to
know whether Alcimede is alive or not; her objection is based on a
reasonable surmise.

consule matrem 'ask your mother's advice'.

106 a gelido ... axe 'from the North Pole': the *axis* properly
was the line drawn through the earth's centre on which the heavens
were supposed to turn, but poets used the word to refer to only the
northern extremity of the *axis,* or pole. Hypsipyle speaks of Colchis
as if it lay in the extreme north, a sentiment echoed by O. when
referring to his place of exile on the Black Sea; cf. *Trist.* 5.2.64 *haec
gelido terra sub axe iacet, Pont.* 2.10.48, 4.14.62, 4.15.36.

107 Tanai (ablative): the mod. river Don. The preposition *a*
found in a late MS and printed by editors is unnecessary: it can be
supplied with both *Tanai* and *paludibus* (ἀπὸ κοινοῦ) from the penta-
meter; cf. Kenney (1962) 11 n. 1, K–S 1 481–2. The region designated
here by its principal river was also known as Sarmatia, and was a
byword for savage life, but O.'s geography is not intended to be
taken literally.

Scythiaeque paludibus udae 'the damp marshes of Scythia':
O. is thinking of the mouth of the river Ister (mod. Danube), a re-
gion known for its marshland; cf. *Trist.* 3.4.49 *Tanais ... Scythiaeque
paludes.* The adjective *udae* is transferred (enallage, 1.10n.) to *Scythiae;*
cf. *Fast.* 6.401 *udae ... paludes.*

108 a patria Phasidos usque 'all the way from the source of
the Phasis': i.e. the remote and savage inland regions of Colchis. For
patria as the source of a river, cf. *Am.* 3.6.40 of the Nile, *qui patriam
... tantae tam bene celat aquae.* In commending Bentley's 'necessary and
certain emendation' *ripa,* Housman (1897) 105 (= *Class. pap.* 386) ob-
jects that *patria Phasidos* 'is the name for nothing on earth' unlike
patria Nili; but that would be true only if the ancients knew the
source of the Nile, and they did not. Hypsipyle is not suggesting that
Medea find a husband from her own country (*ripa Phasidos*) but from
some even more remote and savage place.

109–40 Hypsipyle now turns from the topic of Medea and the threat that she poses to Jason to her own claims on him, recounting again his obligation to her, as well as reciting her many advantages: lineage, nobility and family. But these arguments, too, inevitably lead her back to comparison with her rival.

109 mobilis 'fickle': an attribute more commonly assigned to women in Roman poetry; cf. Calp. *Ecl.* 3.10 *mobilior uentis, o femina*.

110 tua ... uerba: as reported by Hypsipyle at 59–60 above.

pondere ... carent: a variation on the phrase *fide carere* (2.26). For *pondus* in this context, see Fedeli on Prop. 3.7.44. *polliciti* is genitive of the participle to be construed with the possessive *tua* (5.45n.), as Housman (1915) 16 (= *Class. pap.* 1262) notes, i.e. 'your words when you promised in 59–60 above'. Most editors construe as genitive of the neuter noun and take with *pondere*, 'weight of a promise'. But a promise can weigh less or more, and so Heinsius preferred the variant *pollicito*, citing *Fast.* 3.366 *pollicitam dictis ... adde fidem.* But that is not a convincing parallel, since in that passage there is a specific antecedent for *fidem*, while there is none for *pondus* in Jason's words at 59–60.

111 cur non meus: the echo of Jason's promise in 60 is bitter. The parallel at 10.57 *uenimus huc ambo; cur non discedimus ambo*, which resembles this line both rhetorically and rhythmically, militates against the repeated *uir* of most MSS. The pluperfect *ieras* is used for the perfect: 1.34n.

113 generosaque nomina 'high-born titles'.

114 Minoo ... Thoante: Hypsipyle's father, Thoas, was the son of Dionysus and Ariadne, daughter of Minos; hence, the epithet.

feror 'I am spoken of': given the unpleasant association of the name of Thoas with the Lemnian massacre, there is some irony in the way Hypsipyle styles herself here.

115–16 This couplet 'explains' the epithet *Minous* given to Thoas above by naming Bacchus and the Cretan Ariadne as Hypsipyle's grandparents; but the explanation is probably not by O. The lines follow awkwardly on 113–14, with a switch of subject accompanied by ellipse of the verb *est*: *Bacchus auus* looks suspiciously like a 'filler', not unlike *deuictus serpens* in 37. There is a further anomaly in the transitive use of *praeradiat* 'outshine' with an accusative object where one would expect the dative: cf. Hor. *Epist.* 1.1.83 *Baiis praelucet.* The verb is not attested again in Latin until Claudian 10.287, where it is intransitive. It is true that O. coins several new words with the prefix *prae-* (McKeown on *Am.* 1.4.33), but such new formations as are found in the *Her.* occur in poems of disputed authorship: 8.121 *praemori*, 9.98 *praegrauis*, 12.17 *praemedicare*. For interpolations that gloss an allusive name or epithet, see Tarrant (1987) 290–1.

115 Bacchi coniunx redimita corona: only the crown of Ariadne was made a constellation, but Roman poets occasionally speak as if she were set in the stars as well: cf. *Ars* 1.557–8, Prop. 3.17.8.

117 dos tibi Lemnos erit: the kingship of Lemnos will be her dowry. There is an echo of Dido's similar offer to Aeneas at *Aen.* 4.103–4 *liceat Phrygio seruire marito | dotalisque tuae Tyrios permittere dextrae*, cf. 7.149n.

terra ingeniosa colenti 'a land suited by nature to the farmer': a uniquely Ovidian usage; cf. *Fast.* 4.684 *ad segetes ingeniosus ager*. O. recalls Hypsipyle's description of Lemnos in her initial offer to Jason: A.R. 1.830–1 'for it is more fertile than all the rest of the islands in the Aegean sea'.

118 'You can have me, too, among the dotal slaves': a novel application of the motif of the *seruitium amoris*. As a wedding gift to Jason she would offer herself in amorous servitude: *dotales serui* were common components of the dowry. The correction *dotales* (MSS *res tales*) restores Ovidian point to the line. The use of *dotalis* without an accompanying noun is unusual, but not unparalleled (*TLL* s.v. 2054.32ff.).

119 nunc etiam introduces Hypsipyle's next, decisive point, that she has given birth.

gratare ambobus 'be happy for both of us': under the circumstances, an ironic wish, that harks back to Jason's own words at 62. *gratari* is an archaic equivalent of *gratulari*, used by the poets and occasionally in prose after Livy.

120 auctor 'the person responsible': but in O. often simply 'father'; cf. *Met.* 6.172, 13.617.

onus: the child in the womb, as commonly in O.: e.g. 4.58, 11.38, 11.42, 11.64.

121–2 'I've had a lucky throw, too, and I have made my stake with twin offspring by Lucina's favour.' In this context *quoque* is heavily ironic. The word-play is almost untranslatable: *numerus* refers

to the number thrown in a game of dice (cf. *Ars* 3.355), while the
regular idiom for making a wager is *dare pignus* (*OLD* s.v. 2). The
poets make frequent use of *pignora* for children as the guarantee of
a marriage.

121 prolemque gemellam: one of the twins, Euneus, is men-
tioned in the *Iliad*; the name of the other is variously reported as
Nebrophonos (Apollod. *Bibl.* 1.9.17) or Thoas, like his grandfather
(Stat. *Theb.* 5.465). The diminutive (5.45n.) *gemellam*, here and 143, is
affective.

122 Lucina: the goddess, usually identified with Diana or Juno,
who brings children into the world; see Pease on Cic. *De nat. deor.*
2.68. For *Lucina ... fauente*, cf. Virg. *Ecl.* 4.10 *casta faue Lucina*, Call. fr.
7.10 Pfeiffer Ἐλειθυίης ... βουλομένης.

123 cognosceris illis 'you are recognized in them': cf. *Met.*
4.290–1 *cuius erat facies in qua materque paterque | cognosci possent.*

124 norunt 'know how to'.

cetera patris 'all the other traits of their father': cf. *Met.* 6.713
cetera qui matris, pennas genitoris haberent.

125–30 Hypsipyle considers sending her two sons to Jason to en-
treat him to return to her, but concern for their safety with Medea
stops her. In Euripides' play, of course, Medea does use her own
children as 'envoys' and finally murders them: 'it is quite as if Hyp-
sipyle had read Euripides' *Medea*' (Jacobson (1974) 103). Precisely:
this type of reference to a literary source is an integral part of O.'s
conception of his characters in the *Heroides*, who exist not so much as
figures of myth as literary characters: see p. 18.

125 legatos: as a queen Hyspipyle might send envoys to Jason.
The language is somewhat dry: the construction of *dare* with a pre-
dicative gerundive is favoured by O., but avoided by other non-
dramatic poets: cf., e.g., 7.16, 18.164, *Am.* 1.4.12, 1.12.22, *Ars* 3.528,
Fast. 4.548, *Met.* 4.424, 15.472, *ES* 192. These 'envoys' need to be
carried.

126 saeua nouerca 'the thought of their savage stepmother':
i.e. Medea.

127–8 Medeam ... Medea ... | Medeae: the thought of
Medea as stepmother to her children is elaborated in this rising
tricolon with repetition of her name (anaphora) in different cases

(polyptoton). Stepmothers were proverbially cruel (Otto (1890) 245–6), but Medea exceeds them.

128 faciunt ad scelus omne 'are fitted for any crime': O. has many examples of this idiom: e.g. 14.56, 16.192, *Am.* 3.11.42, *Ars* 3.540, *Trist.* 1.10.44, *ES* 8. It is otherwise not common in poetry. Occasionally the dative is used in place of the prepositional phrase: see 2.39n.

129 fratris: Apsyrtus. O. follows an account of his murder and dismemberment by Medea and Jason different from that in Apollonius (4.452–81), in which he is a grown man. According to the version adopted here, he was a young boy, taken hostage and his limbs scattered on the sea in order to delay the pursuit of Aeetes, who stopped to gather them up (Roscher I 3–4). O.'s preference for this version is in part motivated by the rhetorical development of this passage as Hypsipyle thinks of her own children.

130 pignoribus 'children', 122n.

131–2 The disbelief (*diceris*) and indignation of this statement presuppose a clear answer to the question put in 129–30 (no). The language is strongly emotional: *o* is never colourless in Latin, which, unlike Greek, does not require the particle with the vocative.

131 Colchisque ... uenenis: cf. *Met.* 7.394 *Colchis arsit noua nupta uenenis.*

132 Hypsipyles: genitive, a Greek form.

toro: properly the marriage bed. Hypsipyle continues to portray herself as Jason's only legitimate spouse.

133–6 The contrast between the respective claims of Hypsipyle and Medea is made in a series of antitheses grouped as a 'falling' tricolon: 133–4 form the first member, followed by shorter antitheses in the following hexameter (135) and pentameter (136).

133 cognouit: a euphemism for sexual intercourse, 43n.

adultera uirgo: an oxymoron, for *uirgo* is not simply an equivalent of *puella* (5.129n.). Hypsipyle's tone when referring to Medea is bitingly sarcastic.

134 taeda pudica: the torch used in the wedding procession; cf. Cat. 64.302, Virg. *Aen.* 4.18. Again, Hypsipyle insists on the propriety of their liaison: *pudica* implies chastity.

135 Thoanta: accusative, a Greek form (1.5n.). Hypsipyle's second reference to the Lemnian massacre is used only to score a rhetorical point.

136 me mea Lemnos habet: perhaps O's reader may detect a note of irony here, knowing from other texts, like Euripides' *Hypsipyle*, of her subsequent expulsion from Lemnos.

137–8 ipso | crimine: refers generally to Medea's role in taking off the Fleece, a betrayal of her father. The instrumental ablative must be construed with both *dotata est* and *emeruit* : 'the very crime by which she won her husband constituted her dowry'.

137 quid rēfert 'what difference does it make?'

scelerata piam: the juxtaposition is pointed.

138 uirum: here 'husband', in 133 'man'.

139–40 In the preceding couplets Hypsipyle has compared herself to Medea, a topic that is concluded in 137–8, while in 141 she begins a new thought. This couplet was judged spurious by Peters (1882) 34, and his verdict should probably be accepted. He notes the absence of verbal point in contrasting *culpo* and *miror*, and the obscure connection of thought in the pentameter. Housman's emendation *ignauis* does something to improve the sense of the line, which appears to be modelled on *Am.* 1.7.66 *quamlibet infirmas adiuuat ira manus*; but the coherence of the couplet is not enhanced. Interpolations such as this one perhaps originated in marginal annotations, the present elaboration of O.'s thought being prompted by the mention of the Lemnians' crime; cf. Tarrant (1989) 137–52.

141–64 The tone of the epistle now changes abruptly (*dic age*): there is no more mention of return and reconciliation, only of vengeance on Medea and, finally, Jason. In O.'s epistle he has never been portrayed in a positive light, and yet Hypsipyle spares him the worst until the end when she curses both Jason and his new bride.

141 dic age 'Go on, tell me': when used paratactically with another imperative *age* has the force of an interjection (*aduerbium hortantis*, Serv. *Aen.* 2.707), and as such belongs to the conversational idiom; cf. Hofmann (1951) 37, H–S 471.

ut oportuit: 'as you ought to have done': for the peremptory tone of this word, 1.83n.

iniquis 'opposing' winds: the epithet is not without irony.

142 intrasses: a syncopated (5.38n.) pluperfect. For the polysyndetic *-que ... -que*, 1.29n.

143 fetu ... gemello: the twin sons born to Hypsipyle in Jason's absence (121n.). *fetus* for young children, not newborns, is a novelty, used here to evoke sympathy for Hypsipyle.

144 'You would surely (*nempe*, 2.36n.) have prayed for the earth to open up': Hypsipyle positively relishes the thought.

145–6 A rising tricolon, with relative *quo* in anaphora. The first two members are abbreviated by brachylogy, with the one verb for both clauses and *uultu* likewise to be understood in both.

145 quo uultu ... uideres? 'how would you have faced me?': O. adapts the conversational expression *quo ore* to verse; cf. Ter. *Ph.* 917 *quo ore redibo ad eam quam contempserim?*, Cic. *Phil.* 7.21 *quo ore uos ille poterit ... intueri?* The imperfect subjunctive is less regular than the pluperfect for a past potential, but not unusual (H–S 332).

145 scelerate echoes 137 *scelerata* of Medea: Jason is now viewed as a suitable mate for her.

146 'What form of death did you deserve as penalty for your treachery?': the change to indicative *eras* (without potential aspect) is pointed. *perfidiae* signals a return to the theme of Jason's violation of *fides* (41).

147 quidem emphasizes the preceding word *ipse* and, like Greek μέν, introduces a contrast, 'on the one hand you yourself', although the second term *paelicis*, is introduced without the usual adversative conjunction. *quidem* is not common in other poets, but O. is particularly fond of this somewhat prosaic word; cf. Knox (1986a) 39.

per me 'as far as I was concerned'.

tutus sospesque 'safe and sound': the duplication has a colloquial ring; cf. Plaut. *Capt.* 873 *filium tuum modo ... saluom et sospitem uidi*, *Rud.* 631.

148 tu ... ego: the pronouns emphasize the contrast.

149 'As for your mistress, I should have glutted my eyes with the sight of her blood': *uultus* (= *oculos*, *OLD* s.v. 3a) *implere* is certainly figurative, like *uisus implere* (Luc. 9.787) or *oculos implere* (Sil. 3.45), but not without suggestions of the grotesque. Once again (81n.), by referring to her as *paelex*, Hypsipyle emphasizes that she, not Medea, is Jason's legitimate wife.

150 quosque ... tuos 'and the eyes which she has captivated by sorcery – yours': plays upon the familiar amatory topos that love can capture another's sight; cf. *Am.* 3.6.28 *rapuit uultus, Xanthe, Neaera tuos*,

Fedeli on Prop. 1.1.1. The idea of Jason being thus 'carried off' by Medea is echoed from 131 *ablate*. In law *ueneficium* referred to all forms of witchcraft, not only poisoning (*Inst.* 4.18.5): only O. among the poets, with his penchant for appropriate terminology, uses this word.

151 Medeae Medea forem 'I'd have been a veritable Medea to Medea!': the word-play is possible because by O.'s day the name of Medea was a by-word for a sorceress and seductress. Cicero taunts Clodia as a *Palatinam Medeam* (*Cael.* 18), and similar allusive use of figures from myth can be found in Cic. *Sex. Rosc.* 98, *Att.* 1.18.3. For the tense of *forem*, cf. 145n.

153 subnuba 'the one who takes my place as bride': the only occurrence of this word, probably coined by O. on analogy with such words as *innuba, pronuba*.

154 leges ... suas: 5.134n.

155–6 The sense of this couplet is clear: Hypsipyle wishes for Medea to be left alone with two children, as she herself has been. But most MSS begin 156 with *a*, prompting editors to accept *aque* (Burman) for *illa* later in the line even though *orbus* does not govern this preposition: 'so may she one day, bereft of as many children, lose husband too'. But Hypsipyle has her children. The problem lies with the first *a*, which cannot stand in spite of Madvig's best efforts to explain it as temporal, 'after she has lost as many children'. The temptation to construe *natis* with *orba* proved too much for readers at some stage of the transmission who knew that Medea was to lose both children and husband. *cum*, found in some MSS, cuts the knot and *uiro cum totidem natis* means 'her husband and the same number of children [two]'.

157 male parta 'ill-gotten gains': O. is perhaps thinking of the proverbial expression *male partum male disperit* (Plaut. *Poen.* 844); cf. Cic. *Phil.* 2.27.65, Otto (1890) 206.

peiusque relinquat 'and leave them behind even more miserably'.

158 fugam 'refuge': cf. Prop. 2.16.40 *extremo quaerere in orbe fugam*.

159–60 Hypsipyle now includes Jason and any future children by Medea in her curse, with ominous overtones: her father she only betrayed, as she may one day betray Jason, but she murdered her brother. The inference is plain to readers who know what happens next. The adjective *acerba* is construed with *germana* and *filia* (ἀπὸ κοινοῦ).

161 consumpserit: i.e. when she has exhausted all possibility of escape by land or sea.

aera temptet alludes to her future escape from Corinth by air at the end of Euripides' *Medea*.

162 erret inops, exspes: the phrasing recalls a line from the *Medea* of Accius (*TRF* 415 Ribbeck) *exul inter hostes, exspes expers desertus uagus*, a familiar element in curses; cf. *Met.* 14.217 *solus inops exspes leto poenisque relictus*, *Ib.* 113 *exul inops erres*, Eur. *Hipp.* 1028–31.

caede ... sua: because the outcome of the story is known, one thinks immediately of the murder of her children, but O.'s Hypsipyle speaks generally of 'the blood she has shed'.

163 coniugio fraudata 'cheated out of my marriage': flatly stated. The verb is one of the many legal items in O.'s lexicon (2.34n.), but is not otherwise common in poetry.

Thoantias 'daughter of Thoas', whom she saved. The patronymic occurs twice in the *Argonautica* (1.637, 1.712) as an epithet of Hypsipyle.

164 uiuite: there is bitterness in this 'valediction', as in Cat. 11.17 *cum suis uiuat ualeatque moechis*, and irony in the conclusion that the witch Medea and her husband now lie together under a curse (*deuoto ... toro.*). For the polysyndetic *-que ... -que*, 1.29n.

VII Dido Aeneae

The story of Dido's flight from Tyre to the coast of North Africa where she founded the city of Carthage was known to the Greek historian Timaeus (4th–3rd cent. BC), but her encounter with Aeneas may have been Virgil's invention. More precisely, it was probably Virgil who elaborated a tradition that had already been suggested by the synchronism of the foundation of Rome and Carthage, perhaps outlined as the cause of the Punic wars by Naevius in his *Bellum Punicum*; cf. Wigodsky (1972) 29–34, Horsfall (1973–4) 10–13. O.'s epistle is drawn from the portrayal of Dido in books 1 and 4 of the *Aeneid*, on which it forms something of an elegiac commentary. The letter that Dido writes is set after Aeneas has decided to leave Carthage and Dido has confronted him with this fact: Palmer fixes

Aen. 4.413–15 as the moment: *ire iterum in lacrimas, iterum temptare pre-*
cando | cogitur et supplex animos summittere amori, | ne quid inexpertum frustra
moritura relinquat. As a letter, of course, it serves no practical purpose;
in the opening lines Dido confesses her resignation to his departure.
But by refuting the arguments adduced by Virgil's Aeneas to justify
his actions, O. poses a fundamental challenge to the heroic values of
the *Aeneid*. What Lanham (1976) 60–1 has observed of the *Met.* is also
true of this epistle: 'Dido can be left behind [sc. in the *Aeneid*] be-
cause Virgil accepts Rome as an external sanction, the source of all
legitimating explanations. There is no sanction in O.'s poem.'

O.'s other allusions to Dido's story are consonant with the inter-
pretation of the *Aeneid* that forms the basis of this poem. The sly ref-
erence to the founder of Rome and his defining virtue *pietas* in the
third book of the *Ars amatoria*, addressed to female readers, is hardly
in keeping with a reading of the *Aeneid* in terms of rigid Augustan
ideology: *et famam pietatis habet, tamen hospes et ensem | praebuit et causam*
mortis, Elissa, tuae (3.39–40), itself an allusion to the *Aeneid* through
this epistle. It was Virgil who left open the possibility of so reading
Aen. 4, as O. pointedly reminds Augustus in *Trist.* 2.533–4 *et tamen ille*
tuae felix Aeneidos auctor | contulit in Tyrios arma uirumque toros. However
his contemporaries may have interpreted Aeneas' departure from
Carthage, O. leaves no doubt about his view in the four-line 'sum-
mary' of *Aen.* 1 and 4 that he included in his *Metamorphoses* (14.78–81):
excipit Aenean illic animoque domoque, | non bene discidium Phrygii latura
mariti, | Sidonis; inque pyra sacri sub imagine facta | incubuit ferro deceptaque
decipit omnes. In O.'s view Dido was betrayed by the man she took in:
the so-called 'pessimistic' reading of the *Aeneid*, current in so much
modern criticism of Virgil, began with O. It forms the basis for his
portrayal of Dido in this epistle.

1–6 O. states his rhetorical bias in the opening salutation. This
letter begins with a declaration that it is not meant to persuade its
putative recipient. When O.'s Dido says that her words are wasted,
this is not merely a trope: we know, and she knows, from the setting
of this moment in the text of the *Aeneid*, that Aeneas is at this instant
at the harbour making preparations to leave Carthage. As O. him-
self makes clear in his characterization of this poem at *Am.* 2.18.25,
Dido is already intent on suicide as she writes this poem, sword in

hand (*tenens strictum Dido miserabilis ensem*). The epistolary fiction is again only lightly sustained, prompting a medieval reader to prefix to his MS a more 'suitable' epistolary opening (see app. crit.).

1 fata uocant: 6.28n.

abiectus 'casting itself down': passive participle instead of the more common use of the active with the reflexive pronoun; cf. Prop. 1.14.1 *tu licet abiectus Tiberina molliter unda*, Petr. 26 *abiecti in lectis*.

2 Maeandri: a river in Phrygia (mod. Menderoz), famous for its winding course, but not otherwise noted for its swans, as was the Cayster in Lydia. O.'s Dido is perhaps thinking of a river closer to Aeneas' home in Troy.

olor: the native Latin word for 'swan', which survives mainly in poetry and was eventually replaced by the Greek loan-word *cycnus*. The comparison to a swan's final song underlines the note of despair. The belief that the swan has a premonition of its death and marks the moment with an especially beautiful song is as old as Aeschylus, who compares the doomed prophetess Cassandra to a swan (*Ag.* 1444–5). The belief is widely attested in antiquity, especially by poets who found it an irresistible motif in spite of the (somewhat morbid) scepticism of some like the elder Pliny: *Nat.* 10.23.63 *falso, ut arbitror, aliquot experimentis*. See further Fraenkel on Aesch. *Ag.* 1444, *RE* IIA 785.

3–4 The combination of alliteration (*sperem prece posse*) and the repetition *moueri … mouimus*, which is deliberate but not rhetorically effective, perhaps suggests Dido's agitated state.

4 alloquor: Dido addresses Aeneas as if he were present. In antiquity rhetoricians characterized a letter as half a conversation; cf. Demetrios, *Rh. Gr.* III 310–11. This is especially appropriate for Dido who has made it clear that she does not hope for a reply. O. also characterizes this poem as a speech in *Am.* 2.18.25–6 *quod … Dido … dicat.*

aduerso mouimus ista deo 'I have begun [*OLD* s.v. *mouere* 17c] this with a god against me': *ista* refers generally to the complaint that Dido is now making, and the god, who is not specified, we may suppose to be Amor.

5–6 'But having lost what e'er was worth my care, | Why shou'd I fear to lose a dying pray'r?' (Dryden).

5 merita 'my services': cf. *Aen.* 4.317 *si bene quid de te merui*. In this line Dido puts more succinctly the complaint made by Phyllis at 2.107–16.

famam: Virgil's Dido is acutely aware that she has ruined her reputation by her affair with Aeneas; cf. *Aen.* 4.322–3 *extinctus pudor et, qua sola sidera adibam,* | *fama prior*, and in a similar vein, A.R. 4.379 where Medea laments the loss of her good name.

corpusque animumque pudicum 'the modesty of my body and heart'; the adjective is construed with both nouns (ἀπὸ κοινοῦ).

6 male perdiderim 'wretchedly wasted': for the repetition in *perdere* (anastrophe), see 6.29n. Here it combines with the figure of polyptoton (5.12n.), the repetition of a word in a different inflexion. For the sentiment, cf. *Trist.* 1.2.13 *uerba miser frustra non proficientia perdo*.

leue est 'is a small matter'.

7–22 Dido cannot believe that, in spite of her appeals (7 *tamen*), Aeneas really intends to leave Carthage, a city already under construction, for Italy, the whereabouts of which are still unknown. The section opens with a series of incredulous questions (7–12), as punctuated by Bentley, in which Dido draws the contrast between the Rome to come and her own Carthage. This is paralleled by the more important contrast drawn between herself and his future bride, a 'prediction' that plays on the reader's familiarity with the later books of the *Aeneid*. Virgil's Dido says nothing about another woman, and Aeneas has no specific knowledge that he is to wed Lavinia.

7 certus es ire echoes *Aen.* 4.554 *Aeneas ... iam certus eundi*, with variation of the construction. The use of the infinitive with *certus* was an innovation tried once by Virgil at *Aen.* 4.564 (of Dido) *certa mori*. It was adopted by O. (cf. 4.152, 6.51, *Met.* 10.394, 10.428, *Pont.* 4.6.9) and his successors (*ES* 99), but is not found in prose until Tacitus; cf. K–S I 684.

miseramque ... Dido: so Dido styles herself in her first appeal to Aeneas at *Aen.* 4.315 *mihi iam miserae*, and again at 4.420 and 4.429. The Greek accusative in *-o* is the only form attested in Latin (*TLL Onom.* s.v. 146.47–9).

8 uenti uela fidemque ferent: 2.25n. In the preface to his translation of the *Heroides* Dryden remarks on this line, 'What Poet of our Nation is so happy as to express this thought Literally in English, and to strike Wit or almost Sense out of it?'

9 cum foedere soluere naues 'cast off your ships and your pledge': a nearly untranslatable syllepsis; *soluere* properly refers both to untying the cables that hold a ship in port (cf. *ES* 214 *solue ratem*) and to the dissolution of a compact (cf. *Met.* 11.743–4 *coniugiale solutum est | foedus*). O.'s Dido maintains the existence of a marriage bond, which Aeneas denies: *Aen.* 4.338–9 *nec coniugis umquam | praetendi taedas aut haec in foedera ueni.* The metaphorical use of *foedus* is limited to poetry; cf. Reitzenstein (1912) 9–12, Ross (1969) 80–95.

10 ubi sint nescis: in general O. follows Virgil in allowing that Aeneas knows that Italy and the Tiber are his ultimate goal. But there are inconsistencies in the *Aeneid*: for example, before reaching Carthage Aeneas had twice misinterpreted the signs sent him and founded his city in the wrong spot; cf. Pease on 4.345, Heinze (1915) 86–94. O.'s Dido exploits these contradictions in Virgil's text to score a rhetorical point.

Itala regna sequi: the phrase combines two ideas, 'to make for Italy' and 'to seek your kingdom', both drawn from the *Aeneid*. Mercury orders Aeneas to consider Ascanius, *cui regnum Italiae Romanaque tellus | debentur* (*Aen.* 4.275–6), while the verb *sequi* sounds an echo of the famous unfinished line, *Aen.* 4.361 *Italiam non sponte sequor.*

11–12 The first two components of Dido's three-part question were introduced by the repetition (*certus es ... certus es*); the final member itself constitutes a rising tricolon with anaphora (*nec*).

11 noua: O. was surely aware of the interpretation of the city's name reflected in Servius' note on *Aen.* 1.366 *nouae Carthaginis arcem*: *Carthago est lingua Poenorum 'noua ciuitas'.* On such 'etymological' epithets in Propertius, see Shackleton Bailey (1956) 223 and 260 on Prop. 4.1.103 and 4.9.38, and for O., see McKeown (1987) 45–62.

11–12 nec te surgentia tangunt | moenia: as they once did, when he remarked of the Carthaginians (*Aen.* 1.437), *o fortunati quorum iam moenia surgunt.* The work at Carthage, which had lapsed as Dido became distracted by her love for Aeneas (*Aen.* 4.88–9 *pendent opera interrupta minaeque | murorum ingentes aequataque machina caelo*), had been resumed before the composition of this letter by Aeneas himself, who is portrayed by Virgil as occupied in the construction when he is interrupted by Mercury bringing Jupiter's instructions (*Aen.* 4.259–61).

12 summa: sc. *rerum*, 'the fortunes of the state', which O.'s Dido represents as already placed under Aeneas' sovereignty (*sceptro ... tuo*, a familiar poetic metonymy).

13–14 Dido represents Aeneas as a feckless rover, running away from responsibility. The idea is first stated tersely, with word-play and then rephrased more expansively. The two pairs of contrasting verbs are arranged chiastically over the couplet, *facta ... facienda ... quaerenda ... quaesita* (= 'sought and found', *OLD* s.v. 7).

15 ut 'suppose that': concessive; 1.116n.

quis ... tradet habendam 'who will hand it over to your control?': the gerundive is predicative with *tradet*, like *tenenda* with *dabit* in the pentameter.

eam: the Roman poets tended to avoid most forms of the demonstrative pronoun *is*; cf. Axelson (1945) 70–1. This is the only occurrence of the accusative singular (masculine or feminine) in the poetry of O.'s early period. He more freely admits forms of *is* in the *Met.* and his later elegies; of the 23 occurrences in the corpus of *Heroides*, 15 are found in the double epistles (16–21).

16 non notis: a metrically convenient equivalent for *ignotis* which avoids hiatus after the preceding word, as the generalizing plural avoids one before the word following.

17 scilicet alter amor tibi restat 'I suppose you have another woman waiting for you' (Diggle): the sarcastic tone is struck in *scilicet*, as the passage was emended by Diggle (1967) 138, because of metrical anomalies in the MSS. *scilicet* may have indirect MS support in Planudes' version, ἄλλος σοι ὡς ἔοικεν ὑπολέλειπται ἔρως ἔχειν.

18 altera ... fides: at *Aen.* 4.371–3 Dido laments Aeneas' faithlessness: *iam iam nec maxima Iuno | nec Saturnius haec oculis pater aspicit aequis. | nusquam tuta fides.* As Heinze (1915) 135 n. 2 remarks, Virgil echoes Euripides' *Medea* 492 ὅρκων δὲ φροῦδη πίστις, referring to Jason's marriage vows. But Virgil records no promise by Aeneas, and so O. must be viewed as 'interpolating' such an incident in his reading of Dido. In *quamque iterum fallas* the subjunctive is final, 'for you to break a second time'.

19 quando erit ut: a prosaic periphrasis, to judge from the examples collected at K–S II 237, which has here the added force, 'when will it be likely'; cf. R. G. Nisbet on Cic. *Dom.* 65.

instar Carthaginis urbem 'a city as grand as Carthage': *instar*, an indeclinable noun, suggesting equivalence of size or worth, is here in apposition to *urbem*. It is of uncertain etymology; cf. Austin on Virg. *Aen.* 2.15.

20 populos ... tuos: the plural is metrically convenient, avoiding elision before a vowel, but is also vaguely suggestive of Rome's future empire.

21 eueniant 'come true', of an event prophesied or prayed for; cf. Tib. 1.5.57, *Met.* 3.524, 6.37. *ut* is concessive, 1.116n.

nec di tua uota morentur: cf. 18.5, of the gods, *nam cur mea uota morantur?*

22 quae te sic amet 'to love you like this': the subjunctive is generic. The reader is, of course, aware that Dido's suspicions will prove true: Aeneas' marriage to Lavinia will be one of convenience.

uxor: 1.97n.

23–36 Dido diverges from her address to Aeneas to a monologue outlining the intensity of her passion. Throughout this section O.'s heroine writes as if Aeneas were a third party to the 'conversation' (*Aeneas ... ille ... ille*). This is a more extensive diversion from the epistolary fiction than we find elsewhere in the single *Her.*, but the poems so often verge upon the form of a monologue that the reader hardly notices the breach of decorum.

23 uror: perhaps a recollection of *Aen.* 4.68 *uritur infelix Dido*, but O.'s use of the familiar metaphor of the fire of love is ubiquitous; cf. McKeown on *Am.* 1.1.26.

inducto ... sulpure 'coated with sulphur'.

ceratae ... taedae: a unique periphrasis for *cereus*, a wax candle. Dido's choice of image is deliberately ambivalent: the *taeda*, or pine-torch, had familiar associations with the wedding procession, but the *cereus* was used at funerals. She continues to play on the theme of her impending death.

24–5 These lines are found only in a few late MSS. Their omission produces a couplet (23/6) in which the pentameter introduces an entirely new idea, which is not in itself objectionable; but as Housman (1897) 202 (= *Class. pap.* 391) remarks, 'it is surely much more Ovidian to give such different thoughts as the content of 23 and 26 a distich apiece, than to crowd them in a single couplet'. The lines in question are Ovidian in diction and metre, and it is likely that here the later MSS have preserved two lines omitted in the mainstream of the tradition. Accepting them as genuine requires a slight correction in 26 of *dies* to *quies*.

24 pia ... tura focis: cf. *Am.* 3.3.33 *et quisquam pia tura focis imponere curat?* The simile is rounded out in a patterned line (p. 33).

25 uigilantis: the genitive is in agreement with the possessive implied in *oculis*, 2.91n.

26 Aenean animo ... refert: cf. *Aen.* 4.83 *illum absens absentem auditque uidetque. noxque quiesque* amounts to a hendiadys, 'the stillness of the night'.

27 quidem: 6.147n.

male gratus: i.e. *ingratus*. This use of *male* in place of a negative prefix is a colloquialism adopted by the poets because of its metrical convenience; cf. Hofmann (1951) 145; in O. cf. *Am.* 2.18.23 *male gratus*, 3.7.77 *male sane*, *Ars* 2.319 *male firma*, 2.660 *male uiua*, *Fast.* 1.571 *male fortis*, 6.785 *male sobrius*.

ad mea munera surdus 'indifferent to my kindness'.

28 et quo ... carere uelim 'the kind of man I should want to be rid of': the subjunctive is generalizing.

stulta 'an idiot': the adjective is avoided in the high style; cf. 1.75n.

29 non ... odi: O. pointedly rejects the tradition recorded in the *Aeneid* (4.607–29) that Dido laid a curse against Aeneas and his entire race. He reframes Dido's voice in the terms of amatory elegy. In the pentameter, *queror ... questaque peius amo* rings again the note of complaint (1.8n.) and deflates Dido's rage in the epic.

quamuis male cogitat 'though his plans are wicked': the indicative construction with *quamuis* is attested in poetry from Lucretius onwards; it was adopted by post-Augustan prose stylists under the influence of verse (H–S 603–4); cf. 3.8, 4.173, 9.92, 13.119.

30 peius: i.e. *uehementius*, 'I love him worse', again a colloquial usage (Hofmann (1951) 74); cf. 4.26.

queror ... questaque: polyptoton, 5.12n.

31 nurui: Dido refers to herself as daughter-in-law of Venus, the mother of Aeneas (*matris* 36) because she considers her liaison a valid marriage. O. is the first poet to use the longer ending *-ui* of the dative in the fourth declension. Earlier poets preferred the form in -*u* (N–W I 542) or avoided it altogether; cf. 163 *domui*.

fratrem: O. also exploits Aeneas' kinship to Cupid for rhetorical effect at *Am.* 3.9.13–14 *fratris in Aeneae sic illum funere dicunt | egressum tectis, pulcher Iule, tuis,* and, less directly, at *Am.* 1.2.51–2.

32 castris militet ille tuis 'let him be a soldier but in your camp': *tuis* at the end of the line scores the point as Dido plays on the metaphor of love as warfare which O. developed at length in the elegy that begins *militat omnis amans et habet sua castra Cupido* (*Am.* 1.9.1). The motif is common in his poetry; e.g. *Am.* 1.2.32 *castris* ... *Amoris,* 1.9.44, 2.9.4, 2.18.40, *Ars* 2.236, 3.559, McKeown (1989) 258–9.

33 amorem: supply *praebeam* from *praebeat* in the pentameter. If their love cannot be mutual Dido is content to do all the loving and let Aeneas supply only the subject for her care. The same point is found at *Am.* 1.3.2–3 *aut amet aut faciat cur ego semper amem. | a, nimium uolui; tantum patiatur amari.* O. represents Dido as adopting the same strategy; if Aeneas will not truly enlist in Cupid's service, at least he might allow her to love and to preserve the illusion that her love is returned.

34 materiam: a word rarely found in other Augustan poets (Virg. *Aen.* 11.328, Hor. *Carm.* 3.24.49, *Ars* 38, 131), but common in O.'s works (47 instances), where it is often found with a literary reference in the sense of a 'plot' or 'theme'; cf. *Am.* 1.3.20 *te mihi materiam felicem in carmine ... praebe. cura,* too, as well as constituting a standard item in the amatory lexicon, may stand for literary activity. O.'s choice of words is not casual: Dido, cast in the role of the elegiac lover, sounds like the elegiac poet.

35 ista mihi falsae iactatur imago 'that fantasy flits before me in my delusion': Dido recognizes that she is deluding herself. The point is scored by the word-play *fallor ... falsae* (polyptoton, 5.12n.). The passive participle *falsus* is not common in classical Latin in this sense, but cf. *Fast.* 5.494 *falsus eris.* The reading of the MSS *falso* suggests deliberate falsification, which is not quite what O. seems to say here.

37–74 Dido breaks off her reverie and once again directs her speech at Aeneas, pleading with him to postpone his departure. O. expands upon the astonished reaction of Dido in the *Aeneid* (4.309–

11) to Aeneas' determination to leave even in the teeth of contrary winds. Dido imagines him shipwrecked and his final guilty thoughts. Through the prism of O.'s rhetoric the reader is obliged to focus squarely on one question: what is the hurry?

37–8 The mention of Aeneas' parentage leads to a commonplace that is as old as Homer, *Il.* 16.33–5 (Patroclus to Achilles): 'Peleus was never your father nor was Thetis your mother, but it was the grey sea that bore you and the towering rocks.' O.'s more immediate model is Virgil's adaptation of these lines at *Aen.* 4.365–7 *nec tibi diua parens generis nec Dardanus auctor, | perfide, sed duris genuit te cautibus horrens | Caucasus Hyrcanaeque admorunt ubera tigres.* Cf. 10.131n.

innataque ... | robora: Bentley conjectured *elata*, presumably because oaks do not grow from lofty crags, but O. is more interested in the cumulative effect of these images of harshness than he is in botanical precision.

38 progenuere: found only once in Virg. at *Aen.* 4.180, the verb recurs in O. at *Met.* 8.125, 9.670, but is not otherwise attested in Augustan poetry.

39–44 The final member in the list of Aeneas' 'ancestors', the sea, leads to a digression on the dangers of a voyage.

39 nunc quoque: sc. as it was when you first came to these shores.

40 qua 'by which way': the regular Ovidian idiom; cf. Kenney (1970) 177.

tamen 'nevertheless': introducing the apodosis to the concessive clause implied by the ablative absolute *aduersis fluctibus.*

41 hiems: hiemis: anastrophe (6.29n.) and polyptoton (5.12n.).

hiemis ... prosit 'let the winds' partiality do me some good'.

42 euersas concitet ... aquas: the participle is proleptic, 'stirs the waters into violent agitation'. O. echoes with variation Virg. *Aen.* 1.43 *euertitque aequora uentis.*

43 malueram 'I should have preferred if I had had the choice': the indicative for the subjunctive, on the analogy of such constructions as *melius fuerat*, is common in such hypothetical expressions; cf. *Am.* 3.12.20. The infinitive *debere* is understood from the following clause (ἀπὸ κοινοῦ).

44 iustior ... uentus et unda: a reversal of the more familiar comparison of people to the elements, which are conventionally

cruel; cf. 3.133 *matrisque ferocior undis*, *Met.* 14.711 *saeuior illa freto*. The
verb is singular (*est*) in agreement with only the nearer subject.

45 numquid censeris inique? 'you're not being rated unfairly,
I trust': an ironic question. Dido has just said that Aeneas overrates
her worth; in this parenthesis she perhaps implies that she has
estimated *him* too highly. The economic metaphor in *censeor*, which
refers to the rating done by the censors, is continued in the next
couplet. The articulation of 45–6 resembles *Am.* 2.5.1–2 *nullus amor
tanti est (abeas, pharetrate Cupido),* | *ut mihi sint totiens maxima uota mori.*

46 ut pereas depends on *tanti*, a genitive of value.

dum: causal. There is an echo of Dido's exclamation at Virg. *Aen.*
4.314 *mene fugis?* as she at last recognizes the truth of her situation.

47 exerces ... odia 'practise hatred': prompted by Virg. *Aen.*
4.623 *exercete odiis*, the phrase is first attested here, *Met.* 5.245, 9.274–
5, and then in Silver Latin prose. Such expressions with *exercere* used
of an attitude are common, but the poets experimented with new
combinations; cf. Austin on Virg. *Aen.* 4.100. *odia* is a poetic plural
(Maas (1902) 496). The elisions in *pretiosa odia et* are harsh, with the
first coming at the caesura, and probably expressive of Dido's own
anger.

constantia magno: the construction with the ablative of price is
a prosaic idiom introduced to poetry by O. and found only here in
his works; cf. *Am.* 1.8.72 *ne gratis hic tibi constet amor.*

48 dum me careas 'so long as you might be rid of me': the
subjunctive exercises a limiting influence on the main clause.

uile 'of little account': the construction with the infinitive is
attested only here and at Stat. *Silv.* 2.5.29.

49 ponent 'will fall': the intransitive usage was a Virgilian inno-
vation adopted by O. only in this passage; cf. *Aen.* 7.27–8 *cum uenti
posuere*, 10.103.

strataque aequaliter unda 'with the waves spread evenly':
unda is a 'poetic singular' for the waves of the sea. The adverb *aequa-
liter* of a level surface is a technical usage found only in O. in poetry;
cf. Vitr. 9.85 *aequaliter per id cauum influens aqua.*

50 caeruleis ... equis 'Triton will ride through the sea on his
blue-green steeds': i.e. there will be calm, as in the scene depicted
in *Aen.* 1.144–7. The image is framed, so to speak, in the line which
is enclosed by epithet and noun. O. echoes Virgil's description of

Neptune at *Aen.* 5.819 *caeruleo per summa leuis uolat aequora curru*. The depiction of Triton driving a chariot would be unique in Graeco-Roman art and literature, which conceived of him as a minor sea-god, half-man and half-fish: cf. *Aen.* 10.211 *in pristim desinit aluus*, *RE* VIIA 271–6. But O. undoubtedly knew that the Carthaginians worshipped several sea-deities, one of whom was known to outsiders as Triton, as he is listed among the patron gods of Carthage in Polybius' translation (7.9.2) of the treaty between Hannibal and Philip V; cf. Walbank (1967) 49–50. O.'s queen sounds like a real Carthaginian. *caeruleus* is the colour usually attributed to sea-gods, 5.57n.

51 'I wish that you too were changeable with the winds': *mutabilis*, as Lyne (1989) 48–9 notes, is a prosaic word. This is one of only 4 examples in O., who doubtless would have us recall Mercury's words to Aeneas about Dido: *Aen.* 4.569–70 *uarium et mutabile semper | femina*. As Lyne remarks, 'it is pleasant that Ovid makes Dido throw the word "mutabilis" back at Aeneas'.

52 et ... eris: the switch to the indicative reflects Dido's dramatic swings of mood, as she now voices an unexpected note of hopefulness.

duritia: a familiar complaint against hard-hearted lovers; cf. 2.137, 4.85, Prop. 3.12.20.

53–4 'Why, as if you did not know the power of the wild sea, do you put your trust in the waters of which you have so many times had such bad experience?'

54 expertae: sc. *a te*. The passive sense of this deponent is very rare; cf. Stat. *Theb.* 7.722 *experti ... ponti*.

55 ut: concessive, 1.116n.

pelago suadente uiam: *Met.* 13.418 *iamque uiam suadet Boreas*.

57 nec ... prodest 'nor is it advantageous for those who test the waves to break faith': the litotes is ominous. It was an old Greek commonplace that it was dangerous even for an innocent man to risk the perils of the sea in the company of a perjurer; cf. Eur. *El.* 1354–5, Lys. 6.19, Aesch. *Th.* 602–4, Antiphon 5.82, Eur. fr. 852 Nauck, Xen. *Cyr.* 8.1.25, Hor. *Carm.* 3.2.26–8.

temptantibus aequora: for *eis qui temptant*; a unique periphrasis.

58 perfidiae: 6.146n. *poenas exigit* is a common phrase, but it is not attested before O. and Livy; cf. 97, *Met.* 4.190, 8.125.

59 laesus: sc. *fuerit*. For the expression ('wronged love'), cf. Tib. 1.9.1 *si fueras miseros laesurus amores*, *Anth. Lat.* 71.7 SB. There would have been no typographical distinction between *amor* and the god *Amor* for O.'s contemporaries: *laesus Amor* is an offended deity.

mater Amorum: O. recalls the literary tradition of Aphrodite's birth from the waves with *fertur* ('so the story goes'), but the details of this vignette derive from the famous painting of a naked Aphrodite rising from the sea, *Venus Anadyomene*, which Augustus set up in the temple of the deified Julius Caesar. For descriptions, cf. Strabo 14.2.19, Plin. *Nat.* 35.91, and *A.Plan.* 178–82, a series of epideictic epigrams. O. refers to this painting often: *Am.* 1.14.33–4, *Ars* 3.401–2, *Trist.* 2.527–8, *Pont.* 4.1.29–30, and cf. Prop. 3.9.11. Dido lecturing Aeneas on his mother's ancestry is not without irony.

60 Cytheriacis ... aquis: the waters near the island of Cythera, where Aphrodite was said to have come first (Hes. *Theog.* 192–3). The adjective *Cytheriacus* is first attested here and *Fast.* 4.15, and is probably an Ovidian coinage; it is not found in Greek, and is attested later only at Nero, *FPL* fr. 2 Buechner; Mart. 2.47.2, 14.207.1.

61 perdita ... perdam: for the word-play (polyptoton, 5.12n.), cf. *Met.* 14.81, also of Dido, *deceptaque decipit omnes*, Plaut. *Cist.* 686 *perdita perdidit me*; Frécaut (1972) 244. Dido's threats now dissolve into fear as she pictures Aeneas lost at sea.

62 bibat ... aquas: a graphic expression for drowning, cf. *Am.* 2.10.34 *aequora periuro naufragus ore bibat*.

63 uiue, precor: the paratactic combination with the imperative is a colloquialism adopted by the poets for expressive effect. This idiom is not found in prose; cf. K–S 1 200.

sic ... melius: at *Aen.* 4.382–7 Dido prays for Aeneas' death at sea, a prayer that O. here reverses. 'Ovid's Dido is no less eager for Aeneas' punishment than Virgil's, but Ovid represents her, with perhaps more of refinement though less of nature, desire that his punishment should not be death but the pangs that come from remorse and the evil reputation of being the cause of her death' (Shuckburgh).

64 leti causa ... mei: the first explicit mention of suicide. On *leti*, cf. 2.147n., and for the phrasing, cf. *Am.* 2.10.30 *leti causa sit ista mei*.

ferere 'you will be called'.

65 finge, age: the adverbial use of *age* with an imperative is colloquial (6.141) and underlines Dido's urgency here.

nullum ... pondus 'may there be no significance in the omen': cf. *Am.* 2.14.42 *sint ominibus pondera nulla meis.* The euphemism *omen* is standard in such expressions of wish to avoid some unpleasant possibility, the mention of which is considered unlucky; *TLL* s.v. 575.47ff.

66 quid tibi mentis erit? 'what will be your state of mind?'

67 falsae periuria linguae 'the perjuries of your lying tongue': the genitive is subjective. Dido means his false oaths of love and fidelity; the complaint is common in the *Heroides*: cf. 2.32, 6.63. The legal term *periurium* is rare in poetry; it occurs once in the *Aeneid*, when Dido refers to the proverbial faithlessness of the Trojan race: 4.541–2 *necdum | Laomedonteae sentis periuria gentis?*

68 Thoughts of Dido will occur to Aeneas as he faces death. O. compresses the wish of Dido at *Aen.* 4.382–4 *spero equidem mediis, si quid pia numina possunt, | supplicia hausurum scopulis et nomine Dido | saepe uocaturum.*

Phrygia ... fraude 'Trojan treachery': O.'s Dido imputes her lover's treachery to the proverbial perfidy of his people.

69–70 In the *Aeneid* Dido threatens that her spirit will haunt Aeneas after her death: *Aen.* 4.384–6 *sequar atris ignibus absens | et, cum frigida mors anima seduxerit artus, | omnibus umbra locis adero.*

69 coniugis: 1.30n. Dido consistently refers to herself as Aeneas' legitimate spouse; but her words here are eerily reminiscent of Virgil's description of the apparition of Dido's husband Sychaeus to her in a dream: *Aen.* 1.353–4 *uenit imago | coniugis ora modis attollens pallida miris.* We are reminded too that Aeneas has had similar visitations from the shades of Creusa (*Aen.* 2.772–94), Hector (2.270–97), and Anchises (4.351–3, 6.695–6).

deceptae is echoed in 105 *decepit*; cf. *Met.* 14.81 (Dido) *deceptaque decipit omnes.*

70 effusis ... comis: unbound hair is an emblem of uncontrolled grief; cf. Tib. 1.3.8 *et fleat effusis ante sepulcra comis*, Prop. 2.13B.56.

sanguinolenta: rare in poetry other than O., who has it 15 times. Elsewhere in classical verse it is attested only at Tib. 2.6.40, *Epiced. Drusi* 320, Sen. *Ag.* 82.

71 'What can be so important that you would be willing to say "I deserve it; forgive me!"?': the plural imperative is generalizing, and the use of *concedite* without a grammatical object is without exact parallel, but is intelligible in the context as Dido represents Aeneas consumed by a sense of guilt.

73 breue ... spatium 'a brief time to relent': O. recasts Dido's request in the *Aeneid*: 4.433 *tempus inane peto, requiem spatiumque furori*; cf. Sen. *Dial.* 5.39.2 *surda est et amens, dabimus illi spatium.* Dido restates this request below, 178–80.

saeuitiae ... pelagique tuaeque: with the attachment of two possessives O. plays on two senses of *saeuitia* (syllepsis), the savagery of the storm and the hard-heartedness of Aeneas. Dido is thus made to reveal her true motive for urging delay: her hope that Aeneas will relent towards her.

74 morae pretium 'worth the time spent': a common idiom; cf. *Am.* 3.13.5 *grande morae pretium ritus cognoscere*, *Aen.* 4.52–3, *OLD* s.v. *pretium* 2a.

75–110 Dido introduces the boy Ascanius, to whom Aeneas professes an obligation: *Aen.* 4.353–5 *admonet ...| me puer Ascanius capitisque iniuria cari, | quem regno Hesperiae fraudo.* She reverses the arguments made by Aeneas, asserting that the prudent move on his son's behalf is to wait. This serves only as prelude to her accusation that he has never cared for anyone but himself. The tradition that Aeneas left behind a wife at Troy was a problem for Virgil, who treats her loss as emblematic of the sacrifices imposed upon Aeneas by his mission. O.'s negative assessment is a devastating interpretation of the actions of Aeneas in Virgil's epic.

75 ut: concessive (1.116n.); cf. 19.205 *si tibi non parcis, dilectae parce puellae.* 'To the gods Ascanius is the heir to Aeneas' fate who must not be deprived of his destiny; to Dido, Ascanius and his well-being are subjects of Aeneas' paternal concern' (Jacobson (1974) 79).

Iulo: the name was associated with Aeneas' son and established the relation to the Julian *gens*. Virgil uses the two names interchangeably, as does O., who gives him the epithet *binominis* (*Met.* 14.609).

76 titulum mortis habere meae 'the distinction of causing my death': *ES* 190n.

77 Penates: the sacred images rescued from Troy by Aeneas when he carried Anchises out of the burning city: *Aen.* 2.717 *tu, geni-*

tor, cape sacra manu patriosque penatis. In the *Metamorphoses*, O. coined the epithet *penatiger* for Aeneas (15.450). The appellation *di penates* is normal (e.g. Cic. *Sul.* 86), but O. never uses it and, as Palmer notes, *di* of the MSS weakens *deos* in the pentameter.

78 ignibus ereptos: cf. *Aen.* 3.149–50 *quos mecum a Troia mediisque ex ignibus urbis | extuleram.* The paradox is that they should now be threatened with water.

79 quae mihi ... iactas 'that you brag to me about': Virgil's Dido at one point expresses incredulity about Aeneas' exploits: *Aen.* 4.597–9 *en dextra fidesque, | quem secum patrios aiunt portare penatis, | quem subiisse umeris confectum aetate parentem!* But O. makes explicit the note of scepticism implied in Virgil's *aiunt.* We recall that in the *Aeneid* it is the love-sick Dido who asks to hear his story of the fall of Troy over and over again: 4.77–9 *nunc eadem labente die conuiuia quaerit, | Iliacosque iterum demens audire labores | exposcit pendetque iterum narrantis ab ore.*

perfide: 2.78n.

80 sacra paterque: the image is framed by the enclosing noun (*umeros*) and epithet (*tuos*); cf. Pearce (1966). Several times in his later works O. sought to characterize the moment and its meaning in a witty phrase; cf. *Met.* 13.624–5 *sacra et, sacra altera, patrem | fert umeris, uenerabile onus, Cythereius heros, Fast.* 1.527–8, 4.37–8.

81–4 'False was the tale of thy Romantick life; | Nor yet am I thy first deluded wife. | Left to pursuing Foes Creüsa stai'd, | By thee, base man, forsaken and betray'd' (Dryden).

81 omnia mentiris: cf. *Aen.* 4.373 *nusquam tuta fides.* Dido now pretends to believe that Creusa was simply left behind at Troy.

81–2 neque ... -que: 2.90n. Connection is made by *neque*, while *enim* retains its asseverative force ('and indeed ... not').

82 plector: a low word, rare in poetry; only Horace uses it among other Augustan poets. *plecti* means 'to be beaten', hence 'to be punished', and it is commonly used in that sense in comedy.

83 si quaeras: a scathing remark, casting doubt on Aeneas' story of his desperate search for Creusa in *Aen.* 2.747–70.

formosi ... Iuli: Ascanius is referred to as *pulcher Iulus* 4 times in the *Aeneid* (5.570, 7.107, 9.293, 9.310). For reasons of decorum, *formosus* was avoided in the high style; cf. Knox (1986b).

84 occidit: O.'s Dido asserts that she is dead, although in the tradition followed by Virgil she did not die, but was rescued by the Phrygian goddess Cybele (Austin on *Aen.* 2.788). O., who also coined the expression *cadere ab aliquo* (e.g. 9.36, *Fast.* 6.564, *Met.* 5.192) and similar phrases imitating the Greek idiom ἀποθνήισκειν ὑπό τινος (K–S I 100), may have intended a syntactical ambiguity here, creating a moment's hesitation about whether to construe the prepositional phrase with the verb or the participle (amphibole). Cf. *Met.* 13.597 *occidit a forti … Achille*, the only other instance.

sola relicta uiro: the reader's reaction is influenced by recollection of the couplet Prop. 2.24–45–6 from which this half-line is taken: *iam tibi Iasonia nota est Medea carina | et modo seruato sola relicta uiro.*

85 narraras et me mouere 'You told me this story and its effect was not lost on me': Dido scores a point by recalling that Aeneas told her (*Aeneid* 2.738–40) about the disappearance of Creusa himself, and that this ought to have alerted her to his character flaws. She then ironically asserts that she got what she deserved. For the syncopated pluperfect, cf. 5.38n.

86 ure 'torture', but with suggestions also of the metaphor for love (23n.), and the fire of her funeral pyre.

87–8 The transition is not set out logically; its motivation is the thought of her own fault (*culpa*) and punishment (*poena*) just mentioned. Aeneas, too, she now thinks, has been suffering under the condemnation of the gods.

87 tua numina: the Penates he brought from Troy.

88 septima iactat hiems: at the end of the first book of the *Aeneid*, Dido invites Aeneas to tell the story of his wanderings in words that O. here recasts: 1.755–6 *nam te iam septima portat | omnibus errantem terris et fluctibus aestas.* During the time that Aeneas has been in Carthage, the season has changed to winter (cf. *Aen.* 4.309).

89–90 O. recasts Dido's outburst at *Aen.* 4.373–4 *eiectum litore, egentem | excepi et regni demens in parte locaui.*

89 tuta statione 'safe anchorage': cf. Ulp. *Dig.* 43.12.1.13 *stationem dicimus a stando: is igitur locus demonstratur, ubicumque naues tuto stare possunt.*

90 uixque bene audito nomine 'and I barely heard your name when': the ablative absolute enables O. to compress a *cum inuersum* (6.23–5n.). *bene* is little more than filler here, a common colloquial usage; cf. Hofmann (1951) 74.

91 officiis: ironic; she had no obligations to Aeneas; cf. 6.17n.

92 concubitu: this expression for sexual intercourse is common in comedy and elegy (Adams (1982) 177). For sexual favours as an act of *officium*, cf. McKeown on *Am.* 1.10.46, Tränkle (1960) 164, Adams (1982) 163.

sepulta: i.e. 'consigned to oblivion', a striking expression that O. used once again of himself in *Pont.* 1.5.85 *uosque, quibus perii, tum cum mea fama sepulta est.* O. recasts again (5n.) Dido's words at *Aen.* 4.323, here using harsher language.

93–6 O.'s Dido now recalls her retreat to a cave with Aeneas during a storm as described by Virgil in *Aen.* 4.160–72. Because it presupposes familiarity with the text of the *Aeneid*, O.'s recollection of the scene can be brief and focus on selected details.

93 illa dies nocuit: O. abbreviates Virgil's judgement, *Aen.* 4.169–70 *ille dies primus leti primusque malorum | causa fuit.* Cf. 5.33n.

decliue sub antrum 'a sloping cavern': the descriptive detail is O.'s addition; Virgil says nothing about the cave, which he refers to as a *speluncam* (*Aen.* 4.165). O. 'corrects' this to *antrum*, a Greek loan-word introduced by Virgil and decisively preferred by poets afterwards; cf. Norden (1927) 119.

94 caeruleus ... imber 'a dark rain storm': the phrase is Virgilian (*Aen.* 3.194, 5.10), used only here by O., and afterwards only by Val. Fl. 1.82, Stat. *Theb.* 5.362, [Quint.] *Decl.* 12.16. The Latin word came to be associated with Greek κυάνεος; cf. André (1949) 167. The moment is captured in a patterned line.

95 uocem 'a sound': the singular, found in a minority of MSS, is *lectio difficilior*.

nymphas ululasse putaui: see p. 22.

96 Eumenides fati signa dedere mei 'the Eumenides gave the signal for my doom': again, O. reinterprets his Virgilian text: at *Aen.* 4.167 Tellus and Juno are said to signal (*dant signum*) the commencement of Dido's marriage; the signal is here interpreted as one of doom.

97–8 Most MSS omit 97a–b and have something resembling *uiolate Sychaei* at the end of 97; but as Housman (1897) 201 (= *Class. pap.* 390) notes, the resulting couplet is 'compact of vice': the repetition of *pudoris* in a different sense in 98 is intolerable, and the difficulties cannot be put right by emending to *umbraeque Sychaei* with Merkel.

More than one editor has suspected a lacuna in the mainstream of the MS tradition. Housman defended the authenticity of 97a–b, which are found in a few late MSS together with the reading *uiolataque lecti* at the end of 97. If these lines are genuine, their omission could be explained if the scribe's eye jumped from the -*que* in 97 to the one in 97b; the resulting couplet was then emended in the vulgate to save the metre. 97a–b are open to objections, but even if they are not by O. they may stand in the text *exempli gratia*, since they supply the wanted sense: 'if the lines are an interpolation, its ingenuity is amazing' (Housman). Virgil's Dido had vowed not to marry again after the death of her first husband (*Aen.* 4.15–18); the realization that she has broken this resolution to no purpose occupies her thoughts during her last sleepless night: *Aen.* 4.552 *non seruata fides cineri promissa Sychaeo.*

97 exige ... poenas: 58n. For *laese pudor* 'my lost chastity', cf. 5.104, *Met.* 2.450, 7.751.

97–97a pudor ... uiolataque ... | iura: the apostrophe is a recollection of the vow not kept at *Aen.* 4.25–7 *uel pater omnipotens adigat me fulmine ad umbras | ... ante, pudor, quam te uiolo aut tua iura resoluo.*

97b cinisque Sychaei: a striking allusion to Dido's indictment of herself in the *Aeneid*. Alone at night and torn by her emotions, she concludes (4.552), *non seruata fides cineri promissa Sychaeo*, where one ancient MS (M) reads *Sychaei*. The rhythm, with a word-break after the first short of both the fourth and fifth feet, is unusual; cf. Platnauer (1951) 10.

98 me miseram: 5.149n.

99–102 O. recasts the scene in *Aen.* 4.457–61, from which he takes many details: *praeterea fuit in tectis de marmore templum | coniugis antiqui, miro quod honore colebat, | uelleribus niueis et festa fronde reuinctum: | hinc exaudiri uoces et uerba uocantis | uisa uiri.* In Dido's construction of a shrine to her dead husband Servius saw a connection with Roman customs; cf. Serv. on *Aen.* 6.152 *apud maiores ... omnes in suis domibus sepeliebantur, unde ortum est ut lares colerentur in domibus ... inde est quod etiam Dido cenotaphium domi fecit marito.*

99 sacratus ... Sychaeus: the shrine included an image of the deceased.

100 uelleraque alba: woollen strands with which the shrine was garlanded.

appositae: take also with *uellera* (ἀπὸ κοινοῦ). The objects were placed at the shrine as offerings.

101 sensi ... quater ... citari: O. expands Virgil's *uocantis* and adds details. *citari* is a more formal word than *uocari*; rare in poetry, the verb is found again in O. only at *Fast.* 5.683 and it occurs in Augustan poetry only once each in Propertius, Virgil, and Horace. It is regularly used of summoning jurors, magistrates, and the like; cf. *TLL* s.v. 1200.38ff.

102 Elissa: O. uses *Dido* for the nominative and accusative, *Elissa* in the vocative and oblique cases, a convenience made possible by the tradition, which goes back at least to Timaeus, that Dido had formerly gone by a different name. Apparently grammarians disputed over the proper form of the genitive of *Dido*: cf. *GLK* I 127.

103 nulla mora est: an Ovidian variation of the familiar Virgilian expression *haud mora* (Norden (1927) 185–6), which functions almost as an adverb and is usually followed by asyndeton.

debita coniunx: a double-edged phrase in this context, for Dido is 'bound' to Sychaeus as a consequence of her original marriage vow, but also as a result of her pledge to die before taking another husband.

104 admissi 'crime': the substantival use of this participle is another legalism, often found in the *Digest*, but very rare in classical prose. It is found 8 times in O., but not elsewhere in Augustan poetry.

105 culpae: echoes Dido's celebrated pronouncement, *Aen.* 4.19 *huic uni forsan potui succumbere culpae*.

decepit: 69n.

idoneus auctor 'a suitable authority': a literary joke perhaps. The most obvious reference is to Aeneas himself, elsewhere called *pietatis idoneus auctor* (*Fast.* 2.543); but the phrase is most commonly used of trustworthy authors (cf. *TLL* s.v. *idoneus* 234.17ff.) and Dido's affair with Aeneas was largely the product of the imagination of one author, Virgil.

106 inuidiam ... meae 'he removes the ill will that might otherwise attach itself to my offence': *noxae* is dative. Phaedra voices the same sentiment at 4.33–4 *at bene successit, digno quod adurimur igni;* | *peius adulterio turpis adulter obest.*

107 'The fact that his mother is a goddess and that his old father had been carried out of filial piety': *sarcina*, which O. uses frequently in its metaphorical sense, most commonly referred to a soldier's pack. *pia* is in enallage (1.10n.). For the comparative *senior*, cf. 1.38n.

108 mansuri 'who would remain': for the attributive use of the future participle, cf. 5.59n.

rite 'as was proper': cf. *Met.* 7.798–9 *primos rite per annos | coniuge eram felix.* Elsewhere O. uses the word only in religious contexts.

109 si fuit errandum: sc. *mihi*, 'if I had to stray'. The conditional clause provides the basis for the following conclusion and thus takes the indicative.

110 adde fidem 'consider too his reliability': still addressing the shade of Sychaeus, Dido can refer to Aeneas' good character. The imperative here does duty for the protasis of a conditional clause.

nulla parte 'in no respect': the opposite of *omni parte*; cf. *ES* 45n.

pigendus: the gerundive of this impersonal verb is found in a passive sense only here, Prop. 4.1.74 and very rarely in prose (N–W III 659); poets preferred *pudendus*, prose authors *paenitendus* (not possible in hexameters). The subject is *error*, but might easily be thought to be *ille*.

111–38 Dido breaks off her address to her dead husband and, addressing now no one in particular, recounts her life's disappointments, culminating in her preference for Aeneas over other potential suitors. She then addresses him directly again, in tones of increasing vehemence, charging him with impiety against the gods.

111 durat in extremum 'lasts to the end'.

uitaeque nouissima nostrae: a partitive genitive with substantival adjective, 'the final moments of my life'.

112 fati ... tenor 'the course of my destiny': cf. 17.14 *tenor uitae.*

113 internas ... ad aras: O. reconstructs the scene of Pygmalion's crime from *Aen.* 1.349 where he is said to kill Sychaeus *impius ante aras* and 4.21, where Dido speaks of *sparsos fraterna caede penatis. internas* is unparalleled in the sense of 'within a house'; this is the only occurrence of the word in poetry until Neronian verse, which led Heinsius to conjecture *Herceas*, a title of Zeus as household god, comparing Luc. 9.979 *Herceas ... non respicis aras.*

mactatus: as if a sacrificial victim; cf. 1.43n.

114 sceleris ... praemia: the wealth of Sychaeus; cf. Cic. *S. Rosc.* 117 *tribus praediis, hoc est praemiis sceleris, ornatus.*

115–16 exul agor ... patriamque relinquo, | et feror: O.'s
Dido echoes Aeneas' own words describing his departure from Troy
to Dido: *Aen.* 3.10–11 *litora cum patriae lacrimans portusque relinquo | ...
feror exsul in altum.*

115 cineresque uiri: at first glance this contradicts *Aen.* 1.353,
where it is said that Sychaeus was unburied (*inhumati*); but O. has
read Virgil carefully and knows that Dido is accompanied by
Sychaeus in the underworld (6.473–4) and thus that he must have
received burial at some time; cf. Austin on *Aen.* 1.353.

116 dubias ... uias: cf. 16.21 *dubias a litore feci ... uias.*

117 applicor his oris: an echo of Dido's first words to Aeneas;
Aen. 1.616 *quae uis immanibus applicat oris?* For the idiom, cf. 16.128 *ap-
plicor in terras ... tuas, Met.* 3.597–8, *Trist.* 3.9.10.

118 perfide: 2.78n.

litus emo: upon her arrival in North Africa Dido purchased as
much ground as could be enclosed by a bull's hide, as described in
Aen. 1.367–8 *mercatique solum, facti de nomine Byrsam, | taurino quantum
possent circumdare tergo.* Her proud reference to the land as a 'beach'
inverts Iarbas' depreciatory remarks in his complaint at *Aen.* 4.212–
13 *litus arandum | ... dedimus.*

119–20 urbem constitui: *Aen.* 4.655 *urbem praeclaram statui.*

fixi | moenia: a unique expression, as O. 'caps' Virgil's *Aen.*
4.655 *mea moenia uidi.*

inuidiosa 'that provoke jealousy': a favourite adjective with O.
(2.145n.). In *Aen.* 4.39–43, Anna warns her sister of the hostility of
the neighbouring African peoples who threaten the new city. In the
sequel to Dido's suicide her sister Anna must flee Carthage after it is
captured by Iarbas, a story told by O. in the *Fast.* (3.523–696).

121 tument: the metaphor is taken from the swelling of the sea
at the coming of a storm; cf. Virg. *Geo.* 1.465 *operta tumescere bella,*
Vell. 2.15.2, Sen. *Con.* 10.1.8.

bellis ... temptor: the expression occurs only here in poetry; cf.
Cic. *Man.* 23, Sall. *Cat.* 6.4, Tac. *Ann.* 2.79.

peregrina et femina: she is resented as a foreigner and looks an
easy prey because she is a woman; for the construction, cf. 2.65n.

122 'and, all inexperienced I can hardly make ready the city gates
and my troops': *rudis* is nominative singular, not accusative plural,

referring to one untrained for war (and reinforcing *femina*; cf. *OLD* s.v. 5b).

123 mille: often used of an indefinite large number; cf. *Am.* 1.3.15 *non mihi mille placent*, *Ars* 1.63 *iuuenes tibi mille placebunt* (H–S 211, *TLL* s.v. 980.69ff.). Dido, of course, exaggerates the number of her suitors and implies that she rejected them in favour of Aeneas, when a reader familiar with Virgil's text would recognize that she had already done so before his arrival in Carthage: *Aen.* 4.36–7. But O. develops the potential suggested in Iarbas' words at *Aen.* 4.213–14, in which he reacts like a jilted lover. Cf. too *Aen.* 4.320–1 *te propter Libycae gentes Nomadumque tyranni | odere, infensi Tyrii*.

qui me coiere querentes: *me* is the subject of the infinitive phrase governed by *coiere querentes* 'joined in complaining', a slight disjunction of the normal word-order (hyperbaton).

124 nescioquem: contemptuous, often used in elegy of a successful rival in love, e.g. 19.102, *Am.* 2.5.62, Tib. 1.6.6, Prop. 1.11.7. It reflects the dismissive tone of Iarbas' complaint to Zeus, in which he refers to Aeneas as *ille Paris cum semiuiro comitatu* (*Aen.* 4.215); cf. Juvenal's characterization of Aeneas (5.45): *zelotypo iuuenis praelatus Iarbae*.

thalamis ... suis 'marriage to them': *thalamus* is a Greek loanword, found mainly in poetry; cf. McKeown on *Am.* 1.5.11.

125–8 In the *Aeneid* Dido despairs and asks herself, *quid moror? an mea Pygmalion dum moenia frater | destruat aut captam ducat Gaetulus Iarbas?* (4.325–6) O. devotes a couplet to each eventuality, but his Dido transfers the responsibility directly to Aeneas.

125 Gaetulo: i.e. African, from a nomadic tribe of Numidia. Iarbas is the only one of Dido's local suitors named by Virgil.

126 praebuerim: perfect subjunctive for a deliberately vague assertion. *sceleri ... tuo*, as if *uinculis ... tuis*.

127 frater: Pygmalion. *impia* recalls his epithet *impius* at *Aen.* 1.349.

128 respergi ... sparsa: the force of the prefix in *respergi* is carried over to *sparsa*; 6.91n. Construe *cruore* with *nostro* (ἀπὸ κοινοῦ).

129 pone deos 'put down those images of the gods': the Penates which Aeneas brought from Troy; the specific, *deos*, precedes the more general, *sacra* 'sacred objects'; cf. Virg. *Aen.* 2.293 *sacra suosque tibi commendat Troia penatis*.

profanas: the verb in this sense, 'desecrate', is not attested before O. (*Am.* 3.9.19, *Met.* 4.390) and Livy (31.44). In early Latin a verb *profano* is found with the meaning 'to consecrate before an altar'; cf. Cato, *R.R.* 50.

130 non bene: this litotes is not found in the high style, but is a favourite with O.; cf. *Am.* 1.8.96, 1.10.37–8, 1.14.37, 3.7.1, *Bömer* on *Met.* 1.9.

impia dextra: points to a clear parallel with Pygmalion's *manus impia* above (127), and a pointed barb at *pius Aeneas*.

131–2 'In as much as you were fated to atttend to their worship when they had escaped the fire, the gods have reason to regret that they did escape it.' The couplet rather weakly restates the thought of the preceding line to score a verbal point: the effect of the repetition *elapsis igne ... elapsos ignibus* resembles the 'versus serpentinus' (5.117–18n.)

cultor: a rare word in Augustan poetry for a worshipper of the gods; cf. *Met.* 1.327, Cic. *Tusc.* 1.69, Virg. *Aen.* 11.788, Hor. *Carm.* 1.34.1.

133–8 O. reformulates *Aen.* 4.327–30, where Dido expresses her wish that she had had a child by Aeneas. O. does not actually say that she is pregnant, *pace* Austin on *Aen.* 4.329, who finds these lines 'vulgar'. By reminding Aeneas of this possibility, O.'s Dido heightens the reader's sense of his guilt. This point is forcefully driven home by conjuring up the thought of an unborn child, whose death would also be Aeneas' responsibility since he had abandoned her to her enemies.

133 Dido: accusative, 7n.

134 lateat: of a foetus, cf. Hor. *Carm.* 4.6.19–20 *latentes | matris in aluo*, *Am.* 2.13.20 *latens ... onus*, *Met.* 15.217 *spesque hominum primae matris latitauimus aluo*. The image is reinforced in *clausa* 'confined', with which we may compare Seneca's *Thy.* 1041 *clausum nefas* of Thyestes' children.

135 accedet fatis 'will be added to the doom': 1.96n.

infans: in the course of this digression O.'s Dido intensifies her addressee's emotional identification with the unborn (and perhaps unconceived) child through escalation in the language: *pars tui ... infans ... nato ... frater.*

136 nato funeris: the juxtaposition is pointed. The second half-

line is repeated in an address to Cupid at *Rem.* 22. For *nondum nato* as
the foetus, cf. *Am.* 2.14.28 *nondum natis*.

137 frater ... Iuli: a particularly forceful indictment of the an-
cestor of the Julian *gens* by Dido; Augustus would probably not have
been amused.

138 conexos 'joined together': the language is strong; *conecto* is
rare in poetry and almost always retains something of its original
force. And attention is focused on the patterned line.

una duos: O. is fond of such pointed juxtaposing of numerals; cf.
Bömer on *Met.* 3.544. This instance may have occurred to him as he
adapted the motif from Prop. 2.28.41 to his elegy on Corinna lying
near death after an abortion at *Am.* 2.13.15. Cf. *Met.* 2.609, the last
words of Coronis pregnant with Apollo's child, *duo nunc moriemur in
una*.

139–80 In this portion of the epistle Dido approaches the same
question of Aeneas' divine mission from a cooler perspective: she
argues logically the practical advantages of settling instead in Car-
thage. This point is not pressed, however, and her position shifts
again gradually to a request for delay only.

139 sed iubet ire deus: the *horrida iussa* (*Aen.* 4.376–8) of Apollo
and Jupiter reported to Dido by Aeneas at *Aen.* 4.345–59.

uellem uetuisset 'I wish that he had forbidden': parataxis.

140 nec: postponed (1.32n.), as commonly in O.'s works, in the
single *Her.* again only at 4.113 and 12.154.

fuisset: the pluperfect of the auxiliary verb in the passive in
place of the imperfect (both indicative and subjunctive) is apparently
colloquial, and is avoided in poetry before O. and in prose before
Livy; cf. H–S 321. Its increasing use in poetry doubtless owes some-
thing to the metrical convenience afforded by an extra short syllable.

Punica ... humus 'Carthaginian soil': the regular idiom is *terra*
or *tellus* with a geographical epithet; *humus* is an Ovidian variation;
cf. 4.68 *Cnosia ... tellus*, *Fast.* 2.444 *Etrusca ... humo*.

141 hoc duce nempe deo 'of course, this is the god who guides
you': *nempe* (2.36n.) is ironic. O.'s Dido doesn't name the divinity,
but she has in mind Apollo and the oracle given to Aeneas at Delphi
(*Aen.* 3.94–8); cf. *Aen.* 6.59 (Aeneas praying to Apollo): *tot maria intraui
duce te*. The tone derives from *Aen.* 4.379–80 *scilicet is superis labor est,
ea cura quietos | sollicitat*.

142 teris ... tempora longa 'waste such a long time': a pointed reversal of Mercury's complaint to Aeneas: *Aen.* 4.271 *qua spe Libycis teris otia terris?* From Dido's point of view it is rather a waste to wander the oceans.

143–4 'It would hardly be expected that you would expend so much suffering to return to Troy itself, if it were still the city it was when Hector lived.' O. reformulates into a more logical sequence Dido's frantic objections in *Aen.* 4.311–13: *quid, si non arua aliena domosque | ignotas peteres, et Troia antiqua maneret, | Troia per undosum peteretur classibus aequor?*

143 Pergama: 1.32n.

erant repetenda: the apodosis of the condition in the pentameter, indicative because of the hypothetical nature inherent in the gerundive.

144 Hectore ... uiuo: Troy did not fall at Hector's death, but his name was a potent symbol of her greatness.

145 Simoenta: accusative, a Greek form; 1.3n. The epithet *patrium* 'native' is pointed here: the Tiber, addressed as *genitor* at 8.72 and *pater* by Aeneas at Virg. *Aen.* 8.540, echoing an ancient formula (cf. Skutsch on Enn. *Ann.* 26), is not his true ancestral river as Dido sees it.

Thybridis: a Hellenized form of a name apparently of Etruscan origin, the preferred name of the river in the *Aeneid*, and the only one used by O. in the *Met.* For the periphrasis *Thybridis undas*, cf. *Fast.* 1.242, *Met.* 15.432, Virg. *Aen.* 7.436.

146 ut: concessive; 1.116n. For *nempe*, cf. 2.36n.

147 utque latet uitatque: the image of Italy as an unstable and receding goal recurs several times in the *Aeneid*, as in Aeneas' words to Helenus (3.496–7), who has found rest, *arua neque Ausoniae semper cedentia retro | quaerenda*; cf. *Aen.* 5.629, 6.61. In *latet* O. plays upon the contemporary etymology of Latium, whose name was alleged to derive from this verb; cf. *Fast.* 1.238, Virg. *Aen.* 8.322–3. *ut* introduces a qualification, 'considering how' (*OLD* s.v. 22).

149–50 in dotem ... | accipe: a legal phrase attested only here in verse; cf. *TLL* s.v. *dos* 2053.6ff.

ambage remissa 'with no more beating about the bush': a colloquial expression; cf. Hor. *Serm.* 2.5.9 *missis ambagibus*, Plaut. *Cist.* 747 *sed, quaeso, ambages, mulier, mitte.* Dido is bluntly stating her proposition. O. also intends a play on the original sense of *ambages* 'a meandering course'.

150 aduectas Pygmalionis opes: Dido brought with her to Carthage a secret treasure shown to her by the ghost of her husband; cf. *Aen.* 1.363–4 *portantur auari* | *Pygmalionis opes*, a sarcastic reference to the treasure of Sychaeus that his brother Pygmalion thought he had got his hands on.

151 transfer felicius 'you will have better fortune if you resettle': this is a very common Latin idiom, sometimes called the 'adverb of judgement' (H–S 827, K–S I 795); the adverb qualifies not only the action of the verb, but expresses a judgement on the whole phrase; cf. Brink on Hor. *Ars* 40.

152 resque 'affairs of state'.

154 suo partus Marte triumphus 'a triumphal procession secured by his own prowess': the phrase *Marte suo* is idiomatic; cf. *Rem.* 469, Cic. *Phil.* 2.95. The expression *partus ... triumphus* was coined by O. on the analogy of *uictoriam parere*; cf. *Am.* 2.12.16 and, in the spurious Helen episode, *Aen.* 2.578. O.'s use here has point both because he refers specifically to the procession (*eat*), a uniquely Roman institution, and to the Roman god *Mars*.

155 quem superet: the subjunctive is final, 'for him to conquer'.

156 pacis leges 'terms of peace': although this phrase is first attested in *Aen.* 4.618, *lex* is common in a number of combinations for the terms of a *foedus*.

capit 'offers scope for': the verb is construed with the objects of both clauses ἀπὸ κοινοῦ.

157 tu modo: the tone is sharp; the pronoun, emphatic by its separation from the imperative *parce* (163), indicates the urgency of the request. This idiom is common in final appeals to a lover in elegy; cf. Tränkle (1960) 8–9.

matrem: Venus. Dido employs the same oath as Phyllis (2.39), here adapted to the circumstances of Aeneas' family.

fraternaque tela 'the weapons of your brother (Cupid)'.

158 comites ... deos: the word-order is mannered and artificial with an epithet and noun bracketing another pair standing in apposition. This trick of style, which may be termed 'enclosing apposition', was an innovation introduced by the neoteric poets. There is only one other example in the certainly genuine *Her.* of this mannerism (11.19), although O. makes use of it elsewhere; cf. Norden (1927) 116–17, Solodow (1986).

159–62 The long parenthesis postpones the completion of the entreaty begun in 157. The form that it takes, *sic superent* 'so may they remain alive', is a form of bargain in exchange for granting the request, common in petitions (H–S 331, Appel (1909) 152); cf. 4.147–8 *tolle moras ... sic tibi parcat Amor.* O.'s Dido appeals to Aeneas' feelings for his deceased father and young son: astute readers of the *Aeneid* might recall the words of the defeated Rutulian warrior Mago to Aeneas (*Aen.* 10.524–5), *per patrios manes et spes surgentis Iuli, | te precor, hanc animam serues.* Aeneas was not moved on that occasion either.

159 reportat: the correction of the MSS *reportas* is required by Ovidian usage; O. never postpones *et* to the third position and *ille* would then fall flat. Mars may properly be said to escort 'home' the Trojan survivors, a regular use of *reportare* (*OLD* s.v. 2 b).

160 ferus: an obvious epithet for Mars, which, surprisingly, is first attested here.

modus 'limit': *ille* refers to the Trojan war, *Mars ferus.*

161 suos ... impleat annos 'fill out to completion his allotted years': cf. 3.135 *sic omnes Peleus pater impleat annos.*

162 molliter ossa cubent: this sentiment is common in funerary inscriptions, such as *CLE* 428.15, 1458.1; cf. *Am.* 1.8.108 *ut mea defunctae molliter ossa cubent, Trist.* 3.3.76. But this particular formulation with *molliter* is first found in Virg. *Ecl.* 10.33 *molliter ossa cubent*, in the speech of the love-poet Gallus, whose poetry O. may be imitating here; see Clausen *ad loc.*

163 domui: cf. *Aen.* 4.318 *miserere domus labentis.* For the form, see 31n.

tradit habendam: 15n.

164 praeter amasse: this use of the infinitive as a noun with a preposition is a Graecism rarely attested (K–S 1 666); cf. 19.16 *superest praeter amare nihil*, Hor. *Serm.* 2.5.69. *meum* should be construed with *crimen*: 'What accusation do you make against me?': O.'s Dido again slips into legal language (2.28n.). For the syncopated form, 5.38n.

165 Pthia: a city in Thessaly, the home of Achilles. Construe as an ablative with *oriunda* (ἀπὸ κοινοῦ); Pthia is paired with Mycenae at Virg. *Aen.* 1.284 *Pthiam clarasque Mycenas*.

magnisue ... Mycenis: the home of Agamemnon. The epithet is Virgilian: *Aen.* 2.331 *milia quot magnis umquam uenere Mycenis*.

oriunda: the only appearance of the word in poetry after Plautus, Ennius, and Lucilius. The word may have had an archaic flavour: it is very common in Livy and legal texts, but completely avoided by, e.g., Caesar, Sallust, and Tacitus; cf. *TLL* s.v. 1005.75ff.

166 O. produces a more realistic version of Dido's protest to be carried to Aeneas by her sister: *Aen.* 4.425–6 *non ego cum Danais Troianam exscindere gentem | Aulide iuraui classemue ad Pergama misi.* Virgil's Dido speaks as a proud queen who commands armies, O.'s as an ordinary woman. Quintilian cites these lines of the *Aen.* as an example of the rhetorical figure of *auersio: Inst.* 9.2.39 *quae a proposita quaestione abducit audientem.* For other examples in O., cf. 5.156, 21.117, *Rem.* 5.

steterunt in te: i.e. in battle; for the expression, only in O., cf. *Trist.* 1.2.5 *Mulciber in Troiam ... stabat.* For the prosody, cf. 2.142n.

167 si pudet uxoris 'if you are ashamed to have me as wife': Dido pointedly uses the everyday word *uxor*; 1.97n.

hospita cleverly rephrases Virgil's *Aen.* 4.323–4, where Dido gives this name to Aeneas, *cui me moribundam deseris hospes | (hoc solum nomen quoniam de coniuge restat)?*; cf. 2.1, 6.52.

169–80 Once again, as in 39–44 above, she returns to the bad sailing conditions, altering her appeal now. She asks for time to adapt to his decision to leave. Putting Dido's request in this fashion shows Aeneas in an even harsher light, as she now apparently offers no resistance to his eventual departure. It no more reflects her true intentions here than in the model for this passage at *Aen.* 4.433–4.

169 plangentia litus: cf. 19.121 *planguntur litora fluctu.* The verb *plango* normally refers to beating the breast as a sign of mourning; its literal use of the waves beating against the shore is limited to poetry. The MSS read *frangentia* here, but as Heinsius notes in proposing his emendation, the normal idiom in Latin is *fluctus a litoribus franguntur*.

170 temporibus certis 'at fixed times of the year': the language of meteorological observation, as in Vitr. 1.6.10 *flare solent ... certis temporibus etesiae*; cf. *Ars* 2.392, *Rem.* 189, *Fast.* 1.661.

dantque negantque: cf. *Am.* 2.9.50 *dasque negasque*.

171 dabit aura uiam: cf. 19.52 *ut tibi det faciles aura uias*, *Met.* 8.3, *Pont.* 4.9.73, *ES* 214.

carbasa: a Greek loan word (κάρπασος) for 'linen', its use for 'sail' is almost exclusively limited to poetry. It is regularly listed by grammarians as heteroclite, feminine in the singular and neuter in the plural. The neuter plural is first attested here in Latin, and the earliest occurrence in Greek is in an epigram of Augustan date (*AP* 9.415.6): O. is perhaps parading his lexical erudition. Cf. *Aen.* 4.417 *uocat iam carbasus auras*.

172 eiectam 'driven ashore': cf. the definition in Ulp. *Dig.* 47.9.3.6 *eiecta nauis hoc est quod Graeci aiunt* ἐξεβράσθη. Dido reminds Aeneas of the condition of his arrival.

continet alga: the seaweed is said to 'detain' his ships because, piled upon the shore, it is a sign of storms at sea: cf. Hom. *Il.* 9.8, Hor. *Carm.* 3.17.10–11. The image is contained in a patterned line.

173 tempus ut obseruem 'to watch for an opportunity': apparently an everyday phrase; cf. Cic. *Fam.* 11.16.1 *ut tempus obseruaret epistulae tibi reddendae*.

certior: a direct reference to Virgil's description of Aeneas' departure from Carthage: *Aen.* 5.1–2 *interea medium Aeneas iam classe tenebat | certus iter*.

174 This is certainly an unbelievable claim by this point, but that Dido should make it at this juncture is an indication of her deteriorating state of mind.

si: concessive (= *etsi*).

175 laniataque: a strong word, usually reserved for physical mutilation; but cf. Sall. *Hist.* 4.28 *ubi se laniata naufragia fundo emergunt*.

176 postulat 'requires'.

semirefecta: an Ovidian coinage; cf. 1.55n.

177 siqua tibi praebebimus ultra 'anything further I shall give you': a thinly veiled allusion to her possible pregnancy.

178 non: the correction by Hall (1990) 275 eliminates the inconsistency in the MS reading: Dido cannot in one breath say that she wants only time to learn how to endure the separation and in the other still talk of marriage.

coniugii: 2.34n.

tempora parua peto: O. interprets a Virgilian ambiguity: *Aen.*

4.433 *tempus inane peto*, in which the adjective *inane* sparked debate among the ancient commentators: Servius glosses *sine officio coeundi; nam 'sine beneficio' non procedit, cum spatium petat et requiem*, with further observations by Serv. auct. O. clearly thought that the phrase meant 'a trivial amount of time'.

179 dum: not 'until' but 'while' with the indicative.

freta mitescunt et amor: syllepsis (p. 30).

tempore et usu 'by the passing time and by becoming used to the idea': cf. *Rem.* 503 *intrat amor mentes usu, dediscitur usu.*

180 fortiter edisco: by its position the adverb will be construed with *edisco*, although logically it should also be taken with *pati* (amphibole, 1.23n.): it will take courage, Dido implies, to learn endurance.

181–96 Dido announces her intention to commit suicide forthwith: she has suggested as much from the opening of the epistle.

181 si minus 'otherwise': a prosaic and colloquial phrase (H–S 667), occurring 10 times in O., but only once in the other Augustan poets (Prop. 4.4.57).

est animus 'it is my intention': a variation of the usual prosaic idiom *in animo habere*; cf. *Aen.* 4.639 *perficere est animus.*

effundere uitam: a graphic combination, coined by O. after *spiritum effundere* 'breathe one's last', and ventured later only by Val. Fl. 6.706 and Sil. 7.678.

182 crudelis: the Virgilian Dido hurls this epithet at Aeneas with emphasis at *Aen.* 4.311 (cf. Austin *ad loc.*), and again in her dying words: *Aen.* 4.661–2 *hauriat hunc oculis ignem crudelis ab alto | Dardanus.*

183 scribentis imago vividly presents the image of her despair to the mind of the letter's recipient; cf. 11.5.

184 Troicus ensis: in the *Aeneid*, Dido asks her sister to gather the arms that Aeneas left behind in their chamber upon his hurried departure (*Aen.* 4.495), and it is his sword that she uses to kill herself; cf. *Aen.* 4.646–7 *ensemque recludit | Dardanium.* In *Am.* 2.18.25 O. refers to Dido as she writes this letter, *tenens strictum ... ensem.*

187 'How well your gift suits my destiny!' *munera* is bitterly ironic here, as in *Aen.* 4.647 *non hos quaesitum munus in usus.* The sword was not given to her by Aeneas, but left behind (184n.), and *munera* is also the proper word for an offering to the dead. The pentameter then

'explains' the hint in this word: as Shuckburgh notes, its point seems
to be, 'truly this is a cheap way of providing for a wife's obsequies –
you leave her a sword'.

188 instruis ... sepulcra: the phrase is figurative, 'you pro-
vide my funeral service', but retains something of its literal force
'you build my tomb'.

190 uulnus: the metaphor of love as a wound is, of course, as
old as love. O.'s choice here is in part suggested by the opening lines
of *Aen.* 4: *at regina graui iamdudum saucia cura | uulnus alit uenis.* The
weapon (*telo*) is Cupid's dart, aimed at her breast: cf. A.R. 3.286–7
'his arrow burned deep within the girl's heart'.

saeui ... Amoris: the genitive is subjective; it is often difficult to
know when to print with a capital, but O. is clearly thinking of the
god and his weaponry here, and the epithet is conventional for him;
cf. *Am.* 1.1.5, 1.6.34, 2.10.19, *Ars* 1.18, *Rem.* 530, Virg. *Ecl.* 8.47, Fedeli
on Prop. 1.1.6.

191 Anna soror, soror Anna: Dido now addresses her absent
sister Anna, who, though she plays a crucial role in the *Aeneid*, has
not been mentioned by O.'s Dido. The address, in chiastic anaphora
(a characteristic Ovidian pattern, cf. *Ars* 1.99 *spectatum ueniunt, ueniunt
spectentur ut ipsae*), is intended to heighten the pathos here.

meae male conscia culpae 'accomplice in my offence': with
male O.'s Dido attributes a share of the blame to her sister more
clearly than Virgil's character ever does. *culpa* is often a euphemism
for sexual misconduct (105); Virgil exploits the ambiguities inherent
in the word when Dido proclaims at *Aen.* 4.19 *huic uni forsan potui suc-
cumbere culpae*, an ambiguity which he resolves in 4.172 *coniugium uocat,
hoc praetexit nomine culpam.*

192 in cineres: the offerings would consist (for Romans) of liba-
tions of wine and oil poured upon the ashes; hence the prepositional
phrase in place of the expected dative. O.'s Dido ends on a far
gentler note than Virgil's, who asks for revenge: 4.623–4 *cinerique
haec mittite nostro | munera.*

ultima dona: cf. *Am.* 3.9.50 *mater et in cineres ultima dona tulit, CLE*
1302.4 *huic coniux ultima dona dedit.*

193 consumpta rogis: graphic and melancholy; the participle
does duty for a temporal clause, 'when I have been consumed by the
pyre'.

inscribar: 2.145n.

Elissa Sychaei: the use of the genitive alone to indicate marital relationships is old and remains common in sepulchral inscriptions; cf. Luc. 2.343–4 *liceat tumulo scripsisse Catonis Marcia*, H–S 59–60, K–S I 414.

194 hoc tantum ... carmen 'this brief epigram': reformulated by O. in the *Fasti* (3.547–8), when he quotes 195–6, as *tumulique in marmore carmen | hoc breue*; cf. Prop. 2.1.72 *breue in exiguo marmore nomen ero*. O. plays with this motif when he describes the (appropriately) small monument for Corinna's parrot at *Am.* 2.6.59–60.

195–6 O. repeats the epitaph verbatim at *Fast.* 3.549–50, where he describes the epitaph as if Dido's request here had actually been fulfilled. O. recasts the epitaph once more with some variation at *Ars* 3.39–40 *et ensem | praebuit et causam mortis, Elissa, tuae.* He was evidently pleased with the formulation and the figure *praebuit ... et causam ... et ensem* (syllepsis, p. 30). Such reworking of successful formulations is a characteristic of Ovidian style; cf. Ganzenmüller (1911) 398. The parallel with the conclusion of Phyllis' epistle is deliberate: 2.145–8.

195 PRAEBVIT AENEAS ... CAVSAM: when Aeneas meets Dido in the Underworld in the *Aeneid*, he asks incredulously (6.458), *funeris heu tibi causa fui?* O.'s Dido answers.

X Ariadne Theseo

The desertion of Ariadne by Theseus was one of the most celebrated episodes of seduction and betrayal in ancient poetry. As the unknown author of the *Aetna* (*c.* AD 50?) remarked, *quis non periurae doluit mendacia puppis, | desertam uacuo Minoida litore questus?* (21–2). The 64th poem of Catullus is our best-known account of the story, and forms the principal literary backdrop for O.'s epistle. Specific echoes of Catullus' poem (esp. 15, 25–8, 47–50, 59–98, 119–24nn.) clearly show that O. takes his departure from that text. The basic outlines of the story are familiar: Theseus joins the group of fourteen Athenian young men and women regularly sent as tribute to Minos of Crete, where they were offered as sacrifice to the Minotaur. With Ariadne's help Theseus kills the monster and escapes by sea to Athens, stopping en route at the island of Dia, identified in antiquity as Naxos (Call. fr. 601 Pfeiffer). There he abandons Ariadne as she sleeps and returns to Athens. She awakes to find herself alone, but is shortly thereafter carried off by Dionysus. Within these broad outlines there is considerable variation in our sources on almost every detail: on the manner of her meeting with Theseus, on their means of escape from Crete, and on his reason for leaving Ariadne behind (Herter, *RE* Supp. XIII (1973) 1093–1141). The story is as old as Homer, who knew a different account, in which Ariadne dies on Dia (*Od.* 11.321–5); and in the *Cypria* Nestor related to Menelaus, in a digression of course, 'the events concerning Theseus and Ariadne' (*EGF* 31, 38–9).

In the following centuries the affair with Ariadne became a standard item in the mythographical tradition attached to Theseus, but with no general agreement on details, as competing traditions sought to exonerate the Athenian hero for his act of treachery or further implicate him; cf. Plutarch, *Thes.* 20.1. The story was a popular motif in art, appearing frequently in both red-figure and black-figure vase paintings. Already as early as the end of the fifth century BC a painting was displayed in the temple of Dionysus at Athens depicting 'Ariadne asleep, Theseus putting out to sea, and Dionysus on his arrival to carry off Ariadne' (Paus. 1.20.3). The sleeping Ariadne was a popular motif too in Roman wall painting (*LIMC* s.v. 'Ariadne' 55–66), but representations of her awakening to discover Theseus' ship departing were especially popular (*LIMC* 75–90). In part this may be attributable to the success of a literary account of the abandonment, perhaps Cat. 64, although these paintings of a gently weeping Ariadne seem to have little in common with Catullus' hysterical heroine. It has long been suspected that there was another Hellenistic Greek version of the myth, now lost, that served as a model for Catullus; cf. Riese (1866), Maass (1889) 528–9, Barigazzi (1963). This hypothesis would account for similarities between Cat. 64 and the account of the late Greek epic poet Nonnus in book 47 of his *Dionysiaca* as the result of the two poets drawing independently on the same poem. If that is true, some aspects of Catullus' art are unrecoverable for us, and we will miss something in O.'s epistle as well, since it is likely that he too alludes to this lost poem. But the principal focus for O. is Catullus' treatment and an important aspect of his portrayal of Ariadne is the way in which her character is contrasted with the one delineated by his Roman predecessor. O. returns to Ariadne's story three times: in *Ars* 1.527–64, where he concentrates on the sequel to this episode, her rescue by Dionysus, in the *Met.* where a brief summary (8.169–82) forms a bridge to another story, and finally in *Fast.* 3.461–516, where Ariadne is again abandoned, this time by the god.

1–6 The epistle begins so abruptly that some editors have been moved to delete or transpose the first couplet (to follow 110 or 132). It is true that 3–4 look more suitable as an epistolary opening, but 1–2 are unobjectionable in diction and metre, and they do not cohere better after line 6 where they are found in G. Since there is no reason why the first couplet *must* take the form of a salutation, Ariadne's abrupt opening may be read as an indication of her distress, its effect heightened by postponing the identification of the writer, especially since Theseus can hardly have been expecting correspondence from Dia. Ariadne's delusion that her letter will reach Theseus is not only amusing, it is the first of several acts of self-deception in the poem.

1 Mitius ... genus omne ferarum: the comparison of humans with animals to the disadvantage of the former is a familiar conceit; cf. *Am.* 1.10.26 *turpe erit, ingenium mitius esse feris,* Sen. *Oed.* 639, *Phaedr.* 558, Zwierlein (1986) 246–7. It is especially appropriate here for Ariadne, as she finds herself alone on a deserted island.

2 credita ... eram: indicative instead of subjunctive for the past potential. This use is rare in classical prose and poetry, and is perhaps colloquial (H–S 328), thus underlining the indignant tone; contrast 1.108n. The passive here has the force of a reflexive, 'I could have entrusted myself'; cf. K–S 1 104–6.

non ulli: sc. *ferae.*

3 quae: 1.1n.

illo ... litore: the shore of the island of Dia where he abandoned her. With the vocative *Theseu* it is perhaps possible to detect an echo of Cat. 64.133 *deserto liquisti in litore, Theseu.*

4 unde = *ex quo.*

5 -que ... et: the connection is made by *et,* for which *-que* is preparatory. This combination (polysyndeton) was perceived as an archaism by the first century: it is avoided by Cicero and Caesar, and in poetry it is found in the high style (H–S 515). O. uses it once elsewhere in the *Her.* (5.71n.) and the *Ars* (1.95), but otherwise only in the *Met.*, and *Fasti*, and there sparingly: cf. *TLL* s.v. *et* 887.49–51. In this case the anticipatory *-que* prepares the reader for the devastatingly emphatic *et tu* at line-end.

6 per facinus: adverbial, 'criminally', for a metrically intractable (and unattested) *facinerose*; cf. *Rem.* 62, *Ib.* 566. This form of circumlocution is common in Latin poetry, where otherwise common adverbs are generally avoided; cf. Axelson (1945) 62–3.

somnis insidiate meis 'ambushing my sleep': a vivid expression found also at Cic. *Cat.* 1.26 *non solum insidiantem somno maritorum, uerum etiam bonis otiosorum*; cf. Sen. *Phaedr.* 782 *somnis facient insidias tuis.*

7–58 Ariadne tells of her reaction on that morning when she awoke to find herself alone in bed and Theseus' ship gone. The epistolary fiction wears a bit thin here: Theseus is named as a third person in line 10, but Ariadne never fully loses view of the recipient. Theseus cannot know what happened to Ariadne after he left and Ariadne's narrative identifies him with O.'s reader.

7 tempus erat ... quo: Ariadne begins her narrative of events on Naxos in the high style, recalling the appearance of Hector to Aeneas: *Aen.* 2.268 *tempus erat quo prima quies...* As a formula for introducing a narrative, this phrasing is found often in O. and later poets; e.g. *Met.* 6.587, 10.446, *Fast.* 5.497, Luc. 8.467, Stat. *Theb.* 4.680.

uitrea ... pruina: the morning frost (*matutina pruina*, Prop. 2.9.41) is glass-like in its glitter; cf. *Am.* 1.6.55 *uitreoque madentia rore | tempora noctis*. Ariadne obliquely makes the point that she was cold.

8 tectae fronde queruntur aues: echoed with variation at *Fast.* 4.166 *tactae rore querentur aues. queri* is often used of the sound of birds (e.g. 18.82, *Am.* 3.1.4), but it is especially evocative here as Ariadne begins her complaint: Cat. 64. 130 *haec extremis maestam dixisse querellis.* For the expression *tectae fronde,* cf. *Ars* 1.58 *fronde teguntur aues.*

9 incertum uigilans 'half awake': the neuter adjective for adverb is a Graecism; cf. Hor. *Serm.* 2.5.100 *certum uigilans,* Stat. *Theb.* 5.212 *incertumque oculis uigilantibus,* Luc. 6.623, H–S 40.

languida 'sluggish'.

10 prensuras: predicative, with final force, 'to grasp'.

semisupina 'half lying down': a form coined by O. (*Am.* 1.14.20,

Ars 3.788), restored here by Heinsius for the unmetrical *semisopita*, evidently an intrusive gloss influenced by *somno* above.

11–12 nullus erat ... nullus erat: the repetition of the opening of the hexameter at the end of the pentameter is only slightly less extravagant than the type known as the *versus serpentinus* (5.117n.). This trick of style is a favourite with O.; cf. *Am.* 1.4.13–14, 3.2.17–18, *Rem.* 71–2, 705–6, *Fast.* 2.236–7, *Trist.* 4.3.77–8, *ES* 213–14. The couplet is also notable for its entirely dactylic rhythm, together with the threefold repetition of *-que*, creating a light effect. Here *nullus = non* (2.105n.), with emphasis, 'gone without a trace'.

retempto: not attested before O., who then uses it five times in the *Met.* and once in the *Tristia* (5.12.51). The pleonasm with *iterum* is a common type; cf. *TLL* s.v. 556.66ff.

13 conterrita 'thoroughly terrified': the emphatic compound is found in O. only at *Met.* 6.287.

14 sunt ... praecipitata: the passive has a 'middle' sense: 'I threw myself from off ...'

uiduo: not simply 'empty'; by calling the bed 'widowed' she foretells her own condition; cf. 5.106n.

15 adductis sonuerunt pectora palmis 'my breast sounded as I struck it with the flat of my hand': O. varies a Catullan phrase, 64.351 *uariabunt pectora palmis*, a borrowing acknowledged again in O.'s other adaptation of the Ariadne myth: *Ars* 1.535 *tundens mollissima pectora palmis*.

16 utque erat: qualifying *turbida*, an idiomatic expression that captures the suddeness of the moment, 'tangled as it was'; cf. *Fast.* 5.455, *Met.* 4.474, 9.113, 11.60. O. develops only one detail here from Catullus' description of Ariadne, 64.63 *non flauo retinens subtilem uertice mitram*. Her unkempt hair (47, 137, 147) is a standard feature of the scene: *Am.* 1.7.15–16, *Ars* 1.530, 3.153; cf. Cat. 64.56–7 *utpote fallaci quae tum primum excita somno | desertam in sola miseram se cernat harena.*

e somno 'after sleep': a common use of *ex* in prose; for this phrase, cf. Tac. *Germ.* 22, Suet. *Tib.* 68.2, Cels. 2.4.7. O. combines the half-line *utque erat e somno* with *Am.* 1.5.9 *tunica uelata recincta* to form *Ars* 1.529 in his second retelling of Ariadne's tale.

rupta 'torn': 5.141n. The reading of the main tradition produces an unattested and difficult phrase, *comam rapere*.

17 luna fuit 'the moon was shining': in the moment just before dawn as the dew falls (7). O.'s Ariadne is a convincing narrator who explains why she is able to see at this hour; cf. *Fast.* 2.697 *luna fuit: spectant iuuenem.*

specto ... cernam 'I watch to see if I can distinguish': for the construction of a conditional clause with *specto*, cf. 19.27.

18 uideant is a consecutive subjunctive.

19 nunc huc, nunc illuc, et utroque suggests her state of complete confusion. When Cicero describes to his friend Atticus his wretched voyage in the Aegean, he uses similar terms: *Att.* 5.12.1 *hinc Syrum, inde Delum, utroque citius quam uellemus, cursum confecimus.*

sine ordine 'at random': an Ovidian 'formula'; cf. 18.113, *Am.* 2.11.45, *Ars* 2.467, *Met.* 8.389, 14.266, *Pont.* 3.9.53.

20 puellares 'girlish': the adjective is first attested here, but it was probably not coined by O.; cf. *Fast.* 4.433, 4.463, 5.611, *Met.* 5.393, 10.594. It is odd that Ariadne should describe herself as childish, but O. has an image in mind, conveyed here by the 'patterned' line, and he sacrifices verisimilitude to reinforce it.

21 clamanti: sc. *mihi*. O. interprets the scene as set by Catullus: 64.124–5 *saepe illam perhibent ardenti corde furentem | clarisonas imo fudisse e pectore uoces.* The shrill cries reported by Catullus are rendered by O. as a quotation, '*Theseu!*' The allusion is underscored by an echo of the lament recorded immediately thereafter by Catullus (64.133) *deserto liquisti in litore, Theseu?*

22 reddebant 'echoed'; cf. *Met.* 3.361.

24 ipse locus: repeats with variation (chiasmus) the preceding subject, *locus ipse.* The word-play makes a point: Ariadne is alone, and an echo is the only voice she hears.

25–8 Catullus tells us that in the tradition he follows (64.124 *perhibent*) Ariadne first climbs the cliffs and then rushes into the shallow water to call to Theseus (124–31). O. redevelops that scene in a more rational fashion, by making Ariadne spot Theseus' departing ship and ignoring the detail, also recorded by Nonnus (*Dion.* 47.298–300), that she called to him from the edge of the water.

25 mons fuit: cf. Cat. 64.126 *praeruptos ... montes.* Ariadne begins her narrative with an excursus describing the setting; 2.131–48n. The phrasing recalls 5.61, but the function there is different.

apparent 'are visible'.

frutices 'shrubs': an everyday word not much used by poets. It occurs once in Lucretius and Virgil's *Georgics*, but apart from O. (10 occurrences), who is prone to such realistic touches, it is commonplace only in the agricultural writers.

26 hinc: sc. *a uertice.*

pendet 'overhangs'.

adesus: the cliff (*scopulus*) has been worn away by the action of the waves. The compound verb is almost exclusively poetic; O. refines the image, using an even more rare compound, in *Met.* 11.783 *scopulo, quem rauca subederat unda.*

27 uires animus dabat: the witty parenthesis explains why Ariadne was able to scale the cliff, a commentary, so to speak, on Catullus' *praeruptos ... conscendere montes* (64.126). Ariadne relates her story very much as O. would; cf. *Met.* 12.383 *huic ego (nam uires animus dabat) 'adspice' dixi,* also in a narrative attributed to a character.

atque ita 'and after doing so', cf. 6.97n.

28 prospectu metior 'I survey in my view': an unusual phrase for Ariadne scanning the sea, but O. has in mind Catullus' equally unique expression *aciem ... protenderet* (64.127); cf. Hor. *Serm.* 1.2.103 *metiri possis oculo.* The moment is fixed in a patterned line.

29 uentis quoque sum crudelibus usa 'I found the winds cruel, as well as you': cf. 113.

30 praecipiti ... Noto: the epithet is a stock poetic term for winds, but in this context carries a suggestion of the haste of Theseus' departure; in what may be an allusion to this poem, O. scores the same point at *Am.* 1.7.15–16 *talis periuri promissaque uelaque Thesei | fleuit praecipites Cressa tulisse Notos*; cf. McKeown *ad loc.*

carbasa: 7.171n.

31 'As I saw a sight such as I thought I did not deserve to see': i.e. *ut uidi ea quae putarem me esse indignam uidisse.* O. converts to outrage the incredulity reported by Catullus, *necdum etiam sese quae uisit uisere credit* (64.55). The divergent readings of the MSS suggest a meaning along the lines of 18.32 *aut uidet aut acies nostra uidere putat,* but that is not Catullus' point, or O.'s. Ariadne does not doubt that she saw his sail (cf. 43–6), she simply cannot believe it. Housman's emendation restores sense, if not O.'s precise wording.

32 frigidior glacie: 1.22n.

semianimis: scanned as a quadrisyllable. On the form, cf. 1.55n.

33 nec: adversative (2.6n.), 'but grief did not allow'.

languere 'to feel faint', but with a suggestion of idleness: O.'s Ariadne is roused to action by her indignation.

34 excitor: the repetition (epanalepsis) registers an appropriate note of excitement.

uoce uoco 'I call aloud': such pleonasms go back to Ennius (*Ann.* 43 Skutsch) and are common in poetry. The alliterative *uoce uocare* probably has a somewhat old-fashioned and formal tone (Löfstedt (1933) 185-6) and is used elsewhere by O. only at *Met.* 10.3, 10.507.

35-6 O. condenses to a single couplet Ariadne's own report of the complaint she made at Cat. 64.132-201, while watching the departure of Theseus and his companions. In part this is a display of wit, but since the entire epistle constitutes O.'s reworking of that monologue, it suits his programme to abbreviate the words 'actually' spoken on the occasion.

35 quo fugis? puts the matter concisely; in contrast, Catullus' Ariadne begins her address with four rhetorical questions.

scelerate ... Theseu: for Catullus' *perfide ... Theseu* (64.133); cf. 2.78n., 7.133n.

36 numerum ... suum 'its full complement': cf. Cic. *Verr.* 5.51 *si suum numerum naues haberent.*

37-42 O.'s Ariadne describes herself behaving as if she truly believes that she has been abandoned by accident: first she screams wildly, then waves her arms, and finally raises a signal.

37 haec ego: sc. *dixi*. The ellipse is common in the conversational style; cf. 14.67, *Am.* 2.5.33, *Rem.* 39; Hofmann (1951) 169.

quod uoci deerat, plangore replebam 'the defects of my voice, I supplied by beating my breast': the form of expression is striking. The point is perhaps to underline the implausible nature of Ariadne's lament in earlier versions: at the time of Theseus' departure the abandoned woman would more naturally (in the Roman view) incline to lamentation than eloquent statement. The effect is assisted by the sound-play (cacemphaton) *plangore replebam*. *deerat* is scanned as two syllables.

38 uerbera cum uerbis: O.'s Ariadne ironically portrays her frantic behaviour; the word-play has a slightly comical air; cf. Plaut. *Truc.* 112 *me illis quidem haec uerberat uerbis*, *Men.* 978, Ter. *Haut.* 356, Cic. *Tusc.* 3.27.64, and in O., *Am.* 1.6.19-20. O.'s Ariadne likes this figure of speech; cf. 82 *mora mortis*. Elsewhere in the *Her.* only 9.31 *honor ... onus* is comparable.

39 si non audires 'in case you could not hear': the clause depends upon the following *ut* clause.

40 iactatae: she waved her arms, sending a signal far and wide (*late*).

41 candidaque ... uelamina: white, because it could be more clearly seen, but perhaps also a reminder of the white sails which Theseus would forget to raise.

42 scilicet: heavily ironic and to be taken closely with *oblitos*. Ariadne wanted to believe that they had forgotten her, when she had in fact been abandoned.

43 oculis ereptus eras: the parataxis within the couplet, which consists of three independent phrases, reflects the suddenness of Theseus' disappearance over the horizon; cf. *Met.* 7.776 *ipse oculis ereptus erat.*

tum denique 'then and not till then'.

44 genae = *oculi* becomes common in Silver Latin poetry; cf. *TLL* s.v. 1767.63ff. Her eyes, so prone to tears (that is the force of *molles*; cf. *Rem.* 340 *mollibus est oculis, quod fleat illa, refer*), had been numbed (*torpuerant*) by grief.

45 quid potius facerent? 'what better could they do?': the couplet virtually restates the thought of 43-4 in the form of a deliberative question. Although the point falls rather flat, there are no grounds for deleting the couplet as Bentley proposed.

lumina 'eyes', as often in poetry.

47-50 O. 'analyses' the celebrated picture of Ariadne in Cat. 64.61-2 as she gazes after Theseus' ship. There she is also compared to a Bacchante, or rather a likeness of a Bacchante, since a static image conforms to the demands of Catullus' treatment: he is describing a representation of the moment on a tapestry: *saxea ut effigies bacchantis, prospicit, eheu, | prospicit et magnis curarum fluctuat undis.* In the first couplet (47-8) O. represents the comparison to a Bacchante, while he recalls Catullus' image of the statue in the next (49-50). O. describes Phyllis on the beach in similar terms at *Rem.* 593-4 *ibat, ut Edono referens trieterica Baccho | ire solet fusis barbara turba comis .*

47 diffusis: a stereotype for Bacchantes in art and literature; cf.

Am. 1.9.38 *effusis ... comis*, Bömer on *Met.* 3.726. The description recalls Cat. 64.63 *non flauo retinens subtilem uertice mitram.*

48 Ogygio: a rare epithet for 'Theban', first attested here in Latin poetry. It is said to derive from Ogygos, a founder and king of Thebes (Paus. 9.5.1), but the etymology is obscure and the Greek poets used the word as an epithet for both Thebes (Aeschylus, Apollonius) and Athens (Aeschylus). In the *Ars*, when O. reuses this pentameter in his description of Ariadne's mother Pasiphae, the problematic epithet is replaced by one more familiar: 1.311 *fertur ut Aonio concita Baccha deo.* In Greek poetry it is always an epithet of a place; it first occurs here as an epithet of Dionysus, doubtless with Hellenistic precedent.

Baccha: comparisons of women distracted by love to Bacchantes are commonplace (cf. Pease on *Aen.* 4.301); O. reuses this pentameter in his description of Ariadne's mother Pasiphae at *Ars* 1.311.

49 frigida: chilled by the elements, by fear, and because she is without her lover; 1.7n.

50 lapis ipsa fui: a figurative expression for one made numb by fear (Otto (1890) 186), here taken literally.

51 torum: the improvised couch where they had spent the night.

52 non acceptos exhibiturus erat 'was not going to make good its receipts': a legal metaphor. *exhibere* is often used for producing an object (or person) in dispute (*TLL* s.v. 1418.51ff.), with specific reference to the *actio ad exhibendum.*

53 quae possum: i.e. 'which is all I am able to touch'.

uestigia: the imprints on the bed; cf. *Am.* 1.8.97 *ille uiri uideat toto uestigia lecto*, Shackleton Bailey (1956) 81–2.

54 intepuere 'grew warm': the compound becomes current in the early imperial period and may have been coined by Virgil (*Aen.* 10.570), while O. uses it elsewhere only at *Fast.* 5.216. Its meaning 'to grow warm' or 'cool' is determined entirely by the context. The ablative *membris* is instrumental.

55–8 Ariadne falls upon the bed, which she then addresses in a pathetic monologue. The gesture of despair is an echo of the fate of Virgil's Dido, mourning the departure of Aeneas: *postquam Iliacas uestes notumque cubile | conspexit, paulum lacrimis et mente morata | incubuitque toro* (4.648–50). Dido, too, follows with an address to the

objects that remind her of Aeneas. The influence of Greek tragedy
in these contexts is clear (Heinze (1915) 137 n. 2), but Hellenistic nar-
rative verse also placed its heroines in this situation. In Apollonius'
Argonautica, Medea throws herself on her bed to weep for Jason
(3.655–66), and Parthenius tells the story of Polymele, whom Odys-
seus loved and left, weeping over the Trojan spoils he left behind
(*Erot.* 2.2); cf. Clausen (1976).

55 incumbo: sc. *toro*, supplied from the context; cf. *ES* 149.

lacrimisque toro manante profusis 'the bed dripping with
the tears I shed': the ablative *lacrimis* depends upon *manante*; the hy-
perbole lies in the verb *manare* (= *madere*); cf. *Met.* 6.312 *lacrimis etiam
nunc marmora manant*, of Niobe.

57 ambo ... ambo: the anaphora of the pronoun is a manner-
ism adopted by O. from Virgil (e.g. *Ecl.* 7.4, *Geo.* 4.342, *Aen.* 11.291),
probably in imitation of Hellenistic models; cf. [Theocr.] 8.3–4. Ex-
amples in O. are *Met.* 1.327 *innocuos ambos, cultores numinis ambos*, 8.373
ambo conspicui, niue candidioribus ambo; and in later epic, Val. Fl. 7.653
and Stat. *Theb.* 6.374.

58 There is a paradox in the address to the bed, a feature of wed-
ding hymns, as for example in the one by the neoteric poet Ticidas
(*FPL*, fr. 1 Buechner), *felix lectule talibus sole amoribus*; cf. Prop. 2.15.2
lectule deliciis facte beate meis. There is also a competing note from
tragedy, as in Euripides' *Alcestis* 175–80, where the heroine collapses in
tears on her marriage bed and cries, ὦ λέκτρον ... οὗ θνήισκω πέρι.

perfide: the epithet repeatedly applied to Theseus in Catullus'
version (64.132–3) is transferred (enallage, 1.10n.) by O.'s Ariadne
to their marriage 'bed'. Theseus' violation of his oath must always
have formed a prominent part in the tradition: Nonnus, who leans
heavily on Hellenistic models, has his Ariadne call him a 'perjurer'
(ὁρκαπάτην, *Dion.* 47.389).

lectule: a colloquial diminutive, found in O. only here and at
Trist. 1.11.38. *pars nostri ... maior* is a familiar phrase for a close rela-
tionship, amply paralleled in Greek and Latin literature; see Nisbet–
Hubbard (1970) 48, and in O., cf. *Met.* 8.406, *Trist.* 1.2.44, 4.10.32,
Pont. 1.8.2.

59–98 Ariadne laments her condition in 40 carefully articulated
lines. The relationship to Catullus is highlighted by diffuse imitation

of 64.177–87. The opening series of despairing deliberative questions belongs to the style of 'epyllion'. There are many points of contact in details with Catullus; but such laments must have been standard in Hellenistic narrative verse and New Comedy: cf. Plaut. *Rudens* 204–15, the monody of Palaestra: *nunc quam spem aut opem aut consili quid capessam? | ita hic sola solis locis compotita. | hic saxa sunt, hic mare sonat, | neque quisquam homo mi obuiam uenit | ... nec prope usquam hic quidem cultum agrum conspicor. | algor, error, pauor, me omnia tenent.*

59 quid faciam?: deliberative subjunctive rather than future, 'What am I to do?' The question strikes a note familiar from tragedy; cf. Fedeli on Prop. 3.16.5. This portion of the epistle assumes the character of a monologue, until Ariadne again addresses Theseus in 71.

quo sola ferar?: cf. Cat. 64.177 *nam quo me referam?*

cultu 'habitation': cf. Cat. 64.184 *nullo colitur sola insula tecto*, and for the expression, cf. Cic. *Tusc.* 1.45 *regiones omni cultu ... uacantes.* The island is also represented as deserted by Nonnus (*Dion.* 47.354).

60 hominum ... boum: a reminiscence of Homer, *Od.* 10.98 οὔτε βοῶν οὔτ' ἀνδρῶν φαίνετο ἔργα 'the workings of oxen and of men were not seen', cast in a characteristically Ovidian brachylogy, in which one word from each clause (*uideo* and *facta*) must be supplied from the other; cf. Virg. *Geo.* 1.118 *hominumque boumque labores.*

61–2 Ariadne's confusion and urgency are conveyed by the ellipse of the verb and the absence of a connective (asyndeton).

61 omne latus terrae cingit mare: cf. Cat. 64.185 *nec patet egressus pelagi cingentibus undis.*

nauita: 6.48n.

62 ambiguas 'uncertain': O.'s use of this word to describe a course through the sea is unique and it may reflect an awareness of the derivation of the word by contemporary scholars; cf. Paul. *Fest.* p. 15 Lindsay *quod in ambas agi partes animo ... potest.*

itura: predicative 'no ship to journey'.

63–70 Ariadne emphasizes again her isolation by pointing out that even if she could escape the island, she has no one to turn to. The desperation of the heroine who has betrayed all for the sake of a lover who then betrays her was given classic formulation by Euripides in his *Medea* (502–5): 'Now where I am I to turn? To the house of my father which I betrayed along with my country for you when I came here? To the daughters of Pelias? A fine reception they would give me after I killed their father.' The theme recurs in subsequent portrayals of Medea's story (e.g. A.R. 4.378–81, Enn. *Med.* 284–5), and it is not surprising to find echoes in the narratives of other women in a similar predicament. O. found the same lament in Cat. 64. 177–83, but the similar scene in Nonnus' *Dionysiaca* (47.377–80) is probably an indication that an earlier literary version had framed this complaint for Ariadne. O. provides his own distinctive twist by framing the lament as a logical argument.

63 finge 'just suppose': since Ariadne has no physical means of escape, her questions are purely rhetorical. The same rhetorical strategy is employed by O.'s Scylla in *Met.* 8.113–15 *nam quo deserta reuertar? | in patriam? superata iacet. sed finge manere: | proditione mea clausa est mihi.*

64 quid sequar? 'what am I to make for?': 7.10n.

65 ut: concessive, 1.116n.

pacata: cf. *Met.* 13.440 *dum mare pacatum, dum uentus amicior esset.*

66 Aeolus: keeper of the winds; see introd. n. to 11.

67 Crete: the Greek form of the name, preferred by O., but otherwise rare in Latin literature.

centum digesta per urbes 'organized into a hundred cities': acknowledging the Homeric epithet ἑκατόμπολις (*Il.* 2.649); cf. *Ars* 1.297 *centum quae sustinet urbes, Met.* 13.706, Virg. *Aen.* 3.106, Hor. *Carm.* 3.27.33–4.

68 puero cognita ... Ioui: O. refers to the concealment of the infant Zeus from Kronos in a cave on Mt Dicte in Crete. The story is as old as Hesiod (*Theog.* 453–80) and O. makes it a commonplace in describing the island: cf. 4.163 *Iouis insula Crete, Am.* 3.10.20 *Crete nutrito terra superba Ioue, Met.* 8.99 *Iouis incunabula Creten.*

69 tellus iusto regnata parenti: periphrasis for *patria*. Minos' reputation for fairness is as old as Hesiod (fr. 144 M–W), who calls him 'the most kingly of mortal kings'. The passive *regnata* of an intransitive verb with a dative of agent is a Graecism (K–S 1 102), found first in Augustan poetry and later in prose; cf. *Met.* 8.623 *arua ... quondam regnata parenti*, 13.720, *Pont.* 4.15.15, Virg. *Aen.* 6.793–4. In this context, Ariadne's reference to her father might seem a pointed reversal of Catullus' description of Crete: *iniusti regis Gortynia templa* (64.75).

70 nomina cara: in apposition to *pater* and *tellus* (= *patria*), and explained by Bentley (*ad* Hor. *Carm.* 3.27.34) as 'terms of affection', *caritatis nomina.*

71–2 The moment is specified and the treacherous act is limited to providing Theseus with the device by which he could retrace his steps out of the Labyrinth. Other details of the story O. leaves out of account.

71 uictor: predicative, 'after you had won'.

tecto ... recuruo: the Labyrinth; cf. 4.60 *curua ... tecta*, *Met.* 8.158 *caecis ... tectis*, and below 128. The word-play *morerere recuruo* (cacemphaton) is deliberate; cf. *Am.* 2.2.52 *quemquam quamuis.*

72 regerent: final subjunctive. The wording of this pentameter echoes Cat. 64.113 *errabunda regens tenui uestigia filo*; cf. Prop. 2.14.8 *Daedaliam lino cum duce rexit iter.*

fila: the thread to lead him out of the labyrinth, which she gave to Theseus on the advice of Daedalus; cf. 4.59–60, Cat. 64.112–13, Prop. 2.14.7–8, Nonnus, *Dion.* 47.368, 384–5 It is first attested as an element in the story in Pherecydes, *FGrH* 3 F 148 and 150, then in the mythographical tradition, but it figures early in artistic representations; cf. *RE* Supp. xiii 1115–16, *LIMC* s.v. 'Ariadne', nos. 4–8.

73 per ego ipsa pericula: this word-order, with the unstressed pronoun attracted to the second position in the clause ('Wackernagel's Law'), is regular in oaths with *per*, both in Greek and in Latin; cf. *Fast.* 2.841 *per tibi ego hanc iuro ... cruorem*, Eur. *Med.* 324 μὴ πρός σε γονάτων, *Aen.* 4.314 *per ego has lacrimas*, H–S 398–9.

iuro: by reporting Theseus' words verbatim, O.'s Ariadne underscores his treachery; cf. Cat. 64.143 *nunc iam nulla uiro iuranti femina credat.*

74 te ... meam: the pentameter is bracketed by the significant pronouns.

76 periuri: a common epithet for Theseus in O.'s works; cf. *Am.* 1.7.15, *Fast.* 3.473.

sepulta: the metaphorical use 'consigned to oblivion' is well chosen: Ariadne does not know that she will be rescued from this desert island, and might well expect literally to be 'buried' here. The position of *femina* and *uiri* framing the line is pointed.

77 The involved word-order reflects the confusion in her mind.

fratrem: as Phaedra, Ariadne's sister, also calls the Minotaur,

4.115. O. picks up the family connection which Catullus had twice emphasized (64.150, 180–1), because he assimilated Ariadne's situation to that of Medea, who at least conspired in the murder of her brother and in some accounts assisted in the act. O.'s Ariadne, however, attempts to elicit sympathy by a slightly different route and portrays Theseus as her brother's murderer.

mactasses: a strong word (1.43n.), used here and at 101, appropriate to the slaughter of the half-man half-bull. The pluperfect subjunctive is jussive referring to past time (K–S I 187), 'You ought to have slaughtered me'; here it performs the function of the protasis in an unreal condition: 'You ought to have slaughtered me; (if you had) your obligation would have been dissolved.' For the syncopated form, cf. 5.38n.

improbe: a strong word (= Greek σχέτλιος) for a failure of morals, often found in amatory verse after the famous denunciation of Aeneas by Dido: Virg. *Aen.* 4.386 *dabis, improbe, poenas.*

claua: in the earliest representation of the death of the Minotaur, Theseus' weapon is a sword. The club was substituted during the Hellenistic period as his weapon of choice as the result of the assimilation of his career to that of Heracles and probably figured in literary accounts of the period as well; cf. 101, 4.115, Nonnus, *Dion.* 47.436.

78 soluta fides: the promise would have been dissolved, since he had only pledged to love her as long as *both* were alive.

79–80 A statement of the obvious: Ariadne's confused and terrified thoughts are such as would occur to any woman abandoned in similar circumstances. The antithesis posed by the couplet is entirely banal. The situation is improved slightly if we read *et* for *sed*, but the problem is not eliminated: 'the distich, which is entirely otiose, seems spurious' (Palmer). More importantly, the Latinity is suspect: *recordor* with reference to future events, 'to ponder', is unparalleled in the classical period. The couplet perhaps originated in a comment in the margin.

79 quae sum passura: but Ariadne is not thinking about what she will suffer; instead she proceeds to fantasize about different forms of death. Palmer suggested emending to *perpessa*, thus making better grammar with *recordor*, but worse hash of the sense, since nothing has happened to her yet.

81 occurrunt animo 'come to mind': the noun is not required by the idiom.

pereundi mille figurae: cf. Cat. 64.187 *ostentant omnia letum. figurae* is not simply figurative: death appears to her in the shape of visions.

82 mora mortis: for the word-play (38n.), cf. Prop. 1.13.6 *in nullo quaeris amore moram.*

83–8 O. develops and expands the fears expressed by Ariadne at Cat. 64.152–3 *pro quo dilaceranda feris dabor alitibusque | praeda*, a passage where the poet imitates Hom. *Il.* 1.4–5 (96n.). O. eliminates the Homeric allusion and substitutes a rhetorically expansive enumeration of the terrifying creatures.

84 lanient 'to tear apart': final subjunctive. The word-choice is graphic: *laniare* is rarely found in other poets.

lupos: the animal's identity is withheld until the end of the couplet, heightening the suspense.

85–6 A much vexed couplet, which Bentley athetized. The difficulties are lodged in the pentameter, where the MSS present us with an indicative verb after *an* and an impossible elision at the end of the line (Platnauer (1951) 90). No emendation is entirely satisfactory: Housman (1897) 241 (= *Class. pap.* 401) transposed *forsitan* (85) and *quis scit an* (86), but was unable to repair the end of the couplet. The text printed here, which was proposed by Heinsius, is open to objections since it is unexpected for Ariadne now to name the island which she has just called *ista tellus*. None the less it may stand *exempli gratia* for lack of a better alternative.

86 Dia: the name of the island in Homer's account of Ariadne, where she is killed by Artemis (*Od.* 11.325). Later it was identified with Naxos (Callimachus, fr. 601 Pfeiffer), as the place where Theseus abandoned her.

87 dicuntur: Ariadne has only heard of the dangers of the sea before; this is her first actual experience.

expellere 'to cast ashore': the word is usually used for shipwrecks and corpses, but cf. *Met.* 15.511 *corniger hinc taurus ruptis expellitur undis.*

phocas: a 'trick' ending. From the articulation of the preceding lines (*uenturos ... lupos, fuluos ... leones*) we expect some menacing beast to be construed with *magnas*, only to find ... seals.

88 quid uetat ... ?: the phrase has a colloquial air, 'What's to prevent?'; cf. *Fast.* 1.295, *Trist.* 1.2.12, Hor. *Serm.* 1.1.25.

gladios: of pirates; as the next verse shows, she is now thinking of the dangers posed by humans. Ariadne uses the ordinary word for 'swords' for emotional effect, 2.140n.

ire: when used of weapons, the verb is a poeticism; cf. 3.148 *ensis in Atridae pectus iturus, TLL* s.v. 646.34–44.

89–92 Besides being killed by bandits, Ariadne might be made a captive and sold into slavery, a fate she fears even more than death. O. inverts an important point of Ariadne's lament in Catullus, where she declares her willingness to have served Theseus as a slave in his household (64.160–3): *attamen in uestras potuisti ducere sedes, | quae tibi iucundo famularer serua labore, | candida permulcens liquidis uestigia lymphis, | purpureaue tuum consternens ueste cubile.* The corresponding part of Nonnus' version of Ariadne's complaint (*Dion.* 47.390–5) bears a very strong resemblance to Catullus, suggesting that both knew an earlier work in which this figured prominently. O.'s reader is thus a bit surprised to hear that Ariadne abhors servitude.

89 tantum ne: for the more prosaic *modo ne* introducing a restrictive wish, 'if only I am not tied up a captive'.

90 traham ... pensa: of drawing out an allotment (*pensa* from *pendo*) of wool into thread, a slave's task; cf. 3.75 *nos humiles famulaeque tuae data pensa trahemus.* In Nonnus' account, cf. *Dion.* 47.393 'I will work the rattling loom' (πολύκροτον ἰστὸν ὑφαίνειν).

serua: adjective, as at *Fast.* 6.558 *serua manus.*

91–2 A rising tricolon, expressively indignant. The final member comes as something of a surprise: more than her parentage, it is her betrothal to Theseus that she remembers, and values, most.

91 filia Phoebi: Pasiphae, the daughter of the Sun-god identified as Phoebus. O.'s Ariadne is perhaps playing off an earlier version of Ariadne's lament, which may be echoed by Nonnus. His Ariadne also invokes her mother, but as an example of a royal woman who served as a menial (47.396–400): 'my mother too served as a slave' (καὶ ἡμετέρη ποτὲ μήτηρ | ... θήτευε).

92 pacta fui: the 'doubling' of the perfect tense with the past participle is permissible here where the participle has the force of a noun: 'whose betrothed I have been'.

93 uidi: the perfect is frequentative, 'whenever I see'. *porrecta* should also be taken with *mare* and *terras* (ἀπὸ κοινοῦ).

95 restabat 'remained an option' (*OLD* s.v. 4b): i.e. heaven remained in which to place her hope, but she is afraid of it also.

simulacra deorum can only mean 'the images of the gods', such as those placed in temples. Having betrayed her home and family, she fears the gods she would otherwise pray to. Of course, since there are no shrines here, it then occurs to Ariadne that she is on a deserted island.

96 praeda cibusque: O. recasts Ariadne's lament at Cat. 64.152–3 *dilaceranda feris dabor alitibusque | praeda*. His rendering displays an awareness not only of Catullus' formulation, but of Catullus' Homeric model, *Il.* 1.4–5 αὐτοὺς δὲ ἑλώρια τεῦχε κύνεσσι | οἰωνοῖσί τε πᾶσι 'made them the feast of all dogs and birds', which O. probably knew in a variant form with δαῖτα (*cibus*) for πᾶσι, as read by Zenodotus.

97 siue 'if on the other hand': resuming the construction from 93 *si ... uidi*.

colunt habitantque 'if men do cultivate and inhabit this place', a hysteron proteron.

98 externos ... uiros: foreigners; an ironic phrasing, for the threat that they might pose is altogether different from the harm inflicted upon her by falling for Theseus. For *laesa*, cf. 5.4n.

99–132 Ariadne catalogues her regrets: she wishes that she had never helped Theseus in his mission to put an end to the Athenian tribute to Minos. After all that she has done for him, she reflects, she is doomed to die alone and deserted. The rhetorical emphasis falls on her *officia* to Theseus, which he has not properly recompensed.

99 uiueret ... utinam: the imperfect denotes the impossible nature of this wish. Androgeos was the brother of Ariadne. O., like Catullus (64.77), follows the most common version of the myth, in which he was murdered in Athens by rival contestants whom he had defeated in the first Panathenaic games; cf. Apollod. *Bibl.* 2.5.9, 3.1.2, 3.15.7, Paus. 1.27.10, Plut. *Thes.* 10. The story was depicted by Virgil in a description of Daedalus' carvings on the temple of Apollo at Cumae: *Aen.* 6.20–2 *in foribus letum Androgeo; tum pendere poenas | Cecropidae iussi (miserum!) septena quotannis | corpora natorum; stat ductis sortibus urna.* As punishment for this crime (*facta impia*) Minos was

able to impose his demand for an annual human offering to the
Minotaur.

100 funeribus = *mortibus*, a common poeticism, and perhaps
a subtle 'correction' of Catullus' over-bold reference to the 'living
corpses' of the Athenian victims, 64.83 *funera ... nec funera*, a Grae-
cism not reproduced by O.

Cecropi terra: Athens, from Cecrops, the name of its first
legendary king. O. uses many such periphrases with the feminine
adjective in *-is*: cf. 16.30 *Taenaris ... terra, Am.* 1.2.47 *Gangetide terra,
Fast.* 2.663, *Met.* 5.648, 8.153, 9.448, 13.716, *Trist.* 1.2.82, *Pont.* 2.9.54.
For such formations, cf. Bömer on *Met.* 5.303 and 12.34. The ad-
jective *Cecropis* is introduced to Latin by O. from Hellenistic Greek
sources; cf. Antip. Sid. *AP* 7.81.5 (= *HE* 422) Κεκροπὶς αἶα.

101 mactasset: 1.43n.

nodoso stipite: Theseus' weapon (77n.); cf. Virg. *Aen.* 7.507 *stipi-
tis ... grauidi nodis.*

102 ardua ... dextera: raised high to strike; cf. *Met.* 11.482.

parte uirum ... parte bouem: O. seems to have gone out of
his way to avoid using the word *Minotaurus*. It was used by Catullus
(64.79) and Virgil (*Aen.* 6.26), but is not attested in any Greek poetry.
'Presumably it was their sense of Greek usage – and perhaps a desire
to avoid the obvious – that kept Ovid and Statius ... from follow-
ing the example of Catullus and Virgil' (Clausen (1988) 15). O. re-
sponded to the challenge of describing the Minotaur with remark-
able ingenuity. The famous pentameter at *Ars* 2.24 *semibouemque uirum
semiuirumque bouem* was one of those reportedly exempted by O. when
he challenged his critics to select his three most objectionable lines
(Sen. *Contr.* 2.2.12). Cf. *Met.* 8.169 *geminam tauri iuuenisque figuram.*

103 monstrarent: final subjunctive, 'to show you'.

103–4 fila ... | fila: the pathetic repetition (epanalepsis) is a
favourite figure in Catullus' epyllion; cf. Fordyce on 64.26.

104 relecta 'retraced': sc. by repeatedly pulling it in (*adductas*)
with his hands. The reading was restored by Heinsius, who com-
pared *Met.* 8.172–3 *utque ope uirginea nullis iterata priorum | ianua difficilis
filo est inuenta relecto*, where most MSS read *relicto*. The corruption
found in most of the MSS here, *recepta*, probably arose out of an
attempt to construe *saepe* with the verb that follows it rather than
with *adductas*.

105–10 Theseus' victory over the Minotaur may surprise others when they hear of it, but it no longer surprises Ariadne who now knows that he is invincible. The climax of this conceit is the literal interpretation in the final couplet (109–10) of the familiar description of the hard-hearted lover.

105 si stat Victoria tecum 'that Victory sides with you': the personification is assisted by the idiom *stare cum*, which is regularly used for taking sides in a war.

106 The image is set, again, in a 'patterned' line.

belua: the beast is the Minotaur, who is later her 'brother' (115) when it serves her purpose to represent its slaying as a cruel act.

planxit humum 'struck the earth': sc. in its fall; cf. 16.336 *caesaque sanguineam uictima planget humum, Fast.* 1.578, 4.896, *Met.* 3.125.

107 cornu: of the Minotaur.

108 ut: concessive, 1.116n.

pectore tutus eras 'you were protected by your heart [of iron]', explaining the irony of the metaphor in the *praecordia ferrea* above.

109–10 O.'s Ariadne puts a new spin on an old metaphor (e.g. *Am.* 1.11.9, *Met.* 9.614, 14.712, *Tr.* 1.8.41, Tib. 1.1.63) for hard-heartedness by adding an unexpected climax, as did Phyllis in 2.137. The couplet is bound into a rising tricolon by the anaphora of *illic*.

110 qui silices Thesea uincat habes: i.e. *qui silices uincat, Thesea habes*. This dislocation of normal word-order (hyperbaton) is unusually bold for O. (Kenney (1973) 128–30), though some examples can be found in his verse: e.g. 3.19 *si progressa forem, caperer ne, nocte, timebam, Ars* 1.399–400, *Met.* 12.314–15. Such hyperbata are found throughout Latin poetry, and do not appear to be due exclusively to imitation of Hellenistic poets, who also affect this type of word-order; cf. Fordyce on Cat. 66.18.

131–2 This couplet recasts Ariadne's outburst at Cat. 64.154–6 *quaenam te genuit sola sub rupe leaena, | quod mare conceptum spumantibus exspuit undis, | quae Syrtis, quae Scylla rapax, quae uasta Charybdis?* The conceit is as old as Homer, *Il.* 16.33–5 (7.37n.), but after Catullus it is invariably found in amatory contexts in Roman poetry; cf. Virg. *Aen.* 4.365–7, *Met.* 8.120–1. These lines were transposed to their present position by T. Birt (*GGA* (1882) 860) because in their transmitted position they cohere with neither the preceding nor the following lines, while the commonplace fits neatly with the discussion of Theseus' hard heart. A mechanical explanation for their omission here might be the similarity of the opening words (homoearchon) of the pentameters 110 *illi-* and 132 *fili-* in capital script.

131 Pittheidos Aethrae: Theseus' mother, who was the daughter of Pittheus, ruler of Troezen. The genitive *Pittheidos* is a Greek form, scanned as a quadrisyllable.

132 auctores: sc. *generis tui*; cf. *TLL* s.v. 1204.44.

112 at introduces the apodosis to an implied condition in the previous line and has a limiting sense, 'If I had to sleep, at least I could have slept for ever.' *semel* is 'once and for all' (5.104n).

nocte premenda fui: cf. Virg. *Aen.* 6.827 *nocte prementur*, Hor. *Carm.* 1.4.16 *te premet nox.* For the indicative, see 1.108n. *nox* as a poetic metaphor for death is ancient (e.g. Hom. *Il.* 4.659, *Od.* 20.351) and the examples in Latin are numerous.

113 Ariadne's reproachful address to the winds may be a recollection of the lost Greek source of Catullus and Nonnus. The latter reports (*Dion.* 47.303-5) how Ariadne, in her angry speech when she awoke, 'prayed to Boreas and adjured the wind, adjured Oreithyia to bring back the boy to the land of Naxos'. Catullus may recall the same moment in 64.114 *sed quid ego ignaris nequiquam conquerar auris?*

uos quoque crudeles: Ariadne repeats the epithet applied to *somni* above (111) and uses it to build a triad: each of these couplets (111-16) is devoted to the causes of her doom – sleep, wind, and a promise – which are here treated as sentient beings. A couplet (117-18) is then added to explain the point, but the rhetorical effect here is rather weak.

114 in lacrimas officiosa meas 'eager to start my tears': cf. 18.60 *comes in nostras officiosa uias.*

115 dextera: the right hand by which he slew the Minotaur and sealed his promise to Ariadne. She refers more clearly now to the promise sworn by Theseus, to which she had alluded earlier (78). The mythographical tradition records that Ariadne provided him with the secret of the Labyrinth only after extracting from him (*poscenti*) a promise (*fides*) that he would take her away to Athens and make her his wife. This he agreed to do on oath (Apollod. *Epit.* 1.8). Construe *crudelis* with *dextera* and *fides* (ἀπὸ κοινοῦ).

necauit: poets were quite scrupulous in selecting words for killing; cf. Axelson (1945) 65-8, Lyne (1989) 106-8. *necare* is found, e.g., only once in Virgil (*Aen.* 8.488) and not at all in Prop. and Tib. In Roman law it means both 'to execute' and 'to murder'. O., with his predilection for legal language (2.34n.), uses it 16 times; cf. Bömer on *Met.* 9.679. But this is the only occurrence in the *Her.*, for shock effect: the graphic word for 'murder' comes as a surprise at line-end in Ariadne's simultaneous characterization of Theseus' killing of Androgeos and his abandonment of her.

116 nomen inane 'a word without meaning': cf. *Ars* 1.740 *nomen amicitia est, nomen inane fides*, Hor. *Epist.* 1.17.41 *uirtus nomen inane est.*

117–18 The couplet restates and explains the preceding three couplets, repeating the leading item in each (*somnus uentusque fidesque*), in order to score a rhetorical play on the numerical opposition: one girl, *una puella*, surrounded by three causes, *causis ... tribus.*

117 The conceit of the winds conspiring against her is probably echoed from Catullus' source, which was known to Nonnus: *Dion.* 47.309–11 'but even the winds themselves must have borne a grudge against the girl when they carried the ship to Attica'.

in me iurarunt 'have conspired against me': the expression is unique, for the regular sense of *iurare in aliquem* is to swear an oath *to* someone, and the example adduced from Livy 2.45.14 (*TLL* s.v. 676.28) is not a parallel. The syncopated perfect (5.38n.) of *iuro* is more common than the longer form.

119–24 Ariadne laments that she will die alone, far from home, and with no friend or relative to mourn her. O. expands on the fear expressed by Catullus' Ariadne, 64.153 *neque iniacta tumulabor mortua terra*; but he does so by echoing Propertius on the death of Paetus, who was lost at sea: 3.7.9–12 *et mater non iusta piae dare debita terrae* | *nec pote cognatos inter humare rogos,* | *sed tua nunc uolucres astant super ossa marinae,* | *nunc tibi pro tumulo Carpathium omne mare est*; cf. Tib. 1.3.5–10. The sentiment is common in sepulcral epigrams, and reflects the belief that without burial the spirit has no rest.

119 moritura 'when I die'.

120 lumina condat: 1.113n. The subjunctive is final.

122 positos: i.e. *compositos.* Before cremation the body of the deceased would be arranged on the bier and anointed. Somewhat anachronistically, O.'s Ariadne imagines a distinctly Roman funeral.

123 superstabunt replaces Propertius' less straightforward *astant super* (119–24n.).

124 sepulcra: ironic, for she will have none.

125–52 Ariadne directs a final appeal to Theseus, as if her letter could be delivered while he is still on board his ship. She imagines him upon his return to Athens, where there will be no mention of her role in his exploits. The contrast between her expectations of sharing in his triumph and her present condition leads to a final abject appeal.

125 ibis ... portus: the accusative without preposition after verbs of motion, regular with names of cities, is much extended in poetry (H–S 49–50). In this case the usage is perhaps mitigated by the epithet, *Cecropios* (100n.) *portus = Athenas*, as at *Met.* 6.445–6.

126 turbae celsus in ore tuae 'proudly in the sight [*OLD* s.v. *os* 10b] of your followers': describing a triumphant reception in his home city. *celsus* is used metaphorically, as it is in Sil. 15. 257 *ille nitet celsus*, 16.187.

127 taurique uirique: 102n.

128 sectaque per dubias ... uias 'cut into intricate paths'.

saxea tecta: the Labyrinth, which O. depicts as a cavern cut out of rock. Among surviving accounts, only Nonnus has a similar picture: 47.433 πεδοσκαφέος λαβυρίνθου 'the earth-dug labyrinth,' perhaps drawing on the same Hellenistic source as O.

129 narrato: future imperative.

sola tellure relictam: cf. Cat. 64.57 *desertam in sola ... harena.*

130 titulis: 2.73n.

133 di facerent 'I wish the gods had caused you to see me.'

134 mouisset uultus ... tuos 'would have affected your expression', a difficult phrase; cf. Virg. *Aen.* 6.470 *nec magis incepto uultum sermone mouetur.*

135 non oculis, sed, qua potes, aspice mente: cf. Cic. *Balb.* 47 *ut conspiciatis eum mentibus, quoniam oculis non potestis.*

136 haerentem should be taken literally, as Ariadne paints a picture of despair, suggested by Cat. 64.126, where Ariadne scales the cliffs to search for his sails. This is hyperbole, of course: she cannot write a letter while clinging to the rocks.

137 lugentis more 'like one in mourning'. Her hair is unbound because she has just awoken; 47n.

138 sicut ab imbre 'as if with rain': a simile in place of the common metaphor of *imber* for tears, as in O.'s description of

Ariadne at *Ars* 1.532 *indigno teneras imbre rigante genas*. For the causal *ab*, cf. *Am.* 1.13.41 *marcet ab annis*, 2.5.39, *TLL* s.v. 29.76ff.

140 litteraque ... pressa: Ariadne writes her letter on a wax tablet, in which the writing (*littera*) is traced by pressing down (*pressa*) with a stylus.

141 quoniam male cessit: an aside, 'since it has turned out badly', for Ariadne, that is.

adoro 'beseech' is a strong word in this context. It is properly used of petitions addressed to gods, kings, and the like.

143 ne ... quidem 'neither', *OLD* s.v. *quidem* 6 b.

si non ego causa salutis: Ariadne scores a debating point by momentarily yielding her claim to have rescued Theseus: 'Even if it were not true that I rescued you, it is still not right for you to cause my death.'

144 non tamen est cur 'there is no reason why'.

145–7 has tibi ... | hos tibi: the repetition is for emphasis. In these two couplets, Ariadne restates the description she had given earlier of how she beat her breast (15) and tore her hair (16) when she awoke to find Theseus gone.

145 lugubria: beating the breast is a gesture of lamentation, so the transfer (enallage, 1.10n.) of the epithet 'mournful' to *pectora* is comprehensible.

lassas is more common in O.'s elegies (31 instances) than its metrically equivalent synonym *fessus* (20 instances), which is the preferred word in epic poetry and the *Met.* (2.90n.). Its frequency in comedy and infrequence in Republican prose suggest that the word is colloquial; cf. Axelson (1945) 29–30, Austin on Virg. *Aen.* 2.739. O. uses the word to suggest the pathos of Ariadne's exhausted state.

146 trans freta: arms outstretched *towards* the sea are a familiar gesture (e.g. *Met.* 4.556, 8.849); Ariadne reaches out as if she can cross it.

147 qui superant 'that remain,' after tearing out the rest: an extraordinary hyperbole.

ostendo: as if he could see.

148 per lacrimas oro points a contrast with *non per meritum adoro* in 141.

149 flecte ratem: repeated from 36.

uersoque relabere uelo 'reverse your sail and glide back': for *uelum uertere*, cf. 13.134. The MSS read *uento*, but as Burman noted, it was not in Theseus' power to reverse the wind, nor would Ariadne ask it; hence the reading *uelo*, which he found in 'Basileensi codice'. In *uelo* there is perhaps an ironic suggestion (by the poet) of the evil that will come of his not changing sail, the death of his father; cf. Barchiesi (1993) 349–50.

150 ossa feres: i.e. you will bring my bones with you to Athens for burial; cf. *Trist.* 3.3.65–6 *ossa tamen facito parua referantur in urna:* | *sic ego non etiam mortuus exul ero*. At least then Ariadne will not suffer the fate she dreads (119n.) of lying unburied on the barren shore.

XI Canace Macareo

The story of Canace's incestuous love affair with her brother Macareus was made famous by Euripides in his lost tragedy *Aeolus* (frr. 14–41 Nauck). Reconstruction of the plot of this play is a hazardous enterprise, despite the discovery of a fragmentary hypothesis (*P.Oxy.* 2457). It is possible, as many have supposed, that there was another influential treatment of the story composed in Hellenistic times (Rohde (1913) 108 n. 2), but no trace of such a work has been discovered and it is most likely that, as in Phaedra's epistle in *Her.* 4, O. assumed his readers' familiarity with a play by Euripides. In his apology for his poetry O. lists the *Hippolytus* and *Aeolus* in a single couplet as examples of tragedy's propensity to deal with forbidden topics (*Trist.* 2.383–4): *numquid in Hippolyto nisi caeca est flamma nouercae?* | *nobilis est Canace fratris amore sui*. The pairing is surely not a coincidence.

An outline of the plot of Euripides' play is provided in the papyrus: 'Aeolus received from the gods the administration of the winds, and settled in the islands opposite Etruria, having begotten six sons and the same number of daughters. The youngest son, Macareus, fell in love with one of his sisters and seduced her. She became pregnant and hid the birth by pretending sickness. The young man persuaded his father to marry his daughters to his sons, and the latter, falling in with the plan, appointed a marriage ballot for all. The instigator of the scheme failed in the draw, since the lot fell out for the girl he had seduced to become another's wife. Running together ..., the nurse about the baby ...' (trans. E. G. Turner). So much can be recovered from the hypothesis, which breaks off at this point. There can be no certainty about how Euripides presented the concluding events, but a rough impression may be gathered from other accounts, chiefly that attributed by pseudo-Plutarch (*Moralia* 312c–d = *Parallel. min.* 28a) and Stobaeus (*Flor.* 4.20.71) to the *Tyrrhenica* of a certain Sostratus, probably the man mentioned by Strabo (14.1.48) as one of the city of Nysa's distinguished scholars (*RE* IIIA 1200–1). As Stobaeus reports, Canace's pregnancy was discovered and 'when Aeolus learned of this, he sent a sword to his daughter, whereupon she, interpreting the sword as his command, killed herself. When Macareus had appeased his father, he ran to her chamber, but upon finding his beloved dead he ended his own life with the same sword.' Minor discrepancies in other accounts of the story do not diminish the likelihood that Sostratus' report reflects a common tradition founded upon the development of the plot in Euripides' tragedy; cf. Williams (1992). It was certainly Euripides who identified the father of Canace with the keeper of the winds known from the *Odyssey*, perhaps because he is portrayed there in his cave with his six sons married to his six daughters (*Od.* 10.1–9). Such identifications are characteristic of the literary treatments of myth and proved a conundrum for later scholars who knew of other traditions which made Canace the daughter of a different Aeolus, the legendary ancestor of the Aeolians (Diod. 4.67).

Euripides' play caused a scandal: it was parodied repeatedly by Aristophanes (*Ran.* 849, *PCG* III 2 F 1–16) and others. Canace was the subject of a pantomime (*AP* 11.254), and the role was reputed to be a favourite of the Emperor Nero's (Suet. *Nero* 21, Cass. Dio 63.10.2). A likeness of Canace appears in a fresco, preserved in the Vatican, depicting a cycle of female victims of illicit passion: Myrrha, Pasiphae, Phaedra, and Scylla. It is likely that other mythographers or poets related this popular story, but the primary source for O.'s poem was Euripides. He sets the time of 'writing' only moments before her suicide, the irony of the situation being thus deepened by the reader's awareness that Macareus is already rushing to her to countermand her father's order.

1–6 The letter opens abruptly without a salutation; the identity of the correspondents is not provided until the third couplet. The conceit in the opening couplet is an echo of Prop. 4.3.3–4 *si qua tamen tibi lecturo pars oblita derit, | haec erit e lacrimis facta litura meis*; cf. 3.3 *quascumque aspicies, lacrimae fecere lituras*, *Trist.* 1.1.13–14, 3.1.15–16, *ES* 98. The abrupt *tamen* in Canace's epistle has led some editors to accept as genuine the couplet transmitted in some late MSS at the head of the poem (see app. crit.), drawing on the parallel in Prop. 4.3, where *tamen* comes in the second couplet. The abrupt opening, however, is found in one of Cicero's letters (*Fam.* 9.19.1) and suits the emotional tone. The implied thought is that she was trying hard not to blot the page.

1 caecis ... lituris 'illegible smears': the passive use of *caecus* 'blind' for something deprived of light, hence obscure, is a common poeticism; cf. 2.72. We sense that Canace is calling attention to the stains made by her tears. It comes then as something of a shock to learn in the pentameter that the stains will not be made by tears, but by blood.

errabunt 'are unclear': the verb is used by Quintilian (*Inst.* 1.1.27) of the unsteady hand of a child learning to write.

2 a ... caede: the expression vacillates between a temporal and a causal sense, 'after and as a result of the death'; cf. *Met.* 4.163 [*ferrum*] *a caede tepebat.*

dominae: has the effect of personifying the letter by calling Canace its 'mistress'; in his poetry from exile O. often refers to himself as *dominus* of his poetry books, e.g. *Trist.* 1.1.2, 1.7.14, 3.1.5, *Pont.* 1.2.134.

3 calamum: a reed pen for writing with ink on papyrus; Canace's epistle is not a spur-of-the-moment act committed to everyday tablets. The chiastic arrangement of the first five feet (*dextra tenet ... tenet altera*) gives emphasis to the final word of the line: in her other hand she holds unsheathed ... a sword.

4 in gremio 'on my knees': in antiquity the scribe usually rested his writing materials on the knee, the use of desks not becoming common until medieval times.

charta: a papyrus sheet, unfastened (*soluta*) to receive writing; cf. *Trist.* 4.7.7 *chartae sua uincula dempsi.*

5 haec est ... imago: O.'s Canace vividly describes the scene as she would a painting.

Aeolidos: feminine singular. The patronymic is first attested in Parthenius, *Erot.* 2.2, the story of another daughter of Aeolus who was unhappy in love, Polymele.

6 sic: i.e. by intending to kill herself, the purpose of the sword she holds.

uideor ... posse placere patri 'I imagine that I can satisfy my father'. The alliteration in the second half of the line supports the note of indignation.

duro ... patri: the phrase conjures up images of the stern father who was a stock figure in ancient comedy; cf. *Am.* 1.15.17 *durus pater*, in a list of comic stereotypes, Bömer on *Met.* 9.752, *TLL* s.v. *durus* 2307.44. Typically the father earned the epithet *durus* for trying to obstruct the love life of his children: the case of Canace is a bit extreme.

7–20 Canace dwells on the thought of her father's cruelty. This is not simply rhetorical embroidering: the comparison of Aeolus' temperament to the winds that he governs identifies the principal literary text to which O. refers the reader as Euripides' play, since it was he who first identified the father of Canace as the Homeric ruler of the winds; see introd. n.

7 spectator: predicative, 'to witness'; there is perhaps an echo of Virg. *Aen.* 10.443 *cuperem ipse parens spectator adesset*, Turnus' taunt as he turns to attack Pallas.

8 auctorisque oculis exigeretur opus 'the work were examined by the eyes of the one who caused it': Canace continues to describe her suicide scene as a work of art (*opus*). *oculis* is thus instrumental with *exigeretur* (*TLL* s.v. 1463.14ff.). Others interpret the line differently, with the verb meaning 'be accomplished' and *oculis* as an ablative of circumstance 'before the eyes'. But this expression would be unparalleled; the more familiar Latin idiom is *sub oculis*, *ante oculos*, *vel sim.*

9 ut ferus est 'cruel as he is': this use of comparative *ut* shades over to a causal sense. It is common in prose of the classical period, but O. seems to be unique among the poets in adopting the idiom; cf. *Fast.* 1.424 *sicut erat lusu fessa*, *Met.* 13.3 *utque erat impatiens irae*, K–S II 451–2.

truculentior: the word applies equally well to aggressive people and natural forces; cf. Cat. 64.179 *truculentum ... aequor*. Other Augustan poets, with the exception of Hor. *Serm.* 1.3.51, seemed to avoid this word in favour of the unexpanded form *trux*, perhaps because it had a colloquial ring. O. uses it four times; cf. Cooper (1895) 132–3. *suis ... Euris* identifies her father as the ruler of the winds. The east wind stands for all the winds, with no special significance.

10 spectasset: the tense of the verb is 'epistolary'; that is, from the point of view of the recipient Canace is already 'dead'. For the syncopated form, 5.38n.

siccis ... genis 'with dry eyes [10.44n.]': the word-order, with adjective and noun bracketing *uulnera nostra*, makes a poignant juxtaposition.

11 scilicet heightens the note of irony.

est aliquid 'it has some effect': the rhetorical understatement (*litotes*) adds to the ironic tone, underlined by *scilicet*. The idiom *est aliquid* is especially common in O.; cf. 3.131, 4.29, *Ars* 3.755, *Rem.* 480, *Met.* 12.93, *Fast.* 6.27, *Trist.* 1.2.53, 5.1.59, *Pont.* 2.7.65.

12 populi ... sui: sc. the winds, the 'people' he rules.
conuenit: 7.167n.

13–14 The winds indicate the four points of the compass: south (*Notus*), west (*Zephyrus*), north (*Aquilo*), and east (*Eurus*). The expansiveness of this couplet prepares us for the rhetorical point scored in 16: though vast as the sweep of the winds, Aeolus' temporal power is dwarfed by the scope of the defects in his character.

13 Sithonio 'Thracian': because of its (from the Greek point of view) northerly location; 2.6n. The combination of hiatus in the fifth foot after the adjective with a quadrisyllabic word ending the line is in imitation of Greek metrical style. Virgil makes frequent use of this and similar features, which are often highlighted by the presence of Greek nouns or proper names, e.g. *Ecl.* 10.12 *Aonie Aganippe*; cf. Norden (1927) 438. O. cleverly employs it with the only wind that does not receive its Greek name. No other elegist employs this effect, but there are nine instances in O.'s elegies: 4.99 *Maenalia Atalanta*, 9.87, 9.133, 9.141, *Ars* 2.185, 3.13, *Fast.* 2.43, 5.83.

14 pinnis ... tuis: O. varies the construction with an apostrophe for the last-named wind.

proterue: suggests capricious violence; cf. *Am.* 2.16.4 *Icarii stella proterua canis*, Hor. *Epod.* 16.22 *proteruus Africus*, *Carm.* 1.26.2–3 *proteruis ... uentis*. The adjective does not feature in the high style: O. uses it

12 times in his elegies, only 4 times in the *Met*. Among other Augustan poets only Horace (9) and Propertius (1) use it at all.

15–16 The couplet effects the rhetorical point prepared in the previous two lines. The connection is underlined by repetition, while the point that O.'s Canace makes here reflects a commonplace of Stoic philosophy, which placed a premium upon control of the passions; cf. Sen. *Epist*. 113.30 *imperare sibi maximum imperium est*. The point is scored by a slight syllepsis (p. 30) in *imperat*; for the construction with *irae*, cf. *Met*. 9.28.

15 tumidae … irae: the characterization of anger as 'swollen' is familiar; cf. *Met*. 2.602, 8.437, 13.559. The use of *impero* in contexts referring to the command of reason over irrational impulses is common in Latin philosophical discourse, e.g. Cic. *Parad*.

16 et: postponed; 1.32n.

17–20 O. recasts part of the celebrated complaint of the 'epitaph' spoken by the deceased Cornelia, who reminds her husband of the vanity of a noble lineage against the inevitability of death: Prop. 4.11.11–13 *quid mihi coniugium Paulli, quid currus auorum | profuit aut famae pignora tanta meae? | non minus immitis habuit Cornelia Parcas*. O.'s Canace probably also recalls a passage from Euripides' tragedy (fr. 22 Nauck), in which it appears that the heroine plays down the importance of her divine ancestry: τὴν δ' εὐγένειαν πρὸς θεῶν μή μοι λέγε, | ἐν χρήμασιν τόδ' ἐστί, μή γαυροῦ, πάτερ 'don't speak to me of the nobility of our lineage from the gods, father; this ranks with possessions, don't pride yourself on it'.

17 admotam 'promoted': the idiom is common in post-Augustan prose (*TLL* s.v. 775.2ff.). The participle supplies the subject (*me*) of the infinitive *posse*.

18 Iouem: her exact relationship to Jupiter is not known, although the reference to divine genealogy by Euripides (17–20n.) makes it possible that it may have been revealed there. Our other surviving sources tell us that the wind-king was the son of Hippotes (*Od*. 10.2, A.R. 4.778), and there is no apparent connection to Zeus. But the 'other' Aeolus, king of Thessaly, was a son of Hellen, who in turn was, according to some, a son of Zeus and Pyrrha (Apollod. *Bibl*. 1.7.2). O.'s text probably reflects Euripidean or Hellenistic genealogical gerrymandering.

19 num minus: with negative force applying to the entire sentence, 'is the blade I hold less deadly?' For this style of rhetorical question in O., cf. 17.230 *pulsa est Aesonia num minus illa domo?*, 18.174, *Fast.* 1.526, 3.6.

infestum, funebria munera, ferrum: for the apposition, 7.158n. *munera* is ironic, for the sword could only be termed a 'gift' because her father sent it to her; cf. 95–6.

20 feminea: 6.52n. The adjective emphasizes the harshness of her situation: the hands that would usually work the loom (*telam*) now hold a sword (*tela*).

21–32 In a pathetic outburst Canace first reveals that the reason for her distress is her incestuous love for her brother. She then describes the growth of her passion, which she did not recognize at first. O. thus engages sympathy for the seemingly unwitting victim of an uncontrollable passion, who emphasizes her innocence to the end (32n.).

21 o utinam: 1.5n.

Macareu: mention of her brother's name has been postponed to this point, effectively heightening the pathos.

commisit in unum 'joined us as one': might refer to the idea familiar in love poetry that two lovers share one soul (60n.), but in this context it also suggests sexual intercourse, in which case Canace utters the same sentiment as Phyllis in 2.59–60. *committere* is especially graphic: cf. *Met.* 4.369, of Salmacis' rape of Hermaphroditus, *commissaque corpore toto ... inhaerebat*. The preposition with the neuter adjective is used adverbially; cf. *Met.* 4.579–80, of the metamorphosis of Cadmus into a serpent, *commissaque in unum | paulatim tereti tenuantur acumine crura*.

23–4 plus ... quam frater amasti: a turn of phrase that O. recurs to in recounting other tales of illicit passion; cf. *Ars* 1.285 *Myrrha patrem, sed non qua filia debet, amauit, Met.* 9.456 (Byblis) *non soror ut fratrem, nec qua debebat, amabat.* Here too the affectionate vocative *frater* is endowed with heavily ironic undertones by the suggestive repetition of the word. For the syncopated perfect, 5.38n.

25 ipsa quoque incalui: O. pointedly rejects the version of the myth in which Macareus forces himself upon his sister; but *quoque* does suggest that it was Macareus who took the initiative. The metaphorical use of *incalescere* for the fire of love is virtually unique to O.; cf. 18.42, *Am.* 3.6.26, *Fast.* 2.307, *Met.* 2.574, 3.371.

qualem ... audire solebam: implying complete innocence be-forehand; *qualem* suggests that she now begins to experience the full range of love's power.

26 'I felt the presence of a certain god as my heart warmed': *tepere* is less strong than *calere*, and thus more appropriate for the first stirrings of passion; cf. *Rem.* 7, Hor. *Carm.* 1.4.19–20. The god, of course, is Cupid.

27–32 The symptoms felt by Canace – pallor, loss of weight, sleeplessness – are conventional signs of distress in ancient love poetry. Canace experiences all the symptoms of the emotion, but because of her innocence (25n.) and because of the terrible nature of her love for her brother, she cannot bring herself to recognize the cause of her agony.

27 fugerat ore color: a frequent trait of unhappy lovers; cf. Pichon (1902) 224. In Latin *color* refers, as 'colour' does in English, to a healthy complexion.

macies: love produces weight loss, a common motif in O. (e.g. *Am.* 1.6.5–6, 2.9.14, *Ars* 1.733–5) and elsewhere; cf. Fedeli on Prop. 1.5.22. For the expression, cf. *Met.* 3.397 *adduxitque cutem macies*, Virg. *Geo.* 3.483.

28 cibos: the word is rare in Augustan poetry, compared with synonyms such as *epulae*. Virgil uses it but once (*Geo.* 2.216) and Propertius not at all, while O. has it 56 times; cf. *TLL* s.v. 1038.81–3. If the word is then perhaps 'prosaic', its plural is 'poetic' since it allows O. to avoid elision over the caesura.

coacta 'forced [to eat]': *ora* is a poetic plural .

29 nec = *et non*, to be taken with *faciles*, 'and my sleep was dif-ficult'.

nox erat annua 'the night seemed like a year', a familiar con-dition for lonely lovers; cf. 12.58 *acta est per lacrimas nox mihi quanta fuit*, McKeown on *Am.* 1.2.3.

30 gemitum: the unconscious groan betrays her inner turmoil. The force of the participle *laesa* is concessive.

31 reddere causam 'give an account': the phrase, which does not recur in O., has a somewhat technical ring; cf. *Rhet. Her.* 1.2.3, Sen. *Benef.* 2.8.1

32 quid amans esset 'what it was to be in love'.

33–4 The role of the nurse in this story and similar tales inevitably calls to mind the nurse in Euripides' *Hippolytus*. O.'s portrayal of Canace's nurse probably owes something to works that have been lost to us, for such stories seem to have been regarded as standard material in erotic narratives. Parallels for the involvement of the nurse are found both in O. and in the pseudo-Virgilian *Ciris*; cf. Lyne (1979) 185–6. In *Met*.10.298–502 Myrrha's nurse plays a very similar role in first detecting the hidden passion and later in assisting in the progress of the affair. The similar role of the nurse in the *Ciris* may be due to a common model in the neoteric epyllion by Helvius Cinna known as the *Zmyrna*, which might then also have contributed to the development of the plot here. In any event, this set scene is likely to have figured in other stories as well (cf. Knox (1990)) and O.'s reader will have been able to take into account a broader tradition.

33–4 prima ... nutrix ... | prima ... nutrix: the repetition (anaphora) underlines the excitement of the nurse's discovery.

33 praesensit 'had a presentiment': the verb connotes special sensitivity; thus, for example, in the only occurrence of the verb in Virgil (*Aen.* 4.296–7), it is used of Dido in love when she suspects the deceit of Aeneas: *at regina dolos ... praesensit.*

34 Aeoli: 5n.

35 gremioque pudor deiecit ocellos 'and in my shame I cast my eyes down to my bosom'. Expressions such as *deiecit ocellos* for *effecit ut ocellos deicerem* are common; cf. Prop. 1.1.3 *deiecit lumina.* The gesture is a sign of modesty, as in *Am.* 1.8.37 *cum bene deiectis gremium spectabis ocellis,* 2.4.11, Kost on Musaeus 160. For the diminutive *ocellos,* cf. 5.45n.

36 in tacita: literally 'in the case of one who was silent', more idiomatically, 'though I said nothing'.

37 pondera: a common poetic euphemism for pregnancy; cf. *Fast.* 3.42, *Met.* 9.289, Mart. 14.151.1–2 *dulci sed pondere uenter | si tumeat.* The crucial word here is *uitiati* 'deflowered', an explicit term with legal undertones, which the other Augustan poets avoid, though Horace in his *Satires* has it three times and O. twenty-one. The directness of Canace's description is arresting.

38 A patterned line freezes the moment. The adjective *aegra* is proleptic, 'weighed down my limbs and weakened them'. *onus* is another euphemism for the foetus (*TLL* s.v. 646.1ff.).

furtiuum suggests not only her attempts to conceal her pregnancy, but the fact that it was the result of a clandestine love-affair, a common meaning of *furtum* (6.43n.).

39–44 Canace's account of her unsuccessful abortion stands with O.'s two elegies on his mistress' abortion (*Am.* 2.13 and 2.14) as the most direct treatment of the subject in Roman poetry. Under Roman law the foetus was not a person and abortion was not illegal (*Dig.* 35.2.9.1), but it was always subject to social sanction since the practice offended against the traditional Roman concept of marriage as a contract to produce children. If a married woman had an abortion without her husband's consent, it might constitute grounds for divorce, and other penalties were at times imposed in such cases. The practice was a common means of limiting family size, and there is a good deal of literary evidence for abortion among upper-class women for cosmetic reasons: e.g. [O.] *Nux* 23–4 *nunc uterum uitiat quae uult formosa uideri,* | *raraque in hoc aeuo est quae uelit esse parens.* The dangers of abortion in antiquity can hardly be exaggerated: cf. Hähnel (1937), Brunt (1971) 147–8, *RAC* s.v. 'Abtreibung, Beseelung, Geburt'. It is highly unlikely that an attempted abortion figured in any earlier version of the myth; this note of harsh realism is O.'s own and reflects his own sympathies for Canace's predicament; cf. Watts (1973).

39–40 quas … non … quae non … attulit: i.e. she tried them all; for the repetition, cf. Virg. *Aen.* 6.92 *quas gentis Italum aut quas non oraueris urbis,* Juv. 3.309.

39 herbas … medicamina: the former is specific, the latter general. The ancient medical writers list a number of different types of abortifacients.

40 supposuit: the proper medical term (*OLD* s.v. 2b). For the postponement of -*que,* 5.78n.

41 penitus 'from within'.

42 excuteretur: apparently the medical term for aborting a foetus, here again euphemistically termed *crescens onus* (38n.); cf. Cels. 2.7.16, Scrib. Larg. *praef.* 2.29. O. repeats this line almost verbatim to describe abortion at *Fast.* 1.624.

43 a: 5.49n.

nimium uiuax 'too tenacious of life': O.'s Canace writes of the foetus as if it were a child (*infans*) as O. himself does in *Am.* 2.14, reflecting personal sentiment perhaps, but not Roman law.

43–4 admotis ... | artibus perhaps reflects medical jargon; cf. *Rem.* 116 *admoueo ... opem*, *OLD* s.v. *admoueo* 6a.

44 tecto ... ab hoste: the 'foe' is 'concealed' from the point of view of the foetus. The metaphor finds parallels in other references to abortion by O.: *Fast.* 1.623 *ictu ... caeco*, *Am.* 2.14.4 *caecas ... manus*.

45–64 Canace describes the pain of childbirth as she tried to conceal her condition and deliver the infant in secrecy. The birth of the child will expose Canace's incestuous affair, but her reluctance to have the child compounds a difficult delivery. It is only when her brother appears to give her hope that they can be married that she has the will to collaborate in a successful birth.

45–6 nouiens ... | et noua: after nine cycles of the moon (*soror ... Phoebi*) and the beginning of the tenth; i.e. approaching the tenth month, the term most commonly fixed for pregnancy by ancient medical writers; cf. Pease on Cic. *De nat. deor.* 2.69.

soror pulcherrima Phoebi: Diana, by antonomasia; identified as the moon-goddess with her chariot in the pentameter.

46 mouebat 'was driving': cf. *Am.* 1.2.26, Val. Fl. 3.415.

48 O. often compares the life of a lover with that of a soldier and the image is widespread in erotic poetry (7.32n.). In the second of his elegies on his mistress' abortion (2.14), O. extends the metaphor of warfare to childbirth and abortion: 5–6 *quae prima instituit teneros conuellere fetus, | militia fuerat digna perire sua.*

rudis: in the military sense, *rudis* refers to a raw recruit (7.122n.), but the word has other associations as well, suggesting inexperience and lack of sophistication; cf. Prop. 4.3.12 *rudis urgenti bracchia uicta dedi.* The gender of *miles* is, appropriately, feminine; cf. 6.54n.

50 conscia ... anus: the nurse, who was 'in on it'.

51 quid faciam ... ?: deliberative subjunctive (10.59n.).

dolor: a synonym for *labor* in childbirth (*TLL* s.v. 1839.36ff.).

52 timor et nutrix et pudor: fear and shame, which figuratively hold her back, are nicely combined with the nurse who physically restrains her. This type of syllepsis (p. 30), in which the middle term of three is the odd one out, is especially Ovidian: cf. *Ars* 1.551 *et color et Theseus et uox abiere puellae*, 3.614 *hoc leges duxque pudorque iubent*.

53 elapsaque uerba reprendo 'I try to restrain the words which escaped me': impossible, of course, as in the proverbial expression (Hor. *Ars* 390) *nescit uox missa reuerti* (Otto (1890) 367).

54 lacrimas combibere 'to swallow my tears': a figurative phrase for one trying to suppress a powerful emotion; cf. Sen. *Epist.* 49.1 *uideo lacrimas combibentem et affectibus tuis inter ipsam coercitionem exeuntibus non satis resistentem*. The intensive prefix *con-* is characteristic of colloquial compounds (Cooper (1895) 262–71), and this verb, attested 7 times in O. (*ES* 150n.), is used only once by Horace in a decidedly emphatic context: *Carm.* 1.37.28 *corpore combiberet uenenum*.

55 Lucina: 6.122n.

56 'and if I had died, death too would have been a serious indictment of my character', because her pregnancy would then have been revealed. The imperfect indicative in the apodosis of a past condition is quite common (K–S II 404), but the combination with an imperfect subjunctive in the protasis is without parallel.

57 scissa tunicaque comaque: Macareus tears his hair and garments, a gesture of strong emotion.

59–62 Macareus' sudden optimism reflects Aeolus' decision to allow his sons to draw lots for their sisters. Perhaps there was some reason given in Euripides' play why he might have thought his chances better than one in six.

59 soror: the choice of address is poignant, since his attentions are more than brotherly. The pathos is heightened by the pattern of repetition: *soror ... soror; uiue ... uiue*, as well as by the interjection.

dixti: a colloquial syncopation (5.38n.) of the full form of the verb *dixisti*, found in Plautus and later, although this is the only example in O. from a perfect stem in *-si*; cf. N–W III 500–6. The colloquial tone suits her animated report of Macareus' words. Most MSS read *aisti* here, a form not attested otherwise until Augustine: it probably originated as a late gloss on the unfamiliar syncopated form.

60 nec unius corpore perde duos: a poignant remark, since the sentiment is familiar in love poetry that the death of one means death for the other, as in Prop. 2.28.41–2, a prayer for Cynthia who is ill: *si non unius, quaeso, miserere duorum!* | *uiuam, si uiuet; si cadet illa, ca-dam*; cf. Bréguet (1960). Who are the two people to whom Macareus alludes? The parallels in Latin poetry, e.g. *Met.* 2.609, 10.707, 11.388, 12.229, suggest that he means himself, but the context points to the unborn child.

61 spes bona det uires: to a Roman ear this would sound like an invocation of a deity: personified *Spes* had an old and well estab-lished cult in Rome (*RE* IIIA 1634ff.) and her full name was *bona Spes* (Wissowa (1912) 330). Cf. Plaut. *Rud.* 231a *spes bona, obsecro, subuenta mihi.*

62 de quo mater: use of *de* for agent is idiomatic in this context: cf. 9.48, *Am.* 2.19.28, *Fast.* 3.233.

63 crede mihi: the insertion of this phrase in parataxis has a colloquial ring; cf. Tränkle (1960) 9, Hofmann (1951) 126. Canace strikes a note of urgency.

tamen picks up an implied concessive in *mortua*, 'though dead, yet I revived at your words'.

64 crimen onusque 'the criminal burden', by hendiadys, as at *Am.* 3.7.4.

65–92 In vivid terms Canace describes how her father discovered the existence of the child as the nurse was trying to remove it from the palace. At the point where the hypothesis of Euripides' play breaks off there is some mention of the nurse and the infant: we cannot be certain that these events formed part of the plot of the play, but it would have formed an effective scene or 'messenger speech': O. sacrifices verisimilitude in having his Canace relate to Macareus events of which he must be aware, but he is interested in highlighting the despair felt by the mother as she has her child taken from her to be sent to its death.

65 quid tibi grataris?: the natural reaction of a new father would be out of place; cf. 6.119.

66 crimina: Canace refers again to the infant as a 'crime' that must secretly be removed (*subripienda*) so that Aeolus will not discover its existence. This detail enables us to locate the time of Canace's writing after the unsuccessful drawing of lots. She no longer has rea-son to hope that her father will look on this child as legitimate.

67–74 The nature of the feigned religious procession used by the nurse to cover the removal of the infant is not described, suggesting that O. is reporting a familiar scene, perhaps from Euripides' *Aeolus*.

67 frugibus: probably ears of corn, regular components in festivals of Demeter, who is often represented with garlands of corn; cf. Bömer on *Fast.* 4.616.

ramisque albentis oliuae: olive wreaths were used in the festivals of many divinities, not only Athena. The greyish colour of the olive leaf (*albentis*) is often noted; cf. *Met.* 6.81 *fetum canentis oliuae.*

68 uittis: strands of wool to wreath the olive branches.

69 precantia uerba: a Virgilian phrase 'corrected' by O. Virgil uses it in the order *uerba precantia* only once at line-end with synizesis (6.50n.), perhaps following Ennius; cf. Norden on *Aen.* 6.33. O. uses the phrase several times, but only here at verse-end with the word-order reversed. Elsewhere (*Ars* 1.709, *Met.* 2.482, 6.164, 7.590, 9.159, 14.365) the phrase appears in the fourth and fifth feet, providing a fourth-foot trochaic caesura. That effect, which presumably Virgil (and before him, Ennius?) wanted to avoid, is secured here also.

70 dat ... uiam 'give way': both parts of the phrase are construed with each clause (ἀπὸ κοινοῦ).

71 patrias ... ad aures: those of Aeolus, Canace's father, not Macareus.

72 indicio proditur ipse suo: the combination of the reflexive pronoun with *ipse* is emphatic: the infant betrayed himself; cf. *Ars* 3.668 *indicio prodor ab ipse meo, Fast.* 2.172 *proditur indicio ponderis ipsa suo.*

73 reuelat 'lifts the veil from'. The postponement of the subject, Aeolus, to the pentameter with a strong pause following, intensifies the drama of the moment. The verb is first attested here and *Fast.* 6.619; on compounds in *re-*, see McKeown on *Am.* 1.8.75.

75–8 Canace describes how she trembled in fear with a simile, introduced by two comparative *ut*-clauses in asyndeton. The terms of the comparison resemble *Am.* 1.7.53–6 *exanimis artus et membra trementia uidi, | ut cum populeas uentilat aura comas, | ut leni Zephyro gracilis uibratur harundo | summaue cum tepido stringitur unda Noto.* O. found such accumulation effective; cf. Goold (1965) 61.

75 tenui cum stringitur aura 'when it is ruffled by a light breeze': cf. O.'s description of Thisbe upon finding Pyramus dead, *Met.* 4.135–6 *exhorruit aequoris instar, | quod tremit, exigua cum summum stringitur aura.*

76 quatitur tepido fraxinus icta Noto 'the ash-tree trembles

when shaken by the warm south wind': the participle *icta* does duty
for a temporal clause. Most MSS and the corrector of P read *fraxina
uirga* here, but P, which gives nonsense, did not find that in his
archetype. The text printed here is Palmer's emendation, prompted
by the observation that an adjective form *fraxinus* is nowhere attested.
Housman (1899) 174 (= *Class. pap.* 474) dismisses this objection as 'a
characteristic specimen of levity assuming Rhadamanthine airs'; but
the parallels he adduces (e.g. *femina turba*) are not apt, and *uirga* looks
like a stop-gap to fill out a lacuna in the exemplar. Cf. 14.40 *frigida
populeas ut quatit aura comas. tepido* is a natural epithet for the south
wind (*Noto*); cf. *Am.* 1.4.12, 1.7.56.

77 pallentis: pallor accompanies trembling as a sign of fear,
while Canace expects her father's arrival. For the genitive, cf. 5.45n.

78 ab imposito corpore 'by my body as I lay there': the addi-
tion of the preposition where we would expect a simple instrumental
ablative becomes more common in poetry after O.; cf. 4.32 *ab ...
labe notandus, Ars* 1.763, *Met.* 8.514.

79 irruit: sc. Aeolus. The present tense of the narrative has vivid
effect.

81 nihil praeter lacrimas ... profudi: the verb can apply to
pouring forth tears or words. Canace wants to speak but cannot.

pudibunda: a rare word, first attested here and Hor. *Ars* 233, as
well as [Virg.] *Culex* 399. Verbal adjectives with the suffix *-bundus* are
characteristic of less formal Latin (Cooper (1895) 91–6) and are not
frequent in O. This is the only example in *Her.*; elsewhere he uses
fremebundus (*Met.*), *furibundus* (*Met.*, *Ars*), *gemebundus* (*Met.*), *moribundus*
(*Met.*, *Trist.*), *queribundus* (*Met.*), and *tremebundus* (*Met.*); see Clausen on
Virg. *Ecl.* 6.58.

82 torpuerat gelido lingua retenta metu: cf. *Am.* 1.7.20
where the sense of this couplet is expressed more tersely, *ipsa nihil:
pauido est lingua retenta metu*, and Cat. 51.9 *lingua sed torpet*.

83–6 Canace describes the moment when her father orders the
infant to be exposed. Lines 85–6 might be felt as a temporal clause:
'he had given the orders when the child began to wail'. The effect is
that of a *cum inuersum* construction (6.23–5n.), but the parataxis lends
added force to the second couplet: it is the baby's crying that O.
draws our attention to.

83 paruum ... nepotem: the separation of the noun from the epithet adds pathos, for the intervening phrase *canibusque auibusque* makes a pointed juxtaposition. By referring to the baby now as Aeolus' grandson O. underlines the cruelty of his actions.

84 destituique: for the postponement of *-que*, cf. 5.78n.

85 sensisse putares 'you would have thought that he understood'. The remark is an aside by the mother, and thus moving. O. repeats the point in describing the exposure of Romulus and Remus at *Fast.* 2.405 *uagierunt ambo pariter: sensisse putares*.

86 quaque ... poterat uoce 'with such voice as he could', i.e. as best he could without words. The placement of *suum* in the relative clause disrupts the word-order and effectively represents Canace's distressed state of mind.

87 quid mihi tunc animi? 'What do you think my state of mind was then?'

germane 'brother', but the choice of this word is poignant, for as defined by the grammarians (*TLL* s.v. 1914.40ff.) *germanus* differed from *frater* in that the former had to be born of the same two parents.

88 potes ex animo colligere 'you can infer from your own state of mind'.

89 mea me coram: the accumulation of pronouns emphasizes her distress, as does the separation of *mea* from its complement *uiscera* 'flesh'. This is a highly emotional way of referring to the product of Canace's womb, used by O. in other similarly charged contexts such as 118 below and, e.g., *Am.* 2.14.27, *Rem.* 59 (Medea), *Met.* 6.651 (Tereus), 8.478 (Althaea), 10.465 (Cinyras).

inimicus: a harsh reference to Aeolus, so harsh that Palmer suggests it refers to a slave who carried out her father's order, and Bentley softened it by conjecturing *immitis*. But there is no reason to assume anyone else is present and Canace's feelings toward her father are not gentle.

90 Attention is focused on the horrible image in the patterned line.

91–2 Again, the inverse construction makes for vivid narrative: 'he had left the room, when at last ...'

92 contigit: sc. *mihi*.

inque meas unguibus ire genas: an extravagant gesture of grief, 5.71–2n. For the expression, cf. *Am.* 1.7.64 *in uoltus unguibus ire meos*, 2.5.46 *in teneras impetus ire genas*.

93–106 Canace describes the arrival of her father's messenger, who brings the sword with which she is to kill herself. It is likely that this scene was prominently featured in the play, and Θ.'s account sets the time of Canace's writing immediately after the order to commit suicide.

93 patrius ... satelles 'my father's attendant': his mournful expression enlists further sympathy for Canace.

94 indignos edidit ore sonos 'he uttered these shameful words': cf. *Am.* 3.6.72 *edidit indignos ore tremente sonos.*

96 ex merito scire 'judge from your action': *meritum* may be any action, good or bad, which receives compensation (*OLD* s.v. 3b). This is not to be confused with the expression *ex merito* at 5.7.

quid iste uelit 'what its purpose is'.

98 dona paterna: the heavy irony in referring to the sword as her father's 'gift' to her is replayed in the following couplet.

99 genitor: elevated in tone, the word has a formal note as Canace apostrophizes her absent father. *genitor* is rarely attested outside of epic poetry, but it was probably not coined by Ennius, as Tränkle (1960) 39–40 suggests. In the *Her.* it is found only here, 4.157, and 12.109. It is not common in any of his elegiac works, though it is found 42 times in the *Met.*

conubia: the legal term for a formal marriage, which Canace wished for but did not have. For the form, cf. 2.81n.

100 hac ... dote: ironic, of course; cf. 5.92. The juxtaposition of *pater* and *filia* heightens the pathos.

101 decepte ... Hymenaee: Canace thinks herself cheated out of marriage because Aeolus had agreed to Macareus' plan for his six sons to marry their six sisters, but the lot had not fallen out as she wished.

faces ... maritas are the torches carried in the wedding procession.

102 turbato ... pede: as if at an ill omen; for the expression, cf. *Fast.* 2.341–2 *ut saepe uiator | turbatum uiso rettulit angue pedem.* The house of Aeolus is impious (*nefanda*) not because of the incest, which Canace now considers sanctioned, but because of the infanticide and the impending suicide. There is irony here since Hymenaeus is usually addressed in the marriage hymn and Canace's injunction here contrasts sharply with Cat. 61.9–10 *huc ueni, niueo gerens | luteum pede soccum.*

103 faces: the torches of the Furies (Erinyes) are better suited to Canace now, for her funeral pyre not her wedding. The torches are dark (*atras*) as is everything about them: cf. Denniston and Page on Aesch. *Ag.* 462, where they themselves are called black (κελαιναί). Here too the MSS read *atrae* as an epithet of the goddesses, but *atras*, an easy correction, gives better point, for black is especially associated with the flames of a funeral pyre (*TLL* s.v. *ater* 1020.40–50); cf. Stat. *Theb.* 4.133. O.'s readers would surely have recognized a favourite paradox of Hellenistic epigrammatists, the wedding that is also a funeral; cf. Kenney on Apul. 4.33.4.

104 meus ex isto luceat igne rogus: the echo of Tib. 1.1.6 is unmistakable and poignant, *dum meus assiduo luceat igne focus.* Tibullus wishes for a blazing hearth emblematic of his happy relationship with his mistress Delia, but Canace now wishes for death.

105 nubite felices: Canace assumes that the weddings of her sisters will go on. They will marry their brothers with better fortune (*Parca meliore*) because they were not already committed to marriage before the drawing of lots. She is also assuming that Macareus will survive her.

106 amissae memores ... este mei 'remember me when I am gone': some later MSS read *admissi ... mei* 'my crime', a weak moralizing correction prompted by *admisit* in the following line. 'If they are to be married, a warning to beware of her guilt is out of place and useless' (Palmer).

sed tamen: postponed, 1.32n.

107–20 Again, Canace directs her thoughts to her lost child, his innocence of any wrongdoing, and premature death. This whole section has a tragic colouring that can be paralleled in many laments from surviving tragedies, e.g. Eur. *Tro.* 749–65, and it is likely that O. here evokes his Euripidean model. Canace's lament ends with an announcement of her determination to die, which is no longer represented as the harsh judgement of her father, but as her own choice not to survive her baby for long (119–20).

107 tam paucis editus horis 'born so few hours ago': the ablative indicates the time within which the action occurred in the past (K–S I 357).

108 uix bene 'scarcely': 6.24n.

109–10 The couplet restates the point of 107–8 rather weakly: 'if

it is possible for him to deserve death, let him be thought to have
deserved it; but the poor child is wrongly implicated in my crime'.
The verb *plector* (7.82n.) suggests undeserved punishment; cf. 21.53–4
uos pace mouetis | aspera submota proelia, plector ego.

110 a: 5.49n.

admisso: 7.104n.

111 nate, dolor matris: the close parallel with [Eur.]. *Rhes.*
896–7 τέκνον, σ' ὀλοφύρομαι, ὦ ματρὸς ἄλγος 'child, I mourn
for you, grief to your mother', is suggestive: 'it is possible that
Euripides, who so often imitates himself, utilized the same sentiment
in his *Aeolus* and Ovid took it from there' (Jacobson (1974) 162n. 13).

rabidarum: cf. 10.96. The MSS read *rapidarum*, though Burman
reports that he found *rabidarum* in some. It has long been alleged that
rapidus could mean 'savage' because of its derivation from *rapio*, but
certainly in this passage it is more likely that we are dealing with
scribal error.

112 ei mihi: 2.106n.

dilacerate: a graphic verb, 2.90n.

113 nate: the repetition (anaphora) is for emotional effect.

parum fausti 'ill-starred'.

115–18 The anaphora of *non* articulates a sequence of lost mo-
ments contrasted pointedly with the last pentameter.

115 iustis 'fitting'.

116 tonsas ferre … comas: shorn hair as a ritual offering to
the dead is an ancient Greek custom: Achilles cuts off a lock of his
hair and dedicates it at the tomb of Patroclus (*Il.* 23.141), and
Orestes offers a lock to his dead father (Aesch. *Cho.* 6). But the cus-
tom is not Roman, and O. is drawing on Greek traditions to lend
Canace's words a higher tone; cf. Bömer on *Fast.* 3.560.

117 oscula … carpsi: from the corpse (*frigida*). The expression
oscula carpere 'to kiss' is familiar in poetry; cf. Bömer on *Met.* 4.358.

118 uiscera: 90n.

119 infantes … umbras: a striking phrase for the child, for-
merly *onus* (38, 42) or *pondera* (37): she now thinks of it as her baby.

cum uulnere prosequar 'I shall escort him as I strike the
wound': *prosequi* is properly used of the escort of a funeral proces-
sion; cf. *Trist.* 1.8.14 *exsequias prosequerere meas.*

120 fuero dicta: for *dicta ero*. The combination of the future perfect of *sum* and the past participle becomes common in later Latin, assisted by the treatment of the participle as adjective (H–S 324). In the classical period it is rare, and serves to emphasize a temporal distinction: Canace stresses that the period during which she will be called a bereaved mother will have been brief.

121–8 Canace's last words are to her brother, to whom she addresses her final requests (*mandata*, 127).

121 sperate 'longed for' as a bridegroom. As a substantive *speratus* can be used as an equivalent for *sponsus*; cf. *OLD* s.v.

122 sparsa ... collige membra: this grisly injunction may be compared with the scene in Euripides' *Bacchae*, where Cadmus returns home with the dismembered body of his son Pentheus (1216–21). O. may be reflecting part of Euripides' *Aeolus* in incorporating this detail here for shock effect, though he does not take it to the extremes we find later in Seneca's *Phaedra* where Theseus reassembles the mutilated body of Hippolytus in an appalling jigsaw puzzle (1256–61).

nati ... tui: the position of the adjective at the end of the line is effective, reminding Macareus that it is *his* child that has been murdered.

125 lacrimasque in uulnera funde: Canace asks Macareus to weep over her body, as she had not been able to weep over the corpse of her child (115). The phrasing graphically reminds her reader how death will come to her by the sword; cf. *Met.* 4.140 *uulnera suppleuit lacrimis*, 13.490 *lacrimas in uulnera fundit*, *Pont.* 4.11.4.

126 neue reformida 'and do not recoil from the body': the combination of a prohibition with an imperative is usually accomplished by *neque* (K–S 1 203–4), but in poetry *neue* is not infrequent. Such combinations were generally avoided in prose, where the construction of *ne* with the imperative was avoided as archaic and unidiomatic (H–S 340).

amantis amans: polyptoton (5.80n.).

127–8 tu, rogo ... | perfice: an emphatic command. The construction of the imperative with *tu* is a common feature of colloquial Latin (Hofmann (1951) 100–1), but in poetry and formal prose the pronoun usually carries weight. That is underscored here by the parenthetic *rogo*.

127 mandata: the last directive of a dying person, for which the singular *mandatum* is regular in legal language, but elsewhere rare (*TLL* s.v. 267.29–33); cf. 13.165, *Fast.* 4.193, *Pont.* 2.2.43.

128 perfice was found in one MS by Heinsius, where the paradosis gives *perfer* 'do you convey', which gives no sense: Canace is not asking Macareus to do anything other than perform her last request. Heinsius thought this couplet spurious, but Housman's correction of the MSS *persequar* to *obsequar* can be easily justified on palaeographical grounds, and it gives a neat point in the contrast between the *mandata* of sister and father; cf. Housman (1897) 242 (= *Class. pap.* 402–3).

EPISTVLA SAPPHVS AD PHAONEM

There is no trace of the love story that forms the background for this poem in any of the surviving fragments of the poetry of Sappho. The most famous Greek poetess lived and composed on her native island of Lesbos in the early 6th century BC. We first hear of her hopeless love for Phaon in a fragment of the *Leucadia* of Menander (*c.* 310 BC), who refers to it and to her suicide as if they were generally known (fr. 258). If the author of this epistle based it upon a work of literature, then the most likely candidate is one of the many lost comedies that dealt with Sappho. We know of at least six produced in Athens with the title *Sappho*, by Diphilus (frr. 70–1 K–A), Amipsias (fr. 15 K–A), Amphis (fr. 32 K–A), Antiphanes (fr. 194 K–A), Ephippos (fr. 20 K–A), and Timocles (fr. 32 K–A). And at least four other plays, in addition to Menander's, were called *The Leucadian.* Nothing can be discovered about the plot of any of these plays, nor why their authors chose the famous poet of Lesbos as a subject, but the story of Phaon is known to us from other sources (Aelian, *VH* 12.18, Serv. on *Aen.* 3.279, Palaeph. 49, Plin. *Nat.* 22.20). He was a ferryman who worked the route between Lesbos and the mainland. The goddess Aphrodite came to him disguised as an old woman seeking transport, which he provided free of charge. As a reward the goddess endowed Phaon with attractiveness irresistible to any woman. It was almost inevitable that this figure of local lore on the island of Lesbos would eventually be associated with the celebrated female poet who wrote so much about love. In his comedy, Diphilus made the poets Archilochus and Hipponax her lovers. Other traditions had her involved with her fellow countryman Alcaeus or Anacreon (Athen. 13 598b, Hermesianax, *CA* p. 99, fr. 7.47–50) .

This last bit of information is attributed to the Peripatetic grammarian and philosopher Chamaeleon (*c.* 350–280 BC), who wrote a treatise on Sappho. Such 'facts' in Sappho's biography were surely based on inferences drawn from her verses by scholars who had access to her poetry; cf. Lefkowitz (1981). It is reasonable to assume that the story of her love for Phaon originated as a speculative reconstruction derived from a reference in her poetry to the local tradition of the ferryman. No fragment of her poetry refers to this, but one ancient mythographical treatise (Palaeph. *De incred.* 48 = *Myth. Gr.* III (2) 69) explicitly records that Sappho wrote about this Phaon (fr. 211a L–P). Phaon, too, figured in Attic comedy as early as Cratinus (fr. 370 K–A), and the comic playwright Plato (4th cent. BC) produced a play entitled *Phaon* (frr. 188–91 K–A). However, none of these comedies about Sappho or Phaon acquired the prominence that might have led a poet, in the style of O., to seize upon it as a source from which to extract the material for a poem. The author of the *ES*, unlike O. (or the other author(s) of the other non-Ovidian poems in the corpus), struck out on an original path, taking the biographical traditions about a literary figure as the basis for an epistolary fiction.

1–8 The introduction of the epistle develops two motifs, first that the handwriting alone ought to identify Sappho as the author of this letter, unless Phaon has forgotten her. Next, she anticipates his puzzlement that she is writing in elegiac couplets, while he might expect lyric verses from her. None of O.'s *Her.* overtly acknowledge that they are in verse, but the author of this poem plays on Sappho's identity as a poet and represents her letter as another of her literary productions.

1–4 In the opening address Sappho anxiously inquires whether her handwriting looks familiar to Phaon. As commentators such as Burman and de Vries (1885) 36 have noted, the opening of *Pont.* 2.10 develops a similar theme with striking verbal parallels (1–8): *ecquid ab impressae cognoscis imagine cerae | haec tibi Nasonem scribere uerba, Macer? | auctorisque sui si non est anulus index, | cognitane est nostra littera facta manu? | an tibi notitiam mora temporis eripit horum, | nec repetunt oculi signa uetusta tui? | sis licet oblitus pariter gemmaeque manusque, | exciderit tantum ne tibi cura mei.* But the opening of Sappho's epistle is not well developed: the reason for her concern – Phaon is far away in Sicily – is not given until 11. In the intervening lines Sappho passes to a different subject: the unexpected choice of elegiac metre. An explanation might be that the author wanted to combine this idea with that found in *Pont.* 1.7.3–4 *indicat auctorem locus? an nisi nomine lecto | haec me Nasonem scribere uerba latet?*

1 Ecquid, ut: a common Ovidian expression (together with *ecquid* *ubi*), but elsewhere only in his later work; cf. *Met.* 12.588, *Trist.* 3.3.47, 4.3.21, 5.2.1, *Pont.* 1.6.1, 3.5.39.

aspecta est: the verb, though common in O. (160 exx.), is rarely found in the passive (10 exx.) and never in the perfect tense. Its use here is 'flat and lifeless' (Tarrant (1981) 144); O.'s characters write with more vividness and directness.

studiosae 'eager': but when used to describe the writing hand of a poet, the adjective also suggests 'learned'.

2 nostra: predicative, 'as mine'.

3 auctoris: feminine, as often in classical usage. The feminine form *auctrix* 'authoress' is a later concoction of fastidious grammarians. Throughout this opening section the poet's principal concern is with this 'epistle' as a literary work.

Sapphus: the Latinized form of the Greek genitive. O. has one example of this form, *Clius* the genitive of *Clio*, at *Ars* 1.27.

4 hoc breue ... opus: again, Sappho refers to her epistle as a literary work; cf. *Pont.* 3.4.5, where O. refers to that panegyrical epistle as *exiguum opus*.

5–6 alterna ... | carmina 'alternating verses': i.e. the elegiac couplet; cf. *Fast.* 2.121 *alterno carmine*, *Trist.* 3.1.11 *alterno ... uersus*, 3.7.10 *alternos ... pedes*. The spurious opening couplet of 7 (see app. crit.) refers to the following letter as a *carmen*. Sappho's fame in antiquity rested on her accomplishments as a lyric poet, so it is not surprising Phaon did not recognize her elegiac verses. The biographical tradition mentions that she also wrote elegiac poetry (*Suda* s.v. Σαπφώ; *P.Oxy.* 1800, fr. 1). Apparently, in addition to the standard nine-book Alexandrian edition of Sappho's lyrics, there was a book of elegies and epigrams widely believed to be by her. Three epigrams attributed to 'Sappho' are preserved in the *Palatine anthology* (6.269, 7.489, 7.505), and there may have been others. These are certainly later Hellenistic compositions, part of the vogue of writing works under the name of famous literary figures; cf. Page (1981) 127–8. Meleager (*c.* 100 BC) thought them genuine (*AP* 4.1.6 = *HE* 3931) and included them and perhaps others in his *Garland*. The author of the *ES* surely knew of elegiac poems attributed to Sappho, but was discerning enough to see them as anomalous. There is a slight displacement (hyperbaton) of *requiras* to a position within the indirect question.

7 flendus amor ... flebile carmen: an allusion to the connection between elegy and lamentation, which ancient scholars tried to find in the etymology of elegy from Greek ἔλεος 'pity' or εὖ λέγειν 'eulogize' or the like; cf. Harvey (1955) 168–72, West (1974) 7. O. also plays on this association when it suits his purpose. Thus the personification of Elegy in *Am.* 3.9.3 is addressed with the epithet *flebilis* in his poem on the death of Tibullus: *flebilis indignos, Elegia, solue capillos.* And in his exile poetry O. stresses these mournful associations, e.g. *Trist.* 5.1.5–6 *flebilis ut noster status est, ita flebile carmen,* | *materiae scripto conueniente suae;* cf. Hinds (1987) 103–4. The notion that certain metres are appropriate for some topics is a frequently exploited commonplace; cf. Brink (1971) 160–3.

elegia: the Latinized form of the Greek; cf. *Am.* 3.1.7 *uenit odoratos Elegia nexa capillos,* 3.9.3, *Rem.* 379. The readings of F *elegi quoque* and other MSS reflect hesitation over the scansion of the final syllable as long. Palmer's emendation *elegiae* attempts to harmonize this verse with O.'s practice, since he only uses this form to designate the personification of the genre.

8 non facit ad 'does not suit': 6.128n.

barbitos: the lyre, a Greek word, feminine only here in Latin.

9–20 Sappho describes her love for Phaon, comparing the force of her passion to a flame, and recounting how her former pursuits mean nothing to her now.

9–10 The comparison of the 'fire of love' (7.23n.) to a conflagration of dried-out stalks of grain was developed by O. in the *Met.* at 1.492–5, of Apollo's reaction to the sight of Daphne, *utque leues stipulae demptis adolentur aristis,* | *... sic deus in flammas abiit;* cf. 6.455–6. In these passages the point of the comparison lies in the suddenness and violence of the flame: they refer to the effect of love at first sight. Here the comparison is less apt in a description of Sappho's ongoing passion; and in this context *fertilis ... ager* seems odd, too, since [O.] seems also to have Virgil in mind here, who describes the same flame from a technical standpoint: *Geo.* 1.84–5 *saepe etiam sterilis incendere profuit agros* | *atque leuem stipulam crepitantibus urere flammis.* The choice of imagery here here may be owed to Sappho's own poetry, to judge from fr. 48 L–P where she writes of her 'heart which was burning with desire (καιομέναν πόθωι)', and several later authors who refer to 'burning' Sappho, e.g. Plut. *Amat.* 18.

indomitis ... exercentibus Euris 'when the untamed east winds drive on the flame': cf. Hor. *Carm.* 4.14.20–1 *indomitus ... undas | exercet Auster.*

11 'Phaon, you frequent (*celebras*) the faraway fields of Etna.' Phaon, we deduce, is in Sicily, for we know not what reason. There is no other evidence that connects him with that island, but Sappho herself apparently spent some time there in exile. This is recorded in the so-called Parian Marble (*IG* xii 5.444) under a date between 605/4 BC and 591 BC. The reason must have been political, but this event seems to have left no trace in the biographical tradition about Sappho. Since such literary biographies were usually based on inferences drawn from the author's works, it may be that any allusion to the Sicilian exile in Sappho's poetry was vague enough to allow for a connection to be made with Phaon.

Typhoidos: the epithet for Sicily's volcano is unique in Latin. It derives from Typhoeus, the monstrous offspring of Tartaros and Gaia (Hes. *Theog.* 820–2), who was defeated by Zeus and imprisoned under Mt Aetna; cf. *Fast.* 4.491 *alta iacet uasti super ora Typhoeos Aetne*, the ending of which may have influenced the phrasing here.

12 calor: a regular item in the Latin amatory lexicon, but perhaps especially applicable to Sappho, as in Horace's characterization of her poetry at *Carm.* 4.9.10–12: *spirat adhuc amor | uiuuntque commissi calores | Aeoliae fidibus puellae*; cf. *Trist.* 3.7.19–20.

Aetnaeo non minor igne: as the only active volcano with which the Romans were familiar before the eruption of Mt Vesuvius in AD 79, Aetna figures prominently in hyperbolic expressions of burning passion; cf. *Rem.* 491, *Met.* 13.868–9, Otto (1890) 7–8.

13–14 'Nor do songs arise for me to perform to the accompaniment of the well-spaced strings; songs are the product of a mind free from care.' It is 'awkward for Sappho to claim that she cannot compose *carmina* only seven lines after referring to the *ES* itself as *alterna carmina*' (Tarrant (1981) 145). The form of the expression is also inappropriate to the context, since Sappho ought to refer to playing the strings as musical accompaniment, while *dispositis* refers only to the spacing of the strings on the instrument; cf. Vitruvius 5.4.5.

14 proueniunt: the metaphor is derived from agriculture (cf. *OLD* s.v. 3a), as illustrated in *Pont.* 4.2.11–12 *fertile pectus habes, interque Helicona colentes | uberius nulli prouenit ista seges*; cf. *Am.* 1.3.20.

uacuae carmina mentis opus: the notion that poetic composition requires a peaceful setting is developed by O. at *Trist.* 1.1.39 *carmina proueniunt animo deducta sereno*: cf. Luck *ad loc.* The same conceit may also be inverted as a criticism of the life of a poet, as in the objection posed to O.'s art by personified Envy at *Am.* 1.15.2 *ingeniique uocas carmen inertis opus. uacuae* means more than just 'free from care': in love poetry it regularly refers to a heart free from romantic entanglements; cf. Pichon (1902) 287.

15–20 Sappho remarks that she is no longer interested in any of her former female lovers. In some of the surviving poems Sappho addresses women in the same terms as those used by male lovers in homosexual love poetry. The earliest attested remarks about Sappho's homosexual liaisons are contemporary with O. (*Trist.* 2.365, Hor. *Carm.* 2.13.24–5), but some criticism of her sexual preferences is reflected in the biographical tradition: *P.Oxy.* 1800 'she has been accused by some of being licentious (ἄτακτος) and a lover of women (γυναικεράστρια)'. It is likely that discussions of this topic date back at least to the Hellenistic period; cf. Dover (1978) 174–9.

15 Pyrrhiades Methymniadesue: the girls of Pyrrha and Methymna, two cities of Lesbos. The adjectives are otherwise unattested in Latin.

16 Lesbiadum: otherwise unattested; this form supplies the genitive plural for the regular *Lesbis* (cf. 100, 3.36).

cetera turba iuuant: the plural verb is regular with a collective noun.

17–18 uilis 'contemptible': a strong term in the language of love poetry; cf. 3.41 *qua merui culpa fieri tibi uilis, Achille*, 12.187, Cat. 72.6, Prop. 1.2.25. The repetition (anaphora) creates an expectation of a rising tricolon, which is seemingly completed in the pentameter, and then somewhat surprisingly expanded in the following hexameter.

Anactorie ... Gyrinno ... Atthis: girls of Lesbos whom Sappho loved. They are mentioned together by Maximus of Tyre (2nd cent. AD) while comparing Sappho's relationships with young women to those of Socrates with men: 'What Alcibiades and Charmides and Phaedrus were to him, Gyrinno and Atthis and Anactoria were to her' (18.9). The name of Anactoria appears in one fragment (16.15 L–P) as a girl who has gone away and left Sappho forlorn. Atthis' name emerges from a number of fragments as a woman whom Sappho once loved (fr. 49 L–P) and comforted (fr. 96 L–P), but who also deserted her. The third name, Gyrinno, appears in a few fragments (frr. 29, 82 (a), 90 L–P), and was restored by Bentley for the MSS *Cydro*, which is not attested in any fragments or testimonia of Sappho.

19 non sine crimine 'not without incurring censure': criticism of Sappho's homosexual love lyrics apparently was found in part of the ancient biographical tradition; cf. *Suda* s.v. Σαπφώ: 'her companions and friends were Atthis, Telesippa, and Megara with whom she was accused of having disgraceful liaisons (διαβολὴν ἔσχεν αἰσχρᾶς φιλίας)', and above 15–20n. The reading of the vulgate *hic* for *non* is a transparent attempt to deny Sappho's homosexuality. From Sappho's point of view, it is, at the very least, an awkward development in her argument to remind Phaon of her past lovers in such quantity. *centum* stands for an indefinite large number.

20 improbe 'rascal': a standard term of abuse in the lover's lexicon; cf. *Ars* 1.665 *pugnabit primo fortassis et 'improbe' dicet.*

multarum quod fuit, unus habes 'what once belonged to many girls, is yours alone': cf. 16.94 (Paris to Helen) *multarum uotum sola tenere potes.*

21–50 Sappho now turns to flatter Phaon, praising his looks in comparison with her own unattractive features. It was her poetry that made her appealing to Phaon along with her sexual prowess, something of which she now reminds him.

21 This line is borrowed with only a slight change from *Am.* 2.3.13 *est etiam facies, sunt apti lusibus anni.* Such self-imitation is of course characteristic of O., but in this instance the change makes for an awkward and unparalleled expression, *est in te* 'you have'.

22 oculis insidiosa meis 'setting a trap for my eyes': the line is a variation of *Am.* 2.17.12 *o facies oculos nata tenere meos.*

23–4 Comparisons to Apollo and Bacchus as paragons of eternally youthful beauty are commonplace in Roman poetry: e.g. Tib. 1.4.37–8 *solis aeterna est Baccho Phoeboque iuuenta:* | *nam decet intonsus crinis utrumque deum*, Bömer on *Met.* 3.421.

23 sume: the imperative, like the jussive subjunctive in 24, stands for the protasis of a conditional clause.

fidem et pharetras: Apollo's standard equipment; cf. 5.139, *Met.* 10.108 *qui citharam neruis et neruis temperat arcum.* The poetic plural *pharetras*, the reading of F, may stand; cf. *Met.* 4.306 *uel iaculum uel pictas sume pharetras*, Maas (1902) 520n.

manifestus Apollo: the line-ending is repeated from *Ars* 2.493 *haec ego cum canerem, subito manifestus Apollo.*

24 cornua: a frequent attribute of Bacchus; cf. *Ars* 3.348 *insignis cornu Bacche.* His beauty and eternal youth are hymned at *Met.* 4.17–20 *tibi enim inconsumpta iuuenta est; | tu puer aeternus, tu formosissimus alto | conspiceris caelo; tibi, cum sine cornibus astas, | uirgineum caput est.*

25–6 The argument is emotional, not logical: since you could be taken for Apollo and Bacchus, you should love me just as they loved Daphne and Ariadne, even though neither of them was a poet.

25 Daphnen ... Cnosida: Greek accusatives. The antonomasia (2.76n.) for Ariadne, 'the girl from Cnossos', is common: cf. *Ars* 1.523, *Rem.* 745.

26 nec: with adversative sense (2.6n.), 'and yet neither'.

illa uel illa must here be equivalent to *haec uel illa* 'the former or the latter', but where O. uses the phrase it is to register complete indefiniteness, 'this one or that'; cf. *Am.* 1.8.84, *Ars* 1.227, *Fast.* 5.188.

27–50 Sappho excuses her defects and extols her virtues.

27 Pegasides: the Muses; contrast 5.3n. The name, first attested at Prop. 3.1.19, derives from Pegasus, the winged horse whose hoof struck the spot from which flowed the Hippocrene, the spring on Mt Helicon traditionally associated with poetic inspiration.

blandissima carmina: the epithet suggests light verse on erotic subjects; cf. Prop. 1.8.40 *blandi carminis.*

dictant: the Muses 'dictate', the poet is only the mouthpiece; elsewhere O. recognizes a different source of inspiration: *Am.* 2.1.38 *carmina purpureus quae mihi dictat Amor*, *Pont.* 3.3.29.

28 iam canitur toto nomen in orbe meum: virtually identical to *Ars* 2.740 *cantetur toto nomen in orbe meum.* The claim to world-wide fame through poetry is made often in Roman literature; cf. Nisbet–Hubbard on Hor. *Carm.* 2.20.14. O. makes this claim early and often: e.g. *Am.* 1.15.7–8 *mihi fama perennis | quaeritur, in toto semper ut orbe canar*, 1.3.25–6, *Rem.* 363, *Met.* 15.871–9, *Trist.* 2.118.

29 Alcaeus: Sappho's contemporary and the other celebrated lyric poet of Lesbos, hence *consors patriaeque lyraeque.*

30 grandius: the critical verdict reflected here was shared in antiquity by, among others, Horace (*Carm.* 2.13.24–8), in a passage that seems to have been in the mind of [O.]. After a brief reference to the plaintive strains of Sappho's erotic verse he apostrophizes Alcaeus: *et te sonantem plenius aureo,* | *Alcaee, plectro dura nauis,* | *dura fugae mala, dura belli.* In addition to love songs, Alcaeus composed lyrics dealing with contemporary politics, war, and his own exile: sterner stuff, by ancient estimates, than love poetry.

31–40 Sappho concedes her physical defects but argues that her intellectual gifts outweigh them. One ancient biography (*P.Oxy.* 1800, fr. 1) reports that 'in appearance she seems to have been contemptible and ugly, being dark in complexion [35 *candida non sum*] and quite small [33 *breuis*] in stature'. The same details are found elsewhere (Max. Tyr. 18.7; Lucian, *Imag.* 18), and we may suspect that this physical description of Sappho derived from inferences drawn from some lost passage of her poetry.

31 difficilis 'malignant'.

32 'With intellect I compensate for the loss of my beauty.' An odd line in both form and expression. The scansion of *rependo* is impossible for O.: similar examples of shortened *o* in a verb of bacchiac (∪ – –) shape are not attested until the Neronian period; cf. Hartenberger (1911) 56. Most editors print Bentley's *repende*, which is supported by Ausonius, *Prof.* 2.31–2 *quiesce placidus et caduci corporis* | *damnum repende gloria.* But if the author of this epistle is not O., then the metrical objection is not decisive, and in fact the closest parallel in O. tells in favour of *rependo*: *Ars* 2.677 *illae munditiis annorum damna rependunt.* In short, 'if the work is judged spurious, then the more natural *rependo* ought to be preferred' (Tarrant (1981) 137).

33–4 'I am short, but I have a name that fills every land; I am as large as my name.' This couplet is plainly not Ovidian: for Sappho to claim that her size should be measured in quantitative terms by the extent of her reputation is ridiculous. The parallels cited by commentators indicate the origin of these two lines. The couplet owes something to *Met.* 12.617–18 *at uiuit totum quae gloria compleat orbem:* | *haec illi mensura uiro respondet*; the articulation of the hexameter is derived from *Fast.* 1.603 *Magne, tuum nomen rerum est mensura tuarum,* where the play on the name *Magnus* carries the point; cf. *Pont.*1.2.1. Most MSS have this couplet in a different form (see app. crit.), evidence of the survival into the fifteenth century of a tradition independent of F.

35–6 Cepheia ... | Andromede: the daughter of Cepheus, Andromeda, who was rescued by Perseus and brought back to Greece as his bride. Her home was in Ethiopia and so her skin colour was black. She is a standard exemplum in dismissing skin colour as insignificant in matters of love; cf. *Am.* 2.4.40 *est etiam in fusco grata colore uenus*, *Ars* 2.643 *nec suus Andromedae color est obiectus ab illo*, *AP* 5.132.7–8 (Philodemus). The form of Andromeda's name here is unusual: O. does not use the Ionic form Ἀνδρομέδη, which is attested in Greek by Hdt. 7.61, 150, *AP* 5.132.8 (cited above), Nonnus, *Dion.* 1.192. In Latin this form is introduced by Prop. 1.3.4, 2.28.21, 4.7.63, and occurs again only at Germanicus, *Arat.* 201, 640 (cf. N–W 1 69). O. uses only the form Ἀνδρομέδα, with an accusative in -*an*: cf. *Ars* 1.53, *Met.* 4.671, 757. Andromeda was also the name of one of Sappho's rivals, so the choice of this example may not be entirely coincidence.

35 Perseo: scanned as a spondee, by synizesis (6.50n.).

36 patriae: Ethiopia, with a glance at the etymology of Αἰθίοψ as 'burned face'.

fusca colore: the phrase recurs at [Virg.] *Mor.* 32–3 *Afra genus ... et fusca colore*, with no indication of priority.

37 uariis 'those of different colour'.

38 uiridi ... aue: the parrot, whose colour is noted by O. at *Am.* 2.6.21 *tu poteras fragiles pinnis hebetare zmaragdos*. Its affection for the turtle-dove forms the backdrop for a lament in O.'s poem for Corinna's dead parrot: *Am.* 2.6.12 *tu tamen ante alios, turtur amice, dole.*

39–40 'If no woman is to be yours but one who could be deemed worthy of you in her appearance, then no woman will be yours.' Protasis and apodosis of the condition are identical and the first half of the pentameter is repeated verbatim, something which is not attested elsewhere in Latin verse. On the face of it, it is an imitation, not altogether successful, of an Ovidian mannerism which gained notoriety in an anecdote recounted by the elder Seneca (*Con.* 2.2.12) and perhaps known to the author of the *ES*. When a friend asked O. if he could delete three verses from his poetry, O. agreed on the condition that he could except three from the bargain. Each noted separately his choices, and upon inspection they proved to be identical. Two are known: *Ars.* 2.24 *semibouemque uirum semiuirumque bouem* and *Am.* 2.11.10 *et gelidum Borean egelidumque Notum.* In these pentameters there is near repetition, the slight variations scoring a verbal point. There is no such wit in this line; better is 13.166 *si tibi cura mei, sit tibi cura tui.* It is more difficult to judge whether [O.] is imitating Sappho herself. In the late Hellenistic treatise of Demetrius 'On style', Sappho's use of repetition (anadiplosis) receives favourable comment, with the following lines quoted as an example (fr. 114 L–P): παρθενία, παρθενία, ποῖ με λίποισ' ἀποίχηι; | †οὐκέτι ἥξω πρὸς σέ, οὐκέτι ἥξω† 'Virginity, virginity, where have you gone, deserting me?' 'Never again shall I come to you, never again shall I come.' In spite of the corruption in the second line, it is clear that it consisted of a near repetition of the same clause.

41 me cum legeres: cf. *Am.* 2.1.5 *me legat in sponsi facie non frigida uirgo.* Editors have been troubled by the transmitted reading of this line because the pentameter seems to imply that Sappho was reading aloud in Phaon's presence; see Housman (1897) 289 (= *Class. pap.* 409). That she would not do in any case: a lyric poet would sing, as she describes in the next couplet. Here she anachronistically describes the effect of her poetry as written literature, a context in which *loqui* (42) refers to the quality of language; cf. *TLL* s.v. 1662.53ff. Maximus of Tyre (18.7) reports the opinion of Socrates that Sappho was 'beautiful because of the beauty of her songs'. Housman's emendation *sat iam* for *etiam* introduces the rare form *sat*, which is found in O. only in the phrase *sat est*: there is no need to impose it on [O.].

42 usque: take with *iurabas* 'you constantly used to swear'.

43 memini: frequently inserted in parataxis in O., e.g. *Am.* 2.1.11, *Ars* 2.551. The topos that lovers know everything is familiar in O.: e.g. 5.130 *unde hoc compererim tam bene quaeris? amo.*

44 'And while I sang you gave me stolen kisses': the oxymoron *rapta dabas* describes kisses stolen while the girl's attention is diverted; cf. *Am.* 2.4.26 *oscula cantanti rapta dedisse uelim*, perhaps the model for this line.

45–50 Sappho tries to arouse Phaon by reminding him of their sexual encounters.

45 haec: sc. *oscula.*

omnique a parte 'in every respect': a prosaic expression first cultivated in poetry by O.; cf. Bömer on *Met.* 3.70.

46 cum fit amoris opus 'during the act of love': for *opus* as a euphemism for intercourse, cf. *Am.* 1.4.47–8 *saepe mihi dominaeque meae properata uoluptas | ueste sub iniecta dulce peregit opus*, 2.10.36, 3.7.68, *Ars* 2.480, Adams (1982) 157. The present tense *fit* is anomalous: syntax could be restored by reading *dum*, but it does not correspond with *tum* in classical Latin.

47–8 The author appears to have in mind two Ovidian passages: *Am.* 3.14.25–6 *illic nec uoces nec <u>uerba iuuantia</u> cessent, | spondaque <u>lasciua mobilitate</u> tremat* and *Ars* 2.724 *et dulces gemitus <u>aptaque uerba ioco</u>*. This latter passage is varied by O. himself at *Ars* 3.795–6, where O. offers advice on sex to women. Although *iocus* in this context need not always refer to sexual acts, that is plainly the sense here; cf. Adams (1982) 161–2.

47 plus solito 'more than it usually did': an odd expression in this context, implying that her *lasciuia* pleased him when they were not making love, and that it pleased him even more when they were.

lasciuia here suggests sexual freedom. Like other expressions of movement *mobilitas* may be a euphemism for sexual activity; cf. *Am.* 2.4.14 *spemque dat in molli mobilis esse toro*, Adams (1982) 191–3.

49 ubi iam amborum fuerat confusa uoluptas 'when pleasure had just been combined for both of us': *uoluptas*, not surprisingly, often has sexual connotations (Adams (1982) 197–8), but this expression to describe orgasm seems to be without parallel in Latin; however, cf. Theocritus 2.143 ἐς πόθον ἤνθομες ἄμφω 'we both came to our desire', Dioscorides, *AP* 5.55.7 (= *HE* 1489). O. repeatedly insists on the importance of both partners achieving climax; cf. *Ars* 2.682–3 *quod iuuet ex aequo femina uirque ferant. | odi concubitus, qui non utrumque resoluunt*, 2.727–8. For the pluperfect *fuerat* in place of the imperfect, cf. 7.140n.

50 in lasso corpore languor erat: the aftermath of passion; cf. *Am.* 1.5.25 *lassi requieuimus ambo*, *Rem.* 413–15, Apul. *Met.* 2.17, Dioscorides, *AP* 5.55.8 (= *HE* 1490), Adams (1982) 196.

51–70 Thoughts about their past joys together come to an abrupt halt as Sappho reflects on the present (51 *nunc*), when Phaon is lingering in Sicily. Her thoughts then turn to other disappointments in her life – the death of her father, her wayward brother and, somewhat oddly, her daughter – before turning back to Phaon.

51 noua praeda: predicative; cf. *Am.* 1.2.19 *en ego, confiteor, tua sum noua praeda, Cupido.*

52 quid mihi cum: 6.47n.

Sicelis esse uolo: the author is unaware of Sappho's exile in Sicily; 11n.

53 erronem 'runaway': the word is not found in O.; its only other occurrences in poetry are Hor. *Serm.* 2.7.113 and Tib. 2.6.6 *erronem sub tua signa uoca*. It is this latter passage that the author perhaps recalls: the motif is the lover as a runaway. *erro* is usually used of a runaway slave, but it is also defined as (Ulp. *Dig.* 21.1.17.14) *qui non quidem fugit, sed frequenter sine causa uagatur.*

54 Nisiadesque in this context must mean 'Sicilian', but the association is rather tenuous: the Sicilian city of Megara traced its origins to the mainland Greek city of that name and its legendary king Nisus. One wonders whether the unusual epithet occurred in Sappho.

matres ... nurus: a 'polar' expression meaning 'women young and old'. O. uses it frequently in ritual contexts which required the presence of all the women of a community; cf. *Met.* 3.529, 4.9, 12.216, *Fast.* 4.295, *Trist.* 2.23. Its use here is thus a bit hyperbolic: Phaon, Sappho imagines, is pursued by all the women of Sicily. This line is obviously related to *Epiced. Drusi* 204 *Ausoniae matres Ausoniaeque nurus*, though it is impossible to determine priority; cf. also *Am.* 3.4.40 *Romulus Iliades Iliadesque Remus.*

55 nec uos decipiant: an inversion of the elegiac topos of the charming and deceitful mistress; cf. *Am.* 2.9.43–5 *me modo decipiant uoces fallacis amicae | ... et modo blanditias dicat.* The author may have stitched together two Ovidian half-lines: *Am.* 1.8.65 *nec te decipiant ueteres circum atria cerae*, and 3.11.21 *turpia quid referam uanae mendacia linguae*, and may in turn have served as model for [Virg.] *Aetna* 366 *nec te decipiant stolidi mendacia uulgi.*

mendacia: attested once in Prop. (4.5.27), but otherwise only eight times in O. among Augustan poets, including 8.67.

56 An imitation of *Ars* 3.435 *quae uobis dicunt, dixerunt mille puellis.*

57 montes ... Sicanos: modern Erice, a mountain on the west coast of Sicily with an ancient cult of Venus on the summit. The cult was established in Rome by 215 BC and the epithet *Erycina* appears in poetry for Venus as early as Cat. 64.72; cf. Nisbet–Hubbard on Hor. *Carm.* 1.2.33.

58 nam tua sum: the parenthesis, common in appeals to divinities, explains the grounds for addressing a particular deity. Sappho's love poetry marked her out for a close association with Venus.

59–60 'Or is my heavy fortune maintaining the process it first began, and is it always to remain bitter in its course?' The pentameter restates the hexameter, which offers a familiar lament: *Trist.* 5.10.11–12 *an peragunt solitos communia tempora motus,* | *suntque magis uitae tempora dura meae?*

59 tenorem: cf. 7.112 *fati tenor.*

60 in cursu ... suo: the metaphor is from the race-track; cf. *Rem.* 430 *in cursu qui fuit, haesit amor.*

61 sex mihi natales ierant: an unusual expression for 'my sixth birthday had passed'; O. forms this phrase with *ago* or *adesse*; cf. *Met.* 2.497 *natalibus actis,* 13.753 and *Met.* 9.285 *cum iam natalis adesset, Trist.* 3.13.2. The information is so specific that it probably derives from some statement in Sappho's poetry.

61–2 lecta ... | ante diem: cf. Prop. 4.1.127–8 *ossaque legisti non illa aetate legenda* | *patris.* The deceased parent is surely her father, for Sappho's mother is addressed in a fragment (102 L–P) of Sappho's love poetry: 'sweet mother, I cannot weave a web, for I am overcome with desire for a boy because of slender Aphrodite'. His early death may account for the dearth of information about Sappho's father in the biographical tradition: the *Suda* s.v. Σαπφώ records seven alternatives for his name. Herodotus (2.135) reports his name as Scamandronymus; cf. Jacobson (1974) 279–80.

lacrimas ossa bibere meas: cf. *Fast.* 3.561 *mixta bibunt molles lacrimis unguenta fauillae.*

63–8 Sappho touches briefly on the difficulties she had with her brother because of his involvement with a prostitute named Rhodopis. Herodotus (2.135) provides the earliest account: 'Rhodopis was brought to Egypt by Xantheus of Samos; she came to work her trade, but was set free at a high price by a man from Mytilene, Charaxus, the son of Scamadronymus and the brother of the poet Sappho... When Charaxus returned to Mytilene after freeing Rhodopis Sappho thoroughly abused him in a poem.' That poem is lost, but it left its mark on the biographical tradition; cf. *P.Oxy.* 1800, fr. 1; *P.Oxy.* 2506, fr. 48. And one fragment in which she mentions her brother may be related: fr. 5.1–5 L–P '[Cypris and] Nereids, grant that my brother arrive here unharmed and that everything he wishes in his

heart be fulfilled, and grant too that he atone for his past mistakes
...' (Campbell). Another fragment (15 L–P) may also be relevant: it
mentions a woman called Doricha, which was the name by which
Sappho addressed Rhodopis according to ancient sources (e.g.
Athen. 13 596bc, Strabo 17.1.33). It is impossible to tell whether the
sources have conflated two different incidents.

63 carpsit opes 'spent his wealth': this seems to have been Sap-
pho's principal complaint against her brother, as recorded in the
biography *P.Oxy.* 1800, fr. 1. The verb *carpere* usually describes the
act of 'fleecing' a lover of his money; e.g. *Ars* 1.420 *cupidi carpat
amantis opes*, *Am.* 1.8.91. But O. also uses the verb in a neutral sense
of one who spends his own money: *Pont.* 4.9.122 *exiguas carpo munere
pauper opes*. Bentley's conjecture may therefore be preferred to other
suggestions for the *arsit inops* of the MSS, an intrusion from 65 *factus
inops*.

frater: his name was Charaxus, as we learn from Herodotus (63–
8n.).

meretricis: a 'low' word (Tränkle (1960) 120), found only here in
the *Her.* In O.'s other works it is attested 3 times in *Am.*, once only in
Ars, *Pont.*, and *Trist.*, while it is avoided entirely in *Met.* and *Fast.* (but
cf. *Fast.* 5.349 *meretricius*). For the phrase *captus amore*, cf. 1.76, *Fast.*
5.349.

64 'And suffered loss as well as foul shame': cf. *Am.* 3.7.72 *tristia
cum magno damna pudore tuli*.

65 peragit freta caerula: an unusual extension of such famil-
iar phrases as *cursus* or *iter peragere*, without parallel before Petronius,
Sat. 119.3–4 *freta ... peraguntur*. The thought here is oddly expressed:
'it might be pedantry to suggest that the addition of *agili ... remo*
("he traverses the dark-blue seas on a nimble oar") makes Sappho's
brother sound like the first recorded surfer ...' (Tarrant (1981)
141).

66 male quaerit opes: information perhaps inferred from Sap-
pho's poetry, though what this pursuit might be can only be guessed
(piracy?). If not a specific reference to Sappho, then the only point
of this line lies in the repetition of *male*.

67 quod monui: probably in the poem that Herodotus knew
(above, 63–8n.). Since this is not the tone of the surviving fragment

(5 L–P) referring to her brother, Herodotus may have known of a different poem. The information that Charaxus hated his sister may only be an inference drawn from that poem.

bene multa: a colloquial usage, 1.44n.

68 libertas 'frankness': a sense of the word common in prose but not found in O.; cf. Phaedrus 1.2.2, Mart. 6.86.3. In its articulation the line perhaps owes something to Prop. 2.28.14 *hoc tibi lingua nocens, hoc tibi forma dedit.*

69–70 The climactic entry in Sappho's record of woe: she has a daughter! There is no evidence to explain why the author of the *ES* should have thought that Sappho regarded her daughter as a burden. The biographical tradition (*P.Oxy.* 1800, fr. 1, *Suda*) registers her name as Cleis, after Sappho's mother, but that is all. The only substantial fragment in which she is mentioned would be difficult to harmonize with this couplet: 'I have a beautiful daughter who looks like golden flowers, beloved Cleis, for whom I would not [take?] all Lydia or lovely ...' (fr. 132 L–P).

69 'And as if there were lack of things to weary me endlessly': the version of this line found in F contains a number of awkwardnesses uncharacteristic of both O. and the author of this poem: *desit quae me hac sine cura fatiget.* The only undisputed instance of postponed *sine* in O. occurs at *Ars* 2.454 *quo sine non possit uiuere*, where there is no ambiguity since the relative pronoun occurs in anaphora. Another instance occurs in 8.80 *clamabam 'sine me, me sine, mater, abis'*, where the authorship is disputed on other grounds. Here it is unclear whether *hac* is to be understood as *filia* or *cura*. If the poem is not by O. then the smoother reading of the *recentiores* may not be authentic.

70 accumulat curas ... meas 'increases my cares': this construction is not found in O., who uses the verb only once (*Fast.* 2.122), but cf. Petronius, *Sat.* 89.48, Stat. *Theb.* 4.369.

71–96 Her thoughts now turn to Phaon: for her love for him has brought only distress. As she recounts how she has agonized over him, Sappho's thoughts are led back to the reason she fell in love with him in the first place.

71 nostris accedis ... querelis: 1.96n.

72 non agitur uento nostra carina suo 'my ship is not driven by a favouring wind': *suo = secundo*, a common idiom; cf. *Rem.* 14,

264, *Trist.* 3.5.4, Shackleton Bailey (1954). For the metaphor of love as a dangerous voyage, see Henderson on *Rem.* 14.

73–6 The two couplets form a rising tricolon describing her dishevelled hair (73), her lack of interest in jewellery (74), and neglect of her dress (75–6). For O. describing the sophisticated tastes of contemporary Roman women, these are the essentials: *Med.* 18–20 *uultis inaurata corpora ueste tegi,* | *uultis odoratos positu uariare capillos,* | *conspicuam gemmis uultis habere manum.* Such extravagant neglect of appearance was also affected by Laodamia (13.31–2).

73 sparsi sine lege capilli: the line-end is also found at *Ars* 3.133 *non sint sine lege capilli* and *Met.* 1.477 *uitta coercebat positos sine lege capillos.*

74 articulos 'fingers': cf. *Am.* 2.15.4, addressed to a ring, *protinus articulis induat illa suis.*

75 crinibus: this word for 'hair' occurs only here and at 140 in the single epistles, compared with *capillos* (18) and *coma* (16); cf. Axelson (1945) 51.

aurum is the ornament known as *crinale.* In this couplet the author may have had in mind 21.89–90 *ipsa dedit gemmas digitis et crinibus aurum* | *et uestes umeris induit ipsa meis*; cf. *Am.* 3.13.25 *uirginei crines auro gemmaque premuntur, Met.* 5.53, *Pont.* 3.3.15.

76 Arabum ... dona: myrrh, imported from Arabia and prized as a cosmetic; cf. *RE* XXXIA (1933) 1143–5 and, for the phrase, Sen. *Ag.* 806 *Arabumque donis.*

77 'For whom should I adorn myself in my unhappy state, or whom should I endeavour to please?' The passive *colar* has a 'middle' sense. For the perfect infinitive *placuisse,* see 2.28n.; cf. 18.95 *nunc etiam nando dominae placuisse laboro.*

78 ille ... abes: the demonstrative *ille* is often combined with the pronoun *ego* and *tu* to refer to one who is well-known; cf. K–S 1 622.

unicus auctor 'the sole reason': sc. for me to dress up.

79–80 This couplet is at odds with the reasoning of the preceding verses. Sappho has just declared that she is neglecting her appearance because Phaon is away. This statement of fidelity is jarred by the present portrait of fickleness. The couplet may best be explained (Tarrant (1981) 143) as a conflation of two Ovidian passages: *Trist.* 4.10.65–6 *molle Cupidineis nec inexpugnabile telis* | *cor mihi, quodque* *leuis causa moueret, erat* and *Am.* 2.4.10 *centum sunt causae cur ego semper amem*. Each of these passages coheres effectively with its own context in these poems, but that can not be said of this couplet of the *ES*, which is apparently an imitation and must therefore have been composed after the *Tristia*. The repetition *semper ... semper* seems without point.

79 uiolabile: not found in O.

81 siue: elided here and at 83, the only instances of this elision in the *Her.* against eight occurrences of the word without elision in the certainly genuine epistles. *ita* is prosaic: 6.97n.

legem 'terms': the idiom *legem dicere* is common in prose; cf. Bömer on *Met.* 13.72. The passages adduced by de Vries as parallels for the diction in this couplet may well have served as models: *Trist.* 5.3.25–6 *scilicet hanc legem nentes fatalia Parcae | stamina bis genito bis cecinere tibi*, and *Pont.* 1.8.63–4 *at tibi nascenti, quod toto pectore laetor, | nerunt fatales fortia fila deae.*

Sorores: 'a sinister euphemism' (Nisbet–Hubbard on Hor. *Carm.* 2.3.15) for the Parcae who determine the fates of men by spinning.

83 siue abeunt studia in mores 'or my character is influenced by my interests': in Palmer's verdict, 'one of the best sentiments in the *Heroides*', comparing for the sense *Ars* 3.546 *et studio mores conuenienter eunt*. For the expression *abire in*, see Bömer on *Met.* 8.254.

84 ingenium nobis ... facit: cf. *Am.* 3.12.16 *ingenium mouit sola Corinna meum*, 2.17.34. The pentameter is articulated like Prop. 2.1.4 *ingenium nobis ipsa puella facit.*

Thalea: the Muse associated with light verse or comedy. O. calls on her in the *Ars* (1.264) and Virgil in the *Eclogues* (6.2); she is not an inappropriate choice as patron for Sappho's lyrics, but it is extremely unlikely that the choice stems from Sappho's own poetry. In the surviving fragments she addresses the Muses jointly or the eldest of them, Calliope.

85–6 Sappho attempts to rationalize her passion for Phaon, attributing the attraction to his good looks and young age, the same characteristics that would arouse in grown men a homosexual attraction to him.

85 primae lanuginis aetas: the first sign of a beard; cf. *Met.* 12.291 and Bömer *ad loc.*

86 abstulit: 6.131n.

87–92 The same trio, Aurora, Phoebe, and Venus, are found together with their lovers at *Ars* 3.83–5 *Latmius Endymion non est tibi, Luna, rubori,* | *nec Cephalus roseae praeda pudenda deae;* | *ut Veneri, quem luget adhuc, donetur Adonis.* For the thought, cf. McKeown on *Am.* 1.10.7–8.

87 Cephalo: a handsome mortal who, in some accounts, was raped by Aurora (e.g. Hes. *Theog.* 986–7). O. devotes a long narrative to Cephalus, conflating several variants of the myth, at *Met.* 7.661–865. Palmer expressed violent objections to the content of this couplet: 'What a ridiculous bathos is this verse! You would carry off Phaon, but that you like Cephalus better!' The curious defence offered by Purser illustrates the problem: he suggests that *tenet* implies that Aurora is 'prevented by shame' from breaking faith with the man she raped.

89–90 si conspicias ... | iussus erit: a mixed condition, 2.44n.

89 quae conspicis omnia: a conceit conventionally applied to the sun; cf. *Met.* 4.172 *uidet hic deus omnia primus,* and Bömer *ad loc.* The story of Endymion, who was loved by the Moon and slept for ever in a cave on Latmos, was apparently the subject of one of Sappho's poems; cf. fr. 199 L–P.

90 somnos continuare 'to sleep for ever': the passage is apparently imitated by Ausonius, who refers (*Ephem.* 1.15–16) to Endymion, *cui Luna somnos | continuarit.*

91 curru ... eburno: the epithet is strictly ornamental; cf. *Pont.* 3.4.35 *illa ducis facies in curru stantis eburno.*

92 'But she knows that he might be appealing even to her Mars': returns to the note of homosexual attraction with which the series of examples was introduced (86). There do not seem to be any stories about Mars (Ares) being attracted to young men: [O.] appears to be innovating for rhetorical effect.

93 nec adhuc iuuenis, nec iam puer: an elegant description of the point when childhood shades over into adolescence; cf. *Fast.* 3.773–4, of Bacchus, *siue quod ipse puer semper iuuenisque uideris,* | *et media est aetas inter utramque tibi.*

utilis aetas coheres loosely with the context; useful for what?, we may ask. The question is answered only by familiarity with *Ars* 2.667–8, where O. extols the sexual attractions of older women: *utilis, o iuuenes, aut haec, aut serior aetas:* | *iste feret segetes, iste serendus ager.*

94 o decus atque aeui gloria magna: the hyperbole is extravagant, and not particularly effective; cf. *Pont.* 2.8.25, of Augustus, *saecli decus indelebile nostri.*

95 huc ades: a familiar formula in prayers; cf. *Am.* 1.6.54, addressed to Boreas, 2.12.16 (Triumphus), 3.2.46 (Victoria), *Trist.* 5.3.43 (Bacchus).

relabere 'sail back': *labor* and its compounds are often used of sailing, but in O. there is always some mention of the conveying instrument; e.g. 10.149 *flecte ratem, Theseu, uersoque relabere uelo.* There is a play on the two senses of *sinus*, 'bosom' and 'bay'.

96 uerum ut amere sinas: O. allows elision of the second syllable of the second half of the pentameter on only five occasions: 20.178, *Ars* 1.548, *Rem.* 668, *Trist.* 3.6.6, *Pont.* 3.1.90. None of these instances involves elision of *-m*. The unusual metre is not conclusive evidence that O. did not write this line, but such licence would be surprising in an early elegy. The correction of MS *amare* to *amere* by de Vries removes the banality (although de Vries unwisely emended *uerum ut* as well): for the sentiment, cf. *Am.* 1.3.3 *tantum patiatur amari*, with McKeown *ad loc.*

97–122 Sappho describes herself as she writes, not unlike the self-description by Canace in the opening of 11, or by Dido at 7.183. From the context it is clear that Phaon left without a goodbye and that Sappho learned of his departure only from others.

97 lacrimis oculi rorantur obortis 'my eyes grow moist as tears well up': the verb *roro* is not used by O. in the elegies of his early period; it first occurs at 19.124 and in the *Met.* and *Fast.*, and may therefore have had a grand tone. So too the epic tag *lacrimis . . . obortis*; cf. Norden on *Aen.* 6.867, Ogilvie on Livy 1.58.7.

98 litura: 11.1n.

99 certus . . . ire: 7.7n.

modestius isses 'you might have gone in a more becoming fashion': the expression is unusual but paralleled by such instances as Cic. *Fam.* 14.14.1 *modeste uenturus* and Gell. 9.11.6 *modeste progreditur.* A parting at the dock, Sappho suggests, would have been better form.

100 Lesbi: a Greek vocative. It is a somewhat peculiar valediction that Sappho wishes for, 'girl of Lesbos', rather than her name.

101–4 The point is driven home here by the repeated *non* (*nil . . . nec*) and *tu.*

101 tecum oscula ... tulisti: a play on the usual idiom *oscula alicui ferre* (*TLL* s.v. *osculum* 1112.82ff.) 'to kiss', here 'to take with you'.

102 'In short I had no fear of the anguish I was to feel.' As a conclusion this is rather lame: Sappho here complains that in being denied a tearful farewell she was deprived of the apprehensions of heartache that she would suffer.

103 iniuria: a familiar legal term used in amatory poetry for a breach of faith; for this view of love as an implied contract (*foedus amoris*), cf. Reitzenstein (1912) 26–8. The strong sense pause after the fifth foot of the hexameter is unusual; there is no other example in the single *Heroides*.

104 'And you have no token to remind you of your lover': take *amantis* with *admoneat* and *pignus* as object of *habes*. The dislocation of the word-order (hyperbaton) is slight, since *pignus* may also be treated as a case of the antecedent attracted into the relative clause.

105 mandata: what they might have been is unclear (contrast 11.128n.), but Sappho emphasizes the point, repeating the noun and adding the adjective *ulla* in enjambment followed by a sense-pause.

106 ut nolles immemor esse replaces her actual prohibition: *noli immemor esse* 'don't forget me'.

107 per tibi ... Amorem: for the word-order in oaths, see 10.73n. Sappho swears by the divinities who preside over the activities most important to her, love and poetry, that is Amor and the Muses (108 *nouem ... deas*).

discedat: in the parenthetical relative clause Sappho expresses her deepest wish, 'may he [Amor] never leave you!'

108 nouem ... numina nostra, deas: for the word-order, cf. 7.158n.

109 tua gaudia 'the joy of your life': i.e. Phaon. Like the plural *amores*, *gaudia* was sometimes a term of endearment; cf. 19.41, Prop. 1.19.9, Virg. *Aen.* 10.324.

110 nec ... flere ... nec potuisse loqui: the topos of a pain so great that tears are impossible is effectively captured in an epigrammatic pronouncement by Seneca: *Phaedr.* 607 *curae leues loquuntur, ingentes stupent.* See further Bömer on *Met.* 10.538.

111 deerant ... uerba palato 'my throat lacked words': an unusual expression, where O. usually refers to the tongue (*lingua*) as the source of speech; cf. *Met.* 6.584–5 *uerbaque quaerenti satis indignantia linguae | defuerunt.* The line-ending may have been taken from *Am.* 2.6.47 *stupuerunt uerba palato. deerant* is scanned as two syllables.

112 'My heart was gripped by a cold chill': cf. *Fast.* 1.98 *et gelidum subito frigore pectus erat,* with identical line-ending. The symptoms described by Sappho are panic, as sketched by Lucr. 3.152–6, but the author of this poem is probably recalling directly Sappho's famous description of her reaction to the sight of her beloved: 'When I look at you for a moment, it is no longer possible for me to speak; my tongue has snapped, and at once a subtle fire has stolen beneath my flesh' (fr. 31.7–10 L–P). Sappho's poem was adapted in Latin by Catullus (51).

113 postquam se dolor inuenit: O. did not write this line, which is open to objection on metrical grounds. The pattern of caesurae, falling in the second (after *se*) and fourth feet (after *inuenit*) with a spondaic word in the opening foot, is found nowhere in O.; cf. 2.37n. The colloquial expression *se inuenit* is not attested in literature until the Neronian period; cf. Petronius *Sat.* 119.24, Sen. Rhet. *Contr.* 3 praef. 13, Sen. *Benef.* 5.12. The variant *imminuit* found in some MSS is not an improvement, for it does not remove the metrical anomaly. The problem cannot be satisfactorily resolved by obelizing this line, for its removal would necessitate the removal of 111–16 as well, leaving a very harsh transition from 110 to 117. See Tarrant (1981) 138.

pectora plangi: 11.91n.

114 exululare: a strong word, in O. usually reserved for the ritual cries of adherents of ecstatic cults, e.g. *Ars* 1.508, *Fast.* 4.186, *Met.* 6.597, *Trist.* 4.1.42.

115 non aliter quam: a familiar opening tag in a comparison, as de Vries notes. The same comparison of a mother mourning the death of a child is made at *Trist.* 1.3.97–8 *nec gemuisse minus quam si nataeue meumue | uidisset structos corpus habere rogos*; cf. Cat. 39.5.

116 ad exstructos corpus inane rogos: a slightly reworked version of *Am.* 3.9.6 *ardet in exstructo corpus inane rogo.*

117 crescit 'swells with joy': a sense in which the word is not found again until Seneca, *Epist.* 34.1.

maerore: a word attested in Republican prose and drama, but not used by the Augustan poets, with the single exception of Horace, who has it at *Ars* 110, appropriately in a discussion of tragedy. The word recurs in Neronian literature.

118 itque reditque: a familiar Ovidian tag (e.g. *Trist.* 5.7.14), together with *it redit* (*Fast.* 1.126) and *redit itque* (*Ars* 1.93, *Met.* 2.409).

119 'And so that the cause of my distress might be seen to be shameful': Sappho's demeanour is like that of a mother in mourning for a deceased daughter. Out of spite her brother calls attention to the fact that this is not the case with Sappho, whose daughter is alive. Earlier Sappho had referred to the birth of her daughter as a source of grief for her (69–70n.). This second rather curious reference to her daughter provokes suspicion that the poet is recalling a specific passage in Sappho's poetry.

121 non ueniunt in idem 'do not combine': a Graecism (εἰς τὸ αὐτό) found in O. only at *Fast.* 1.395, where it has a different meaning 'to assemble in one place'. The author of this line perhaps had in mind *Met.* 2.846–7 *non bene conueniunt nec in una sede morantur | maiestas et amor.*

pudor atque amor: their contrasting pull is a frequent motif in O.; cf. 19.171–2, *Am.* 3.10.28, *Met.* 1.618–19.

omne: nominative, 'the whole town was looking'.

122 lacero pectus aperta sinu: *pectus* is object of *aperta* used in a 'middle' sense, 'exposing my breast', another gesture of mourning; cf. *Fast.* 1.408 *dissuto pectus aperta sinu*, Tib. 1.6.18.

123–34 Phaon occupies her thoughts day and night, as Sappho now describes them, digressing on her erotic dreams of him. This scene is reminiscent of Hero's dream that she is sleeping with Leander (19.59–64): *nam modo te uideor prope iam spectare natantem, | bracchia nunc umeris umida ferre meis, | nunc dare, quae soleo, madidis uelamina membris, | pectora nunc nostro iuncta fouere sinu | multaque praeterea linguae reticenda modestae, | quae fecisse iuuat, facta referre pudet.* This passage also seems to betray familiarity with the end of *Ars* 3, where O. offers advice to women on sex (769–808), and the dream of Byblis in *Met.* 9.468–86 in which she imagines having intercourse with her brother.

123 te somnia nostra reducunt: cf. 7.26.

124 somnia: the repetition (epanalepsis) heightens the pathos.

formoso candidiora die 'brighter than the handsome day': the phrase *formosus dies* is somewhat unusual, but not so odd as has been thought; cf. *Rem.* 187 *formosa ... aestas, Fast.* 4.129 *formoso tempore, Ars* 2.315 *formosissimus annus.* But the adjective was chosen because the poet could not accommodate to the metre the phrase he wanted to make, *candido candidiora die,* a familiar type of expression, for which cf. Nisbet–Hubbard on Hor. *Carm.* 1.16.1.

125 illic: i.e. in her dreams.

quamuis regionibus absis: the ablative indicates measure, 'by wide regions'. The line-ending recurs at *Met.* 12.41 *quamuis regionibus absit.*

126 The conceit that the night is too short for lovers is one that occurs often in O. It is developed extensively in *Am.* 1.13; cf. McKeown (1989) 337–8. The scene here closely resembles Hero's letter to Leander (19.65–6) *me miseram! breuis est haec et non uera uoluptas;* | *nam tu cum somno semper abire soles.*

gaudia: the joys of sex; cf. *Met.* 9.483, Adams (1982) 197–8.

127 ceruice onerare lacertos: a variation of a common periphrasis for 'embrace'; cf. *Am.* 2.16.29 *tu nostris niueos umeris impone lacertos,* Tib. 1.8.33.

128 tuae: sc. *ceruici,* and with *meos* supply *lacertos,* a common type of ellipse with possessive pronouns.

129 lingua: the ablative is instrumental; cf. *Am.* 2.5.23–4 *improba tunc uero iungentes oscula uidi:* | *illa mihi lingua nexa fuisse liquet,* 3.7.9 *osculaque inseruit cupida luctantia lingua,* 3.14.23, 2.5.57–8.

130 aptaque ... accipere, apta dare: the accusatives are predicative, 'to take and to give closely'; cf. Tib. 1.4.53–4 *tum tibi mitis erit, rapias tum cara licebit* | *oscula: pugnabit, sed tamen apta dabit.*

131–2 Sappho remembers that she spoke as she made love to Phaon in her dream and that it seemed 'almost real', *ueris simillima;* earlier (48) she had recalled that Phaon was fond of such 'pillow talk'.

131 blandior: cf. *Ars* 3.795 *blandae uoces.*

132 uigilant sensibus ora meis 'my lips are alert to my sensations': a difficult phrase, but under the circumstances we should not be surprised at the lack of a parallel: there are few such explicit dreams about intercourse in Latin poetry.

133–4 The couplet opens with a false dodge, *ulteriora pudet narrare* 'I am ashamed to tell the rest', which is immediately followed by the details. This is not unlike the end of *Ars* 3.769, where instruction on sexual technique is introduced with *ulteriora pudet docuisse*; cf. *Rem.* 359, *Fast.* 5.532, *Met.* 14.18. In 19.63–4 (above, 123–34n.) O.'s Hero is more delicate. *omnia fiunt* is not an uncommon euphemism: cf. Theocr. 2.143 ἐπράχθη τὰ μέγιστα 'all was accomplished'.

134 siccae non licet esse mihi 'I cannot stay dry': i.e. she climaxes. The explicitness of *siccae* contributed to the corruption of most MSS, which read *sine te*, and the embarrassment of editors. A significant exception is Burman, who provides the relevant parallels: *Ars* 2.686, Mart. 11.81.2.

135–56 When morning comes to dispel her dreams Sappho looks for comfort in nature, the woods where she had been with Phaon. This motif is common in Hellenistic and Roman love poetry, e.g. Phanocles, *CA* pp. 106–7, Theocr. 11, Virg. *Ecl.* 2.1–5. O.'s predecessor in the genre of elegy, Cornelius Gallus, seems to have adapted a similar scene in Callimachus' *Acontius and Cydippe* (frr. 72–3 Pfeiffer) to describe himself looking for consolation in his troubled love affair. This, at least, is how Virgil describes Gallus in *Ecl.* 10.52–4, and Prop. 1.18 is in the same line of descent; cf. Ross (1975) 71–4. In Sappho's case the woods provide no solace because they only remind her of Phaon. O. warns against this in *Rem.* 725–6: *et loca saepe nocent; fugito loca conscia uestri | concubitus: causas illa doloris habent.*

135 Titan: Helios, the Titan, Hyperion's son (Hes. *Theog.* 371–3), the sun. The metonymy is common in Latin poetry.

136 queror: 1.8n. and below 152 where we see that Sappho's complaint finds no echo in the world around her.

137–40 The frantic wanderings of women distracted with love are common in ancient narrative. These lines seem to recall the cases of Phaedra (e.g. Eur. *Hipp.* 215–22) or Pasiphae; cf. *Ars* 1.311–12 *in nemus et saltus thalamo regina relicto | fertur ut Aonio concita Baccha deo.* But the poet here diverges from the familiar comparison of the distracted woman to a Bacchante (11.48n.), replacing it with a more sinister type.

138 conscia deliciis 'witness to our delights': in elegy *deliciae* is frequently used of love-making or trifling. It is avoided in the high style; O., for example, has it only once in the *Met.*; cf. Knox (1986a) 34.

139 mentis inops 'devoid of sense': an Ovidian phrase; cf. *Ars* 1.465, 3.684, *Rem.* 127, *Fast.* 4.457, *Met.* 2.200, 6.37.

furialis Enyo: the 'Cappadocian goddess of hysterics' (Housman) known as Ma, an Earth-goddess who was identified by the Greeks with their female war deity Enyo and by the Romans with their Bellona. The Romans first encountered her cult in Komana during the campaigns of Sulla in 92 BC. Tibullus describes the fanatic behaviour of a priestess in the practice of the cult, which involved self-mutilation and ecstatic celebration (1.6.43–56), and there are frequent references in Latin literature, especially in the early Empire; cf. Wissowa (1912) 348–50. For Sappho this comparison is a transparent anachronism.

140 feror 'I am carried away', as if under external impulse; cf. O. *Medea* fr. 2 *feror huc illuc ut plena deo*.

141 uident oculi: as if her eyes were not under her control.

scabro pendentia tofo 'arched with rough volcanic rock': the description is conventional; cf. *Am.* 3.1.3 *speluncaque pumice pendens*, *Met.* 13.810–11 *uiuo pendentia saxo | antra*.

142 Mygdonii marmoris instar 'like Phrygian marble': from Mygdonia, a region in Asia Minor, where the Phrygian town of Synnada was famous for its marble. *instar* is an indeclinable neuter (7.19n.). The Asiatic epithet is in keeping with the reference to Enyo. The point of the comparison is that the rough stone grotto seems more beautiful to her than an artificial one made out of cut stone.

143–4 cubilia nobis | praebuit: a familiar pastoral scene, 5.14n.

145 dominum siluaeque meumque 'the forest's lord and mine': the pairing of a genitive with a possessive adjective is a common brachylogy. While *dominus*, like its feminine counterpart, is a familiar term of endearment for one's lover (*OLD* s.v. 4b), the point of referring to Phaon as *dominus siluae* is less clear unless the author knew of some reference to Phaon as a hunter.

146 uile solum locus est 'the place is cheap ground': the thought is the same as O.'s description of the Palatine at *Pont.* 2.8.18 *qui locus ablato Caesare uilis erit*, while the expression resembles that of *Met.* 15.428 *uile solum Sparte est*, a passage which is also perhaps an interpolation.

dos erat ille loci 'he was the charm of the place': the sense of *dos*, literally 'dowry', was greatly extended by O., who uses it, e.g., for the natural gifts of mind and body; cf. Bömer on *Met.* 5.562. There is no example in O., however, where it is applied to a place.

147–50 The change to the perfect tense abruptly sets the moment in the past. The details of this couplet closely resemble the scene at 10.53–5.

148 The pentameter repeats and amplifies the hexameter, adding the point that the grass was flattened by their weight. The effort to avoid verbal repetition here leads to what Palmer noted as a somewhat unusual use of *curuum*, which seems more applicable to bent trees (*TLL* s.v. 1550.74).

149–50 Sappho seeks consolation in the place where Phaon had been, like Hero, who weeps over Leander's garments (19.31), or Laodamia, who embraces a bust of Protesilaus (13.151–4), or Dido (Virg. *Aen.* 4.648–50). [O.] may have been inspired by Prop. 4.3.30 *siqua relicta iacent, osculor arma tua*; but the motif was also common in Hellenistic romantic narrative: cf. 10.55–8n.

`**150 lacrimas combibit herba meas** 'the grass absorbed my tears': the phrasing resembles 11.54 and *Ars.* 2.326, though neither passage is parallel in sense.

151 The 'pathetic fallacy' in these lines that the natural world shares in the poet's emotions is found in early Greek poetry, but is especially common in Hellenistic verse, e.g. Theocr. 1.71, 7.74, Bion 1.31, Mosch. 3.1. In Roman poetry Virgil depicts nature mourning for Gallus as he perishes from love, in lines that imitate Theocritus (*Ecl.* 10.13–15): *illum etiam lauri, etiam fleuere myricae, | pinifer illum etiam sola sub rupe iacentem | Maenalus et gelidi fleuerunt saxa Lycaei.* O. imitates this passage in representing the aftermath of the death of Orpheus (*Met.* 11.44–9), and includes the detail, found here too, of the trees losing their leaves, the arboreal equivalent of cutting one's hair as a sign of mourning: *Met.* 11.46–7 *positis te frondibus arbor | tonsa comas luxit.*

152 dulce queruntur aues = *Am.* 3.1.4; cf. 10.8, *Fast.* 4.166.

153–4 The only bird singing is the nightingale, identified allusively (antonomasia) as 'the most mournful mother who took impious (*non ... pie*) vengeance on her husband'. The poet alludes to the most common version of the myth of Procne and Philomela (Apollod.

Bibl. 3.14.8, Ov. *Met.* 6.412–674), daughters of Pandion. Procne married Tereus, a Thracian king, and had a son Itys. Tereus raped Philomela and cut out her tongue to prevent her from revealing the crime, but she contrived to communicate the truth to her sister by weaving the story into a tapestry. Procne took vengeance by killing her own son Itys and serving him up as a meal to Tereus. When Tereus realized what had happened he attacked the sisters, but the gods intervened to turn them all three into birds, Procne into the nightingale, Philomela the swallow, and Tereus the hoopoe.

154 This line looks like a reworking of *Am.* 3.12.32 *concinit Odrysium Cecropis ales Ityn*, but if so, the imitation is not inert. For *Odrysius* 'Thracian' the poet substitutes an equivalent epithet *Ismarius*, from Mt Ismarus in southern Thrace. For the nightingale *Cecropis ales* the poet restores an older epithet *Daúlias ales*. According to Thucydides 2.29.3, Tereus ruled in the city of Daulis in Phocis, and 'in references to the nightingale the bird has been called "Daulias" by many poets'. No example has been preserved in Greek poetry, but Catullus, who translated one of Sappho's most famous poems, refers to Procne using this epithet: 65.13–14 *qualia sub densis ramorum concinit umbris | Daulias, absumpti fata gemens Ityli.* It is not unreasonable to suppose that one of the poets Thucydides had in mind was Sappho, and that this passage reflects familiarity with one of her lost poems. Fr. 135 L–P shows that she knew the myth. The recherché epithet was picked up by the bookish imitators of Augustan poetry: *Epiced. Drusi* 106, [Virg.] *Ciris* 200, [Sen.] *HO* 192.

Ityn: the lament of the nightingale for her son is a familiar topos in Greek and Roman poetry, often with onomatopoeic repetition of the boy's name, as here: cf. Aesch. *Ag.* 1144 'she bewails, a nightingale, with "Itys, Itys"', Soph. *El.* 148, [Virg.] *Culex* 252, Sen. *Ag.* 672.

156 hactenus 'so far and no more': 6.63n.

157–84 As Sappho wanders alone she comes upon a sacred spring. She describes how she was visited there by a nymph who advised her to seek a cure for her love by journeying to the island of Leucas, one of the more northerly of the Greek islands of the Ionian Sea, there to leap from the promontory where Apollo's temple was located. This passage is full of detailed incidents that are otherwise unattested and prompt suspicions that the poet is interpreting passages in Sappho's poetry.

157–8 est ... | fons: a familiar form of topographical excursus in imitation of epic models; cf. 2.131–48n. Descriptions of idyllic spots are a common type of digression, and O. has many examples. He sets the scene for his story of Narcissus by describing first the spring where he will see his reflection: *Met.* 3.407 *fons erat inlimis, nitidis argenteus undis*; cf. *Am.* 3.1.1–4. Such descriptions were recommended by rhetoricians and it is probably not pure coincidence that one, Hermogenes (2nd cent. AD), quotes from Sappho's description of a sacred grove as a prime example (*Id.* 2.4): fr. 2.5–6 L–P 'and within it cold water babbles through apple branches'. The author of *ES* may have had this in mind or another piece by Sappho no longer extant.

157 uitroque magis perlucidus: a familiar comparison; cf. Hor. *Carm.* 3.16.1 *o fons Bandusiae splendidior uitro*, Call. fr. 238.16 Pfeiffer, Otto (1890) 376.

158 The parenthesis anticipates the appearance of the nymph of the fountain. Sacred groves were considered numinous places, and strange things could happen in them.

159 expandit: the verb is found only once elsewhere in Latin poetry at Lucr. 1.126 in a metaphor.

aquatica lotos: the Indian lotos, or clove-tree, with rose-coloured blossoms rising high above the water, described by Plin. *Nat.* 16.30.53. The adjective *aquaticus* is first attested in O. and describes this tree: *Met.* 9.341, 10.96.

160 una nemus 'a grove all by itself': a clever phrase found also at *Met.* 8.743–4, where the hyperbole describes Demeter's sacred oak before its violation by Erysichthon: *stabat in his ingens annoso robore quercus, | una nemus*; cf. Plin. *Nat.* 16.44, of an ilex, *siluamque sola facit*.

tenero caespite terra uiret: cf. *Ars* 3.688 *fons sacer et uiridi caespite mollis humus.*

161–72 Sappho relates how she learned from a fountain nymph of a way to escape her feelings for Phaon by jumping from a cliff on the island of Leucas into the sea below. The story that Sappho made this leap is at least as old as Menander (fr. 258 Körte), but its orgins are obscure; cf. Wilamowitz (1913) 25–33. The tradition that lovers who made the leap – and survived – would be cured of their passion is much older: Photius, *Bibl.* 153 provides an extensive discussion derived from Ptolemy Chennos (*c.* AD 100), complete with a list of people who made the jump which does not include Sappho. Other references illustrate how widely the tradition was known (e.g. Anacr. fr. 31 Page, Eur. *Cycl.* 166–7). After Menander, we do not hear of Sappho making this leap until Stat. *Silv.* 5.3.154–5, and later acquaintance with the story (e.g. Serv. on *Aen.* 3.279; Auson. *Epigr.* 103.13, *Cup. cruc.* 24) might be due to this poem.

161 cum lassos posuissem flebilis artus 'when in tears I had lain down to rest my weary limbs': for the expression *artus ponere*, cf. Virg. *Aen.* 1.173 *sale tabentis artus in litore ponunt.* Sappho is asleep when the Naiad appears to her.

162 constitit ante oculos … meos: the pentameter has the same articulation as [O.] *Am.* 3.5.10, the pseudo-Ovidian *Somnium*, which describes the appearance of a cow to the poet in a dream: *constitit ante oculos candida uacca meos.* Both passages perhaps derive from *Ars* 3.44 *et ante oculos constitit ipsa meos*, describing an epiphany of Aphrodite. The repetition of *constitit* (anadiplosis) in 163 is a familiar Ovidian device; cf. *Fast.* 2.306–7 *uidit … | uidit et incaluit.*

163 ignibus aequis 'with equal passion': a widespread motif in Greek New Comedy and Latin amatory verse; cf. 19.5 *urimur igne pari*, Kost (1971) 160–1.

164 ureris: 9–10n.

Ambracia … terra 'the region of Ambracia', a city in Epirus which lent its name to the Gulf of Ambracia, opposite Leucas.

165 ab excelso 'from a height': cf. *Fast.* 2.369.

quantum patet aspicit aequor 'looks upon the sea as far as it stretches'.

166 Actiacum … Leucadiumque: the epithets apply to Apollo, not the sea. There were temples of Apollo both at Actium, the promontory at the opening of the Gulf of Ambracia (e.g. Thuc. 1.29.3) and Leucas, the site of Sappho's leap (Strabo 10.9). The poet here seems to conflate the two, but he was not the first to do so: cf. Prop. 3.11.69 *Leucadius uersas acies memorabit Apollo*, where he is probably referring to the temple at Actium which was enlarged by Augustus after his victory over Antony in the sea battle fought there; cf. Shackleton Bailey (1956) 175 n. 1.

167–70 No other writer mentions the story of Deucalion's leap from the Leucadian rock. It is a guess, but only a guess, that the story grew from an etymological association of the name Δευκαλίων with Λευκαδίων (Birt (1877) 432). The names Deucalion and Pyrrha are otherwise associated only in the story of the primeval flood and the regeneration of mankind in its aftermath (*Met.* 1.313–415). Deucalion's name thus guarantees the ancient pedigree of the cure for love described by the Naiad.

167–8 se ... | misit 'threw himself': a poetic idiom.

168 pressit aquas: an unparalleled expression for 'struck the water'.

169 nec mora: used in asyndeton it is adverbial ('at once'), a familiar Ovidian phrase; cf. Bömer on *Met.* 1.167, McKeown on *Am.* 1.6.13.

uersus Amor fugit 'Love turned and fled': cf. 3.139 *uersus amor tuus est in taedia nostri.*

mersi 'when he was immersed': the reading of the vulgate (see app. crit.) *Pyrrhae* introduces a unique variant to the tradition attached to the leap from Leucas, that it transfers the feelings of one to the other. This variant is probably an interpolation designed to make this letter conform to the context suggested by *Am.* 2.18.34; cf. 181–4n.

169–70 lentissima ... | pectora ought to mean 'his unfeeling heart', as the phrase does at [Tib.] 3.17.6 *nostra potes lento pectore ferre mala*; and it should probably be understood as a sort of prolepsis: i.e. love fled from the heart that no longer responded.

171 hanc legem locus ille tenet: the 'law' that governs the spot made the promontory at Leucas 'the most famous Lover's Leap that there has been anywhere' (Palmer).

172 nec ... time: connection of a prohibition to an imperative with *nec* is rarely found in Latin prose, but is a common usage among poets, who also made considerable use of *ne* with the imperative in prohibitions; cf. H–S 340, K–S 1 204.

desiluisse: for the perfect infinitive, 2.28n.

173 cum uoce abiit: cf. *Met.* 15.663–4 *extemplo cum uoce deus, cum uoce deoque | somnus abit.* The final syllable of *abiit* is scanned long, 6.31n.

frigida 'chill', with fear.

surgo: as if from sleep, 161n.

174 The pentameter is transmitted in two different forms by the MSS, with F offering the text printed here and all others having the

line in the form *nec grauidae lacrimas continuere genae*. This interpolation
is based on *Ars* 2.70 *nec patriae lacrimas continuere genae*. The adjective
grauidus is used also of eyes heavy with tears in [O.] *Epiced. Drusi* 115–
16 *erumpunt iterumque grauant gremiumque sinusque | effusae grauidis uberi-
busque genis*. In such cases, when authorship is in dispute, it is difficult
to determine which reading to prefer in the text, for if O. is not the
author of the epistle, the version found in the majority of the MSS
may be original: the reading of F would then be an interpolation to
conform to O.'s more regular form of expression, for which cf. *Am.*
1.14.51, 3.9.46. For *genae = oculi*, cf. 10.44n.

175 monstrataque 'prescribed': perhaps suggesting a medical
metaphor; cf. *Rem.* 252 *Apollo ... monstrat opem, Trist.* 2.270 *quaeque* [sc.
herba] *iuuet monstrat, OLD* s.v. 3b.

177 quidquid erit, melius quam nunc erit: a frigid ex-
pression without real parallel in O. or elsewhere. The strong sense
pause after the fourth foot is unusual; cf. Platnauer (1951) 25.

177–8 aura, subito | et ... habe 'Ye gentle gales, beneath my
body blow, | And softly lay me on the waves below' (Pope): the cor-
rection of MS *habent* is required by the sense. Construe *non magnum
... pondus* in apposition to *mea ... corpora* with interlocking word-
order.

179 tu quoque, mollis Amor, pennas suppone cadenti:
Sappho imagines that a winged Cupid will soften her fall. Palmer
detects an allusion to the scapegoat ritual which took place on the
cliffs of Leucas in the precinct of Apollo's temple as described by
Strabo (10.2.9). According to him, the criminal who was tossed into
the sea below was equipped with wings and an attempt was made to
pull him out of the water. If there is such an allusion here, the effect
is bathetic.

180 ne sim ... mortua crimen 'lest by my death I bring re-
proach': cf. *Trist.* 3.10.42 *non foret angustae mors tua crimen aquae*.

181–4 Sappho vows to dedicate her lyre to Apollo if she survives
the leap and is released from her love for Phaon. In *Am.* 2.18.34
there is a reference to a reply to Sappho's letter to Phaon composed
by O.'s friend Sabinus, *dat uotam Phoebo Lesbis amata lyram*. But this
cannot refer to a reply to our *ES*, since it supposes that Sappho
vowed her lyre to Phoebus if Phaon reciprocated her love. Either
Am. 2.18.34 refers to a lost poem by O., or it is an interpolation.

181 inde: with causal force, 'in consequence' (*OLD* s.v. 10a).

chelyn: a lyre, the common instrument (*communia munera*) of Sappho and Apollo. This Greek loan-word is not found in O. or the other Augustan poets, but is common in Seneca and the Flavian poets.

ponam 'I shall dedicate': 1.26n.

182 ea: forms of the pronoun *is* are generally avoided in poetry (7.15n.); the feminine ablative singular is found in O. only at *Met.* 14.641 and *Trist.* 2.429.

unus et alter: elsewhere in O. this combination is either deprecatory, 'only one or two' (*Am.* 1.8.54, 2.5.22, *Trist.* 1.3.16), or indefinite, 'someone or other' (*Rem.* 364, *Fast.* 2.394). As a description of an elegiac couplet, consisting of two verses of unequal length, it is oddly inappropriate; but cf. 20.238 *causaque uersiculis scripta duobus erit*, Tarrant (1981) 147.

183–4 To include a dedicatory inscription in the poem is entirely in O.'s manner (cf. 2.147–8n.) but this one is curiously inept in its context, its sole point apparently being to elaborate the conceit just alluded to (181) that Sappho and Apollo employ the same musical instrument. We expect the dedication to be in gratitude for rescuing her from her torture.

POETRIA: it is no objection to Ovidian authorship that this Greek loan-word, attested in Cicero, is not found elsewhere in Augustan poetry: Roman poets rarely touch on the subject of female writers. In Ter. Maur. *GLK* VI 390 she is also styled *poetria Sappho*.

184 CONVENIT ILLA MIHI CONVENIT ILLA TIBI: for the repetition with slight variation, cf. 40n. The formulation is similar to *Am.* 2.5.31 *haec tibi sunt mecum, mihi sunt communia tecum*.

185–206 Sappho's resolve to seek the cure from the waters of Leucas weakens as her thoughts turn to Phaon again. She develops the idea that only his return can save her, and reveals a premonition that her leap from the cliff will only bring death. And once again she returns to the effect that her passion has had on her art.

185–6 The apostrophe to Phaon is abrupt; in the hexameter it is not clear that he is addressed as the reason for her trip to Leucas, as opposed to the Naiad who actually sent her.

185 Actiacas oras: identifies Actium with the cliffs of Leucas; 166n.

187 'You could be more conducive to my good health than the waters of Leucas': the use of medical terminology (*salubrior*) recurs to describe the curative effect of the leap and plays upon the obvious notion that longing for an absent lover may also be satisfied by his/ her return.

188 et forma et meritis 'both in beauty and healing power' (Palmer): referring to two of Apollo's attributes: Sappho is no longer thinking of Apollo as a poet, as she was above (181–4).

189 scopulis undaque ferocior omni 'more cruel than any cliff or wave': comparisons of a hard-hearted lover to rocks and waves are conventional in ancient love poetry: e.g. 3.133 *sis licet immitis matrisque ferocior undis*, *Met.* 13.801, Virg. *Aen.* 4.365–7, all drawing on Hom. *Il.* 16.33–5; cf. Kost (1971) 371. Here, of course, it aptly recalls the rocks and waves of the anticipated leap from Leucas.

190 titulum mortis habere meae: repeated from 7.76 and 21.176; cf. *Trist.* 1.11.30 *haec titulum nostrae mortis habere uelit*. The figurative use of *titulus* is easily understood from its literal meaning of 'an inscription': instead of being commemorated as the 'Apollo' who saved her, Phaon might be inscribed as the cause of her death; cf. *Met.* 9.562 *neue merere meo subscribi causa sepulcro*.

191 tecum mea pectora iungi 'my breast to be pressed to you': the idiom calls for joining like with like, and therefore *tecum* is a surprise; cf. *Met.* 2.604–5 *cum pectore iuncta ... pectora*, and the examples collected at *TLL* s.v. *iungo* 658.13ff.

192 poterant: the imperfect indicative is regular in unreal expressions with verbs indicating possibility, such as *posse, debere*; cf. H–S 328.

praecipitanda: predicative with *dari*, 'abandoned to be cast down from the rocks'.

193 haec sunt illa: sc. *pectora*. The poet plays on *pectus* in the hexameter as a physical attribute which might be praised for its beauty (e.g. *Pont.* 2.5.37–8) and in the pentameter as the seat of the intellect (e.g. *Trist.* 1.3.7–8, 3.7.44). The combination here seems almost coarse; cf. Tarrant (1981) 147.

195 facunda: the word is somewhat prosaic, avoided by most poets, but common in O., who has it 16 times.

dolor artibus obstat: peace of mind is an essential concomitant of poetic composition; cf. *Trist.* 1.2.32 of O. himself, *ambiguis ars stupet ipsa malis.*

196 substitit 'came to a halt': the metaphor, as Palmer notes, 'may be from a river's flow being checked'; for the phrasing, cf. *Trist.* 1.1.48 *ingenium tantis excidet omne malis.*

197 non mihi respondent 'do not respond to my call': the expression has a technical ring, as of failing health; cf. *OLD* s.v. *respondeo* 10a. O. uses the same metaphor of his own failing powers in *Pont.* 4.2.15 *nec tamen ingenium nobis respondet ut ante.*

ueteres in carmina uires 'my former capacity for poetry'; the prepositional phrase expresses purpose.

198 plectra ... lyra: the *plectrum* is the instrument used to strike the strings of the lyre. The pentameter thus takes the familiar form in which the second hemistich repeats with variation the sense of the first.

199–202 The two couplets are addressed to all the women of Lesbos who used to hear Sappho sing. The triple anaphora of the Greek substantive (100n.) *Lesbides ... Lesbides ... Lesbides* is emphatic, a reminder that it is the women named in her poetry who made Sappho famous as a love poet. Dörrie (1975) 177 calls attention to an epigram in the *Palatine anthology* (9.189) which is a call to the women of Lesbos (*Lesbides*) to come to the sanctuary of Hera to dance there and to hear Sappho sing. The epigram is of Hellenistic date (Page (1981) 337–8), and it may well be that if its author was inspired by a lost poem of Sappho's calling the women of Lesbos, then the poet of the *ES* may have that in mind here as that call is reversed.

199 aequoreae: like many other formations in *-eus*, this one has a poetic colouring (5.62n.), but as an epithet for the women of Lesbos it is a bit odd, even though O. also refers it to island inhabitants: *Met.* 15.752 *aequoreos ... Britannos.* The author may well have had in mind a passage (in Sappho?) referring to sea nymphs; cf. Cat. 64.15 *aequoreae ... Nereides.*

200 Aeolia ... lyra: the ablative is obviously instrumental. Sappho composed in the Aeolic dialect; cf. *Am.* 2.18.26 (perhaps spurious) *Aeoliae Lesbis amica lyrae,* Hor. *Carm.* 2.13.24 *Aeoliis fidibus,* Nisbet–Hubbard *ad loc.*

201 amatae 'because you were loved by me'. For the Lesbian women whose names are found in the fragments, see 17–18n.

202 ad citharas turba uenire meas 'to come trooping to my lyre': for the plural with the collective noun, cf. Prop. 1.19.13 *illic formosae ueniant chorus heroinae*. Housman (1897) 290 (= *Class. pap.* 410–11) proposed *mea* on the grounds that '*chorus caterua turba manus* and similar words are not placed in apposition without an adjective in agreement', but there are sufficient parallels besides the example in Propertius (where Housman emends to *formosus*) to guarantee the construction; cf. Fedeli (1980) 448–9.

203 omne ... quod uobis ante placebat: i.e. her poetry, as we infer from the following couplet.

204 dixi quam modo paene 'meus' 'how close I just came to saying "my Phaon"': for the exclamatory accusative *me miseram*, cf. 5.149n.

205 efficite ut redeat stands for a *si*- clause; cf. 23n.

uates quoque uestra redibit: i.e. Sappho will regain her poetic talent. It is not at all clear how the girls of Lesbos could effect Phaon's return.

206 ingenio uires ille dat, ille rapit: the conceit is the same as Prop. 2.1.4 *ingenium nobis ipsa puella facit*, though the phrasing may owe something to *Trist.* 2.532 *ingenio uires ... dedit*.

207–20 Sappho closes on a note of doubt. Does her pleading move Phaon, or will he stay away? Her final request is for clarity, a letter at least so that she may know whether she should seek the cure at Leucas.

207 ecquid ago precibus pectusue ... 'am I accomplishing anything at all by begging and ...': the conjunction *-ue* is cumulative, not disjunctive 'or', like *an* below cf. *OLD* s.v. *-ue* 3.

agreste 'churlish': the more common adjective in this context is *rusticus*, which is opposed to the sophistication O. and the Roman love poets associate with *amor*; cf. *Met.* 11.767–8 *non agreste tamen nec inexpugnabile amori | pectus*.

208 an riget: sc. *pectus*; cf. 3.96 *rigida mente*, *Am.* 1.4.3 *rigido pectore*, *Trist.* 1.8.42.

Zephyri uerba caduca ferunt: a familiar image to suggest the futility or meaninglessness of words; cf. *Am.* 2.16.45–6 *uerba puellarum, foliis leuiora caducis, | irrita, qua uisum est, uentus et unda ferunt*.

209 qui: sc. *Zephyri*. The conceit in this line is familiar, 2.25n.

210 si saperes 'if you had any sense': 5.99n.

lente: 1.1n.

decebat: for the imperfect indicative, cf. 192n. The sentiment is spectacularly flat: 'this deed would become you'.

211 siue redis 'if you are intending to return'.

211–12 uotiua ... | munera: votive garlands to decorate the stern, to be dedicated on Phaon's departure from Sicily. Such garlanding usually takes place after port has been reached; on departure it is a sign of special joy; cf. Pease on Virg. *Aen.* 4.418.

laceras ... mora: cf. 3.138 *nec miseram lenta ferreus ure mora.*

213–14 solue ratem ... solue ratem: 5.117n.

213 Venus orta mari mare praestat amanti: Aphrodite was reckoned among the gods of the sea and was in fact worshipped under the epithet Εὔπλοια 'Fair-sailing' at Cnidos (Paus. 1.1.3); cf. 16.23–4 *illa dedit faciles auras uentosque secundos: | in mare nimirum ius habet orta mari*; Musaeus 249–50 'do you not know that Kypris is offspring of the sea, and rules over the sea and our sufferings?' The same motif is found in Hero's epistle to Leander: 19.159–60 *quod timeas non est: auso Venus ipsa fauebit, | sternet et aequoreas aequore nata uias.* For the polyptoton *mari mare*, cf. 5.12n. *praestat* 'renders secure' is a verb that is avoided by the other Augustan poets except in its participial form, although O. has it 60 times; cf. *Met.* 11.747–8 *uentos custodit et arcet | Aeolus egressu, praestatque nepotibus aequor.*

214 aura dabit cursum: 7.171n.

215–16 Cupid will himself steer the ship and handle the sails. The image of Cupid as helmsman appears to be unique, but not inappropriate to the context since sailing is a frequent metaphor for love in Roman poetry and Greek epigram; cf. Nisbet–Hubbard on Hor. *Carm.* 1.5.16.

215 gubernabit: the word is entirely avoided by the Augustan poets with a single exception in O.'s exile poetry, *Trist.* 5.14.29.

216 dabit ... uela legetque 'will spread and shorten the sail'.

tenera: the adjective is appropriate to any attribute of Cupid, e.g. *Am.* 2.18.4 *tener ... Amore, Ars* 1.7. For the distribution of epithet and noun over two clauses, 1.92n.

217 Pelasgida: the epithet may be applied to Sappho since Lesbos was once inhabited by Pelasgians and was known as Pelasgia; cf. Diod. 5.81, Plin. *Nat.* 5.31.39. The specificity of this bit of learning seems irrelevant here, perhaps an indication that it is taken from Sappho's poetry. For the Greek form of the accusative, 7.7n.

fugisse: for the perfect infinitive, 2.28n.

218 'You will not find a good reason to run away from me': the construction of *digna* with the passive infinitive is common and, as de Vries notes, the correction of MS *fuga* is required by sense: *digna fuga* can only mean 'deserving of exile'. The objection (*tamen*) posed by this parenthesis is not strictly logical and simply restates a point elaborated at great length in the epistle.

219 hoc saltem resumes the construction interrupted by the parenthesis.

miserae: sc. *mihi*.

220 ut mihi Leucadiae fata petantur aquae: the only occurrence of *fata petere* in O. means 'to seek death': 19.117 *iamdudum pecca, si mea fata petis*; cf. Sen. *Tro.* 390, Luc. 7.652, 8.652. Here it must mean 'to seek my destiny', a sense not found elsewhere. The genitive *Leucadiae . . . aquae* is loosely defining.

BIBLIOGRAPHY

The following list provides abbreviations for frequently cited reference works and editions of Ovid. It also gives details for all works cited in the introduction and commentary by author and date. Abbreviations for journals follow *L'Année philologique*.

I. ABBREVIATIONS

CA
(ed.) J. U. Powell, *Collectanea Alexandrina*. Oxford 1925.

CIL
Corpus Inscriptionum Latinarum. Berlin 1863– .

EGF
(ed.) M. Davies, *Epicorum Graecorum Fragmenta*. Göttingen 1988.

FGrH
F. Jacoby, *Die Fragmente der griechischen Historiker*. Leiden 1923–58.

FIRA
(ed.) S. Riccobono et al., *Fontes Iuris Romani Anteiustiniani*, 2nd ed. 3 vols. Florence 1968–9.

GLK
(ed.) H. Keil, *Grammatici Latini*. 7 vols. Leipzig 1855–80.

HE
(edd.) A. S. F. Gow and D. L. Page, *The Greek Anthology. Hellenistic epigrams*. 2 vols. Cambridge 1965.

H–S
J. B. Hofmann and A. Szantyr, *Lateinische Syntax und Stilistik*. Munich 1965.

K–S
R. Kühner and C. Stegmann, *Ausführliche Grammatik der lateinischen Sprache. Zweiter Teil: Satzlehre*. 3. Auflage ed. A. Thierfelder. 2 vols. Leverkusen 1955.

LIMC
Lexicon Iconographicum Mythologiae Classicae. Zurich and Munich 1981– .

N–W
F. Neue and C. Wagener, *Formenlehre der lateinischen Sprache*, 3. Auflage. 4 vols. Leipzig and Berlin 1902–5.

OCD²
(edd.) N. G. L. Hammond and H. H. Scullard, *The Oxford Classical Dictionary*. 2nd ed. Oxford 1970.

OLD	(ed.) P. G. W. Glare, *Oxford Latin Dictionary*. Oxford 1982.
RAC	(ed.) T. Klauser, *Reallexikon für Antike und Christentum*. Stuttgart 1950– .
RE	(edd.) A. Pauly, G. Wissowa et al., *Real-Encyclopädie der classischen Altertumswissenschaft*. Stuttgart 1893–1980.
Roscher	(ed.) W. H. Roscher, *Ausführliches Lexicon der griechischen und römischen Mythologie*. Leipzig 1884–1937.
SH	(edd.) H. Lloyd-Jones and P. Parsons, *Supplementum Hellenisticum*. Berlin and New York 1983.
TLL	*Thesaurus Linguae Latinae*. Munich 1900– .

2. EDITIONS, COMMENTARIES, ETC.

Bentley	E. Hedicke (ed.), *Studia Bentleiana*. v. *Ovidius Bentleianus* (Freienwald 1905).
Burman	P. Burman (ed.), *P. Ovidii Nasonis opera omnia* (Amsterdam 1727).
Dörrie	H. Dörrie (ed.), *P. Ovidii Nasonis Epistulae Heroidum* (Berlin 1971).
Goold	G. P. Goold, rev. ed. of Showerman (Cambridge, Mass. 1977).
Heinsius	N. Heinsius (ed.), *P. Ovidii Nasonis opera* (Amsterdam 1661).
Housman	A. E. Housman, unpublished lecture notes on *Her.* 1–10 (Cambridge Univ. Library Add. 6897; 6898, 3–13).
Loers	V. Loers (ed.) *P. Ovidii Nasonis Heroides et A. Sabini Epistolae* (Cologne 1829).
Palmer	A. Palmer (ed.), *P. Ovidi Nasonis Heroides*, 2nd ed. (Oxford 1898).
Papathomopoulos	M. Papathomopoulos (ed.), Μαξίμου Πλανούδη Μετάφρασις τῶν Ὀβιδίου Ἐπιστολῶν (Ioannina 1976).
Showerman	G. Showerman (ed.), *Ovid, Heroides and Amores* (Cambridge, Mass. 1914).

Shuckburgh   E. S. Shuckburgh (ed.), *P. Ovidii Nasonis Heroidum*
                    Epistulae XIII (London 1905).

3. OTHER WORKS

Adams, J. N. (1982). *The Latin sexual vocabulary*. London.

André, J. (1949). *Etudes sur les termes de couleur dans la langue latine*.
    Paris.

Appel, G. (1909). *De Romanorum precationibus*. Giessen.

Audollent, A. (1904). *Defixionum tabellae*. Paris.

Austin, C. and Reeve, M. D. (1970). 'Notes on Sophocles, Ovid and
    Euripides', *Maia* 22: 3–18.

Axelson, B. (1945). *Unpoetische Wörter. Ein Beitrag zur Kenntnis der lateini-
    schen Dichtersprache*. Skrifter utgivna av Vetenskaps-societeten i
    Lund 29. Lund.

Barchiesi, A. (1984). 'Ovidio, *Her.* 1, 95', *M.D.* 13: 159–60.

    (1992). *P. Ovidii Nasonis epistulae Heroidum 1–3*. Florence.

    (1993). 'Future reflexive: two modes of allusion and Ovid's *Hero-
    ides*', *H.S.C.P.* 95: 333–65.

Barigazzi, A. (1963). 'Il Dionysos di Euforione', *Miscellanea di studi
    alessandrini in memoria di Augusto Rostagni*: 416–54. Turin.

Bednara, E. (1906). 'De sermone dactylicorum Latinorum quaes-
    tiones', *A.L.L.* 14: 317–60, 532–604.

Bell, A. J. (1923). *The Latin dual and poetic diction. Studies in numbers and
    figures*. London.

Berger, A. (1953). *Encyclopedic dictionary of Roman law*. Philadelphia.

Betz, H. D. (1986). *The Greek magical papyri in translation*. Chicago.

Birt. T. (1877). 'Animadversiones ad Ovidi heroidum epistulas',
    Rh.M. 32: 388–432.

Bömer, F. (1969–86). *P. Ovidius Naso: Metamorphosen*. Heidelberg.

Bréguet, E. (1960). 'In una parce duobus', *Hommages Herrmann* (Coll.
    Latomus 44): 205–14. Brussels.

Brink, C. O. (1971). *Horace on poetry. The 'Ars poetica'*. Cambridge.

Brunt, P. A. (1971). *Italian manpower 225 B.C. to A.D. 14*. Oxford.

Büchner, W. (1940). 'Die Penelopeszenen in der Odysee', *Hermes* 75:
    146–59.

Clairmont, C. (1951). *Das Parisurteil in der antiken Kunst*. Zurich.

Clausen, W. (1955). 'Silva coniecturarum', *A.J.P.* 76: 47–62.

(1976). 'Virgil and Parthenius', *H.S.C.P.* 80: 179.

(1987). *Virgil's Aeneid and the tradition of Hellenistic poetry*. Berkeley.

(1988). 'Catulliana', *B.I.C.S.* Supp. 51: 13–17.

(1994). *A commentary on Virgil, Eclogues*. Oxford.

Cooper, F. T. (1895). *Word formation in Roman sermo plebeius*. New York.

Courtney, E. (1965). 'Ovidian and non-Ovidian Heroides', *B.I.C.S.* 12: 63–6.

Delz, J. (1986). 'Heroidibus Ovidianis argutiae restitutae', in U. Stache, W. Maaz, F. Wagner (edd.), *Kontinuität und Wandel*: 79–88. Hildesheim

de Vries, S. (1885). *Epistula Sapphus ad Phaonem apparatu critico instructa commentario illustrata et Ovidio vindicata*. Leiden.

Diggle, J. (1967). 'Notes on the text of Ovid, *Heroides*', *C.Q.* 17: 136–44.

Dörrie, H. (1960a). *Untersuchungen zur Überlieferungsgeschichte von Ovids epistulae Heroidum* I. Göttingen.

(1960b) *Untersuchungen zur Überlieferungsgeschichte von Ovids epistulae Heroidum* II. Göttingen.

(1972). *Untersuchungen zur Überlieferungsgeschichte von Ovids epistulae Heroidum* III. Göttingen.

(1975). *P. Ovidius Naso: Der Brief der Sappho an Phaon*. Zetemata 58. Munich.

Dover, K. J. (1978). *Greek homosexuality*. Cambridge, Mass.

Dutoit, E. (1936). *Le thème de l'adynaton dans la poésie antique*. Paris.

Eitrem, S. (1941). 'La magie comme motif littéraire chez les Grecs et les Romaines', *S.O.* 21: 39–83.

Ernout A. and Meillet, A. (1959, 1960). *Dictionnaire étymologique de la langue latine*. 2 vols. Paris.

Faraone, C. (1991). 'The agonistic context of early Greek binding spells', in Faraone, C. and Obbink, D. (edd.), *Magica hiera: ancient Greek magic and religion*: 3–32. Oxford.

Fauth, W. (1980). '*Venena amoris*: die Motive des Liebeszaubers und der erotischen Verzauberung in der augusteischen Dichtung', *Maia* 33: 265–82.

Fedeli, P. (1980). *Sesto Properzio: Il primo libro delle elegie*. Florence.

(1985). *Properzio: Il libro terzo delle elegie*. Bari.

Fischer, U. (1969). *Ignotum hoc aliis ille novavit opus. Beobachtungen zur Darstellungskunst Ovids in den Heroiden unter besonderer Berücksichtigung der Briefpaare her. 16 und 17 (Paris und Helena) und her. 20 und 21 (Acontius und Cydippe).* Diss. Berlin. Augsburg.

Fraenkel, E. (1957). *Horace.* Oxford.

(1964). *Kleine Beiträge zur klassischen Philologie.* 2 vols. Rome.

Frécaut, J.-M. (1972). *L'esprit et l'humour chez Ovide.* Grenoble.

Ganzenmüller, C. (1911). 'Aus Ovids Werkstatt', *Philol.* 70: 274–311, 397–437.

Goold, G. P. (1965). 'Amatoria critica', *H.S.C.P.* 69: 1–107.

Hähnel, R. (1937). 'Der künstliche Abortus im Altertum', *Archiv f. Geschichte der Medizin* 29: 224–55.

Hall, J. B. (1990). 'Conjectures in Ovid's *Heroides*', *I.C.S.* 15: 263–92.

Hartenberger, R. (1911). *De 'o' finali apud poetas latinos ab Ennio usque ad Iuvenalem.* Diss. Bonn.

Harvey, A. E. (1955). 'The classification of Greek lyric poetry', *C.Q.* 5: 157–75.

Heinze, R. (1915). *Virgils epische Technik.* Leipzig & Berlin.

Hill, D. E. (1973). 'The Thessalian trick', *Rh.M.* 116: 221–38.

Hinds, S. (1987). *The metamorphosis of Persephone. Ovid and the self-conscious muse.* Cambridge.

Hofmann, J. B. (1951). *Lateinische Umgangssprache.* Heidelberg.

Hopkinson, N. (1982). 'Juxtaposed prosodic variants in Greek and Latin poetry', *Glotta* 60: 162–77.

Horsfall, N. (1973–4). 'Dido in the light of history', *P.V.S.* 13: 1–13.

Housman, A. E. (1897). 'Ovid's *Heroides*', *C.R.* 11: 102–6, 200–4, 238–42, 286–90, 425–31 (= Diggle, J. and Goodyear, F. R. D. (edd.), *The classical papers of A. E. Housman* (Cambridge 1972) 380–421).

(1899). Review of Palmer, *C.R.* 13: 172–8 (= *Class. pap.* 470–80).

(1910). 'Greek nouns in Latin poetry from Lucretius to Juvenal', *J.Ph.* 31: 236–66 (= *Class. pap.* 817–39).

(1915). 'Ovid, *Her.* vi 110', *P.C.P.S.* 16 (= *Class. pap.* 1262).

(1922). '*Attamen* and Ovid, *Her.* 1.2', *C.Q.* 16: 88–91 (= *Class. pap.* 1052–5).

Jacobson, H. (1974). *Ovid's Heroides.* Princeton.

Kennedy, D. C. (1984). 'The epistolary mode and the first of Ovid's *Heroides*', *C.Q.* 34: 413–22.

Kenney, E. J. (1959). 'Notes on Ovid: II', *C.Q.* 9: 240–60.

(1962). 'The manuscript tradition of Ovid's *Amores*, *Ars amatoria*, and *Remedia amoris*', *C.Q.* 12: 1–31.

(1969). 'Ovid and the law', *Y.C.S.* 21: 241–63.

(1970). 'Notes on Ovid, III: Corrections and interpretations in the *Heroides*', *H.S.C.P.* 74: 169–85.

(1973). 'The style of the *Metamorphoses*', in J. W. Binns (ed.), *Ovid*: 116–53. London.

(1982). 'Ovid', in E. J. Kenney and W. V. Clausen (edd.), *The Cambridge history of classical literature*. Vol. II. *Latin literature*: 420–57. Cambridge.

Knox, P. E. (1986a). *Ovid's 'Metamorphoses' and the traditions of Augustan poetry*, Cambridge Philolological Society Suppl. vol. II. Cambridge.

(1986b). 'Adjectives in *-osus* and Latin poetic diction', *Glotta* 64: 90–101.

(1990). 'Scylla's nurse', *Mnem.* 43: 158–9.

Kost, K. (1971). *Musaios. Hero und Leander*. Bonn.

Kraus, W. (1968). 'Ovidius Naso', in *Ovid*, ed. M. von Albrecht and E. Zinn: 67–166. Darmstadt.

Lachmann, K. (1848). 'De Ovidi epistulis', *Progr. Univ. Berolinense* (= *Kleinere Schriften* (Berlin 1876) II 56–61).

Lanham, R. A. (1976). *The motives of eloquence*. New Haven.

Lefkowitz, M. R. (1981). *The lives of the Greek poets*. London.

Leumann, M. (1977). *Lateinische Laut- und Formenlehre*. Munich.

Lilja, S. (1965). *The Roman elegists' attitude to women*. Annales Academiae Scientiarum Fennicae Ser. B, 135.1. Helsinki.

Linse, E. (1891). *De P. Ovidio Nasone vocabulorum inventore*. Leipzig.

Löfstedt, E. (1933). *Syntactica. Studien und Beiträge zur historischen Syntax des Lateins, Zweiter Teil*. Lund.

(1942). *Syntactica. Studien und Beiträge zur historischen Syntax des Lateins, Erste Teil*, 2nd ed. Lund.

Luck, G. (1962). *Hexen und Zauberei in der römischen Dichtung*. Zurich & Stuttgart.

Lyne, R. O. A. M. (1978). *Ciris. A poem attributed to Vergil*. Cambridge.

(1979). '*Seruitium amoris*', *C.Q.* 29: 117–30.

(1989). *Words and the poet. Characteristic techniques of style in Vergil's Aeneid*. Oxford.

322   BIBLIOGRAPHY

Maas, P. (1902). 'Studien zum poetischen Plural bei den Römern', *A.L.L.* 12: 479–550.

Maass, E. (1889). 'Alexandrinische Fragmente', *Hermes* 24: 520–9.

Madvig, J. N. (1873). *Adversaria critica.* Vol. II. Copenhagen.

Martini, E. (1933). *Einleitung zu Ovid.* Prague.

Maurer, J. (1990). *Untersuchungen zur poetischen Technik und den Vorbildern der Ariadne-Epistel Ovids.* Frankfurt am Main.

McKeown, J. C. (1987). *Ovid: Amores. Text, prolegomena and commentary.* Vol. I: *Text and prolegomena.* Liverpool.

(1989). *Ovid: Amores. Text, prolegomena and commentary.* Vol. II: *A commentary on Book One.* Leeds.

Nisbet, R. and Hubbard, M. (1970). *A commentary on Horace: Odes, Book I.* Oxford.

(1978). *A commentary on Horace: Odes, Book II.* Oxford.

Norden, E. (1927). *P. Vergilius Maro: Aeneis, Buch VI,* 3rd ed. Berlin.

Otto, A. (1890). *Die Sprichwörter und sprichwörtlichen Redensarten der Römer.* Leipzig.

Page, D. L. (1981). *Further Greek epigrams.* Cambridge.

Pearce, T. E. V. (1966). 'The enclosing word order in the Latin hexameter', *C.Q.* 16: 140–71, 298–320.

Peters, W. (1882). *Observationes ad P. Ovidii Nasonis Heroidum epistulas.* Leipzig.

Pichon, R. (1902). *Index verborum amatoriorum.* Paris.

Platnauer, M. (1951). *Latin elegiac verse.* Cambridge.

Reeve, M. D. (1973). 'Notes on Ovid's *Heroides*', *C.Q.* 29: 117–30.

Reitzenstein, R. (1912). 'Zur Sprache der lateinischen Erotik', *Sitzb. der Heidelberger Akad. der Wiss.* 3.

Renehan, R. (1977). 'Compound-simplex verbal iteration in Plautus', *C.P.* 72: 243.

Riese, A. (1866). 'Catull's 64tes Gedicht aus Kallimachos übersetzt', *Rh.M.* 21: 498–509.

Robert, L. (1960). *Hellenica* XI–XII. Paris.

Rohde, E. (1913). *Der griechische Roman und seine Vorläufer,* 3rd ed. Leipzig.

Ross, D. O. (1969). *Style and tradition in Catullus.* Cambridge, Mass.

(1975). *Backgrounds to Augustan poetry. Gallus, elegy and Rome.* Cambridge.

Ruhnken, D. (1831). *Dictata ad Ovidii Heroidas et Albinovani elegiam,* ed. F. T. Friedmann. Frankfurt.

Sedlmayer, H. S. (1880). *Kritischer Commentar zu Ovids Heroiden.* Vienna.

Shackleton Bailey, D. R. (1954). 'On an idiomatic use of possessive pronouns in Latin', *C.R.* 4: 8–9.

(1956). *Propertiana.* Cambridge.

Smith, K. F. (1913). *The Elegies of Albius Tibullus.* New York.

Solimano, G. (1970). 'Il mito di Apollo e Admeto negli elegiaci latini', in *Mythos: scripta in honorem M. Untersteiner:* 255–68. Genoa.

Solodow, J. (1986). '*Raucae, tua cura, palumbes:* study of a poetic word order', *H.S.C.P.* 90: 129–53.

Stanford, W. B. (1963). *The Ulysses Theme. A study in the adaptability of a traditional hero,* 2nd ed. Oxford.

Stinton, T. C. W. (1965). *Euripides and the judgement of Paris.* London. (= *Collected papers on Greek tragedy* (Oxford 1990) 17–75.)

(1973). '*Quid ergo Athenis et Hierosolymis?, quid mihi tecum est?* and τί ἐμοὶ καὶ σοί;', *Rh.M.* 116: 84–90.

Syme, R. (1978). *History in Ovid.* Oxford.

Tarrant, R. J. (1981). 'The authenticity of the letter of Sappho to Phaon (*Heroides* xv)', *H.S.C.P.* 85: 133–53.

(1983). 'Ovid. *Heroides, Epistula Sapphus*', in L. D. Reynolds (ed.), *Texts and transmission. A survey of the Latin classics:* 268–73. Oxford.

(1987). 'Toward a typology of interpolation in Latin poetry', *T.A.P.A.* 117: 281–98.

(1989). 'The reader as author: collaborative interpolation in Latin poetry', in J. N. Grant (ed.), *Editing Greek and Latin texts:* 121–62. New York.

Traina, A. (1991). 'Soror alma (Verg. *Aen.* x 439)', *Maia* 43: 3–7.

Tränkle, H. (1960). *Die Sprachkunst des Properz und die Tradition der lateinischen Dichtersprache,* Hermes Einzelschriften 15. Wiesbaden.

Tupet, A.-M. (1976). *La magie dans la poésie latine.* I *Des origines à la fin du règne d'Auguste.* Paris.

Vian, F. (1969). *Quintus de Smyrne: La suite d'Homère.* Tome III: *Livres X–XIV.* Paris.

(1976). *Apollonios de Rhodes: Argonautiques.* Tome I: *Chants I–II.* Paris.

Walbank, F. W. (1967). *A historical commentary on Polybius.* Vol. II. Oxford.

Watkins, C. (1966). 'An Indo-European construction in Greek and Latin', *H.S.C.P.* 71: 115–19.

Watts, W. J. (1973). 'Ovid, the law and Roman society on abortion',
    A.C. 16: 89–101.
West, M. L. (1974). *Studies in Greek elegy and iambus.* Berlin and New
    York.
Wheeler, A. L. (1925). 'Topics from the life of Ovid', *A.J.P.* 46: 1–28.
Wigodsky, M. (1972). *Vergil and early Latin poetry.* Hermes Einzel-
    schriften 24. Wiesbaden.
Wilamowitz-Moellendorff, U. von (1913). *Sappho und Simonides.* Berlin.
Wilkinson, L. P. (1955). *Ovid recalled.* Cambridge.
Williams, Gareth (1992). 'Ovid's Canace: dramatic irony in *Heroides*
    11', *C.Q.* 42: 201–9.
Williams, Gordon (1968). *Tradition and originality in Roman poetry.* Ox-
    ford.
Winkler, J. (1990). *The constraints of desire.* New York and London.
Wissowa, G. (1912). *Religion und Kultus der Römer.* Leipzig.
Zwierlein, O. (1986). *Kritischer Kommentar zu den Tragödien Senecas* (Akad.
    der Wissen. und der Lit. Mainz; Abhandlungen der Geistes-
    und Sozialwissenschaftlischen Klasse; Einzelveröffentlichung
    6). Wiesbaden.

INDEXES

References are to lemmata in the Commentary.

1 Latin words

a, 5.49, 5.123, 11.43, 11.110
adulter, 1.6
age, with imperative, 6.141, 7.65
alius (in dative), 5.59
arbitrium, 5.36

bene (with adjectives), 1.44, *ES* 67

careo (passive), 1.50
certus (+ infinitive), 6.51, 7.7, *ES* 99
concubitus, 7.92
coniunx, 1.30, 7.69
conubium, conubialis, 2.81, 6.41, 11.99
crede mihi, 11.63
cura (= *curator*), 1.104

deuoueo, 2.13, 6.91

ei mihi, 2.106, 5.60, 11.112
et (postponed), 1.32
ex (for agency), 6.61; (for instrumental), 5.152, (= 'after'), 10.16

facere (intransitive), 1.103, 2.39, 6.128, *ES* 8; (w. subjunctive in asyndeton) 2.66, 2.98
forsitan, 2.14, 2.104
fruor (euphemism), 2.79
furtum, 6.43, 11.38

genitor, 11.99
gladius, 2.140, 10.88

heres, 2.78
hostis (fem.), 6.82

in (final), 6.12
insimulare, 6.22

is (forms in poetry) 5.69, 5.141, 7.15, *ES* 182
ita, 6.97, 10.27, *ES* 81
iuro (passive), 2.23–4

lassare, lassus, 1.10, 10.145
letum, 2.147
longaeuus, 1.103, 5.40

mactare, 1.43, 7.113, 10.77, 10.101
maeror, *ES* 117
male (privative), 7.27
meretrix, *ES* 63

namque (postponed), 1.37
ne … quidem (= 'neither'), 10.143
nec (adversative), 2.6, 2.55, 10.33, *ES* 23; (postponed) 7.140
neco, 10.115
nempe, 2.36, 6.144, 7.141, 7.146
nescioquis (contemptuous), 7.124
nex, 2.148
nimium quoque, 6.53

o ego, 6.15
obses, 2.34
olor, 7.2
oportet, 1.83, 6.141
oriundus, 7.165

pacisco, 2.4, 6.5
parce (+ imperative), 5.43

-que (adversative), 6.71; (inferential), 6.79; (displaced), 2.70, 5.78, 11.40, 11.84; (after *neque*) 2.90, 7.81–2; (in polysyndeton), 1.29, 1.103, 6.142, 6.164

-que ... et ... et, 5.71, 6.70, 6.142, 10.5
quidem, 6.147

scilicet (ironic), 5.58, 6.87, 10.42, 11.11
sed tamen (postponed), 11.106
siue (elided), *ES* 81, 83
socius, socialis, 2.33, 6.41
sponsor, 2.34

stultus, 1.75, 7.28
stuprum, 5.143
subnuba, 6.153

uirgo, 5.129, 6.133
ut (concessive), 1.116, 7.15, 7.75, 7.146
ut qui (+ subjunctive), 1.105
uxor, 1.97, 7.22

2 General

ablative
   absolute, w. *quamlibet*, 6.7; w.
     tamen, 7.40
   instrumental, 2.89, 2.112, 5.126,
     5.152, 6.54, 10.54, 11.8, *ES* 129,
     200
   locative, 2.19
   of price, 7.47
   of result, 2.3
   in Greek names, 5.29, 6.48
abortion, 11.39–44
accusative
   exclamatory, 5.149, 7.98
   Greek form of, 1.5, 1.13, 2.84,
     5.57, 5.73, 5.105, 6.65, 7.7,
     ES 217
   of place to, 1.63, 10.125
   retained, 1.60, 5.137, 6.3–4
adjectives
   for genitive, 1.14, 2.112, 5.68
   in *-ax*, 2.116
   in *-bilis*, 5.149, 6.49
   in *-bundus*, 11.81
   in *-eus*, 5.62, 5.87, 6.52, *ES* 199
   in *-osus*, 1.9, 2.45, 2.121, 5.28, 7.83
adverbs
   of 'judgement', 5.144, 7.151
   neuter adjectives for, 10.9
   prepositional phrases for, 10.6,
     11.21
adynaton, 5.29–30
amphibole, 1.23, 2.1, 7.84, 7.180
anachronism, 1.35, 1.52, 1.53–6, 2.4,
   2.83, 5.2, 5.12, 10.122, *ES* 41, 139

anaphora, 1.74, 2.53–4, 2.109, 5.49,
   6.47–8, 6.127–8, 6.145–6, 7.11–12,
   7.191, 10.57, 10.109–10, 11.33–4,
   11.115–18
anastrophe, 6.29, 7.6, 7.41
antonomasia, 2.76, 11.45
Apollonius, 6 intr., 6.5, 6.9–54,
   6.11–12, 6.25–6, 6.32, 6.41–6,
   6.51, 6.57, 6.59, 6.105, 6.129,
   10.55–8
apposition, enclosing, 7.158, 11.19,
   ES 108
archaisms, 1.37, 1.55, 2.147, 5.96,
   6.48, 6.119, 10.5, 11.126

brachylogy, 1.70, 2.109, 2.148, 6.145–
   6, 10.60, *ES* 145

Callimachus, 2 intr., 2.1, 2.6, 2.29,
   2.45, 2.78, 2.121–48, 5.21–30, 5.25,
   5.151–2, 10.86, *ES* 135–56
Catullus, 6.71, 10 intr., 10.15, 10.16,
   10.21, 10.25–8, 10.31, 10.35, 10.47–
   50, 10.58, 10.59–98, 10.69, 10.77,
   10.89–92, 10.96, 10.100, 10.102,
   10.131–2, 10.119–24, *ES* 112, 154
compound adjectives
   in *-fer, -ger*, 2.84, 5.137
   in *semi-*, 1.55
   poetic, 1.103, 2.18
cum inuersum, 6.23–5, 6.57, 7.90

dative
   of agent, 10.69

'ethic', 5.122
of 4th declension, 7.31
separative, 6.67
with verbs, 2.4, 2.39
declension, heteroclite, 7.171
diction
    colloquialisms, 1.23, 1.41, 1.44,
        1.50, 1.75, 1.103, 1.110, 2.27,
        2.28, 2.32, 2.36, 2.53, 2.98,
        2.105, 2.129, 2.130, 5.70, 5.99,
        5.149, 6.21, 6.47–8, 6.147, 7.27,
        7.30, 7.63, 7.65, 7.90, 7.140,
        7.149, 7.181, 10.2, 10.58, 10.88,
        11.9, 11.59, 11.63, 11.127–8,
        ES 67, 113
    diminutives, 5.45, 6.121, 10.58,
        11.35
    epicisms, 1.30, 1.33, 1.55, 1.103,
        2.84, 2.90, 5.56, 11.99, ES 97
    prosaic, 1.83, 1.105, 2.140, 5.108,
        5.141, 6.88, 6.97, 6.147, 7.19,
        7.47, 7.51, 7.181, 10.89, 11.28,
        ES 45, 195

ellipse, 1.1, 1.63–4, 2.129, 5.41–2,
    5.81–2, 6.115–16, 10.37, 10.61–2,
    ES 128
enallage, 1.10, 1.59, 1.92, 2.89, 2.123–
    4, 2.142, 5.26, 5.101, 6.107, 7.107,
    10.58, 10.145
epitaphs, 2.147–8, 7.195–6, 11.17–
    20
etymology, 1.39–40, 5.111, 7.11, 7.147,
    ES 7, 36, 167–70
Euripides, 2.31, 5 intr., 5.29–30,
    5.41, 6 intr., 6.125–30, 6.136,
    6.161, 7.18, 10.58, 10.63–70, 11
    passim
excursus, topographical, 2.131–48,
    10.25, ES 157–8

Gallus, 5.17–20, 7.162, ES 135–56,
    151
genitive
    Greek form of, 6.132, ES 3
    in -ii, 2.34, 7.178

agrees with possessive, 5.45, 6.110,
    7.26, 11.77
    of respect, 1.80
    of value, 1.4, 7.46
Graecism, 1.27, 2.23–4, 5.60, 7.124,
    7.164, 10.9, 10.69, 10.100, ES 121

Homer, 1 passim, 6 intr., 7.37–8, 10
    intr., 10.60, 10.67, 10.83–8, 10.96,
    10.131–2
hyperbole, 2.137, 5.56, 10.55, 10.136,
    10.147, ES 12, 160

infinitive
    with adjectives, 2.112, 6.51, 7.7,
        ES 218
    adnominal, 1.109
    as noun, 7.164
    perfect for present, 2.28, 2.142,
        ES 77, 172, 217
    of purpose, 1.37

legal language, 1.96, 2.34, 2.44, 2.78,
    2.112, 5.4, 5.36, 5.51, 5.58, 5.78,
    5.91, 5.144, 6.22, 6.163, 7.104,
    7.149, 7.164, 10.52, 10.115, 11.37,
    11.127, ES 103

magic, 2.13, 5.39, 6.83–4, 6.91
medical language, 5.149–50, 5.154,
    11.39, 11.40, 11.42, 11.43–4,
    ES 175, 187
metre
    caesura or word-break, 1.5, 1.95,
        2.37, 7.97b, 11.69, ES 113
    elision, 1.115–16, 2.137, 7.49,
        ES 96; (avoided) 1.24, 2.40,
        5.105, 7.20, 11.28
    hiatus, 1.5, 6.15, 6.41, 7.16, 11.13
    prosody, 1.87, 2.81, 2.120, 2.142,
        5.23–4, 5.135, 6.31, 6.74, 7.166,
        ES 32
    spondaic lines, 6.103
military imagery, 6.82, 7.32, 11.48
mood
    indicative (in apodosis of con-

mood (*cont.*)
    dition), 11.56; (potential), 1.108,
    2.28, 7.43, 10.2, 10.112, *ES* 192;
    (w. *quamuis*), 7.29; (w. *usque …*
    dum), 1.45
    subjunctive (causal), 2.13–14, 2.96;
    (in cautious assertion), 6.93,
    7.126; (deliberative), 10.59,
    11.51; (generalizing) 5.7; (in
    parataxis) 1.2, 1.111, 2.65–6;
    (in subordinate clauses by
    analogy), 2.81–2
Musaeus, 6.45, *ES* 213

Nonnus, 2.6, 10 intr., 10.25–8, 10.
    58, 10.63–70, 10.89–92, 10.113,
    10.117, 10.128

parenthesis, 1.37, 2.79, 2.105, 5.61,
    7.45, 7.159–62, 10.27, *ES* 58, 107,
    158, 218
participle
    in '*ab urbe condita* construction',
    6.8
    with concessive force, 5.10, 5.12,
    11.30
    future as attributive, 2.99, 5.59,
    5.116, 7.108, 10.10
    proleptic, 7.42
    temporal, 11.76
    perfect, syncopated, 5.38, 5.43, 6.11,
    6.142, 7.85, 7.164, 10.77, 10.117,
    11.10, 11.59
    plural, 'poetic', 1.78, 2.40, 2.131,
    7.20, 7.47, 11.28, *ES* 23
polyptoton, 5.80, 6.127–8, 7.6, 7.30,
    7.35, 7.41, 7.61, 11.126, *ES* 213
prepositional phrases
    adnominal, 1.97
    final, 5.58, *ES* 197
    for instrumental abl., 11.78
    word-order in, 2.15, 6.20
Propertius, 1.7–10, 1.42, 1.59–62,
    1.75, 2.1, 5.13–32, 5.17–20, 5.21–
    30, 5.149–50, 10.119–24
proverbial expressions, 1.79, 2.9–10,

2.48, 5.29–30, 5.96, 5.103–4,
    5.109, 5.115, 6.157, 11.53

relative clauses
    causal, 1.105
    loosely connected, 1.75
    final or consecutive, 2.46, 2.84,
    7.18, 7.155, 10.18, 10.72, 10.84,
    10.103, 10.120
    generic or generalizing, 1.78, 5.77,
    6.102, 7.22, 7.28
repetition, pointless, 1.3

Sappho, *ES passim*
sense-pauses, 1.56, 5.33, 5.90, 5.130,
    11.73, *ES* 177
syllepsis, 2.25, 2.107–8, 2.148, 6.55,
    7.9, 7.73, 7.179, 7.195–6, 11.15–16,
    11.52
synizesis, 6.50, 11.69, *ES* 35

tenses
    future (periphrasis for), 2.144
    future perfect (with past par-
    ticiple), 11.120
    perfect (frequentative), 10.93;
    (with past participle), 10.92
    pluperfect (for imperfect or per-
    fect), 1.34, 1.115, 5.69, 6.112;
    (with past participle), 7.140,
    ES 49
    present (with *cum*), *ES* 46; (con-
    ative) 1.82
Tibullus, 1.31–2, 2.70, 5.13–32,
    5.151–2, 11.104, *ES* 139

Virgil, 1.53–6, 1.87, 2 intr., 2.45,
    2.81–6, 2.111, 5.94, 7 *passim*,
    10.55–8, 10.99, 11.69, *ES* 135–56,
    151

word-order
    ἀπὸ κοινοῦ, 1.14, 1.73, 2.26, 2.75,
    2.148, 5.111, 6.67, 6.107, 6.159–
    60, 7.5, 7.43, 7.100, 7.128, 7.156,
    7.165, 10.93, 10.115, 11.70

chiasmus, 2.26, 2.95, 6.67, 7.13–
    14, 7.191, 10.23–4, 11.3
enclosing, 1.32, 2.37–8, 2.65–6,
    6.13, 7.50, 7.80
hyperbaton, 7.123, 10.110, *ES* 5–6,
    104
noun and epithet distributed,
    1.92, *ES* 216

in oaths, 10.73, *ES* 107
postponed conjunctions, 1.32,
    2.37–8, 2.65–6, 6.13, 7.50, 7.80
word-play, 2.9–10, 2.12, 2.29, 5.12,
    5.59, 5.111, 5.123–4, 6.121–2,
    6.151, 7.13–14, 7.149, 10.38, 10.71,
    10.82, *ES* 95, 193

Lightning Source UK Ltd.
Milton Keynes UK
UKOW040500190912

199247UK00001B/13/A